Fodor's

CHICAGO

WELCOME TO CHICAGO

Chicago is a city with an appetite—for food, of course, but also for design, history, and culture. Come here to marvel at the cutting-edge architecture or take in the gorgeous views of Lake Michigan; to spend a day cheering with baseball fans and a night laughing at a comedy show; to shop, to visit renowned institutions like the Field Museum and the Adler Planetarium, and to experience the legendary blues scene. To do all this, you'll need nourishment: taste deep-dish pizza, piled-high hot dogs, Italian beef sandwiches, and more.

TOP REASONS TO GO

★ **Architecture:** The skyline dazzles with some of the country's most iconic buildings.

★ **Local Eats:** Cheap ethnic bites and gourmet chefs make Chicago a great food town.

★ **Art:** See everything from old masters at the Art Institute to outdoor sculptures in Millennium Park.

★ **Jazz and Blues:** Music venues are filled with both big-name legends and up-and-comers.

★ **Shopping:** Stop at designer shops on the Magnificent Mile or funky Wicker Park boutiques.

★ **Comedy:** Chicago improv venues are well-known training grounds for comedy superstars.

Fodor's CHICAGO

Publisher: Amanda D'Acierno, *Senior Vice President*

Editorial: Arabella Bowen, *Editor in Chief*; Linda Cabasin, *Editorial Director*

Design: Tina Malaney, *Associate Art Director*; Chie Ushio, *Senior Designer*

Photography: Jennifer Arnow, *Senior Photo Editor*; Mary Robnett, *Photo Researcher*

Production: Linda Schmidt, *Managing Editor*; Evangelos Vasilakis, *Associate Managing Editor*; Angela L. McLean, *Senior Production Manager*

Maps: Rebecca Baer, *Senior Map Editor*; Mark Stroud (Moon Street Cartography), David Lindroth, *Cartographers*

Sales: Jacqueline Lebow, *Sales Director*

Marketing & Publicity: Heather Dalton, *Marketing Director*; Katherine Punia, *Publicity Director*

Business & Operations: Susan Livingston, *Vice President, Strategic Business Planning*; Sue Daulton, *Vice President, Operations*

Fodors.com: Megan Bell, *Executive Director, Revenue & Business Development*; Yasmin Marinaro, *Senior Director, Marketing & Partnerships*

Copyright © 2016 by Fodor's Travel, a division of Penguin Random House LLC

Writers: Jenny Berg, Joseph Erbentraut, Carly Fisher, Neil Munshi, Roberta Sotonoff

Editors: Amanda Sadlowski, Mark Sullivan, Sue MacCallum-Whitcomb

Production Editor: Jennifer DePrima

30th Edition

ISBN 978-1-101-87853-8

ISSN 0743–9326

All details in this book are based on information supplied to us at press time. Always confirm information when it matters, especially if you're making a detour to visit a specific place. Fodor's expressly disclaims any liability, loss, or risk, personal or otherwise, that is incurred as a consequence of the use of any of the contents of this book.

SPECIAL SALES

This book is available at special discounts for bulk purchases for sales promotions or premiums. For more information, e-mail specialmarkets@penguinrandomhouse.com.

PRINTED IN THE UNITED STATES OF AMERICA

10 9 8 7 6 5 4 3 2 1

CONTENTS

A Guide to the Art Institute. 56
The Sky's the Limit. 80
Frank Lloyd Wright. 137
Chicago Sings the Blues 265

CONTENTS

MAPS

ABOUT THIS GUIDE

Fodor's Recommendations

Everything in this guide is worth doing—we don't cover what isn't—but exceptional sights, hotels, and restaurants are recognized with additional accolades. Fodor's Choice★ indicates our top recommendations; and **Best Bets** calls attention to notable hotels and restaurants in various categories. Care to nominate a new place? Visit Fodors.com/contact-us.

Trip Costs

We list prices wherever possible to help you budget well. Hotel and restaurant price categories from **$** to **$$$$** are noted alongside each recommendation. For hotels, we include the lowest cost of a standard double room in high season. For restaurants, we cite the average price of a main course at dinner or, if dinner isn't served, at lunch. For attractions, we always list adult admission fees; discounts are usually available for children, students, and senior citizens.

Hotels

Our local writers vet every hotel to recommend the best overnights in each price category, from budget to expensive. Unless otherwise specified, you can expect private bath, phone, and TV in your room. For expanded hotel reviews, facilities, and deals, visit Fodors.com.

Top Picks

★ Fodor's Choice

Listings

- ✉ Address
- ✉ Branch address
- ☎ Telephone
- 📠 Fax
- 🌐 Website
- 📧 E-mail
- 🎟 Admission fee
- 🕒 Open/closed times
- [M] Subway
- ✢ Directions or Map coordinates

Hotels & Restaurants

- 🏨 Hotel
- 🛏 Number of rooms
- 🍽 Meal plans
- 🍴 Restaurant
- ✍ Reservations
- 👔 Dress code
- 💳 No credit cards
- [$] Price

Other

- ⇨ See also
- ☞ Take note
- ⛳ Golf facilities

Restaurants

Unless we state otherwise, restaurants are open for lunch and dinner daily. We mention dress code only when there's a specific requirement and reservations only when they're essential or not accepted. To make restaurant reservations, visit Fodors.com.

Credit Cards

The hotels and restaurants in this guide typically accept credit cards. If not, we'll say so.

EUGENE FODOR

Hungarian-born Eugene Fodor (1905–91) began his travel career as an interpreter on a French cruise ship. The experience inspired him to write *On the Continent* (1936), the first guidebook to receive annual updates and discuss a country's way of life as well as its sights. Fodor later joined the U.S. Army and worked for the OSS in World War II. After the war, he kept up his intelligence work while expanding his guidebook series. During the Cold War, many guides were written by fellow agents who understood the value of insider information. Today's guides continue Fodor's legacy by providing travelers with timely coverage, insider tips, and cultural context.

1

EXPERIENCE CHICAGO

CHICAGO TODAY

A century ago, poet Carl Sandburg called Chicago "stormy, husky, brawling/city of the Big Shoulders" in an eponymous poem that still echoes city life today. Indeed, Chicago is stormier and huskier than ever, with political scandals breaking more frequently than the El train circles the Loop. But it's also cleaner, greener, and more urbane than expected—with bold new architecture, abundant green space, and a vibrant dining scene. So what will you find when you visit: a rough-and-tumble Midwestern town or a sophisticated metropolis? The answer is both, and much, much more.

Building and Rebuilding

The iconic skyline dominates postcards and tourist snapshots—and for good reason. Architecture fans are excited to see the city that Daniel Burnham, Louis Sullivan, and Frank Lloyd Wright built, but modern development has also brought new energy. Recent years have seen the birth of the Millennium Park lakefront, the 92-story Trump Tower Chicago, and the innovative Aqua, an 82-story tower with balconies designed to look like waves. Development doesn't come without controversy, however. Some older buildings have been torn down to make

way for the new, and preservationists decry each loss of a historic building to the wrecking ball.

Politics as Usual

Speaking of controversy, Chicago's political scene has witnessed the highest highs and the lowest lows in recent years. The high point: when about a quarter-million Chicagoans of every age, shape, and ethnicity gathered downtown to celebrate Illinois Senator Barack Obama's historic presidential election in 2008. The low point: pick one. Governor (and Chicago resident) Rod Blagojevich's 2011 conviction for trying to sell Obama's vacated Senate seat? Illinois Representative Jesse Jackson Jr.'s 2013 guilty plea to criminal charges of diverting campaign funds for personal use? Cook County Commissioner William Beavers's 2013 conviction for tax evasion? The Associated Press reported that there were 1,531 convictions for public corruption here between 1976 and 2010, the most of any district in the country.

Foodie's Paradise

Visitors expecting deep-dish pizza and Italian beef sandwiches won't be disappointed, but they will have to elevate their expectations a hundredfold. Chicago

WHAT'S NEW

Picking the perfect hotel is suddenly going to get a whole lot harder. Chicago is in the middle of a building boom that will bring an esitmated 3,200 more rooms to the city over the next year or so. That doesn't even count celebrated newcomers like the Virgin

Hotel (the first in the world for this new concept), the Godfrey Hotel Chicago, and the Soho House Chicago.

If we're not waiting for the CTA (Chicago Transit Authority, that is), we're talking about it—complaining about the new high-capacity El cars

or praising the Transit Stop estimated-arrivals app. We're uploading pics of the notable characters we encounter to the "People of the CTA" Facebook page. Equal measures funny, sad, and disgusting, the page had 144,000 "likes" at last count.

is—dare we say it?—the most exciting city in the country for dining right now. It seems like there's a Food & Wine Best New Chef or *Top Chef* winner on every block. Sample cutting-edge cuisine from chef Grant Achatz at Next and Alinea, Homaro Cantu at Moto, and Stephanie Izard at Girl & the Goat. Or just spend your entire visit in Logan Square, where you'll have your pick of Lula Café, Longman & Eagle, and Belly Shack. Satisfied yet? We didn't even mention the hundreds of neighborhood ethnic eateries that let you dine across the globe without ever leaving the city.

Changing Landscape

Mayor Richard M. Daley's 22-year reign was a period of incredible resurgence for the city, complete with environmental development, sustainable building, and a failed Olympics bid. But it wasn't always diplomatic or even democratic, and the jury's still out on his replacement, another tough-talking Democrat—this time Obama's former chief of staff, Rahm Emanuel. His administration's hard-line tactics led to a highly contentious teachers' union strike in 2012, and kicked off 2013 with an unpopular decision to close 54 schools, the most in the city's history.

The economy is still flailing, and devastating gun violence plagues the city's South and West sides.

Full of Pride

Sure, Chicagoans like to complain—about the weather, about our sports teams, and especially about our politicians. But if an out-of-towner dares to diss our beloved city, you can bet there will be fireworks bigger than the ones over Navy Pier in summer. Sandburg was right again about Chicago when he wrote, "come and show me another city with lifted head singing/ so proud to be alive and coarse and strong and cunning."

We rejoiced when the city lifted its ordinance banning onboard cooking on food trucks. Although other restrictions have stopped some would-be operators from getting their mobile food vehicles rolling, there are still a slew of trucks offering already-prepared goodies. Our favorites include the Tamale Spaceship, Flirty Cupcakes, and the Slide Ride (gourmet sliders).

We're also big beer drinkers. If we're not busy home-brewing, we're heading to the local brewery to fill our growlers with the latest batch from Half Acre, Metropolitan Brewing, Piece, Haymarket, Revolution Brewing, and Finch's Beer Co.

CHICAGO PLANNER

When to Go

June, September, and October are mild and sunny. November through March the temperature ranges from crisp to bitter, April and May can fluctuate between cold/soggy and bright/warm, and July and August can either be perfect or serve up the deadly combo of high heat and high humidity. That said, the only thing certain about Chicago's weather, according to locals, is that it can change in an instant. If you head to Chicago in warmer months, you'll be able to catch some of the fantastic outdoor festivals; during the holiday season the city's decked out in lights.

Getting Around

Chicago has an excellent network of buses and trains, which are collectively called the El (for "elevated," which many of them are). The combination should bring you within ¼ mile of any place you'd like to go. Those accustomed to cities will likely be comfortable on any train, anytime. Others may want to take extra caution after 11 pm. Buses are almost always safe; there are several express buses running from downtown to destinations like the Museum of Science and Industry.

As of this writing, the fare for the bus is $2, the train is $2.25, and a transfer is 25¢ with a Transit Card; if you're paying cash, all rides are $2.25. Travelers may want to get a Ventra ticket at airport CTA stations or any visitor center.

For directions to specific places via public transportation, for public transportation maps, and for places to buy Ventra Cards, see ⊕ *www.transitchicago.com*.

If you drive downtown, park in one of the giant city-owned parking lots underneath Millennium Park or by the Museum

Campus, which charge a flat fee. Private lots usually cost double.

Visitor Centers

Chicago Cultural Center. ⊠ *77 E. Washington St.* ☎ *312/744–6630* ⊕ *www.cityofchicago.org* ⊗ *Mon.–Thurs. 9–7, Fri. and Sat. 9–6, Sun. 10–5.*

Millennium Park Welcome Center. ⊠ *201 E. Randolph St., in the Northwest Exelon Pavilion, between Michigan Ave., and Columbus Ave., Loop* ☎ *312/742–1168* ⊕ *www.millenniumpark.org* ⊗ *Daily 6 am–11 pm.*

Street Smarts

Chicago is a city of about 2.8 million people, most of whom have good intentions. Still, it is a big city. It pays to be cautious and aware of your surroundings at all times.

Put down the cell phone and remove your earphones when strolling city streets or riding public transit. Hide valuables and flashy jewelry when you're out and about, or, better yet, leave them at home. Keep your purse or bags close to you and in clear view in restaurants and in bars. Never leave your belongings unattended, especially on trains or buses. Be polite but insistent with panhandlers. Legitimate vendors of *StreetWise*—the city's nonprofit magazine benefiting the homeless—should be able to provide an official badge. (The magazine sells for $2.)

Expect to have your bags and purses searched when entering sports stadiums, museums, and city buildings. You may be asked to show a photo ID at certain downtown buildings.

At night do what you would in any city: know your destination ahead of time, plan your route, and walk with confidence and purpose. Avoid dark or empty streets and skip those tempting shortcuts through the city's many alleys.

Saving Money

Chicago is a city of choices: you can splash out on the fanciest meals and pricey theater tickets or opt for fun activities that don't cost a dime.

If you plan to hit several major attractions, consider a **Chicago cityPASS** at participating locations or online (⊕ *www. citypass.com/chicago*). It will save you a combined total of about $80 on admission to these major attractions: Shedd Aquarium, the Field Museum, Skydeck Chicago at Willis (Sears) Tower, either the Museum of Science and Industry or John Hancock Center Observatory, and either Adler Planetarium or the Art Institute of Chicago. To save even more, time your museum visit for a day or time when admission is free.

From spring to fall, neighborhood fests and free concerts abound. The most stunning place to catch a free concert is the Frank Gehry–designed Jay Pritzker Pavilion at Millennium Park. Daytime and evening concerts showcase everything from classical to jazz to punk rock.

Open Hours

Most businesses in Chicago are open 10–6. Some shops stay open as late as 10. Restaurants can be closed Monday and usually stop serving around 10 pm on weeknights, 11 pm or later on weekends. There are a number of 24-hour diners, but they are rarer than you might expect. Bars close at 2 am or 4 am.

Tickets

You can avoid the long lines at Chicago museums by buying tickets online at least a day in advance. The most popular architecture tour, led by the Chicago Architecture Foundation, always sells out—be sure to buy tickets in advance.

WHAT'S WHERE

Numbers refer to chapters.

2 The Loop, West Loop, and South Loop. Bounded by looping El tracks, the city's business center pulses with professionals scurrying between architectural landmarks. Restaurants and galleries dominate the West Loop; the once-desolate South Loop now teems with college students and condo dwellers.

3 Near North and River North. Shoppers stroll the Magnificent Mile between the John Hancock Center and the Chicago River, passing landmarks such as the Water Tower and Tribune Tower. Just north, stately mansions dominate the Gold Coast. Anchored by the Merchandise Mart, River North juxtaposes tourist traps with a thriving gallery scene.

4 Lincoln Park and Wicker Park. Beyond the 1,200-acre park and the zoo, Lincoln Park boasts cafés and high-end boutiques. Starving artists used to call Wicker Park/Bucktown home until skyrocketing rents killed the arty vibe. Most of the hipsters have decamped to nearby Logan Square, where wide boulevards are lined with organic cafés, cocktail bars, and taquerias.

5 Lakeview and Far North Side. Baseball fans pilgrimage to Wrigley Field: just south of the ballpark, on Clark Street, are memorabilia shops and sports bars; a block east is Halsted Street, site of gay enclave Boystown. Farther north on Clark is Swedish-settled Andersonville, which has a quiet, residential feel.

6 Pilsen, Little Italy, and Chinatown. Mexican restaurants, mom-and-pop shops, and Spanish signage line 18th Street, the heart of Pilsen. Gone are many of the Near West Side's Italian groceries and shops, but you can still get a mean veal marsala on Taylor Street. In Chinatown skip the souvenir shops and head for the restaurants, teahouses, and bakeries.

7 Hyde Park. The main draw of this South Side neighborhood is the University of Chicago. Promontory Point has breathtaking lake and skyline views.

8 Day Trips From Chicago. Just north of the city, Evanston is the site of Northwestern University and its leafy campus. To the west suburban Oak Park is best known for native sons Frank Lloyd Wright and Ernest Hemingway; Wright's home and studio are here, along with many notable examples of his architecture.

CHICAGO
TOP ATTRACTIONS

Skydeck Chicago at Willis (Sears) Tower

(A) Take the ear-popping ride to the 103rd-floor observatory, where on a clear day you can see as far as Michigan, Wisconsin, and Indiana. Fearless folks can step out onto the Ledge, twin glass boxes extending 4.3 feet from the Skydeck and suspended a dizzying 1,353 feet above the city.

John Hancock Center

(B) The third-tallest building in Chicago has the most impressive panoramic views of the lake and surrounding skyline—it's high enough to see the tops of neighboring buildings, but not so remote that you feel as if you're looking out from a plane. The observatory recently changed its name to 360 Chicago, and added a new attraction on the 94th floor called Tilt, in which brave visitors lean against full-length windows (while holding onto metal support bars). If you'd like to skip the observatory, head to the bar that adjoins the Signature Room restaurant on the 95th floor—you'll spend your money on an exorbitantly priced cocktail instead of the observatory entrance fee and enjoy a great view.

The Magnificent Mile

(C) Exclusive shops, department stores, and boutiques line the northern half of swanky Michigan Avenue. Even better, the concentration of prestigious stores in vertical malls means you can get a lot of shopping done in winter without venturing into the bluster outside.

Navy Pier

(D) Yes, it's a little schlocky, but Navy Pier is fun, especially for families. Everyone can fan out to shop in the mall, play 18-hole minigolf in Pier Park in summer, see a movie at the IMAX Theatre, or explore the Chicago Children's Museum. Plus, there's a stained-glass museum, a fun-house maze with scenes of Chicago landmarks, and an old-fashioned swing ride.

Art Institute of Chicago

(E) This Chicago cultural gem has the country's best collection of impressionist and postimpressionist art, as well as the Renzo Piano–designed modern wing. It's also a great place to see all those paintings you've seen only on postcards, like *American Gothic* and *Nighthawks*.

Field Museum

(F) Say hello to Sue, the Field's beloved gigantic *T. rex*, before immersing yourself in this extraordinary museum's collection of anthropological and paleontological artifacts and animal dioramas. The dinosaurs are the thing here, but surprising collections of Tibetan Buddhist altars, mummies, and re-creations of famous gems may entice you to linger for hours.

Shedd Aquarium

(G) We find the experience of watching entire universities—not just schools—of fantastically colored fish, as well as dolphins and whales, completely mesmerizing.

Don't miss the Wild Reef exhibit, where stingrays slide quietly under the Plexiglas at your feet.

Millennium Park

(H) Make a beeline for Frank Gehry's **Jay Pritzker Pavilion,** where an incredible sound system allows audiences to enjoy concert-hall sound in the great outdoors. The Bean, formally known as *Cloud Gate*, is a luminous polished-steel sculpture that plays tricks with the reflection of Chicago's skyline. In warmer months children of all ages can't resist a splash in the Crown Fountain, twin 50-foot towers that project close-up video images of Chicagoans "spitting" jets of water.

TOUR THE TOWN

Chicago Architecture Tours

Every great city has great buildings, but Chicago *is* its great buildings. Everything Chicagoans do is framed by some of the most remarkable architecture to be found anywhere. The best way to see the sky-scraping Loop towers or the horizontal sweep of the Prairie School is on one of these top tours.

Chicago Architecture Foundation. The foundation conducts excellent docent-led boat, walking, and bus tours of the Loop and beyond. To get a panoramic view of Chicago's magnificent skyline, try the boat tours. ⊠ *Santa Fe Bldg., 224 S. Michigan Ave.* ☎ *312/922–3432* ⊕ *www.architecture.org* ✏ *$10 walking tours* ☉ *Walking tours run year-round; boat tours available Apr.–Nov., daily.*

Chicago Greeter. Savvy local volunteers run free two- to four-hour walking tours of the city's neighborhoods and areas of interest, such as fashion, film, and public art. Tours run daily at 10 am and 1 pm and should be booked well in advance. Those who don't sign up in advance for a Chicago Greeter tour can show up for an on-the-spot InstaGreeter tour, offered Friday through Sunday 10 to 4. Tours depart from the visitor information center at Chicago Cultural Center. ⊠ *77 E. Randolph St.* ☎ *312/744–8000* ⊕ *www.chicagogreeter.com* ✏ *Free.*

Chicago Trolley and Double Decker Co. This hop-on, hop-off ride takes visitors to many downtown and Loop highlights and allows you the flexibility to stop at attractions that catch your fancy. ⊠ *Chicago* ☎ *773/648–5000* ⊕ *www.chicagotrolley.com* ✏ *$35.*

River and Lakefront Tours

Hop into a boat and sail down the Chicago River for some of the prettiest views of the city. Some tours even head out to the lake for a skyscraper-studded panorama.

You can also hop on a Shoreline water taxi and cruise down the river or on the lake. You won't get running narration, but it's not crowded and it's affordable—single rides range from $5 to $8 with stops at the Michigan Avenue Bridge, Union Station/Willis (Sears) Tower, Navy Pier, and the Museum Campus.

Mercury Chicago's Skyline Cruiseline. This company does Canine Cruises, where dogs are welcome, and a Chicago by Night tour at sunset. ⊠ *112 E. Wacker Dr.* ☎ *312/332–1353* ⊕ *mercuryskylinecruise line.com* ✏ *$28.*

Shoreline Sightseeing. Shoreline's been plying these waters since 1939, and has tours of both the river and Lake Michigan. ⊠ *Chicago* ☎ *312/222–9328* ⊕ *www.shorelinesightseeing.com* ✏ *$35.*

Tall Ship Adventures of Chicago. Adventure and education meet on lake tours that illuminate Chicago's maritime history, the life of lake sailors, and environmentalism. Former Mayor Richard M. Daley declared the tall ship *Windy* the flagship of Chicago. ⊠ *Chicago* ☎ *312/595–5555* ⊕ *www.tallshipadventuresofchicago.com* ✏ *$30.*

Wendella. See the city at dusk on the Chicago at Sunset tour. There's also a river architecture tour and a combined river and lake tour. ⊠ *400 N. Michigan Ave., at the Wrigley Bldg.* ☎ *312/337–1446* ⊕ *www.wendellaboats.com* ✏ *$35.*

Kayaking and Canoeing Tours

For a more adventurous spin down the river, rent a canoe or a kayak. Just beware of large boats and crew shells.

Chicago River Canoe and Kayak. This company offers a wide variety of trips, from floats among the skyscrapers to sunset paddles to a nearby island. ⊠ *3400 N. Rockwell* ☎ *773/704–2663* ⊕ *www.chicagoriverpaddle.com* ⊠ *$50.*

Kayak Chicago. Tours focusing on everything from the city's varied architecture to the nighttime skyline are available at this well-regarded outfit. ⊠ *1501 N. Magnolia Ave.* ☎ *312/852–9258* ⊕ *www.kayakchicago.com* ⊠ *$65.*

Urban Kayaks. At this popular outfitter you can join 90-minute tours of the main branch of the Chicago River. ⊠ *260 Chicago Riverwalk* ☎ *312/965–0035* ⊕ *www.urbankayaks.com* ⊠ *$45.*

Wateriders. A "Ghosts and Gansters of Shadytown" tour is one of the unique offerings at Wateriders. ⊠ *Kingsbury Yacht Club, 950 N. Kingsbury St.* ☎ *312/953–9287* ⊕ *www.wateriders.com* ⊠ *$65.*

Special-Interest Tours

Whether you're a foodie, a history buff, or a shopaholic, there's a custom tour for you.

Chicago Food Planet Food Tours. Sample local delicacies like deep-dish pizza, Polish pastries, Chicago-style hot dogs, and Szechuan cuisine on a Near North, Bucktown–Wicker Park, or Chinatown food-and-cultural tour. ⊠ *Chicago* ☎ *312/818–2170* ⊕ *www.chicagofoodplanet.com* ⊠ *$35.*

Untouchable Tours: Chicago's Original Gangster Tour. Your guides, in character as Prohibition era goons, take you on a bus tour through Chicago's checkered mafia past. Though the kitsch factor is high, the tours are stuffed with history and will take you to neighborhoods you might otherwise miss. ⊠ *Chicago* ☎ *773/881–1195* ⊕ *www.gangstertour.com* ⊠ *$30.*

Behind the Scenes

For a look at what (or who) makes the city tick, check out the following activities.

Federal Reserve Bank of Chicago. The facility processes currency and checks, scanning bills for counterfeits, destroying unfit currency, and repackaging fit currency. A visitor center in the lobby has permanent exhibits of old bills, counterfeit money, and a million dollars in $1 bills. One-hour tours at 1pm every weekday explain how money travels and show a high-speed currency-processing machine. ⊠ *230 S. LaSalle St., Loop* ☎ *312/322–2400* ⊕ *www.chicagofed.org* ⊠ *Free.*

Goose Island Brewery. Follow a brewer on a tour of this well-known Chicago brewery producing handcrafted lagers, ales, and vintage ales. During the tour you'll sample six beers from the current rotation and receive a souvenir pint glass to take home. Reserve at least a week in advance. Tour participants must be 21 or older with valid ID. ⊠ *1800 N. Clybourn Ave., Lincoln Park* ☎ *312/915–0071* ⊕ *www.gooseisland.com* ⊠ *$10.*

Graceland Cemetery. A comprehensive guide available at the entrance walks you by the graves and tombs of the people who made Chicago great, including merchandiser Marshall Field and railroad-car magnate George Pullman. ⊠ *4001 N. Clark St., Far North Side* ☎ *773/525–1105* ⊕ *www.gracelandcemetery.org* ⊠ *Free.*

CITY ITINERARIES

Two Hours in Town

If you've got only a bit of time, go to a museum. Although you could spend days in any of the city's major museums, two hours will give you a quick taste of Chicago's cultural riches. Take a brisk walk around the **Art Institute** to see Grant Wood's *American Gothic,* Edward Hopper's *Nighthawks,* and one of the finest impressionist collections in the country. Or check out the major dinosaur collection or the gorgeous Native American regalia at the **Field Museum.** Take a close look at the sharks at the **Shedd Aquarium.** If the weather's nice, stroll along the lakefront outside the **Adler Planetarium**—you'll see one of the nicest skyline views in the city. Wander down State Street or the Magnificent Mile or around Millennium Park. If you're hungry, indulge in one of Chicago's three famous culinary treats—deep-dish pizza (head to Pizzeria Due to avoid the lines at Giordano's, Gino's, and Pizzeria Uno); garden-style hot dogs; or Italian beef sandwiches. After dark? Hear some music at a local club. Catch some blues at Blues Chicago to get a taste of authentic Chicago.

■TIP→ Remember that many of the smaller museums are closed Monday.

A Perfect Afternoon

Do the zoo. Spend some time at the free **Lincoln Park Zoo and Conservatory** (the tropical plants will warm you up in winter), take a ride on the exotic animal–themed carousel, and then spend a couple of hours at the nearby **Chicago History Museum** for a quirky look at the city's past. If you'd like to stay in the Lincoln Park neighborhood a bit longer, have dinner at one of many great local restaurants, and then head to **The Second City,** the sketch-comedy troupe

that was the precursor to *Saturday Night Live.*

■TIP→ The Second City offers free improvisation after the last performance every night but Friday.

Sightseeing in the Loop

State Street, that Great Street, is home to the old **Marshall Field's,** which has been reborn as Macy's; Louis Sullivan's ornate iron entrance to the **Sullivan Center;** and a nascent theater district; as well as great people-watching. Start at Harold Washington Library at Van Buren and State streets and walk north, venturing a block east to the beautiful **Chicago Cultural Center** when you hit Randolph Street. Grab lunch at the Museum of Contemporary Art's serene Wolfgang Puck café, Puck's at the MCA, and then spend a couple of hours with in-your-face art. Go for steak at Morton's or the Palm before a night of Chicago theater. Broadway touring shows are on Randolph Street at the Ford Center for the Performing Arts Oriental Theatre or the Cadillac Palace, or head elsewhere for excellent local theater—the Goodman, Steppenwolf, Lookingglass, and Chicago Shakespeare will each give you a night to remember.

Get Outdoors

Begin with a long walk (or run) along the lakefront, or rent a bike or in-line skates and watch the waves on wheels. Then catch an El train north to **Wrigley Field** for Cubs baseball; grab a dog at the seventh-inning stretch, and sing your heart out to "Take Me Out to the Ball Game." Afterward, soak up a little beer and atmosphere on the patio at one of the local sports bars. Finish up with an outdoor concert in **Grant or Millennium Park.**

Family Time

Start at **Navy Pier**—or heck, spend all day there. The **Chicago Children's Museum** is a main attraction, but there's also an IMAX theater, a Ferris wheel, a swing ride, a fun house, a stained-glass museum, and, in summer, Chicago-themed miniature golf in Pier Park. If the crowds at the Pier get to be too much, walk to **Millennium Park**, where kids of all ages can ice-skate in winter and play in the fountain in summer, where giant digital portraits of Chicagoans spit streams of water to help cool you off. Whatever the weather, make sure to get your picture taken in the mirrored center of the Bean—the sculpture that's formally known as *Cloud Gate*. At night in summertime, take a stroll by Buckingham Fountain, where the dancing sprays jump to music and are illuminated by computer-controlled colored lights, or take a turn on the dance floor during Chicago's SummerDance celebration.

■ TIP→ Fireworks explode near Navy Pier every Wednesday at 9:30 pm and Saturday at 10:15 pm Memorial Day through Labor Day.

Cityscapes

Start at the top. Hit the heights of the **John Hancock Center** or **Skydeck Chicago** at the Willis (Sears) Tower for a grand view of the city and the lake. Then take a walking tour of downtown with a well-informed docent from the **Chicago Architecture Foundation.** In the afternoon, wander north to the **Michigan Avenue Bridge,** where you can take an informative boat tour of the Chicago River. Enjoy the architecture as you float by, resting your weary feet.

Shop Chicago

Grab your bankroll and stroll the **Magnificent Mile** in search of great buys and souvenirs. Walking north from around the Michigan Avenue Bridge, window-shop your way along the many upscale stores. Hang a left on **Oak Street** for the most elite boutiques. **Accent Chicago** (⊠ *875 N. Michigan Ave.*) is where serious souvenir hunters spend their cash. Dedicated shoppers will want to detour a little farther south to **State Street** in the Loop for a walk through the landmark Marshall Field's building, now Macy's. For a culture buzz, check out the **Museum of Contemporary Art** (closed Monday). After making a tough restaurant choice (prime rib at Smith & Wollensky's or Lawry's? or deep-dish pizza at Giordano's?), consider a nightcap at the Signature Room at the 95th-floor bar on top of the John Hancock Center—the city will be spread beneath your feet.

AUTHENTIC CHICAGO

So you've done the Art Institute and the Willis (Sears) Tower—now it's time to put away your tourist hat and make like a local. Luckily, it's not hard to figure out what Chicagoans like to do in their spare time. Here's how to follow in their footsteps.

Get Out of Downtown

Chicago is a city of neighborhoods, and in many of them you can see traces of each successive immigrant group. Each neighborhood in the city has its own flavor, reflected in its architecture, public art, restaurants, and businesses, and most have their own summer or holiday festivals. Here are a few standout 'hoods.

Andersonville. The charming diversity of the Swedish/Middle Eastern/gay mélange of Andersonville means you can have lingonberry pancakes for breakfast, hummus for lunch, and drinks at a gay-friendly bar after dinner.

Bronzeville. Bronzeville's famous local historic figures include Ida B. Wells—a women's-rights and African-American civil-rights crusader—the trumpeter Louis Armstrong, and Bessie Coleman, the first African-American woman pilot. The area has nine landmark buildings and is rapidly gentrifying.

Chinatown. The Chinese New Year dragon parade is just one reason to visit Chinatown, which has dozens of restaurants and shops and a quiet riverfront park.

Devon Avenue. Devon Avenue turns from Indian to Pakistani to Russian Orthodox to Jewish within a few blocks. Try on a sari, buy a bagel or electronics, or just people-watch—it's an excellent place to spend the afternoon.

Little Italy. Though most Italians moved to the West Side a couple of generations ago, Little Italy's Italian restaurants and lemonade stands still draw them back.

Pilsen/Little Village. The best Mexican restaurants are alongside Pilsen's famous murals. Be sure to stop into the National Museum of Mexican Art, which will give you an even deeper appreciation of the culture.

Brave the Cold

The city's brutal windy winters are infamous, but that doesn't keep Chicagoans from making the best out of the long cold months. Throw on lots of layers, lace up your ice skates, and show those city dwellers what you're made of.

The rink at **Millennium Park** has free skating seven days a week from mid-November to mid-March and a dazzling view of the Chicago skyline. Just north lies Chicago's latest green space, Maggie Daley Park, which features a skating ribbon and a playground.

On the snowiest days some hardy souls **cross-country ski** and snowshoe on the lakeshore—bring your own equipment.

Holiday-walk Chicago's windows during the **Magnificent Mile Lights Festival,** in November, the Saturday before Thanksgiving. The celebration includes music, ice-carving contests, and stage shows, and ends in a parade and the illumination of more than 1 million lights.

FREE THINGS TO DO

It's easy to spend money in Chicago, what with shopping, museum-entrance fees, restaurants, and theater, but if you'd like to put your wallet away for a while, here are some options. The Lincoln Park Zoo is also free.

Free Art

Chicago has some of the most famous public art in the country, including a **Picasso** in Daley Plaza, **Alexander Calder's** *Flamingo* in Federal Plaza, and Anish Kapoor's *Cloud Gate* sculpture in Millennium Park. For a fairly comprehensive list, see ⊕ *cityofchicago.org/publicart* or pick up a *Chicago Public Art* guide at a visitor center.

The **City Gallery** (⊠ *806 N. Michigan Ave.*) in the Historic Water Tower has rotating exhibits of Chicago-themed photography. Five different galleries showcase contemporary visual art by local artists at the **Chicago Cultural Center** (⊕ *www.chicago culturalcenter.org*).

Free Concerts

Grant Park and Millennium Park host regular classical and pop concerts in summer. For a schedule, pick up the *Chicago Reader* or visit the *TimeOut Chicago* website at ⊕ *www.timeoutchicago.com*.

Chicago is a festival town, celebrating blues, jazz, and world music during the warm months. For a schedule, see ⊕ *www.explorechicago.org*.

Free concerts—from classic and jazz to electronica and world beat—are performed most weekdays at 12:15 in the **Chicago Cultural Center** (⊕ *www.chicago culturalcenter.org*).

Free Movies

Local library branches and parks across the city show free movies throughout the summer—check the Chicago Park District website for details (⊕ *www.chicagopark district.com*).

Free Fireworks

Every Wednesday and Saturday night in summer, Navy Pier puts on a showy display of colorful explosives. Watch from the pier or along the waterfront opposite Buckingham Fountain.

Free Improv

The world-famous Second City comedy troupe has a free improv set after the last performance every night but Friday. For more information, go to ⊕ *www. secondcity.com* or call ☎ *312/664–4032*.

Free Museum Days

Always Free: Jane Addams Hull-House Museum, Museum of Contemporary Photography, National Museum of Mexican Art, Oriental Institute Museum, Smart Museum of Art

Sunday: DuSable Museum of African-American History

Tuesday: Swedish American Museum Center (second Tuesday of each month)

Thursday: Chicago Children's Museum (5–8 pm only), Peggy Notebaert Nature Museum

■ TIP➔ The Shedd Aquarium, the Museum of Science and Industry, and the Field Museum, among others, offer free admission on certain weekdays in the winter; call the museums or visit their websites for specific dates.

CHICAGO WITH KIDS

Chicago sometimes seems to have been designed with kids in mind. There are many places to play and things to do, from building sand castles at one of the lakefront's many beaches to playing 18-hole minigolf at Navy Pier in summer. Here are some suggestions for ways to show kids the sights.

Museums

Several area museums are specifically designed for kids. At the **Chicago Children's Museum**, three floors of exhibits cast off with a play structure in the shape of a schooner, where kids can walk the gangplank and slide down to the lower level, and make a splash with a water playground, featuring a scaled-down river and a waterwheel.

Also at **Navy Pier** you'll find a Ferris wheel and Viennese swings (the kind that go around in a circle like a merry-go-round). In summer, crowds of kids make the most of Pier Park's 18-hole minigolf course, musical carousel, and remote-control boats.

Many other Chicago museums are also kid-friendly, especially the butterfly haven and the animal habitat exhibit with its climbable tree house at the **Peggy Notebaert Nature Museum,** the replica coal mine and hands-on Idea Factory at the **Museum of Science and Industry,** the dinosaur exhibits at the **Field Museum,** and the sharks and dolphins at the **John G. Shedd Aquarium.**

Parks, Zoos, and Outside Activities

Chicago's neighborhoods are dotted with area play lots that have playground equipment as well as several ice-skating rinks for winter months. On scorching days, visit the **63rd Street Beach House,** at 63rd Street and Lake Shore Drive in Woodlawn. The interactive spiral fountain in the courtyard jumps and splashes, leaving

---

MORE IDEAS FOR FAMILY FUN

- Holiday Lights Festival on Michigan Avenue
- Bulls, Cubs, or White Sox game
- Day trip to Oak Park
- Gospel Brunch at House of Blues
- Chicago Architecture Foundation Cruise

---

kids giggling and jumping. The **North Park Village Nature Center** on the Far Northwest Side (on Pulaski Road north of Bryn Mawr Avenue) is a wilderness oasis, serving up 46 acres of trails and a kid-oriented Nature Center with hands-on activities and fun educational programs. Deer sightings are common here.

Millennium Park has a 16,000-square-foot ice-skating rink. Skaters have an unparalleled view of downtown as they whiz around the ice.

For more structured fun, there are two zoos: the free **Lincoln Park Zoo** and the large, suburban **Brookfield Zoo**, which has surprising exhibits such as a wall of pulsing jellyfish.

FABULOUS FESTIVALS

Chicago festivals range from local neighborhood get-togethers to citywide extravaganzas. Try to catch a neighborhood street fair for some great people-watching if you're in town between June and September. For details, see ⊕ *www.chicago reader.com* or ⊕ *timeoutchicago.com*.

Chicago Air & Water Show. Thrill-seekers and families flock to the Chicago Air & Water Show, a lakefront spectacle featuring aerial acrobatics and daredevil water acts. See the U.S. Navy Blue Angels perform precision flying maneuvers at the two-day event in mid-August. ✉ *Lakeshore, Fullerton Ave. to Oak St.; focal point at North Ave. Beach* ☎ *312/744–3315* ⊕ *www.cityofchicago.org/city/en/depts/dca/supp_info/chicago_air_and_watershow.html*.

Chicago Blues Festival. The Chicago Blues Festival, in Grant Park, is a popular three-day, four-stage event in June starring blues greats from Chicago and around the country. If you see only one festival in Chicago, this is the one. ✉ *Chicago* ☎ *312/744–3315* ⊕ *www.cityofchicago.org/city/en/depts/dca/supp_info/chicago_blues_festival.html*.

Chicago Jazz Festival. The Chicago Jazz Festival holds sway for four days during Labor Day weekend in Millenium and Grant Parks. ✉ *Chicago* ☎ *312/744–3315* ⊕ *www.cityofchicago.org/city/en/depts/dca/supp_info/chicago_jazz_festival.html*.

Magnificent Mile Lights Festival. The holiday season officially starts with the Magnificent Mile Lights Festival, a weekend-long event at the end of November with tons of family-friendly activities including musical performances, ice-carving contests, and stage shows. The fanfare culminates in a parade and the illumination of more than 1 million lights along Michigan Avenue.

✉ *Chicago* ⊕ *www.themagnificentmile.com/events/lights-festival*.

Northalsted Market Days. Street fairs are held every week in summer. Northalsted Market Days, in August, is the city's largest street festival. It's held in the heart of the gay community of Lakeview and has blocks and blocks of vendors as well as some wild entertainment such as zany drag queens and radical cheerleaders. ✉ *Chicago* ⊕ *www.northalsted.com*.

St. Patrick's Day Parade. The St. Patrick's Day Parade turns the city on its head: the Chicago River is dyed green, shamrocks decorate the street, and the center stripe of Dearborn Street is painted the color of the Irish from Wacker Drive to Van Buren Street. This is your chance to get your fill of bagpipes, green beer, and green knee socks. It's more than four hours long, so you probably won't see the whole thing. ✉ *Chicago* ☎ *312/942–9188* ⊕ *www.chicagostpatsparade.com*.

Taste of Chicago. Taste of Chicago dishes out pizza, cheesecake, and other Chicago specialties to 3.5 million people after the Fourth of July holiday. ✉ *Grant Park, Columbus Dr. between Jackson and Randolph Sts.* ☎ *312/744–3315* ⊕ *www.cityofchicago.org/city/en/depts/dca/supp_info/taste_of_chicago.html*.

World Music Festival. At the weeklong World Music Festival in September, international artists play traditional and contemporary music at venues across the city. ✉ *Chicago* ⊕ *www.worldmusicfestivalchicago.org*.

CHICAGO THEN AND NOW

The Early Days

Before Chicago was officially "discovered" by the team of Father Jacques Marquette, a French missionary, and Louis Jolliet, a French-Canadian mapmaker and trader, in 1673, the area served as a center of trade and seasonal hunting grounds for several Native American tribes, including the Miami, Illinois, and Pottawattomie. Villages kept close trading ties with the French, though scuffles with the Fox tribe kept the French influence at bay until 1779. That year, black French trader Jean Baptiste Point du Sable built a five-room "mansion" by the mouth of the Chicago River on the shore of Lake Michigan.

The Great Fire

The city grew until 1871, when a fire in the barn of Catherine and Patrick O'Leary spread across the city, killing hundreds. (Contrary to the legend, it was probably not started by a cow kicking over a lantern.) A recent drought coupled with crowded wooden buildings and wood-brick streets allowed the blaze to take hold quickly, destroying 18,000 structures within 36 hours.

Gangsters to the Great Migration

World War I (aka the Great War) changed the face of Chicago. Postwar—and especially during Prohibition (1920–33)—the Torrio–Capone organization expanded its gambling and liquor distribution operations, consolidating its power during the violent "beer wars" from 1924 to 1930. Hundreds of casualties include the seven victims of the infamous 1929 St. Valentine's Day Massacre. In 1934 the FBI gunned down bank robber and "Public Enemy No. 1" John Dillinger outside the Biograph Theater on the North Side, now a theater venue and a Chicago landmark.

The Great War also led to the Great Migration, when African-Americans from the South moved to the northern cities between 1916 and 1970. World War I slowed immigration from Europe but increased jobs in Chicago's manufacturing industry. More than 500,000 African-Americans came to the city to find work, and by the mid-20th century African-Americans were a strong force in Chicago's political, economic, and cultural life.

IMPORTANT DATES IN CHICAGO HISTORY

1673	Chicago discovered by Marquette and Jolliet
1837	Chicago incorporated as a city
1860	First national political convention. Abraham Lincoln nominated as the Republican candidate for president
1871	Great Chicago Fire

The Notorious 1968 Democratic Convention

The Daley dynasty began when Richard J. Daley became mayor in 1955. He was reelected five times, and his son Richard M. Daley ran the city until opting out in 2011, when President Barack Obama's former chief of staff, Rahm Emanuel, won.

The first Mayor Daley redrew Chicago's landscape, overseeing the construction of O'Hare International Airport, the expressway system, the University of Illinois at Chicago, and a towering skyline. He also helped John F. Kennedy get elected.

Despite these advances, Mayor Richard J. Daley is perhaps best known for his crackdown on student protesters during the 1968 Democratic National Convention. Americans watched on their televisions as the Chicago police beat the city's youth with sticks and blinded them with tear gas. That incident, plus his "shoot-to-kill" order during the riots that followed the assassination of Dr. Martin Luther King Jr., and his use of public funds to build giant, disastrous public housing projects like Cabrini–Green, eventually led to the temporary dissolution of the Democratic machine in Chicago. After Daley's death, Chicago's first black—and beloved—mayor, Harold Washington, took office in 1983.

Chicago Today

The thriving commercial and financial "City of Broad Shoulders" is spiked with gorgeous architecture and set with cultural and recreational gems, including the Art Institute, Millennium Park, 250 theater companies, and 30 miles of shoreline. Approximately 2.8 million residents live within the city limits, and tens of thousands commute from the ever-sprawling suburbs to work downtown.

The last Mayor Daley gave downtown a makeover, with his focus on ecofriendly building initiatives that led to a green roof on City Hall and new bike paths throughout town. But parts of the South and West sides remain mired in poverty and suffer the brunt of the gun violence that has made international headlines.

There are always controversies (former governor Rod Blagojevich was convicted of federal corruption charges in 2011 and current Mayor Emanuel is no stranger to contention), but most Chicagoans are fiercely proud to call the city home.

IMPORTANT DATES IN CHICAGO HISTORY

1886	Haymarket Riot
1893	World's Columbian Exposition
1968	Democratic National Convention
1973	Sears (now Willis) Tower, tallest building in North America, completed
2008	Then–Illinois Senator Barack Obama elected 44th president of the United States

FOR "DA FANS"

You can't talk about Chicago for long without hearing the name of at least one of its storied sports legends: Michael Jordan, Scottie Pippen, Walter "Sweetness" Payton, William "The Refrigerator" Perry, Ernie Banks, "Slammin'" Sammy Sosa, "Shoeless" Joe Jackson. Sports fandom runs through the city's veins, win or lose. One of the best ways to experience the true spirit of Chicago is to join its fiercely loyal fans at a game.

Chicago Bears

Even people who don't know the gridiron from a nine iron are familiar with "Da Bears," as immortalized in the famous *Saturday Night Live* sketch. Chicago's hard-fought, smash-mouth brand of football has made the Monsters of the Midway the winningest franchise in NFL history; they won their 700th game in 2010. The team made it to the Super Bowl in 2006, eventually losing to the Colts, but has not fared particularly well in the nearly decade since, and in 2015 overhauled its coaching and management staff.

Where They Play: ⊠ *Soldier Field, 1410 South Museum Campus Dr., Near South Side.*

Season: August–December

How to Buy Tickets: Ticketmaster ☎ *312/559–1212* ⊕ *www.chicagobears.com.*

Most Notable Players: Dick Butkus, Mike Ditka, Sid Luckman, Bronko Nagurski, Walter Payton, Gale Sayers

Past Highlights: Jim McMahon's "statement" headbands and eventual Hall of Famer Richard Dent's stellar play helped the team shuffle right up to the Vince Lombardi Trophy after winning Super Bowl XX.

Chicago Bulls

Although the days of Air Jordan, three-peats, and Dennis Rodman in wedding dresses may be firmly in the rearview mirror, the legacy established by winning six championships in eight years has sustained the team's popularity, even through the leaner years that followed. Now, a new squad of fresh faces, led by consensus 2011 MVP Derrick Rose, is looking to put its stamp on the next Bulls dynasty. While Rose missed the entire 2012–13 season due to an injury, the team still made the Eastern Conference Finals. They lost to the Miami Heat. Rose then missed most of the 2013–14 season with another injury, but has since roared back to form, and but six consecutive years of playoff appearances indicate that the Bulls are back in the game for good.

Where They Play: ⊠ *United Center, 1901 W. Madison St., Near West Side.*

Season: October–April

How to Buy Tickets: Ticket office ☎ *312/455–4000* ⊕ *www.bulls.com.*

Most Notable Players: Michael Jordan, Dennis Rodman, Scottie Pippen, Toni Kukoc

Past Highlights: The Bulls owned the 1990s, becoming the only team in NBA history to win more than 70 games in a season in 1995–96 with an incredible 72–10 record.

Chicago Cubs

Cubbies fans are certainly loyal, sticking by their "boys in blue" for more than 100 championship-free years. Some blame the record losing streak on a curse made by Billy Sianis, owner of the Billy Goat Tavern, after he and his ticket-holding goat were booted from Wrigley during Game 4 of the 1945 Cubs–Tigers World Series. The ensuing years have had their share of goats; but with new ownership, a new

manager in Joe Maddon, and several promising young players, hope springs eternal for the Lovable Losers.

Where They Play: ✉ *Wrigley Field, 1060 W. Addison St., Lakeview.*

Season: April–September

How to Buy Tickets: Ticket office ☏ 773/404–2827 ⊕ *chicago.cubs.mlb.com.*

Most Notable Players: Ernie Banks, Ron Santo, Ryne Sandberg, Sammy Sosa

Past Highlights: "Slammin'" Sammy Sosa played a major role in reawakening Americans' interest in baseball in 1998 as he battled Mark McGwire in a historic chase for the home-run record, finishing with 66 home runs during the height of the steroid era.

Chicago White Sox

The South Side favorites won the World Series in 2005, sweeping the Astros in four games. Since then, though, the Sox have made the playoffs only once, when they won the AL Central in 2008. In 2011 manager Ozzie Guillen was replaced by former third baseman Robin Ventura, but so far performance has been uneven. Despite recent struggles, the Sox's young squad is expected to be in contention for the title sooner rather than later.

Where They Play: ✉ *U.S. Cellular Field, 333 W. 35th St., South Side.*

Season: April–September

How to Buy Tickets: Ticket office ☏ 312/674–1000 ⊕ *www.whitesox.mlb.com.*

Most Notable Players: "Shoeless" Joe Jackson, Nellie Fox, Luis Aparicio, Harold Baines, Frank Thomas

Past Highlights: In July 2009 Mark Buehrle, a veteran pitcher who has spent his entire career with the White Sox, notched the second perfect game in the team's history, earning him a congratulatory phone call from President Obama (an avowed Sox fan).

Chicago Blackhawks

Though the Hawks have led the NHL in attendance for the last three seasons, they too were hit by the seemingly city-wide championship drought, having failed to win a Stanley Cup since 1961. But that's all changed: seven straight years in the playoffs have seen three championships, with the Cup coming back to the Windy City in 2010, 2013, and 2015. Owner Rocky Wirtz, the son of much-maligned owner William "Dollar Bill" Wirtz, deserves credit for changing ownership policies to attract elite talent—and fans—back to the United Center.

Where They Play: ✉ *United Center, 1901 W. Madison St., Near West Side.*

Season: October–April

How to Buy Tickets: Ticket office ☏ 800/745–3000 ⊕ *blackhawks.nhl.com.*

Most Notable Players: Stan Mikita, Pierre Pilote, Bobby Hull, Denis Savard, Tony Esposito

Past Highlights: The Hawks brought the Cup home to Chicago in 2010 on a thrilling sudden-death overtime goal by Patrick Kane to beat the Flyers in Game 6. Even the Chicago Picasso donned a hockey mask in celebration.

A GOOD PUBLIC ART WALK

Chicago's museums house some of the most famous art anywhere, but don't forget the city's great outdoors. Some of the most impressive art here is outside, in plazas, parks, and other public spaces. The best part? It's all free.

Michigan Avenue and Millennium Park

Start your tour in front of the **Art Institute of Chicago** on Michigan Avenue at Adams Street, where you'll see the two iconic bronze lion statues that guard the entrance. Head north to the well-manicured paths of the museum's two public gardens, filled with fountains and sculptures, including Alexander Calder's **Flying Dragon.**

Exit at the south end of Millennium Park and check out the **Crown Fountain,** two 50-foot glass block towers separated by a granite reflecting pool. The towers project a collection of video images of the faces of 1,000 Chicagoans filmed by artist Jaume Plensa. From time to time, one of the faces sports pursed lips and "spits" water down, showering the shrieking crowd below. Don't miss Anish Kapoor's first public outdoor piece, **Cloud Gate** (affectionately called "the Bean" by locals). The shiny surface is like a giant fun-house mirror reflecting and distorting the skyline. Also of note is the Frank Gehry–designed **Jay Pritzker Pavilion,** an outdoor concert venue with curling ribbons of steel that frame the opening to the stage and connect to a trellis sound system.

Enter the Loop

Pass the Greek-inspired peristyle at the park's northwest corner to exit the park at Randolph Street. Head west on Randolph to **We Will,** a contemporary steel sculpture that's local artist Richard Hunt's ode to the city's diversity. Continue west until you reach the plaza of the James R. Thompson Center at LaSalle Street to see Jean DeBuffet's graffiti-inspired 1984 sculpture **Monument with Standing Beast.** Across LaSalle Street to the north, look up to see Richard Hunt's **Freeform** on the entrance of the State of Illinois building. The sculpture weighs 3 tons and is 2½ stories tall.

Daley Plaza

Next, head to Daley Plaza to see Picasso's **unnamed sculpture.** Opinions vary about whether the abstract installation represents a woman's head or one of the artist's Afghan hounds. Across the street is Joan Miró's **Chicago,** originally titled *The Sun, the Moon and One Star.* Stand behind the 39-foot mixed-media sculpture to see the blue mosaic work at its back.

Chase and Federal Plazas and the Federal Building

Walk east to Dearborn Street, then south to Chase Plaza to see **The Four Seasons** by Marc Chagall, a 70-foot-long mosaic/mural that depicts six Chicago-specific scenes. Continue two blocks south to Federal Plaza, where the **Flamingo** by Alexander Calder is a striking, 53-foot vermillion red contrast to the black and steel buildings around it. End your tour with a peek through the glass of the lobby of the Federal Building here to see the **Town-Ho's Story,** a crazy conglomeration of steel and aluminum that's part of Frank Stella's *Moby-Dick* series.

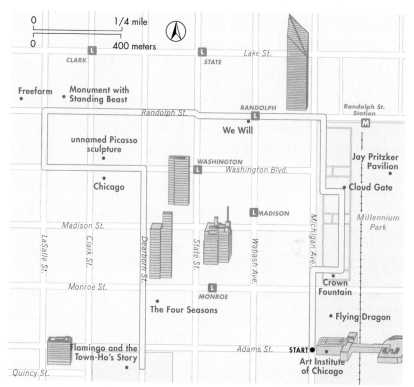

Highlights:	The Picasso, Joan Miró's Chicago, Cloud Gate, Crown Fountain.
Where to Start:	The Art Institute of Chicago (El Red and Blue lines at Jackson; Orange, Green, Pink, Brown, and Purple lines at Adams).
Length:	Two to four hours, depending on stopping times.
Where to Stop:	The Federal Building (El Red and Blue lines at Jackson; Brown, Orange, and Purple lines at LaSalle and Van Buren).
Best Time to Go:	A weekday morning in fall, when the weather is good and crowds tend to be light.
Worst Time to Go:	A frigid winter day or a busy summer weekend.
Good in the 'Hood:	The "Chicago Mix" of cheese and caramel popcorn at any of the handful of Garrett's Popcorn shops (26 W. Randolph St. at State St. and other locations) scattered around downtown.

A GOOD ARCHITECTURE WALK

The Great Fire of 1871 could have been the death of Chicago, but instead it proved to be a grand rebirth. Renowned architects treated the decimated urban landscape as a fresh palette for their innovative ideas, sparking a revolution that has never really ended. Chicago's skyline is one of the city's most precious attributes, ever-changing but always awe-inspiring.

Tall Buildings of Every Size

Chicago is the home of the modern skyscraper, so start your tour at Wacker Drive and Adams Street at the city's tallest building, the **Willis Tower** (aka the Sears Tower). The 1,454-foot giant was the tallest building in the world when it was finished in 1973. Then head to the famous **Rookery Building.** This 12-story stunner, completed in 1888 by Daniel Burnham and John Welborn Root, is the oldest standing high-rise in town. On Jackson, check out the 45-story art deco **Chicago Board of Trade**, designed by Holabird & Root in 1930.

Chicago School and Modern Contrasts

Also on Jackson Street is Burnham and Root's 17-story **Monadnock Building.** Built in 1891, it's the last and tallest skyscraper built with masonry load-bearing walls. Head to Congress Parkway and Wabash Avenue to see Louis Sullivan and Dankmar Adler's **Auditorium Building,** a grand theater completed in 1889 that still hosts performances. These buildings are evidence of Chicago School architecture, which combined modern design practices of the time with traditional ideas like brick facades and ornamentation.

For a lesson in contrast, double back to Jackson and Dearborn streets to see the orderly, geometric 4.6-acre **Federal Center,** which was completed in the early 1970s by Mies van der Rohe. Don't miss the graceful slopes of **Chase Tower,** built in 1969 as the First National Bank of Chicago Building.

Stores and Centers

The **Sullivan Center,** at State and Madison streets, was Louis Sullivan's last major work in Chicago; note the elaborate cast-iron entryway ornamentation and three-part "Chicago Window," allowing plenty of light. Walk along State Street, past the **Reliance Building** (now the Hotel Burnham). This building is considered the first-ever glass-and-steel skyscraper. On the northeast corner of State and Washington streets, stop and admire **Macy's,** designed by Burnham in 1907 and most famous for the multistory atriums inside, one domed with a Tiffany mosaic.

Walk west on Randolph Street to reach the 648-foot **Richard J. Daley Center** at Clark Street, the tallest building in Chicago for four years until the John Hancock Center was built in 1969. Across Randolph is Helmut Jahn's dome-shape **James R. Thompson Center.**

Corncobs and High-Profile Towers

Head north on Clark Street, then east along the Chicago River to see **Marina City,** Bertrand Goldberg's pair of 61-story corncob-like apartment towers. Along the river at Kinzie Street is **Trump International Hotel & Tower,** a 1,389-foot skyscraper condo-hotel complex that was initially designed to be the world's tallest building before the events of 9/11.

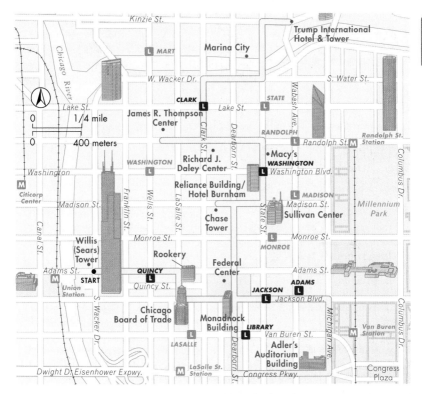

Highlights:	Willis Tower, Sullivan Center, Marina City.
Where to Start:	Willis Tower (El Brown, Orange, Pink, and Purple lines at Quincy).
Length:	Three to four hours, depending on stops.
Where to Stop:	Trump International Hotel & Tower (El Red Line at Grand).
Best Time to Go:	Late morning in the fall, when tourists are fewer and workers have settled in at their desks.
Worst Time to Go:	Summer weekends during one of the many downtown festivals.
Good in the 'Hood:	Browsing the shops on the ground floor of the Monadnock Building is like stepping back in time; eye vintage-inspired clothing and shoes at Florodora and Florodora Shoes, try on a fedora at Optimo Hats, or get a close shave at Frank's old-timey barbershop.

CLARK STREET PUB CRAWL

Once a Native American trail, Clark Street is one of Chicago's major arteries, running roughly 12 miles from Chinatown on the South Side to the border with Evanston at the north. A Clark Street pub crawl, with stops in three distinct neighborhoods, gives you a taste of this vibrant, diverse city that plays as hard as it works.

Downtown/River North

Begin your pub crawl where Clark Street meets the Chicago River. From the Clark Street Bridge, the city spreads out in all directions. On your left are the iconic corncob structures of Marina Towers, with Lake Michigan in the far distance, and a series of bridges spans the river on both sides.

If you're kicking off your walk during the day, head to **Fado** (⊠ *100 W. Grand Ave.* ☎ *312/836–0066*), an ornate Irish pub featuring decor imported from the Emerald Isle. Relax with a perfectly poured pint of Guinness and a hearty boxty. ■TIP➜ Blues fans should check the night's lineup at Blue Chicago just up the street at 536 N. Clark Street to see whether it's worth heading back downtown for music and a nightcap. After knocking back a pint or two, take a five-minute walk to the Grand Avenue Red Line station, where you'll hop on a northbound El train. You can also flag a cab or grab a northbound bus on Dearborn.

Lakeview/Wrigleyville

Exit the Red Line at Addison and walk to **Murphy's Bleachers** (⊠ *3655 N. Sheffield Ave.* ☎ *773/281–5356*), directly across from Wrigley Field's bleacher entrance. The historic sports bar's rooftop is the best place to watch a Cubs game outside of the Friendly Confines. With sports memorabilia lining the walls and numerous brews on tap, it's the quintessential Wrigleyville experience. Finish getting your sports fix and head back to the Red Line stop at Addison.

Andersonville

Exit the Red Line at Berwyn and whet your thirst with a stroll through Andersonville. Beer aficionados flock to **The Hopleaf** (⊠ *5148 N. Clark St.* ☎ *773/334–9851*) for its mind-boggling selection of international drafts and bottled beers. Note that the bar area gets very crowded on weekends and there's almost always a wait for a table. Energy flagging by this point? Luckily it's just a quick stumble north to your last stop, **Simon's Tavern** (⊠ *5201 N. Clark St.* ☎ *773/878–0894*). Look for the neon sign depicting a fish hoisting a martini—a play on "pickled herring." This slightly divey bar is steeped in local history. The original owner, a bootlegger during Prohibition, used to cash paychecks in a bulletproof booth on the premises. When you're ready to call it a night, hail a cab or hike it back to the 24-hour Red Line.

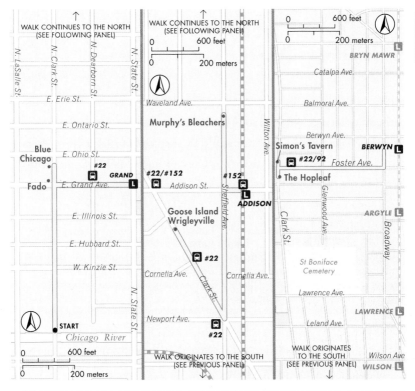

Highlights:	**River North**: View downtown in all its splendor from the Clark Street Bridge, memorialized in a Carl Sandburg poem of the same name. This neighborhood boasts boutiques, galleries, clubs, trendy restaurants, and businesses all concentrated within a few square blocks. **Wrigleyville:** Sports reign supreme in this North Side neighborhood, where Wrigley Field and sports bars surrounding it are the primary draw. **Andersonville:** Unpretentious bars, restaurants, and antiques shops line this stretch of Clark Street on the Far North Side, and side streets are quiet and tree-lined.
Where to Start:	Clark Street at the Chicago River (El Brown and Purple lines at the Merchandise Mart).
Length:	Three to four hours, depending on how long you mull over your beer (7 miles).
Where to Stop:	Simon's Tavern in Andersonville (El Red Line at Berwyn).
Best Time to Go:	Late afternoon or early evening.
Worst Time to Go:	Morning.

A GOOD GALLERY WALK IN RIVER NORTH

River North is the granddaddy of Chicago's gallery districts, a more established and refined neighborhood of art-centric businesses than other trendy
areas like Pilsen and the West Loop. It's an easy walk to River North from
most downtown hotels, and there's a bevy of hip restaurants and clubs
interspersed with the galleries here, making it a one-stop destination for
a great time out.

Superior Street: The Epicenter of It All

Start at the heart of the action, at the intersection of Superior and Wells streets. A walk in any direction from here can't go wrong if you're looking for galleries to browse, but we suggest heading west on pretty Superior Street to hit a huge cluster of galleries on this block right off the bat. The first among our favorites on this street is **Ann Nathan Gallery** (⊠ *212 W. Superior St.* ☎ *312/664–6622*), which showcases both established and emerging sculptors and painters in a spacious, bright space with high ceilings and exposed wood beams. Just a few doors down is **ECHT Gallery** (⊠ *222 W. Superior St.* ☎ *312/440–0288*), the go-to place for contemporary glass sculpture by artists including Dale Chihuly and Martin Blank. At 300 West Superior Street you'll find several notable galleries, including **Catherine Edelman Gallery,** well known for its breathtaking collection of contemporary photography and mixed-media photo-based art, most in black and white. Vintage black-and-white photographs can be found directly across the street at **Stephen Daiter Gallery** (⊠ *230 W. Superior St.* ☎ *312/787–3350*), which specializes in experimental works.

Franklin Street: Contemporary Curb Appeal

Head north to Franklin Street and take time to stop at the many shops and galleries with massive windows showcasing their wares. Don't miss **Architech Gallery of Architectural Art** (⊠ *730 N. Franklin St.* ☎ *312/475–1290*); their collection includes lithographs from Frank Lloyd Wright's Wasmuth Portfolio and some of Daniel Burnham's original plans and construction documents. **Stephen Kelly Gallery** (⊠ *750 N. Franklin St.* ☎ *312/867–1931*) showcases the colorful abstracts of the owner as well as a handful of other contemporary artists.

Wells Street: More Art and Tourist Hot Spots

Head back toward Wells Street, where you'll find a curious mix of sophisticated galleries and iconic restaurants (including '50s diner-style Ed Debevic's and Chicago-pizza classic Gino's East). Duck into **Roy Boyd Gallery** (⊠ *739 N. Wells St.* ☎ *312/642–1606*), one of the oldest galleries in the neighborhood. Most of what you'll find here is abstract painting, drawing, and sculpture. Across the street is **Carl Hammer Gallery** (⊠ *740 N. Wells St.* ☎ *312/266–8512*), known for its collection of outsider art by Chris Ware and Hollis Sigler, among others.

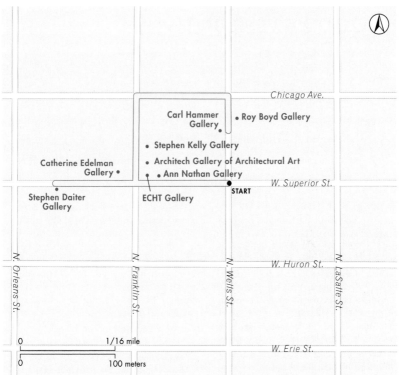

Highlights:	Ann Nathan Gallery, Architech Gallery of Architectural Art, Carl Hammer Gallery.
Where to Start:	Intersection of Superior and Wells (El Red and Brown lines at Chicago Ave.).
Length:	Two to three hours, depending on your browsing pace, and about half a mile.
Where to Stop:	Wells Street. The El Red and Brown lines at Chicago Ave. are a quick walk away.
Best Time to Go:	Friday evening, when new exhibitions open and area galleries stay open late.
Worst Time to Go:	Sunday or Monday, when most galleries are closed. Most galleries are open Tuesday through Saturday from noon to 5 pm. The crowd-averse should avoid this area in early May, when throngs of art lovers descend on galleries during the annual Expo Chicago fair.

A GOOD LAKEFRONT BIKE RIDE

There are few better ways to fall instantly in love with Chicago than by touring its lakefront path. You could do it on foot or by Rollerblade, but the best way to take in the sights is by bicycle. You'll cover the most ground, get in some decent exercise, and — if you're lucky — get a nice tailwind to help you along courtesy of Lake Michigan.

First Things First: Getting a Bike

The entire lakefront path is just over 18 miles long. Your best bet is to start in the middle, at Navy Pier, where you can rent some wheels from **Bike and Roll Chicago** (⊠ *600 E. Grand Ave.* ☎ *312/729–1000* ⊕ *www.bikechicago.com*); the company has additional locations at Millennium Park, the Riverwalk, and the 53rd Street Bike Center in Hyde Park. **Bobby's Bike Hike** (⊠ *465 N. McClurg Ct.* ☎ *312/915–0995* ⊕ *www.bobbysbikehike.com*) is another option. Bobby's also books guided tours, including a kids' cycle and a historic Hyde Park tour. (*For more on Lakefront Activities, see Experience the Lakefront in this chapter.*)

North or South?

Either direction you head from Navy Pier will not disappoint. The north part of the trail hugs Lincoln Park and affords beautiful views, but it can be heavy with runners and skaters, and it might prove hard to navigate the traffic. Instead opt to head south. ■TIP➔ **Addresses are painted on the pavement—"500S" for 500 South—so you can keep tabs on where you are.**

Downtown Chicago

After five minutes or so, you'll be pedaling past downtown and the big and small boats bobbing in the bay at **Chicago Yacht Club,** which hosts the famous Race to Mackinac each July. At Randolph Street you can take a detour to check out **Millennium Park,** including the show-stopping Crown Fountain and *Cloud Gate* (Bean)

sculpture. Just a few blocks south is **Buckingham Fountain** in Grant Park, one of the city's most recognizable landmarks. If you're here between April and October, wait to see the water show that happens every hour on the hour for 20 minutes starting at 9 am, with the final display ending at 11 pm; evening shows are set to lights and music.

Museum Campus

Less than a mile away is **Museum Campus,** a 57-acre lakefront park that's home to the **Shedd Aquarium, the Field Museum,** and **Adler Planetarium.** Solidarity Drive is a quiet, pretty detour with a promenade and access to **Northerly Island.** Actually a peninsula, it was home to Meigs Field airport until 2003, but is now a nature area with a small beach (12th Street Beach, a little-known downtown gem) and a concert venue.

Soldier Field, Chinatown, and Beyond

Back on the path, you'll pass **Soldier Field,** home of the Chicago Bears football team, and **Burnham Skate Park,** a 20,000-square-foot expanse of ramps, rails, and straightaways for aspiring skateboarders, then **McCormick Place,** a massive exhibition center and trade show hall. Continue south on a much more serene trail. Stop for a quick dip at **Hyde Park,** home to the University of Chicago and the massive **Museum of Science and Industry,** or continue to the larger **63rd Street Beach** in Jackson Park, where you'll find the city's oldest beach house. The trail ends at 71st Street.

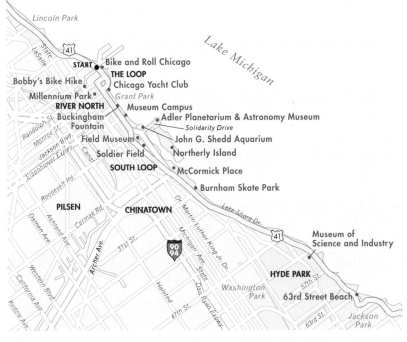

Highlights:	Buckingham Fountain, Millennium Park, Museum Campus, Northerly Island, Soldier Field, 63rd Street Beach.
Where to Start:	Navy Pier (El Red Line at Grand Ave.).
Length:	One to four hours, depending on stops.
Where to Stop:	71st Street (6 Jackson Park express bus has a bike rack).
Best Time to Go:	A warm and sunny weekday morning, when the crowds are light and the lake is peaceful.
Worst Time to Go:	An unseasonably warm weekend when it will feel like the entire city decided to join you to take advantage of the weather.
Good in the 'Hood:	McDonald's Cycle Center in Millennium Park offers free bike parking, fee-based repairs, and lockers and showers for members.

EXPERIENCE THE LAKEFRONT

Enjoy the Lake

San Diego and Los Angeles may have the ocean, and New York its Central Park, but Chicago has the peaceful waters of Lake Michigan at its doorstep. Bikers, dog walkers, boaters, and runners crowd the lakefront paths on warm days; in winter the lake is equally beautiful, with icy towers formed from frozen sheets of water.

For information on biking along the lakeshore, see A Good Lakefront Bike Ride in this chapter.

Hit the Beach

One of the greatest surprises in the city is the miles of sandy beaches that Chicagoans flock to in summer. The water becomes warm enough to swim in toward the end of June, though the brave will take an icy dip through the end of October. Chicago has about 30 miles of shoreline, most of it sand or rock beach. Beaches are open to the public daily from 11 am (a handful at 9:30 am) to 7 pm, Memorial Day through Labor Day, and many beaches have changing facilities; all are wheelchair-accessible.

The **Chicago Park District** provides lifeguard protection during daylight hours throughout the swimming season.

All references to north and south in beach listings refer to how far north or south of the Loop each beach is. In other words, 1600 to 2400 North means the beach begins 16 blocks north of the Loop (at Madison Street, which is the 100 block) and extends for eight blocks.

⚠ Along the lakefront you'll see plenty of broken-rock breakwaters with signs that warn "No swimming or diving." Although Chicagoans frequently ignore these signs, you shouldn't. The boulders below the water are slippery with seaweed and may hide sharp, rusty scraps of metal, and the water beyond is very deep. It can be dangerous even if you know the territory.

Boating

Nothing beats the view of the Chicago skyline from the water, especially when the sun sets behind the sparkling skyscrapers. Plenty of boats are available to rent or charter, though you might want to leave the skippering to others if you're not familiar with Great Lakes navigation.

Sailboat lessons, rentals, and charters are available from **Chicago Sailing** (☎ 773/871–7245 ⊕ *www.chicagosailing. com*). Chicago Sailing focuses on sailing instruction for all levels and includes a program on keeping your boat in tip-top shape.

Sailboats, Inc. (☎ 800/826–7010 ⊕ *www. sailboats-inc.com*), one of the oldest charter-certification schools in the country, prepares its students to charter any type of boat.

2

THE LOOP

GETTING ORIENTED

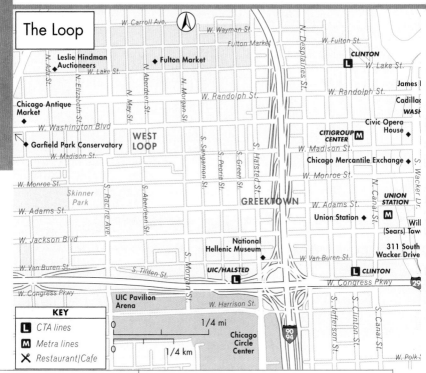

KEY

- **L** CTA lines
- **M** Metra lines
- **✕** Restaurant/Cafe

0 ———— 1/4 mi

0 ———— 1/4 km

MAKING THE MOST OF YOUR TIME

The Loop has many "must-sees," including the Art Institute and the architectural boat tour (⇨ *Experience Chicago chapter*), so prepare for a long day. Browse the shops on State Street, then take a trip out on the Ledge at Willis Tower and snap a selfie at Millennium Park's "Bean." Later, catch a play or a Chicago Symphony concert. Set aside another full day to explore the South Loop's Museum Campus: the Field Museum, Shedd Aquarium, and Adler Planetarium are all top-notch choices.

GETTING HERE

If you're driving, you'll probably be taking the expressways—Kennedy from the northwest, Edens/Kennedy from the north, Dan Ryan from the south, and Congress from the west. Lake Shore Drive runs north and south along Lake Michigan.

If you're relying on public transportation, you can come by CTA bus, by El, or by rail. In the suburbs, hop on the Metra or South Shore Line and arrive at Union Station (Canal and Jackson streets). CTA's Red, Green, Blue, Yellow, Purple, Brown, and Pink lines link the city with the Loop.

SAFETY

Some parts of the South Loop feel sketchy, so stick to well-lighted streets at night. In the West Loop near Ashland Avenue and the United Center, gentrification comes to a halt; streets around the Fulton Market area are deserted during off times. Exercise caution in both areas.

TOP REASONS TO GO

Get cultured: Spend an afternoon at the Art Institute perusing everything from ancient mosaics and old master paintings to contemporary photographs.

See fabulous fountains: Watch the faces screened onto Millennium Park's Crown Fountain spit at delighted onlookers, then admire the rococo splendor of Grant Park's Buckingham Fountain.

Appreciate architecture: From late 19th-century beauties, like the Rookery, to late 20th-century marvels, such as the Willis Tower, the Loop contains some of the country's architectural gems.

Get a taste of Chicago: Order a deep-dish pizza at Pizzeria Uno, where it was invented, or opt for authentic Mediterranean food in the West Loop's Greektown district.

Explore the world and beyond: Spot stars at the Adler Planetarium, spy your favorite fish at the John G. Shedd Aquarium, and see Sue the *T. rex* at the Field Museum.

QUICK BITES

Caffè Baci. For breakfast, lunch, or a quick snack, this is a great find. Try a "Jojo," the bistro's signature sandwich—it's a *filone* (an Italian baguette) stuffed with prosciutto, mozzarella, artichoke hearts, basil, and plum tomatoes. ⊠ *2 N. LaSalle, Loop* ☎ *312/629–2216* ⊕ *www.caffebaci.com* ⊗ *Closed weekends.*

Garrett Popcorn. Lines form early and stay throughout the day. The popcorn is so popular that there are nine other Chicago outlets plus branches in Dubai, Hong Kong, Singapore, Japan, Kuwait, and Malaysia. ⊠ *26 W. Randolph St., Loop* ☎ *888/476–7267* ⊕ *www.garrettpopcorn.com.*

Heaven on Seven. This Loop legend is famous for casual Cajun breakfasts and lunches that have area office workers gladly lining up to be served. ⊠ *111 N. Wabash Ave., 7th fl., Loop* ☎ *312/263–6443* ⊕ *www.heavenonseven.com* ⊗ *Closed Sun.*

Defined by the El (the elevated train that makes a circuit around the area), the Loop is Chicago at its big-city best. Noisy and mesmerizing, it's a living architectural museum alongside shimmering Lake Michigan. Gleaming modern towers vie for space with late 19th- and early 20th-century buildings, and striking sculptures by Picasso, Miró, and Chagall watch over plazas that come alive with music and farmers' markets in summer.

THE LOOP

Updated by Roberta Sotonoff

The Loop oozes with charm and culture—it has a world-class symphony, top-rate theaters, fine restaurants, tempting shops, and swinging nightlife. There's no shortage of sights to see either. A slew of impressive buildings representing different styles and eras makes it feel like a theme park for architecture enthusiasts.(⇨ *The Good Architecture Walk in the Experience Chicago chapter for architecture highlights.*) Internationally known landmarks, including Millennium Park's *Cloud Gate* sculpture, blanket the Loop landscape, and visitors and locals alike gush over the masterpieces displayed inside the renowned Art Institute, this country's second largest art museum.

TOP ATTRACTIONS

150 North Michigan Avenue. Some wags have pointed out that this building, with its diamond-shape top, looks like a giant pencil sharpener. Built in 1984 as the Smurfit-Stone Building and later known as the Crain Communications Building, it has a slanted top that carves through the top 10 of its floors. In the plaza is Yaacov Agam's *Communication X9*, a painted, folded-aluminum sculpture. You'll see different patterns in the sculpture depending on your vantage point. ⌧ *150 N. Michigan Ave., Loop.*

190 South LaSalle Street. This 40-story postmodern office building, resembling a supersized château, was designed by John Burgee and Philip Johnson in the mid-1980s. The grand, gold-leaf vaulted lobby is spectacular. ⊠ *190 S. LaSalle St., at W. Adams St., Loop.*

224 South Michigan Avenue. This structure, designed in 1904 by Daniel Burnham, who later moved his office here, was once known as the Railway Exchange Building and the Santa Fe Building, for a "Santa Fe" sign on its roof that has since been removed. The **Chicago Architecture Foundation** uses the building's atrium for rotating exhibits about the changing landscape of Chicago and other cities. The organization also offers a variety of tours via foot, bus, and boat. ⊠ *224 S. Michigan Ave., Loop.*

> ### GRID CITY
>
> Getting around the Loop is easy. It's laid out like a grid. The intersection of State Street, which runs north–south, and Madison Street, which runs east–west, is the zero point from which the rest of the city fans out.

FAMILY **Art Institute of Chicago.** ⇨ *See highlighted feature in this chapter for more information.* ⊠ *111 S. Michigan Ave., Loop* 🕾 *312/443–3600* ⊕ *www.artic.edu/aic* 🖎 *$23* ⊙ *Fri.–Wed. 10:30–5, Thurs. 10:30–8, weekends 10:30–5.*

Fodor's Choice ★

Chicago Board of Trade. Home of the thriving financial district, relatively narrow LaSalle Street earned the moniker "The Canyon" (and it feels like one) because of the large buildings that flank either end. This one was designed by Holabird & Root and completed in 1930. The streamlined, 45-story giant recalls the days when art deco was all the rage. The artfully lighted marble lobby soars three stories, and Ceres (the Roman goddess of agriculture) stands atop its roof. Trading is no longer done here, but it's worth a look at what was the city's tallest skyscraper until 1955, when the Prudential Center topped it. ⊠ *141 W. Jackson Blvd., Loop* 🕾 *312/435–3590* ⊕ *www.cbotbuilding.com.*

Fodor's Choice ★ **Chicago Cultural Center.** Built in 1897 as the city's original public library, this huge building houses the Chicago Office of Tourism Visitor Information Center, as well as a gift shop, galleries, and a concert hall. Designed by the Boston firm Shepley, Rutan & Coolidge—the team behind the Art Institute of Chicago—it's a palatial affair notable for its Carrara marble, mosaics, gold leaf, and the world's largest Tiffany glass dome. ⊠ *78 E. Washington St., Loop* 🕾 *312/744–6630* ⊕ *www.chicagoculturalcenter.org* ⊙ *Mon.–Thurs. 8–7, Fri. 8–6, weekends 9–6; tours Wed., Fri., and Sat. at 1:15; concerts Sun. at 3.*

Chicago Theatre. When it opened in 1921, the grand and glitzy Chicago Theatre was tagged "the Wonder Theatre of the World." Its exterior features a shrunken version of the Arc de Triomphe, and its lobby is patterned after the Royal Chapel at Versailles with a staircase copied from the Paris Opera House. Murals decorate the auditorium walls and ceiling. The seven-story, 3,600-seat space has served as a venue for films and famed entertainers ranging from John Philip Sousa and Duke Ellington to Ellen DeGeneres and Beyoncé. Tours let you stand on the stage where they performed, go backstage, and peruse its autographed walls.

LaSalle Street (the Cavern) is Chicago's financial hub.

✉ *175 N. State St., Loop* ☎ *312/462–6318* ⊕ *www.thechicagotheatre. com* ✉ *Tours $15* ☉ *Tours daily at noon.*

Civic Opera House. The handsome home of the Lyric Opera of Chicago is grand indeed, with pink-and-gray Tennessee-marble floors, pillars with carved capitals, crystal chandeliers, and a sweeping staircase to the second floor. Designed by Graham, Anderson, Probst & White, the second-largest opera house in North America combines lavish art deco details with art nouveau touches. Tours are given a few times a year. ✉ *20 N. Wacker Dr., Loop* ☎ *312/419–0033 Civic Opera House, 312/332–2244 Lyric Opera* ⊕ *www.civicoperahouse.com.*

Fine Arts Building. This creaky building was constructed in 1895 to house the showrooms of the Studebaker Company, then makers of carriages. Publishers, artists, and even architect Frank Lloyd Wright have used its spaces. Today the principal tenants are professional musicians. Take a look at the handsome exterior; then step inside the marble-and-wood-work lobby, noting the motto engraved in marble as you enter: "All passes—art alone endures." The building has an interior courtyard, across which strains of piano music and sopranos' voices compete with tenors' as they run through exercises. Visitors can get a peek at the studios and hear live music during "Open Studios" events, held on the second Friday of each month between 5 and 9 pm. ✉ *410 S. Michigan Ave., Loop* ☎ *312/566–9800* ⊕ *www.fineartsbuilding.com* ☉ *Weekdays 7 am–10 pm, Sat. 7 am–9 pm, Sun. 10 am–5 pm.*

FAMILY **Grant Park and Buckingham Fountain.** Two of Chicago's greatest treasures reside in Grant Park—the Art Institute and Buckingham Fountain. Bordered by Lake Michigan to the east, a spectacular skyline to the west, and the Museum Campus to the south, the ever-popular park serves as the city's front yard and unofficial gathering place. This pristine open space has walking paths, a stand of stately elm trees, and formal rose gardens, where Loop dwellers and 9-to-5-ers take refuge from the concrete and steel. It also hosts many of the city's largest outdoor events, including the annual Taste of Chicago, a vast picnic featuring foods from more than 70 restaurants.

The park's centerpiece is the gorgeous, tiered **Buckingham Fountain** (*between Columbus and Lake Shore Drs. east of Congress Plaza*), which has intricate pink-marble seashell designs, water-spouting fish, and bronze sculptures of sea horses. Built in 1927, it was patterned after one at Versailles but is about twice the size. See the fountain in all its glory between May 1 and October 1, when it's elaborately illuminated at night and sprays colorfully lighted waters. Linger long enough to experience the spectacular display that takes place every hour on the hour, and you'll witness the center jet of water shoot 150 feet into the air. ⊠ *Loop* ☎ *312/742–7529* ⊕ *www.chicagoparkdistrict.com/parks/clarence-f-buckingham-memorial-fountain* ⊗ *Park daily 6 am–11 pm. Fountain Apr.–mid-Oct., daily 8 am–10:45 pm.*

James R. Thompson Center. People either hate or love this state-government building. Former governor James Thompson, who selected the Helmut Jahn design, hailed it in his 1985 dedication speech as "the first building of the 21st century." For others, it's a case of postmodernism run amok. A bowl-like form topped by a truncated cylinder, the 17-story building's sky-blue-and-salmon color scheme screams 1980s. But the 17-story atrium, where exposed elevators zip up and down and sunlight casts dizzying patterns through the metal-and-glass skin, is one of the most animated interiors anywhere in the city. The sculpture in the plaza is Jean Dubuffet's *Monument with Standing Beast*. It was once nearly as controversial as the building itself. The curved shapes, in white with black traceries, have led it to being nicknamed "Snoopy in a blender." The **Illinois Artisans Shop** (*312/814–5321*), on the second level of the center, sells crafts, jewelry, and folk art by Illinois artists; it's open weekdays 9–5. ⊠ *100 W. Randolph St., Loop* ☎ *312/814–3000* ⊕ *www2.illinois.gov/cms/About/JRTC.*

FAMILY **Maggie Daley Park.** Named after former Mayor Richard M. Daley's late wife, this park offers a place to play between Lake Michigan and the city's skyline. Opened in late 2014, it includes 40-foot-high rock-climbing sculptures, an Enchanted Forest with a kaleidoscope and mirrored maze, a Slide Crater, a Wave Lawn, and an area strictly for

DID YOU KNOW?

The BP Bridge is the first (and so far only) to be designed by Frank Gehry. Pretty as the gently sloping, brushed steel structure is, the bridge also serves a practical purpose: it helps keep nearby traffic noise from interfering with concerts held at the Jay Pritzker Pavilion.

BP BRIDGE

toddlers. A seasonal ice-skating ribbon winds around the park (skates can be rented for $12). ⊠ *337 E. Randolph St., at northeastern edge of Grant Park, Loop* ☎ *312/742–3918* ⊕ *www.chicagoparkdistrict. com/parks/maggie-daley-park/* ⊗ *6 am–11pm.*

Marquette Building. Like a slipcover over a sofa, the clean, geometric facade of this1895 building expresses what lies beneath: in this case, a structural steel frame. Sure, the base is marked with roughly cut stone and a fancy cornice crowns the top, but the bulk of the Marquette Building mirrors the cage around which it is built. Inside is another story. The intimate lobby is a jewel box of a space, where a single Doric column stands surrounded by a Tiffany glass mosaic depicting the exploits of French Jesuit missionary Jacques Marquette, an early explorer of Illinois and the Upper Midwest. From its steel skeleton to the terra-cotta ornamentation, this Holabird & Roche structure is a clear example of the Chicago style. ⊠ *140 S. Dearborn St., Loop* ☎ *312/422–5500* ⊕ *www.marquette.macfound.org.*

FINDING FACTS

For information about the city's architectural treasures, contact the **Chicago Architecture Foundation** (☎ *312/922–3432* ⊕ *www. architecture.org*) or the **Chicago Convention and Tourism Bureau** (☎ *312/567–8500* ⊕ *www.choosechicago.com*).

FAMILY
Fodor's Choice
★

Millennium Park. "The Bean," the fun fountains, the Disney-esque music pavilion—all the pieces of this park quickly stole the hearts of Chicagoans and visitors alike when it opened 2004. The showstopper is Frank Gehry's stunning **Jay Pritzker Pavilion.** Dramatic ribbons of stainless steel stretching 40 feet into the sky look like petals wrapping the music stage. The sound system, suspended by a trellis that spans the great lawn, provides concert-hall sound outside. Notable events presented here include the Grant Park Music Festival (a classical-music series with free concerts every Wednesday, Friday, and Saturday from mid-June to late August), June's jam-packed Chicago Blues Festival, and the Chicago Jazz Festival on Labor Day Weekend. The 1,525-seat Harris Theater for Music and Dance provides an indoor alternative for fans of the performing arts.

Visitors who appreciate public art will be equally impressed by supersize works like the curvaceous *Cloud Gate* located between Washington and Madison streets. Affectionately dubbed "the Bean," the 110-ton, polished-steel sculpture by noted British artist Anish Kapoor was unveiled in 2006, and its gleaming reflective surface provides a fun-house-mirror view of Chicago's storied skyline. After taking the obligatory selfie beneath it, you can head to the **Crown Fountain** in the park's southwest corner and have a local spit at you. Okay, it's just a giant image of a Chicagoan's face—actually, dozens of Chicagoans' faces rotating through on two 50-foot-high glass block–tower fountains. The genius behind the Crown Fountain, Spanish sculptor Jaume Plensa, lined up the mouths on the digital photos with an opening in the fountain. When a face purses its lips, water shoots out its "mouth." Kids love it, and adults feel like kids watching it.

More conventional park perks include the lovely **Lurie Garden** (a four-season delight) and the seasonal **McCormick Tribune Ice Rink,** which opens for public skating each winter. ⊠ *Between Michigan Ave. and Columbus Dr., Randolph and Monroe Sts., Loop* ☎ *312/742–1168* ⊕ *www.cityofchicago.org/city/en/depts/dca/supp_info/millennium_ park.html* ▣ *Free* ☉ *Daily 6 am–11 pm.*

Prudential Plaza. There are two architecturally notable buildings at the plaza. Directly west of the Aon Center and across from Millennium Park is **One Prudential Plaza.** Designed by Alfonzo Lanelli and completed in 1955, this limestone-and-ridged-aluminum structure was once the city's tallest building (barring the statue of Ceres atop the Board of Trade). At the time, it had the world's fastest elevators and an observation deck that became passé once some of the city's other behemoths were completed. Attached to One Prudential is its sibling **Two Prudential Plaza,** nicknamed "Two Pru," a towering glass-and-granite giant with an address of 180 North Stetson Avenue. Along with their neighbors they form a block-long business-oriented minicity. Two Prudential is the tallest reinforced concrete building in the city, and its blue detailing and beveled roof are instantly recognizable from afar. ⊠ *One Prudential, 130 E. Randolph St., Loop* ☎ *312/565–6700* ⊕ *www.prudentialplaza.info.*

Reliance Building. The clearly expressed, gleaming verticality that characterizes the modern skyscraper was first and most eloquently articulated in this trailblazing steel-frame tower, built by Burnham, Root, and Charles Atwood. Completed in 1895 and now home to the stylish Hotel Burnham, the building was a crumbling eyesore until the late 1990s, when the city initiated a major restoration. In the early and mid-1900s, it was a mixed-use office building. Al Capone's dentist reportedly worked out of what's now Room 809. Don't be misled when you go looking for this masterpiece—a block away, at State and Randolph streets, a dormitory for the School of the Art Institute of Chicago shamelessly mimics it. Once you've found the real thing, admire the mosaic floor and ironwork in the reconstructed elevator lobby. The building boasts early examples of the Chicago Window, which define the entire facade by adding a shimmer and glimmer to the surrounding white terra-cotta. ⊠ *1 W. Washington St., Loop* ☎ *312/782–1111* ⊕ *www.burnhamhotel.com.*

Richard J. Daley Center. Named for late mayor Richard J. Daley, this boldly plain high-rise is the headquarters of the Cook County court system, but it's best known as the site of a sculpture by Picasso. Simply dubbed the *Picasso,* this monumental piece provoked an outcry when it was installed in 1967; baffled Chicagoans tried to determine whether it represented a woman or an Afghan hound. In the end, they gave up guessing and simply embraced it as a unique symbol of the city. The building itself was constructed in 1965 of Cor-Ten steel, which weathers naturally to an attractive bronze. In summer, its plaza is the site of concerts, political rallies, and a Thursday farmers' market. In December, the city's official Christmas tree is erected here, and Christkindlmarket (a traditional German market selling food and gifts) takes over the area. For building tours, call the Circuit Court's Office of Public

Affairs at *312/603–1928.* ✉ *50 W. Washington St., Loop* ☎ *312/603–7980* ⊕ *www.thedaleycenter.com* ⊘ *Weekdays 8–5:30.*

Fodor's Choice **The Rookery.** This 11-story struc-
★ ture, with its eclectically orna-
mented facade, got its name from
the pigeons and politicians who
roosted at the temporary city hall
constructed on this site after the
Great Chicago Fire of 1871; the
structure didn't last long, and the
Rookery replaced it. Designed in
1885 by Burnham & Root, who
used both masonry and a more
modern steel-frame construction,
the Rookery was one of the first
buildings in the country to feature a
central court that brought sunlight
into interior office spaces. Frank

Lloyd Wright, who kept an office here for a short time, renovated the
two-story lobby and light court, eliminating some of the ironwork and
terra-cotta and adding marble scored with geometric patterns detailed
in gold leaf. The interior endured some less tasteful alterations after
that, but it has since been restored to the way it looked when Wright
completed his work in 1907. ✉ *209 S. LaSalle St., Loop* ☎ *312/553–6100* ⊕ *therookerybuilding.com.*

Sullivan Center (*Carson, Pirie, Scott & Co.*). From 1899 to 2007 this was
the flagship location for the department store Carson, Pirie, Scott & Co.
The work of one of Chicago's most renowned architects, it combines
Louis H. Sullivan's visionary expression of modern design with intricate
cast-iron ornamentation. The eye-catching rotunda and the 11 stories
above it are actually an addition Sullivan made to his original building.
In later years D.H. Burnham &Co. and Holabird &Root extended Sullivan's smooth, horizontal scheme farther down State Street. In 2012,
the Sullivan Center became a shopping mall, with tenants that include
Target and DSW. ✉ *1 S. State St., Loop* ☎ *312/675–5500* ⊕ *www.the sullivancenter.com.*

Symphony Center. Now home to the acclaimed Chicago Symphony
Orchestra (CSO), this complex includes Orchestra Hall, built in 1904
under the supervision of Daniel Burnham. The Georgian building has
a symmetrical facade of pink brick with limestone quoins, lintels,
and other decorative elements. An interior renovation, completed in
1997, added a seating area that is behind and above the stage, allowing patrons a unique vantage point. Backstage tours are available by
appointment for groups of 10 or more; the $10 fee is waived for groups
buying concert tickets. ✉ *220 S. Michigan Ave., Loop* ☎ *312/294–3000* ⊕ *www.cso.org.*

FAMILY
Fodor's Choice
★

Willis Tower. Designed by Skidmore, Owings & Merrill in 1974, the former Sears Tower was the world's tallest building until 1996. The 110-story, 1,730-foot-tall structure may have lost its title and even changed its name, but it's still tough to top the Willis Tower's 103rd-floor Skydeck—on a clear day it offers views of Illinois, Michigan, Wisconsin, and Indiana. Enter on Jackson Boulevard to take the ear-popping ride up. ■ TIP➜ **Check the visibility ratings at the security desk before you decide to ascend.** Video monitors turn the 70-second elevator ride into a thrilling trip. Interactive exhibits inside the observatory bring Chicago's dreamers, schemers, architects, musicians, and sports stars to life; and computer kiosks in six languages help international travelers key into Chicago hot spots. For many visitors, though, the highlight (literally) is stepping out on the Ledge, a glass box that extends 4.3 feet from the building, making you feel as if you're suspended 1,353 feet in the air. Before leaving the tower, check out Calder's spiraling mobile sculpture *The Universe* in the ground-floor lobby on the Wacker Drive side. ⊠ *233 S. Wacker Dr., Loop* ☎ *312/875–9696* ⊕ *www.willistower. com, www.theskydeck.com* ✉ *Skydeck $19.50* ☺ *Skydeck Apr.–Sept., daily 9 am–10 pm; Oct.–Mar., daily 10 am–8 pm.*

WORTH NOTING

311 South Wacker Drive. The first of three towers intended for the site, this pale pink edifice is the work of Kohn Pedersen Fox, who also designed 333 West Wacker Drive, a few blocks away. The 1990 building's most distinctive feature is its Gothic crown, brightly lit at night. During migration season so many birds crashed into the illuminated tower that management was forced to tone down the lighting. An inviting atrium has palm trees and a splashy, romantic fountain. ⊠ *311 S. Wacker Dr., at W. Jackson Blvd., Loop* ☎ *312/692–8200* ⊕ *www.311 southwacker.com.*

333 West Wacker Drive. This green-glazed beauty doesn't follow the rules. Its riverside facade echoes the curve of the Chicago River just in front of it, while the other side is all business, conforming neatly to the straight lines of the street grid. The 1983 Kohn Pedersen Fox design, roughly contemporary to the James R. Thompson Center, enjoyed a much more positive public reception. It also had a small but important role in the 1986 movie *Ferris Bueller's Day Off* as the location of Ferris's dad's office. ⊠ *333 W. Wacker Dr., between W. Lake St. and N. Orleans St., Loop* ⊕ *www.emporis.com/building/333wackerdrive-chicago-il-usa.*

Aon Center. With the open space of Millennium Park at its doorstep, the Aon Center really stands out. Originally built as the Standard Oil Building, the 83-story skyscraper (first referred to as Big Stan) has changed names and appearances twice. Not long after the building went up in 1972, its marble cladding came crashing down, and the whole thing was resheathed in granite. The vertically striped structure sits on a handsome (if rather sterile) plaza, where Harry Bertoia's wind-chime sculpture in the reflecting pool makes interesting sounds when a breeze blows. ⊠ *200 E. Randolph Dr., Loop* ☎ *312/381–1000.*

Continued on page 59

A GUIDE TO THE ART INSTITUTE

The Art Institute of Chicago, nestled between the contemporary public art showplace of Millennium Park and the Paris-inspired walk-ways of Grant Park, is both intimate and grand, a place where the rooms are human-scale and the art is transcendent.

Come for the sterling collection of Old Masters and Impressionists (an entire room is dedicated to Monet), linger over the extraordinary and comprehensive photography collection, take in a number of fine American works, and discover paintings, drawings, sculpture, design, and photography spanning the ages.

The Art Institute is more than just a museum; in fact, it was originally founded by a small group of artists in 1866 as a school with an adjoining exhibition space. Famous alumni include political cartoonist Herblock and artists Grant Wood and Ed Paschke. Walt Disney and Georgia O'Keeffe both took classes, but didn't graduate. The School of the Art Institute of Chicago, one of the finest art schools in the country, is across the street from the museum; occasionally there are lectures and discussions that are open to the public.

Top: Pose with one of the two bronze lions; Bottom: Millefiori paperweight, French, 1845/55

BEST PAINTINGS

AMERICAN GOTHIC (1930). GALLERY 263
Grant Wood won $300 for his iconic painting of a solemn farmer and his wife (really his sister and his dentist). Wood saw the work as a celebration of solid, work-based Midwestern values, a statement that rural America would survive the Depression and the massive migration to cities.

American Gothic (1930).

NIGHTHAWKS (1942). GALLERY 262
Edward Hopper's painting of four figures in a diner on the corner of a deserted New York street is a noir portrait of isolated lives and is one of the most recognized images of 20th-century art. The red-haired woman is the artist's wife, Jo.

THE CHILD'S BATH (1893). GALLERY 273
Mary Cassatt was the only American to become an established Impressionist and her work focused on the daily lives of women and children. In this, her most famous work, a woman gently bathes a child who is tucked up on her lap. The piece was unconventional when it was painted because the bold patterns and cropped forms it used were more often seen in Japanese prints at the time.

Nighthawks (1942).

SKY ABOVE CLOUDS IV (1965). GALLERY 249
(not pictured) Georgia O'Keeffe's massive painting, the largest canvas of her career, is of clouds seen from an airplane. The rows of white rectangles stretching toward the horizon look both solid and ethereal, as if they are stepping stones for angels.

THE OLD GUITARIST (1903/04). MODERN WING
(not pictured) One of the most important works of Pablo Picasso's Blue Period, this monochromatic painting is a study of the crooked figure of a blind and destitute street guitarist, singing sorrowfully. When he painted it, Picasso was feeling particularly empathetic toward the downtrodden—perhaps because of a friend's suicide—and the image of the guitarist is one of dignity amid poverty.

The Child's Bath (1893).

GRAINSTACK (1890/91). GALLERY 243
The Art Institute has the largest collection of Monet's Grainstacks in the world. The stacks rose 15 to 20 feet tall outside Monet's farmhouse in Giverny and were a symbol to the artist of sustenance and survival.

Grainstack (1890/91).

THE MODERN WING

The Modern Wing

In May 2009 the Art Institute unveiled its highly anticipated Modern Wing. Designed by Pritzker Prize–winning architect Renzo Piano, designer of Paris's Pompidou Center, the 264,000-square-foot addition is almost a separate museum unto itself, providing 65,000 square feet of display space for the museum's extensive collection of modern and contemporary art. With the addition, the Art Institute became the country's second largest art museum.

THE DESIGN
The rectangle of glass, steel, and limestone cost just under $300 million and took nearly four years to build. The airy, ultra-modern structure provides abundant natural light and dramatic views of Millennium Park through floor-to-ceiling windows. Green building features include a "flying carpet" canopy that filters sunlight through skylights in the third-floor galleries and a sophisticated lighting system that self-adjusts based on available light and temperature.

North facade of the Modern Wing

THE COLLECTION
View works from major art movements of the 20th and 21st centuries, ranging from painting and sculpture to video and installation art. Notable artists represented in the collection include Eva Hesse, David Hockney, Jasper Johns, Kerry James Marshall, Joan Mitchell, Jackson Pollock, Gerhard Richter, and Andy Warhol.

GRIFFIN COURT
The light-filled central corridor provides a dramatic passageway to the three-story pavilions flanking it on both sides and to the street-level Pritzker Garden. Griffin Court also houses a ticket area, gift shop, coat check, education center, garden café, and balcony café.

Griffin Court

NICHOLS BRIDGEWAY
A 625-foot pedestrian bridge soars over Monroe Street and the Lurie Gardens, connecting the third floor of the Modern Wing's West Pavilion to the southwest corner of Millennium Park—and providing stunning views of the park, skyline, and lake.

BLUHM FAMILY TERRACE
Rotating sculpture installations occupy the free, 3,400-square-foot outdoor space on the West Pavilion's third floor, adjacent to the seasonally focused restaurant Terzo Piano (reservations recommended).

A painting by Gerhard Richter

The Modern Wing of the Art Institute, which was designed by Renzo Piano and opened in 2009, is a stunning home for the renowned collection within.

Bank of America Theatre. On Monroe, near State Street, the ornate Bank of America Theatre (formerly the LaSalle Bank Theatre and before that the Shubert Theatre) stages major Broadway plays and musicals. It was the tallest building in Chicago when it opened in 1906. ⊠ *18 W. Monroe St., Loop* ☎ *800/775–2000* ⊕ *broadwayinchicago.com/about/theatre-history/.*

Cadillac Palace Theatre. Opened in 1926 as a vaudeville venue, the theater was designed to evoke the Palace of Versailles. As time went on, its popularity waned. During the 1970s, it became a banquet hall; in the '80s, it hosted rock concerts. Renovated in the '90s and reopened in 1999 as a performing arts space for long-run Broadway shows, the Cadillac Palace Theatre has recaptured some of its former glory. ⊠ *151 W. Randolph St., Loop* ☎ *312/977–1702* ⊕ *broadwayinchicago.com/theatre/cadillac-palace-theatre/.*

Carbide and Carbon Building (Hard Rock Hotel). Designed in 1929 by Daniel and Hubert Burnham, sons of the renowned architect Daniel Burnham, this is arguably the jazziest skyscraper in town. A deep-green terra-cotta tower rising from a black-granite base, its upper reaches are embellished with gold leaf. The original public spaces are a luxurious composition in marble and bronze. The story goes that the brothers Burnham got their inspiration from a gold-foiled bottle of champagne. So perhaps it's fitting that the building now houses the Hard Rock Hotel Chicago, party central for those who wouldn't be caught dead at the Four Seasons. ⊠ *230 N. Michigan Ave., Loop* ☎ *312/345–1000* ⊕ *www.hardrockhotelchicago.com.*

Chase Tower. This building's graceful swoop—a novelty when it went up—continues to offer an eye-pleasing respite from all the surrounding right angles; and its spacious, sunken bi-level plaza, with Marc Chagall's mosaic *The Four Seasons*, is one of the most enjoyable public spaces in the neighborhood. Designed by Perkins & Will and C.F. Murphy Associates in 1969, Chase Tower has been home to a succession of financial institutions. Name changes aside, it remains one of the more distinctive buildings around, not to mention one of the highest in the heart of the Loop. ✉ *10 S. Dearborn St., Loop.*

Chicago Temple. The Gothic-inspired headquarters of the First United Methodist Church of Chicago, built in 1923 by Holabird &Roche, comes complete with a first-floor sanctuary, 21 floors of office space, a sky-high chapel (free tours are available), and an eight-story spire, which is best viewed from the bridge across the Chicago River at Dearborn Street. Outside, along the building's east wall at ground level, stained-glass windows relate the history of Methodism in Chicago. Joan Miró's sculpture *Chicago* (1981) is in the small plaza just east of the church. ✉ *77 W. Washington St., Loop* ☏ *312/236–4548* ⊕ *www.chicagotemple.org* ✆ *Tours Mon.–Sat. at 2, Sun. after services.*

Federal Center and Plaza. This center is spread over three separate buildings: the Everett McKinley Dirksen Building; the John C. Kluczynski Building (*230 S. Dearborn*), which includes the Loop's post office; and the Metcalfe Building (*77 W. Jackson*). Designed in 1959, but not completed until 1974, the severe constellation of buildings around a sweeping plaza was Mies van der Rohe's first mixed-use urban project. Fans of the International Style will groove on this pocket of pure modernism, while others can take comfort in the presence of the Marquette Building, which marks the north side of the site. In contrast to this dark ensemble are the great red arches of Alexander Calder's *Flamingo*. The area is bounded by Dearborn, Clark, and Adams streets and Jackson Boulevard. ✉ *Dirksen Building, 219 S. Dearborn St., Loop* ☏ *312/353–6996* ⊕ *www.gsa.gov/portal/content/101841.*

Ford Center for the Performing Arts–Oriental Theatre. An opulent "hasheesh-dream decor" of Buddhas and elephant-type chairs made this a popular spot for viewing first-run movies starting in 1926. Though listed on the National Register of Historic Places in 1978, the building continued to crumble for some time after. In 1998 it was restored to its past splendor and since then has had a second life as a home to Broadway shows.

CHICAGO THEATER DISTRICT

On State, just north of Randolph Street, is the old theater district. The ornate 1921 Beaux-Arts **Chicago Theatre**, a former movie palace, now hosts live performances. Across the street is the **Gene Siskel Film Center**, which screens art, foreign, and classic flicks. West on Randolph Street the long, glitzy neon sign of the **Ford Center for the Performing Arts–Oriental Theatre** shines. The **Goodman Theatre**, on Dearborn, presents new productions in the 1925 art deco landmark Harris & Selwyn Twin Theaters. One block west is the **Cadillac Palace Theatre**, built as a vaudeville venue in 1926.

✉ *24 W. Randolph St., Loop* ☎ *312/977–1702* ⊕ *broadwayinchicago. com/theatre/chicagos-oriental-theatre/.*

Hyatt Center. At 48 stories, the headquarters of this hotel and resort company is no giant, but it more than makes its mark on South Wacker Drive with a bold elliptical shape, a glass-faced street-level lobby rising 36 feet, and a pedestrian-friendly plaza. It displays a noticeable tweaking of the unrelieved curtain wall that makes many city streets forbidding canyons. Designed by Pei Cobb Freed & Partners, the Hyatt Center was completed in 2004. ✉ *71 S. Wacker Dr., Loop* ⊕ *www.hyatt centerinfo.com.*

Inland Steel Building. A runt compared to today's tall buildings, this sparkling 19-story high-rise from Skidmore, Owings & Merrill was a trailblazer when it was built in the late 1950s. It was the first skyscraper erected with external supports (allowing for wide-open, unobstructed floors within), the first to employ steel pilings (driven 85 feet down to bedrock), the first in the Loop to be fully air-conditioned, and the first to feature underground parking. ✉ *30 W. Monroe St., Loop* ⊕ *www. inlandsteelbuilding.com.*

FAMILY **Macy's.** This neoclassical building, designed by Daniel Burnham, opened in 1907 as one of the world's earliest department stores, Marshall Field's. Macy's acquired the chain in 2005 and changed the store's name. An uproar ensued, and many Chicagoans still refer to the flagship as Marshall Field's. A visit is as much an architectural experience as a retail one. The building has distinct courtyards (one resembling an Italian palazzo), a striking Tiffany dome of mosaic glass, a calming fountain, and gilded pillars. Its green clock at the State and Randolph entrance is a Chicago landmark. For lunch, try the Walnut Room, and make sure to sample Frango mints—the store's specialty, they were once made on the 13th floor. ✉ *111 N. State St., Loop* ☎ *312/781–1000* ⊕ *www.visitmacyschicago.com* ☉ *Mon. and Thurs.–Sat. 10–8, Tues. 9–9, Wed. 9–10, Sun. 11–6.*

Monadnock Building. Built in two segments a few years apart, the Monadnock captures the turning point in high-rise construction. Its northern half, designed in 1891 by Burnham & Root, was erected with traditional load-bearing masonry walls (6-feet deep at the base). In 1893 Holabird & Roche designed its southern half, which rose around the soon-to-be-common steel skeleton. The building's stone-and-brick exterior, shockingly unornamented for its time, led one critic to liken it to a chimney. The lobby is equally spartan: lined on either side with windowed shops, it's essentially a corridor, but one well worth traveling. Walk it from end to end and you'll feel as if you're stepping back in time. ✉ *53 W. Jackson Blvd., at S. Dearborn St., Loop* ☎ *312/922–1890* ⊕ *www.monadnockbuilding.com.*

SOUTH LOOP

The South Loop's main claim to fame is the Museum Campus—the Field Museum, Shedd Aquarium, and Adler Planetarium. Jutting out into the lake, it affords amazing skyline views. To the north, giant

The lighting around Buckingham Fountain was designed to evoke soft moonlight.

gargoyles (actually stylized owls signifying wisdom) loom atop the Harold Washington Library. East on Congress at Michigan Avenue is the Romanesque Revival–style Auditorium Theatre, designed by architects Sullivan and Adler. Farther south at Printers Row, lofts that once clattered with Linotype machines now contain condos. The South Loop begins more or less where the Loop itself ends, starting south of Van Buren, extending down to Chinatown, and including everything between Lake Michigan and the Chicago River.

TOP ATTRACTIONS

FAMILY **Adler Planetarium and Astronomy Museum.**

Fodor's Choice ⇨ *See highlighted feature in this chapter.*
★

Fodor's Choice **Auditorium Theatre.** Hunkered down across from Grant Park, this
★ 110,000-ton granite-and-limestone behemoth was an instant star when it debuted in 1899, and it didn't hurt the careers of its designers, Dankmar Adler and Louis H. Sullivan, either. Inside were offices, a 400-room hotel, and a 4,300-seat state-of-the-art theater with electric lighting and an air-cooling system that used 15 tons of ice per day. Adler managed the engineering—the theater's acoustics are renowned—and Sullivan ornamented the space using mosaics, cast iron, art glass, wood, and plaster. During World War II the building was used as a Servicemen's Center. Then Roosevelt University moved in and, thanks to the school's Herculean restoration efforts, the theater is again one of the city's premiere performance venues. Tours are offered on Monday and Thursday. ⊠ *50 E. Congress Pkwy., South Loop* ☎ *312/922–2110* ⊕ *www.*

auditoriumtheatre.org 🖳 *Tours $10* ⊙ *Tours Mon. at 10:30 and noon, Thurs. at 10:30.*

Fodor'sChoice **Field Museum.**
★ ⇨ *See highlighted feature in this chapter.*

FAMILY **Harold Washington Library Center.** Opened in 1991 and named for Chicago's first African-American mayor, this library was primarily designed by architect Thomas Beeby, of Hammond, Beeby & Babka. Gargantuan and almost goofy, the granite-and-brick edifice is a uniquely postmodern homage to Chicago's great architectural past. The heavy, rusticated ground level recalls the Rookery; the stepped-back, arched windows are a reference to the great arches in the Auditorium Theatre; the swirling terra-cotta design is pinched from the Marquette Building; and the glass curtain wall on the west side is a nod to 1950s modernism. The huge, gargoyle-like sculptures atop the building include owls, a symbol of wisdom. The excellent **Children's Library**, an 18,000-square-foot haven on the second floor, has vibrant wall-mounted figures by Chicago imagist Karl Wirsum. Works by noted Chicago artists are displayed along a second-floor walkway above the main lobby. There's also an impressive Winter Garden with skylights on the ninth floor. Free programs and performances are offered regularly. ⊠ *400 S. State St., South Loop* 🕾 *312/747–4300* ⊕ *www.chipublib.org/locations/15/* ⊙ *Mon.–Thurs. 9–9, Fri. and Sat. 9–5, Sun. 1–5.*

FAMILY **John G. Shedd Aquarium.**
Fodor'sChoice ⇨ *See highlighted feature in this chapter.*
★

WORTH NOTING

Dearborn Station. Part of Printers Row, this is Chicago's oldest-standing passenger train station, designed in the Romanesque Revival style in 1885 by New York architect Cyrus L.W. Eidlitz. Now filled with offices and stores, it has a wonderful 12-story clock tower and a red-sandstone and redbrick facade ornamented with terra-cotta. Striking features inside are the marble floor, wraparound brass walkway, and arching wood-frame doorways. ⊠ *47 W. Polk St., South Loop* 🕾 *312/554–8100* ⊕ *www.dearbornstation.com.*

Franklin Building. Built in 1888 as the home of the Franklin Company, one of the largest printers at the time, this building has intricate decoration. The tile work on the facade leads up to *The First Impression*—a medieval scene illustrating the first application of the printer's craft. Above the entryway is a motto: "The excellence of every art must consist in the complete accomplishment of its purpose." The building was turned into condos in 1989. ⊠ *720 S. Dearborn St., South Loop* ⊕ *www.thefranklinbuilding.com.*

Museum of Contemporary Photography. "Contemporary" is generally defined here as work made in the past two or three decades. Curators constantly seek out new talent and underappreciated established photographers, which means that there are artists here you probably won't see elsewhere. Rotating exhibits have included explorations of infrastructure, crime, and American identity. ⊠ *600 S. Michigan Ave.,*

ADLER PLANETARIUM AND ASTRONOMY MUSEUM

✉ *1300 S. Lake Shore Dr., South Loop* ☎ *312/922–7827* ⊕ *www.adlerplanetarium. org* 🎫 *$12, $29.95 all-access pass* ⏱ *Weekdays 9:30–4, weekends 9:30–4:30, plus 3rd Thurs. of month 6–10 pm for ages 21 and up.*

TIPS

■ Additional charges apply for the Grainger Sky Theater, Definiti Space Theater, and Samuel C. Johnson Family Star Theater, but don't skip them—they're the most important reasons to go. Package prices are available.

■ Take a quick ride in the Atwood Sphere, the nation's very first planetarium experience.

■ Stop in at the Adler's café for simple fare like paninis and salads, with breathtaking views of the Chicago skyline.

Taking you on a journey through the stars to unlock the mysteries of our galaxy and beyond, the Adler tells amazing stories of space exploration through high-tech exhibits and immersive theater experiences. Artifacts and interactive elements bring these fascinating tales of space and its pioneers down to earth.

Highlights

Feel like you are flying through the universe at the technologically advanced Grainger Sky Theater. You'll get an up-close view of stunning space phenomena, and the magnificent imagery is so realistic that it might only be surpassed by actual space travel.

Experience how the universe evolved more than 13.7 billion years ago—from the Big Bang to modern day—in the Adler's newest permanent exhibit, "The Universe: A Walk Through Space and Time." A spectacular projection showcases the enormity of the universe, and touch screens let you investigate diverse and beautiful objects from deep space.

Turn your kids into modern-day space adventurers in "Planet Explorers," which lets them sense what it's like to climb, crawl, and fly through space.

Journey into space in the Definiti Space Theater, or don 3-D glasses to view celestial phenomena in the Samuel C. Johnson Family Star Theater.

FIELD MUSEUM

✉ *1400 S. Lake Shore Dr., South Loop* ☎ *312/922–9410*
⊕ *www.fieldmuseum.org*
💳 *$18, $31 all-access pass*
⊙ *Daily 9–5; last admission at 4.*

■ Don't hesitate to take toddlers to the Field. In the Crown Family PlayLab, kids two- to six-years old can play house in a re-created pueblo and compare their footprints with a dinosaur's.

■ It's impossible to see the entire museum in one visit. Try to get tickets to the special exhibit of the season and then choose a couple of subjects you'd like to focus on, like North American birds or Chinese jade.

■ The Sue Store sells a mind-boggling assortment of dinosaur-related merchandise.

■ Tucked in the back, the dining room comes with wonderful views of the lake and the Museum Campus.

More than 400,000-square feet of exhibit space fill this gigantic museum, which explores cultures and environments from around the world. Interactive displays examine such topics as the secrets of Egyptian mummies, the art and innovations of people living in the Ancient Americas, and the evolution of life on Earth. Originally funded by Chicago retailer Marshall Field, the museum was founded in 1893 to hold material gathered for the World's Columbian Exposition; its current neoclassical home opened in 1921.

Highlights

Explore one of the world's best dinosaur collections in "Evolving Planet," an awe-inspiring journey through 4 billion years—and don't miss 65-million-year-old "Sue," the largest and most complete *Tyrannosaurus rex* fossil ever found. At the McDonald's Fossil Preparation Laboratory, you can watch paleontologists cleaning bones.

Shrink to the size of a bug to burrow beneath the soil in "Underground Adventure" (additional fee). You'll come face-to-face with a giant, animatronic wolf spider and listen to the sounds of gnawing insects.

Travel to ancient Egypt via a working canal, a living marsh where papyrus is grown, a shrine to the cat goddess Bastet, burial-ceremony artifacts, and 23 mummies. Or spend a couple of hours taking in contemporary and ancient Africa. Dioramas reproduce the homes and lives of Africans from Senegal, Cameroon, and the Sahara.

See nature at its most sparkly in the Grainger Hall of Gems, with magnificent jewels and jewelry.

Learn how museum scientists are preserving biodiversity at "Restoring Earth," in the Abbott Hall of Conservation.

Check out the 3-D theater, screening movies on dinosaurs, mummies, and Ice Age animals.

JOHN G. SHEDD AQUARIUM

✉ *1200 S. Lake Shore Dr.,*
South Loop ☎ *312/939–2438*
⊕ *www.sheddaquarium.org*
⌨ *$8, $35.95 all-access pass*
⊙ *Memorial Day–Labor Day,*
daily 9–6; Tues. after Labor
Day–Sun. before Memorial
Day, weekdays 9–5, weekends
9–6.

TIPS

■ Lines for the Shedd often
extend all the way down the
neoclassical steps. Buy a
ticket in advance to avoid the
interminable wait, or spring
for a cityPASS.

■ Soundings restaurant makes
an elegant (albeit pricey) stop
for lunch. The quiet tables
look over Lake Michigan—and
there are very few Chicago
eateries that can say that. The
food court, Bubble Net, offers
more moderately priced family
fare, and Deep Ocean Café,
in the Polar Play Zone, caters
to kids.

■ June through early September, catch live jazz on the
Shedd's north terrace on
Wednesday evenings from 5
to 10. It coincides with Navy
Pier's fireworks. A gorgeous
view of the lake and skyline
can make for a magical night.

One of the most popular aquariums in the country, the Shedd houses more than 32,500 creatures from around the world.

Highlights

Get an up-close look at piranhas, snakes, and stingrays at "Amazon Rising." The 8,600-square-foot exhibit resembles a flooded forest and re-creates the rise and fall of floodwaters.

Shiver as sharks swim by in their 400,000-gallon tank as part of "Wild Reef," which explores marine biodiversity in the Indo-Pacific. The exhibit also has colorful corals, stingrays that slide by under your feet, and other surprising creatures, all from the waters around the Philippines.

Stare down the knobby-headed beluga whales (they love to people-watch), observe Pacific white-sided dolphins at play, and follow the simulated Pacific Northwest nature trail in the spectacular Oceanarium, which has pools that seem to blend into Lake Michigan. The aquatic show here stars dancing belugas, leaping dolphins, and comical penguins. Be sure to get an underwater glimpse of the dolphins and whales through the viewing windows on the lower level, where you can also find a bunch of information-packed, hands-on activities.

Head to the 90,000-gallon "Caribbean Reef" exhibit to see sharks, stingrays, sea turtles, and other denizens of the deep dart around. It's most fun to observe when divers swim within, feeding the animals and talking to the crowd gathered outside. Kids have their own Polar Play Zone, where they can dress in penguin suits or peruse Arctic waters in a miniature submarine.

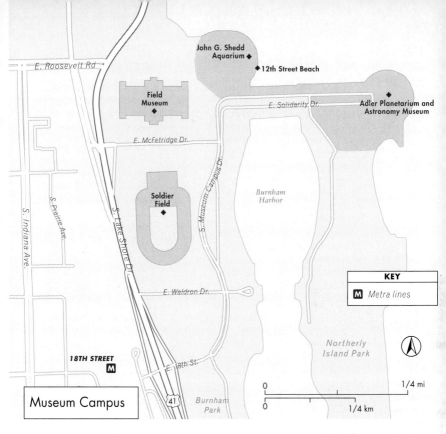

South Loop ☎ *312/663–5554* ⊕ *www.mocp.org* ✉ *Free* ⏱ *Mon.–Wed.,
Fri., and Sat. 10–5, Thurs. 10–8, Sun. noon–5.*

Pontiac Building. Built in 1891, the simple, redbrick Pontiac is an early
Chicago School skyscraper—note the classic rectangular shape and flat
roof. It is the city's oldest existing Holabird & Roche building. ⊠ *542
S. Dearborn St., South Loop.*

Printers Row. Bounded by Congress Parkway on the north, Polk Street
on the south, Plymouth Court to the east, and the Chicago River to the
west, this district fell into disrepair in the 1960s, but a neighborhood
resurgence began in the late 1970s. Bibliophiles flock in for the Printers
Row Lit Fest, a weekend-long literary celebration held each June. But,
at any time of year, you can admire examples of buildings by the group
that represented the First Chicago School of Architecture (including
Louis Sullivan). ⊠ *Between Congress Pkwy. and Polk St., Plymouth
Ct.and the Chicago River, South Loop.*

FAMILY **Soldier Field.** Opened in 1924 as the Municipal Grant Park Stadium,
the facility was renamed in 1925 to commemorate American soldiers
who died during World War I. Just south of the Museum Campus, the
building and its massive columns are reminiscent of ancient Greece.
Since 1971 it's been the home of the Chicago Bears. It is also a venue
for college games and concerts. A controversial modern glass expansion,

MUSEUM CAMPUS TIPS

The parklike, pedestrian-friendly Museum Campus is home to the Big Three—the **Field Museum**, the **John G. Shedd Aquarium**, and the **Adler Planetarium and Astronomy Museum**. If you're driving, park in one of the lots just past the Field Museum on McFetridge Drive; alternately, you can arrive via the **Chicago Trolley HOP ON HOP OFF Tour** (*773/648–5000*), which connects sites on the 57-acre campus with other downtown tourist attractions and train stations. Just east of the Field Museum is the Shedd Aquarium, on the lakefront;

farther still, at the end of a peninsula jutting into Lake Michigan, is the Adler. Look north from here for a fantastic view of the city skyline.

If you're visiting all three museums plus other major attractions, consider a Chicago cityPASS ($96, valid for nine consecutive days). You'll avoid long lines and get access to the Field, the Shedd, and the Willis Tower Skydeck, plus the Adler or the Art Institute, and 360° Chicago (formerly the John Hancock Center Observatory) or the Museum of Science and Industry.

which looks like a spaceship that landed on the arena, was completed in 2003. Behind-the-scenes tours feature the Doughboy Statue, Colonnades, field, South Courtyard, visitors' locker room, the suites, and the United Club. ⊠ *1410 S. Museum Campus Dr., South Loop* ☏ *312/235–7000* ⊕ *www.soldierfield.net* ✉ *Tours $15 (check website for times).*

WEST LOOP

For an especially good meal, head to the West Loop, along the Chicago River. What was once skid row and meatpacking warehouses is now a vibrant community with trendy restaurants. Greektown, a five-block stretch of Halsted Street, serves up authentic *saganaki* (appetizers). A thriving art scene has emerged around Fulton Market.

Chicago Antique Market. This famed indoor-outdoor flea market, held on the third Saturday and Sunday of the month from late March through mid-December, is Chicago's answer to London's Portobello Road Market. Centered on Randolph Street and Ogden Avenue at Plumber's Hall, it offers midcentury furniture, vintage handbags, ephemera, and much more. May through September, free shuttles head back and forth between the Hall and Water Tower Place on the hour, from 10 to 4. ⊠ *1340 W. Washington Blvd., West Loop* ☏ *322/666–1200* ⊕ *www. chicagoantiquemarket.com* ✉ *$8 online, $10 at gate* ⊗ *Weekends 10–5.*

Fulton Market. This stylish neighborhood is filled with chic restaurants, trendsetting galleries, shops, and showrooms for cutting-edge design and green living. Be aware, though, that it remains a bustling commercial district. During the day the seafood, produce, and meatpacking plants swarm with heavy vehicles helmed by harried drivers. Exercise caution while driving or, better yet, take a cab. At night, be alert: this can still be an iffy area. ⊠ *Along Fulton Market and Lake St. between Desplaines St. and Ashland Ave., West Loop* ⊕ *www.explorefultonmarket.com.*

OFF THE BEATEN PATH

Garfield Park Conservatory. Escape winter's cold or revel in summer sunshine inside this huge "landscape art under glass" structure, which houses tropical palms, spiny cacti, and showy blooms. A children's garden has climbable leaf sculptures and a tube slide that winds through trees. The "Sugar from the Sun" exhibit focuses on the elements of photosynthesis—sunlight, air, water, and sugar—in a full-sensory environment filled with spewing steam, trickling water, and chirping sounds. Don't miss the historic Jens Jensen–designed Fern Room with its lagoon, waterfalls, and profusion of ferns. On-site events include botanical-themed fashion shows, seasonal flower shows, and great educational programing. ⊠ *300 N. Central Park Ave., Garfield Park* 🕾 *312/746-5100* ⊕ *www.garfield-conservatory.org* 🖃 *Free* ☉ *Thurs.–Tues. 9–5, Wed. 9–8.*

Greektown. This small strip may as well be half a world away from the rest of the West Loop. Greek restaurants are the main draw here. Continue west on Madison, past the slew of new condo developments and vintage conversions in progress, and you'll come to one of Chicago's popular dining and nightlife destinations. On a stretch of Madison roughly between Sangamon and Elizabeth streets, you'll find boutiques, trendy bars and lounges, and popular restaurants. The National Hellenic Museum, at 333 South Halsted, explores the Greek immigrant experience and the influence of Greek culture. ⊠ *Halsted St. between Madison and W. Van Buren Sts., West Loop* ⊕ *www.greektownchicago.org* 🖃 *Free.*

NEAR NORTH AND RIVER NORTH

GETTING ORIENTED

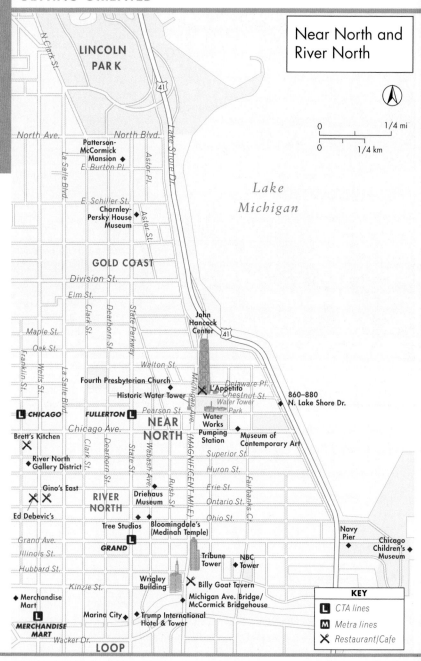

Near North and
River North

0   1/4 mi
0   1/4 km

LINCOLN PARK

North Ave.   North Blvd.

Lake Michigan

N. Clark St.

La Salle Blvd.

Astor Pl.

Lake Shore Dr.

Patterson-McCormick Mansion
E. Burton Pl.

E. Schiller St.
Charnley-Persky House Museum

Astor St.

GOLD COAST

Division St.

Elm St.

John Hancock Center

Maple St.

Oak St.

Clark St.

Dearborn St.

State Parkway

Franklin St.

Wells St.

La Salle Blvd.

Walton St.

Fourth Presbyterian Church
Historic Water Tower

Michigan Ave.

Delaware Pl.
× L'Appetito
Chestnut St.

860-880 N. Lake Shore Dr.

Pearson St.

Water Tower Park

L CHICAGO   FULLERTON **L**

NEAR NORTH

Chicago Ave.

Water Works Pumping Station

Brett's Kitchen
×

(MAGNIFICENT MILE)

Museum of Contemporary Art

River North Gallery District

Superior St.

Clark St.

Dearborn St.

State St.

Wabash Ave.

Rush St.

Huron St.

Fairbanks Ct.

Gino's East
× ×

Erie St.

RIVER NORTH

Driehaus Museum

Ontario St.

Ed Debevic's
×

Ohio St.

Tree Studios

Bloomingdale's (Medinah Temple)

Navy Pier

Grand Ave.

L GRAND

Illinois St.

Hubbard St.

Tribune Tower

NBC Tower

Chicago Children's Museum

Kinzie St.

Wrigley Building

× Billy Goat Tavern

Merchandise Mart

Michigan Ave. Bridge/ McCormick Bridgehouse

Marina City

Trump International Hotel & Tower

L MERCHANDISE MART

Wacker Dr.

LOOP

KEY	
L	*CTA lines*
M	*Metra lines*
×	*Restaurant/Cafe*

GETTING HERE

Near North: If you're arriving from the north by car, take Lake Shore Drive south to the Michigan Avenue exit. From the south, exit at Grand Avenue for Navy Pier. The prepaid parking app SpotHero can save you money.

The 3, 4, 144, 145, 146, 151, and 167 buses run along Michigan Avenue. Buses 29, 65, and 66 all service Navy Pier. If you're using the El, take the Red Line to Chicago Avenue or Clark and Division.

River North: The Merchandise Mart has its own stop on the El's Brown and Purple lines. For drivers, there is a parking lot at 350 North Orleans Street. If you are heading to the northern tip of the neighborhood, take Wells Street to Chicago Avenue. You can also walk west from the Mag Mile a few blocks to get to the area.

MAKING THE MOST OF YOUR TIME

If you have kids, factor in at least a day for Navy Pier's family-friendly attractions. Art lovers can pass a day at the Museum of Contemporary Art and assorted galleries, while dedicated shoppers can easily spend the same amount of time flexing their wallets on the Magnificent Mile, *the* Chicago shopping spot. Along the way, get a bird's-eye view of Chicago, including the Tribune Tower, Trump Tower, and Marina City, from the State Street Bridge.

TOP REASONS TO GO

Enjoy the views: Have a drink at the John Hancock Center's Signature Lounge, or just drink in the vista at 360° Chicago.

Kick back with the kids: The engaging Chicago Children's Museum is just one reason why families flock to Navy Pier.

Get your retail fix: Browse the shops of the Magnificent Mile, pausing for world-class people-watching en route.

QUICK BITES

Billy Goat Tavern. Behind and a level down from the Wrigley Building is the inspiration for *Saturday Night Live*'s classic "cheezborger, cheezborger, cheezborger, cheeps, no fries, no Coke, Pepsi" skit. Grab a greasy burger at this no-frills grill, or just have a beer and absorb the comic undertones. ⊠ *430 N. Michigan Ave., Lower Level, Near North* ☎ *312/222–1525* ⊕ *www.billygoattavern.com.*

Brett's Kitchen. Under the El at Superior and Franklin, Brett's Kitchen is an excellent spot for a pastry, sandwich, or omelet. It's open until 4 am. ⊠ *233 W. Superior St., River North* ☎ *312/664–6354* ⊕ *www.bretts kitchen.com* ☉ *Closed Sun.*

Ed Debevic's. The purposefully sassy waiters and waitresses at this touristy '50s-style diner keep the crowds entertained. ⊠ *640 N. Wells St., River North* ☎ *312/664–1707* ⊕ *www.ed debevics.com.*

Gino's East. Fill up on yummy Chicago deep-dish pizza at the graffiti-covered Gino's East. ⊠ *500. N LaSalle Street, River North* ☎ *312/988–4200* ⊕ *www. ginoseast.com.*

L'Appetito. For great Italian sandwiches, try this deli and grocery off the John Hancock Center's lower-level plaza. ⊠ *875 N. Michigan Ave., Near North* ☎ *312/337–0691* ⊕ *www. lappetito.com.*

Sightseeing
★★★★★

Dining
★★★★☆

Lodging
★★★★☆

Shopping
★★★★☆

Nightlife
★★★★☆

River North, the Magnificent Mile, the Gold Coast: this area holds some of the city's greatest attractions. Navy Pier and the Chicago Children's Museum are top stops for families, and serious shoppers can seriously exercise their credit cards along Michigan Avenue's most famous stretch. Impressive architecture, compelling art, and top-notch restaurants also await.

NEAR NORTH

Updated by Roberta Sotonoff

The Near North Side begins north of the Chicago River and runs north on and around Michigan Avenue—including the neighborhoods of River North (*see separate section, below*), Streeterville, and the Gold Coast—all the way up to North Avenue and the verdant green of Lincoln Park.

Near North has some of the city's best shopping and most crowd-pleasing restaurants, as well as some of its most distinctive buildings. To get a taste, start at the beginning of the Mag Mile and check out the architecture of the Tribune Tower. Then browse the shops on Michigan Avenue as well as the chichi boutiques on Oak and many other side streets. The John Hancock Center offers one of the best sky-high views of Chicago. Instead of shelling out bucks at the observatory, get a drink at its Signature Lounge for about the same price; the view comes free.

Hugging the lakeshore north of Oak Street and east of Clark Street is the Gold Coast. Potter Palmer (the developer of State Street and the Palmer House Hotel) transformed this area when he built a mansion here, and his social-climbing friends followed suit. The less fortunate residents thought the new arrivals must have pockets lined with gold.

To the east of the Mag Mile on Grand Avenue, Navy Pier stretches a half mile into Lake Michigan. Packed with restaurants, souvenir stalls, and folks out for a stroll, this perpetually busy wonderland is adored by kids and adults alike. You'll find the Chicago Children's Museum, a

150-foot-high Ferris wheel, an IMAX theater, and the Chicago Shakespeare Theatre here. It is also the starting point for many lake cruises. Make sure to dedicate an evening to seeing and being seen at one of the chic local restaurants.

TOP ATTRACTIONS

860–880 N. Lake Shore Drive. These twin apartment towers overlooking Lake Michigan were an early and eloquent realization of Mies van der Rohe's "less is more" credo, expressed in high-rise form. I-beams running up the facade underscore their verticality; inside, mechanical systems are housed in the center so as to leave the rest of each floor free and open to the spectacular views. Completed in 1951, the buildings are a prominent example of the International Style, which played a key role in transforming the look of American cities. ⊠ *860–880 N. Lake Shore Dr., at E. Chestnut St., Near North.*

FAMILY **Chicago Children's Museum.**
Fodor's Choice ⇨ *See the highlighted feature in this chapter.*
★

FAMILY **John Hancock Center and 360° Chicago.** Designed by Skidmore, Owings
Fodor's Choice & Merrill, this multipurpose skyscraper is distinguished by its taper-
★ ing shape and enormous X braces, which help stabilize its 100 stories. Soon after it went up in 1970, it earned the nickname "Big John." No wonder: it's 1,127 feet tall (1,502 feet counting its antennae). Packed with retail space, parking, offices, a restaurant, and residences, it has been likened to a city within a city. Like the Willis Tower, which was designed by the same architectural team, the John Hancock Center offers views of four states on clear days. To see them, ascend to the 94th-floor observatory—now dubbed 360° Chicago ($19). While there, thrill seekers can pay an additional fee to take advantage of the tower's newest feature, The Tilt ($7), which has eight windows that tilt downward to a 30-degree angle, giving you a unique perspective on the city below. Those with vertigo might prefer a seat in the bar of the 95th-floor Signature Lounge; the tab will be steep, but you don't pay the observatory fee and you'll be steady on your feet . ⊠ *875 N. Michigan Ave., Near North* ☎ *888/875–8439* ⊕ *www.johnhancockcenterchicago. com, www.360chicago.com* ⊡ *Observatory $19* ⊙ *Observatory daily 9 am–11 pm; last ticket sold at 10:30 pm.*

FAMILY **Magnificent Mile.** Michigan Avenue, or Mag Mile as some call it, is a
Fodor's Choice potpourri of historic buildings, upscale boutiques, department stores,
★ and posh hotels. (It is also the city's most popular place for people-watching.) Among its jewels are the Tribune Tower, the Wrigley Building, the John Hancock Center, the Drake Hotel, and the Historic Water Tower. ⊠ *Michigan Ave., between Chicago Ave. and Lakeshore Dr., Near North* ☎ *312/642–3570* ⊕ *www.themagnificentmile.com.*

McCormick Bridgehouse. Located in the southwest tower of the Michigan Avenue Bridge, this engaging museum provides a glimpse into the history of movable bridges (and some great city views, too). Until the 1960s, the five-story bridgehouse was home to the family of a man hired to tend the bridge. On lift days visitors can see the gears that still

CHICAGO CHILDREN'S MUSEUM

✉ Navy Pier, 700 E.
Grand Ave., Near North
☎ 312/527–1000 ⊕ www.
chicagochildrensmuseum.
org 🎟 $14, free Thurs. 5–8
pm and 1st Sun. of month
for children 15 and younger
🕙 Fri.–Wed. 10–5, Thurs. 10–8.

TIPS

■ The museum issues readmission bracelets that let you leave and come back on the same day—a great idea for weary families who want to grab a bite or simply explore other parts of Navy Pier before returning to take in more of the museum.

■ Stop for lunch at the nearby space-themed McDonald's; alternately, you can bring a picnic and snag a seat outside (in warm weather) or inside amid the Crystal Ballroom's tropical plants and fountains.

■ Artabounds workshops are free with admission.

■ Most families spend an average of three hours here.

■ The museum is designed for kids 12 or younger. Adults may not enter without a child.

Hands-on is the operative concept at this brightly colored Navy Pier anchor. Kids can tinker with tools, climb through multilevel tunnels and ship riggings, play at being a firefighter, dig for dinosaur fossils, and, if their parents allow it, get soaking wet.

Highlights

Oversize water tubs with waterwheels, pumps, colorful pipes, and fountains are all part of the splashy fun at "WaterWays" (raincoats for kids are provided). If everyone pumps hard enough, water squirts 50 feet in the air.

The "Tinkering Lab" lets children ask their own questions and test their own ideas using real tools and materials.

Kids can don authentic firefighter gear, operate a replica fire truck, slide down a pole, or practice escaping from a smoke-filled bedroom in "Play It Safe."

With real tools and wooden struts, little ones can construct their own building in the "Skyline" exhibit.

Children—and adults who act like ones—can scurry up a three-story-high rigging complete with crow's nest and gangplank on the "Kovler Family Climbing Schooner," which is reminiscent of the boats that once sailed Lake Michigan.

"Dinosaur Expedition" lets families brush away dirt to discover the bones of a *Suchomimus*, a fish-eating dinosaur. The exhibit re-creates a trip to the Sahara led by University of Chicago paleontologist Paul Sereno.

"Creativity" is the watchword at Kraft Artabounds Studio, where kids participate in rotating art activities like creating a castle out of clay or painting with marbles.

raise the bridge put to work. This is the only bridgehouse in Chicago that is open to the public. See the website for a lift schedule; reservations are recommended. ⊠ *376 N. Michigan Ave., at Wacker Dr., Chicago* ⊕ *www.bridgehousemuseum. org* ⊠ *$4, $10 on lift days* ⊘ *Mid-May–Oct., Thurs.–Mon. 10–5.*

DID YOU KNOW?

The base of Tribune Tower is studded with pieces from more than 120 famous sites and structures around the world, including the Parthenon, the Taj Mahal, Westminster Abbey, the Alamo, St. Peter's Basilica, the Great Wall of China, and Bunker Hill.

3

Michigan Avenue Bridge. Chicago is a city of bridges—and this one, completed in 1920, is among the most graceful. The structure's four pylons are decorated with impressive sculptures representing major Chicago events: its exploration by Marquette and Joliet, its settlement by trader Jean Baptiste Point du Sable, the Fort Dearborn Massacre of 1812, and the rebuilding of the city after the Great Chicago Fire of 1871. The site of the fort, at the southeast end of the bridge, is marked by a commemorative plaque. As you stroll Michigan Avenue, be prepared for a possible delay; the bridge rises about hundred times a year between April and November to allow boat traffic to pass underneath. ⊠ *River North.*

Fodor'sChoice ★ **Museum of Contemporary Art.**
⇨ *See the highlighted feature in this chapter.*

FAMILY **Navy Pier.** No matter the season, Navy Pier is a fun place to spend a few hours, especially with kids in tow. Constructed in 1916 as a commercial-shipping pier and part of Daniel Burnham's Master Plan of Chicago, it stretches half a mile into Lake Michigan. Redesigned and reopened in 1995, it's a major tourist draw. Outside, there's a landscaped area with gardens, a fountain, a carousel, a 15-story Ferris wheel, and a beer garden. Inside you'll find the Crystal Gardens, a six-story glass atrium that serves as an indoor event venue and botanical park; the Smith Museum of Stained Glass Windows; the Chicago Children's Museum; an IMAX theater; the Chicago Shakespeare Theatre; and a bevy of souvenir shops, restaurants, and bars. ⊠ *600 E. Grand Ave., Near North* ☎ *312/595–7437* ⊕ *www.navypier.com.*

Fodor'sChoice ★ **Tribune Tower.** To create a home for his newspaper, *Chicago Tribune* publisher Colonel Robert McCormick held a design competition in which entrants were judged anonymously. After rejecting a slew of functional modern designs by such notables as Walter Gropius, Eliel Saarinen, and Adolf Loos, McCormick chose the work of architects Raymond Hood and John Mead Howells, who were inspired by the cathedral in Rouen, France. The result, which opened in 1925, was a soaring Gothic building with flying buttresses in its crown. Embedded in the exterior walls are chunks of material taken from famous sites, including the Taj Mahal. On the ground floor are the studios of WGN radio, part of the *Chicago Tribune* empire, which also includes WGN-TV, cable-television stations, and the Chicago Cubs. (Modesty was not one of Colonel McCormick's prime traits: WGN stands for the

MUSEUM OF CONTEMPORARY ART

✉ *220 E. Chicago Ave., Near North* ☎ *312/280–2660*
⊕ *www.mcachicago.org*
🎫 *$12 suggested donation; free daily for Illinois residents and Tues. for nonresidents*
⊙ *Tues. 10–8, Wed.–Sun. 10–5.*

A group of art patrons who felt the great Art Institute was unresponsive to modern work founded the MCA in 1967, and it has remained a renegade art museum ever since. It doesn't have any permanent exhibits; this lends a feeling of freshness but also makes it impossible to predict what will be on display at any given time. Special exhibits are devoted mostly to original shows you can't see anywhere else.

Highlights

The MCA building looks like a home for contemporary art— designed by Berlin architect Josef Paul Kleihues, it's made of square metal plates with round bolts in each corner.

The 7,000-piece collection, still growing, includes work by Alexander Calder, Jeff Koons, Bruce Nauman, Sol LeWitt, Kerry James Marshall, Cindy Sherman, and many others. Exhibitions that draw from this collection make up about a quarter of the museum; the rest is devoted to special exhibits and artist projects.

The museum showcases work in all mediums, including paintings, sculpture, works on paper, photography, video, film, and installations.

Guided "Exhibition Focus" tours, dedicated to short-run exhibits, are offered daily. Tours that provide a balanced sweep of the entire museum are also available, as are ones geared specifically to families with young children.

The MCA Store carries well-designed jewelry and quirky items for the home, from porcelain eggshells that sprout flowers to goggles aimed at onion choppers.

The John Hancock Center offers some of the best panoramic views of the city.

Tribune's self-bestowed nickname: World's Greatest Newspaper.) ✉ *435 N. Michigan Ave., Near North* ☎ *312/222–3994* ⊕ *www.tribune.com.*

Fodor's Choice **Wrigley Building.** The gleaming white landmark headquarters of the
★ chewing-gum company—designed by Graham, Anderson, Probst & White—was instrumental in transforming Michigan Avenue from an area of warehouses to one of the most desirable spots in the city. Its two structures were built several years apart and later connected, and its clock tower was inspired by the bell tower of the grand cathedral in Seville, Spain. Be sure to check it out at night, when lamps bounce light off the 1920s terra-cotta facade. Its interior is undergoing a renovation. ✉ *400–410 N. Michigan Ave., Near North* ⊕ *www.thewrigley building.com.*

WORTH NOTING

Charnley-Persky House Museum. Designed by Louis Sullivan and his protégé Frank Lloyd Wright, this almost austere residence is one of the few extant buildings that displays the combined talents of these two architectural innovators. Historians still squabble about who contributed what here, but it's easy to imagine that the young go-getter had a hand in the cleanly rendered interior. Note how the geometric exterior looks unmistakably modern next to its fussy neighbors. Public tours of both the interior and exterior are available and last about one hour. The complimentary Wednesday tours are less comprehensive than the $10 ones on Saturday; reservations are a good idea for large groups. ✉ *1365*

Continued on page 84

THE SKY'S THE LIMIT

Talk about baptism by fire. Although Chicago was incorporated in 1837, it wasn't until *after* the Great Fire of 1871 that the city really started to take shape. With four square miles gone up in flames, the town was a clean slate. The opportunity to make a mark on this metropolis drew a slew of architects, from Adler & Sullivan to H. H. Richardson and Daniel H. Burnham—names renowned in the annals of American architecture. A Windy City tradition was born: the city's continuously morphing skyline is graced with tall wonders designed by architecture's heavy hitters, including Mies van der Rohe; Skidmore, Owings & Merrill; and, most recently, Santiago Calatrava. In the next four pages, you'll find an eye-popping sampling of Chicago's great buildings and how they've pushed—and continue to push—the definition of even such a lofty term as "skyscraper."

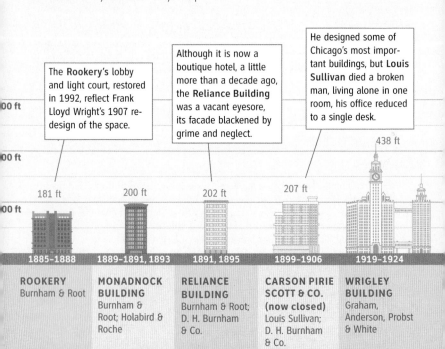

The **Rookery's** lobby and light court, restored in 1992, reflect Frank Lloyd Wright's 1907 re-design of the space.

Although it is now a boutique hotel, a little more than a decade ago, the **Reliance Building** was a vacant eyesore, its facade blackened by grime and neglect.

He designed some of Chicago's most important buildings, but **Louis Sullivan** died a broken man, living alone in one room, his office reduced to a single desk.

00 ft

00 ft

438 ft

181 ft	200 ft	202 ft	207 ft	

00 ft

1885–1888	1889–1891, 1893	1891, 1895	1899–1906	1919–1924
ROOKERY Burnham & Root	**MONADNOCK BUILDING** Burnham & Root; Holabird & Roche	**RELIANCE BUILDING** Burnham & Root; D. H. Burnham & Co.	**CARSON PIRIE SCOTT & CO. (now closed)** Louis Sullivan; D. H. Burnham & Co.	**WRIGLEY BUILDING** Graham, Anderson, Probst & White

THE BIRTH OF THE SKYSCRAPER

Houses, churches, and commercial buildings of all sorts rose from the ashes after the blaze of 1871, but what truly put Chicago on the architectural map was the tall building. The earliest of these barely scrape the sky—especially when compared to what towers over us today—but in the late 19th century, structures such as William Le Baron Jenney's ten-story Home Insurance Building (1884) represented a bold push upward. Until then, the sheer weight of stone and cast-iron construction had limited how high a building could soar. But by using a lighter yet stronger steel frame and simply sheathing his building in a thin skin of masonry, Jenney blazed the way for ever taller buildings. And with only so much land available in the central business district, up was the way to go.

Although the Home Insurance Building was razed in 1931, Chicago's Loop remains a rich trove of early skyscraper design. Some of these survivors stand severe and solid as fortresses, while others manifest an almost ethereal quality. They—and their descendants along Wacker Drive, North Michigan Avenue, and Lake Shore Drive—reflect the technological, economic, and aesthetic forces that have made this city on the prairie one of the most dramatically vertical communities in the country.

Bits and bobs of famous sites are embedded in the exterior of the building and are easy to spot. Check out the Taj Mahal.

Soul Train, the wildly popular dance program, first aired from WCIU–TV studios atop the **Chicago Board of Trade.**

With its restaurants and other amenities—and initially reasonable rents—**Marina City** was designed to help stem the flood of urbanites to the suburbs.

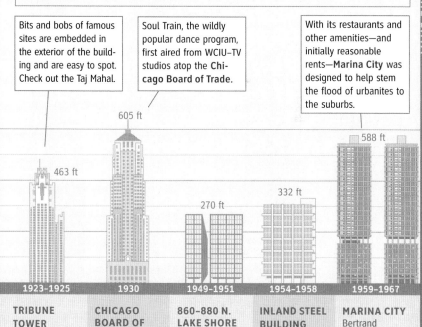

605 ft

463 ft

270 ft

332 ft

588 ft

1923–1925	1930	1949–1951	1954–1958	1959–1967
TRIBUNE TOWER Howells & Hood	**CHICAGO BOARD OF TRADE** Holabird & Root	**860–880 N. LAKE SHORE DRIVE** Ludwig Mies van der Rohe	**INLAND STEEL BUILDING** Skidmore, Owings & Merrill	**MARINA CITY** Bertrand Goldberg Associates

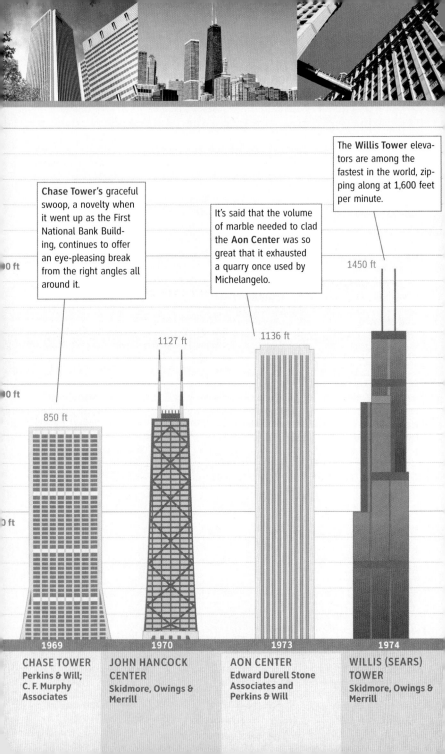

Chase Tower's graceful swoop, a novelty when it went up as the First National Bank Building, continues to offer an eye-pleasing break from the right angles all around it.

It's said that the volume of marble needed to clad the **Aon Center** was so great that it exhausted a quarry once used by Michelangelo.

The **Willis Tower** elevators are among the fastest in the world, zipping along at 1,600 feet per minute.

0 ft

0 ft

0 ft

850 ft

1127 ft

1136 ft

1450 ft

1969

CHASE TOWER
Perkins & Will;
C. F. Murphy
Associates

1970

**JOHN HANCOCK
CENTER**
Skidmore, Owings &
Merrill

1973

AON CENTER
Edward Durell Stone
Associates and
Perkins & Will

1974

**WILLIS (SEARS)
TOWER**
Skidmore, Owings &
Merrill

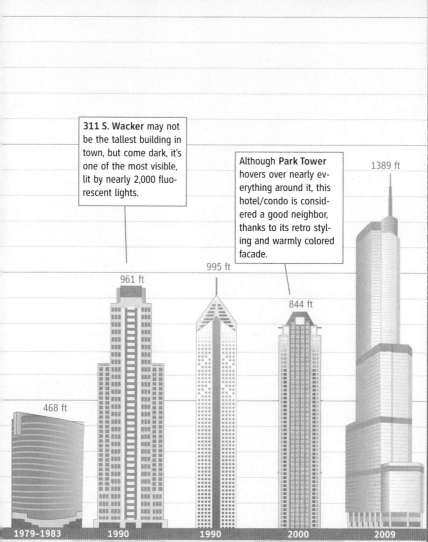

311 S. Wacker may not be the tallest building in town, but come dark, it's one of the most visible, lit by nearly 2,000 fluorescent lights.

Although **Park Tower** hovers over nearly everything around it, this hotel/condo is considered a good neighbor, thanks to its retro styling and warmly colored facade.

1389 ft

995 ft

961 ft

844 ft

468 ft

1979–1983	1990	1990	2000	2009
333 W. WACKER DRIVE Kohn Pedersen Fox and Perkins & Will	**311 S. WACKER DRIVE** Kohn Pedersen Fox	**2 PRUDENTIAL PLAZA** Loebl, Schlossman & Hackl	**PARK TOWER** Lucien LaGrange Architects	**TRUMP TOWER** Skidmore, Owens, and Merrill

Kids and kids-at-heart get their thrills at Navy Pier.

N. Astor St., Gold Coast ☎ 312/573–1365 ⊕ *www.charnleyhouse.org* 🖾 *Tours Wed. free, Sat. $10* ☿ *Tours Wed. and Sat. at noon.*

Fourth Presbyterian Church. A welcome visual and physical oasis amid the high-rise hubbub of North Michigan Avenue, this Gothic Revival house of worship was the first big building erected on the avenue after the Chicago Fire. Designed by Ralph Adams Cram, the church drew many of its congregants from the city's elite. Local architect Howard van Doren Shaw devised the cloister and companion buildings. ■ TIP → In July and August, free concerts are staged every Friday at 12:10 beside the courtyard fountain off Michigan Avenue; other months they're performed in the sanctuary. ⊠ *126 E. Chestnut St., Near North* ☎ 312/787–4570 ⊕ *www.fourthchurch.org.*

Historic Water Tower. This famous Michigan Avenue structure, completed in 1867, was originally built to house a 137-foot standpipe that equalized the pressure of the water pumped by the similar pumping station across the street. Oscar Wilde uncharitably called it "a castellated monstrosity" studded with pepper shakers. One of the few buildings that survived the Great Chicago Fire, it remains a civic landmark and a symbol of the city's spirit. The small gallery inside hosts rotating art exhibitions of local interest. ⊠ *806 N. Michigan Ave., at Pearson St., Near North* ☎ 312/744–3315 🖾 *Free* ☿ *Daily 10–6:30.*

NBC Tower. This 1989 limestone-and-granite edifice by Skidmore, Owings & Merrill looks back to the art deco days without becoming a victim of fashion's past. Four floors of the 38-story tower are dedicated to a radio and television broadcasting facility. ⊠ *455 N. Cityfront Plaza Dr., Near North* ☎ 312/222–9611 ⊕ *www.nbc-tower.com.*

A REVERED SCHOOL

The **Chicago School** had no classrooms and no curriculum, nor did it confer degrees. In fact, the Chicago School wasn't an institution at all but rather a name given to the collection of architects whose work, beginning in the 1880s, helped free American architecture from the often rigid styles of the past. Nonetheless, a number of their buildings echoed a classical column, the lower floors functioning as the base, the middle floors as the shaft, and the cornice on top being the equivalent of a capital. In pioneering the "tall building," these architects used steel-frame construction; they also reduced ornamentation. Alumni include Daniel Burnham, William Le Baron Jenney, Louis Sullivan, Dankmar Adler, John Root, William Holabird, and Martin Roche.

Patterson-McCormick Mansion. On the northwest corner of Astor and Burton places in the swanky Gold Coast, you'll find this Georgian building. It was commissioned in 1891 by *Chicago Tribune* chief Joseph Medill and built by Stanford White. You can't go inside because it's been converted into condos—Billy Corgan of the Smashing Pumpkins is said to own one of the units. ⊠ *20 E. Burton Pl., Gold Coast.*

Water Works Pumping Station. Water is still pumped to some city residents at a rate of about 250 million gallons per day from this Gothic-style structure, which, along with the Water Tower across the street, survived the 1871 conflagration. The **Lookingglass Theatre** now calls this place home. ⊠ *163 E. Pearson St., at Michigan Ave., Near North* ☎ *312/337–0665* ⊕ *lookingglasstheatre.org.*

RIVER NORTH

Once the warehouse district and for a time a place where many Chicago artists had their lofts, River North is now known for its large, often touristy restaurants, art galleries, and the enormous Merchandise Mart, which still serves as a neighborhood landmark. River North lies immediately north of the Loop and the Chicago River, south of Chicago Avenue, and west of the Mag Mile.

TOP ATTRACTIONS

Bloomingdale's (Medinah Temple). Built in 1912 for the Shriners, the former Medinah Temple is a Middle Eastern fantasy, with horseshoe-shape arches, stained-glass windows, and intricate geometric patterns around windows and doors (it once also held a 4,200-seat auditorium). Vacant for many years, it was transformed into a Bloomingdale's Home & Furniture Store in 2003. ⊠ *600 N. Wabash Ave., River North* ☎ *312/324–7500* ⊕ *www.bloomingdales.com* ⊗ *Mon.–Thurs. 10–7, Fri. and Sat. 10–8, Sun. noon–6.*

Driehaus Museum. Curious about how the wealthy built their urban palaces during America's Gilded Age? Steps away from the Magnificent Mile, the former Samuel Mayo Nickerson mansion has lavish

DID YOU KNOW?

Marina City has served as a backdrop for many films, including *The Blues Brothers*, *Batman Begins*, and *The Dark Knight*. But it's best remembered for the supporting role it played in Steve McQueen's final flick, *The Hunter*. in that movie's famous chase scene, the criminal that McQueen is pursuing drives off the top floor of the parking garage and into the Chicago River.

interiors with 19th-century furniture and objets d'art, including pieces by Louis Comfort Tiffany and the Herter brothers. ✉ *40 E. Erie St., River North* ☎ *312/482–8933* ⊕ *www.driehausmuseum.org* 🎫 *$20; $5 for tour* ⊙ *Tues.–Sun. 10–5; tours Tues.–Sun. at 10:30, 11:30, 1:30, and 3:30.*

The Merchandise Mart. The massive Merchandise Mart, on the river between Orleans and Wells streets, takes up nearly two square blocks. It was the world's biggest building when it opened in 1930 and remains large enough to have its own stop on the El's Brown and Purple lines. Miles of corridors on the top floors are lined with trade-only furniture and home-design showrooms. LuxeHome, a collection of 30 or so upscale stores with an emphasis on home design and renovation, takes up the bottom two floors. ✉ *222 Merchandise Mart Plaza, River North* ☎ *800/677–6278* ⊕ *www.mmart.com* ⊙ *Showrooms weekdays 9–5; LuxeHome weekdays 9–5, Sat. 10–3.*

River North Gallery District. North of the Merchandise Mart and south of Chicago Avenue, between Orleans and Dearborn, is a concentration of art galleries carrying just about every kind of work imaginable. Virtually every building on Superior Street between Wells and Orleans houses at least one gallery, and visitors are welcome to stop in. Free tours leave from Chicago and Franklin every Saturday at 11; galleries also coordinate their exhibitions to showcase new works on some Friday evenings (check the *Chicago Gallery News* for dates). Although many artists have ditched this high-rent district for the cheaper, more industrial West Loop, there is still a lot to see. ✉ *Between Chicago Ave. and Merchandise Mart, Orleans and Dearborn Sts., River North* ☎ *312/649–0064 Chicago Gallery News* ⊕ *www.chicagogallerynews.com.*

GOLD COAST

North of Oak Street, hugging Lake Shore Drive, is the Gold Coast neighborhood. Astor Street is the grande dame of Gold Coast promenades, and homes like the Patterson-McCormick Mansion and the Charnley-Persky House still impress. Where Dearborn Street meets Oak Street is the Gold Coast's famous shopping district. Past the former **Playboy Mansion** (*1340 N. State St.*), all the way to North Boulevard, is a beautiful view of Lincoln Park. This is a lovely area to stroll around on a sunny, summer afternoon.

WORTH NOTING

Marina City. Likened to everything from corncobs to the spires of Antonio Gaudí's Sagrada Familia in Barcelona, these twin towers were a bold departure from the severity of the International Style, which began to dominate high-rise architecture beginning in the 1950s. Designed by Bertrand Goldberg and completed in 1964, they contain condominiums (all pie-shaped, with curving balconies); the bottom 19 stories of each tower are given over to exposed spiral parking garages. The complex is also home to four restaurants, the House of Blues nightclub, the Hotel

Sax Chicago, a huge bowling alley, and the titular marina. ⊠ *300 N. State St., River North* ⊕ *www.marinacity.org.*

Tree Studios. Built in 1894 with a courtyard and annexes constructed in 1911 and 1912, the nation's oldest surviving artist studios have been restored and designated a Chicago landmark. Shops, galleries, and event spaces now fill the studios. ⊠ *4 E. Ohio St., at State St., River North.*

Trump International Hotel & Tower. The Chicago Sun-Times Building was torn down to make way for this 92-story tower, which was designed by Skidmore, Owings & Merrill and opened in 2008. A spire that elevates its height to a whopping 1,392 feet makes it the city's second-tallest building. The concrete-reinforced structure (the former Sears Tower and John Hancock Center are reinforced by steel) is a glassy, tiered monolith whose biggest attribute is an idyllic riverfront location. Although there's no viewing deck, the public can get picturesque views of downtown through the floor-to-ceiling windows of its 16th-floor restaurant, Sixteen, or the Terrace (open seasonally); Rebar, on the mezzanine level, provides lovely views of the Chicago River and Michigan Avenue Bridge. ⊠ *401 N. Wabash Ave., River North* ☎ *312/588–8000* ⊕ *www.trumphotelcollection.com/chicago.*

4

LINCOLN PARK
AND WICKER PARK

with Bucktown and Logan Square

GETTING ORIENTED

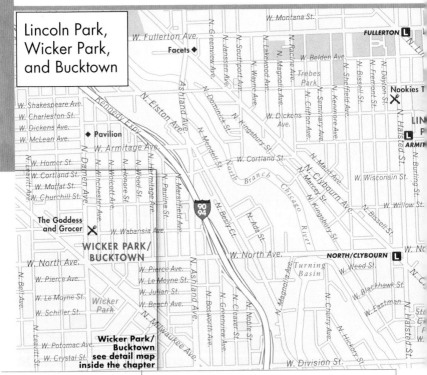

Lincoln Park, Wicker Park, and Bucktown

GETTING TO LINCOLN PARK

Ride the CTA Red Line or Brown Line train to either Armitage or Fullerton Avenue. Buses 11, 22, 36, and 151 take you through the area, too. If you're driving, take Lake Shore Drive to Fullerton Avenue and go west to Sheffield Avenue.

GETTING TO LOGAN SQUARE

Take the Kennedy Expressway to California Avenue (Exit 46A). By El, take the Blue Line toward O'Hare to Logan Square. From the Loop, take Bus 20 to Homan and Bus 82 north to Logan Square.

MAKING THE MOST OF YOUR TIME

Lincoln Park can be done in two ways—with or without kids. Highlights for the little ones include the Lincoln Park Zoo, the Peggy Notebaert Nature Museum, and the beach; adults enjoy the area's shops, eateries, and entertainment options. Lincoln Park's Steppenwolf Theatre and Old Town's Second City (the club that launched countless comedians) are quintessential Chicago experiences. Wicker Park/Bucktown is good for funky shopping, people-watching, and cool restaurants, while Logan Square has morphed from an immigrant neighborhood into a hip urban enclave.

GETTING TO WICKER PARK/BUCKTOWN

Take the Kennedy Expressway to North Avenue, and then head west to the triangular intersection of North, Milwaukee, and Damen avenues. Metered street parking is limited, and side-street parking is by resident permit only, so it's worth it to take advantage of restaurants' valet service. By El train, take the Blue Line to the Damen–North Avenue stop.

KEY

L CTA lines

✗ Restaurant/Cafe

Peggy Notebaert Nature Museum

Green City Market (winter)

W. Fullerton Pkwy.

Lincoln Park Conservatory

St. Valentine's Day Massacre site

Oz Park

Lincoln Park Zoo

W. Dickens Ave.

R.J. Grunt's

LINCOLN PARK

RMITAGE W. Armitage Ave.

W. Wisconsin St.

41 North Avenue Beach

Green City Market (summer)

Lincoln Park

Louis Sullivan row houses

W. Eugenie St.

Chicago History Museum

The Second City

W. North Blvd.

North Ave.

L SEDGWICK

OLD TOWN

W. Schiller St.

Stanton Schiller Park

W. Scott St.

W. Goethe St.

W. Scott St.

E. Scott St.

W. Division St.

E. Elm St.

Lake Michigan

TOP REASONS TO GO

Enjoy the lakefront: Walk— or run or bike—on the path heading south from North Avenue Beach, and take in the breathtaking views of the city along Lake Michigan.

Laugh: Catch the free improv after the show at the famed Second City comedy club every night except Friday.

Shop: Browse the boutiques along Lincoln Park's Armitage Avenue or shop for funky finds on Division Street, Milwaukee Avenue, and Damen Avenue.

Visit the animals: Say hello to the apes and other animals at the Lincoln Park Zoo. The added bonus is that it's free.

QUICK BITES

Goddess and Grocer. Tasty sandwiches and salads that please vegans and carnivores alike are served at Goddess and Grocer. ⊠ *1649 N. Damen Ave., Bucktown* ☎ *773/342–3200* ⊕ *www.goddessandgrocer.com.*

Nookies Too. Heaping breakfasts, available anytime, make this spot a favorite with the neighborhood's late-night crowd. There are also branches in Old Town, Lakeview, and Edgewater. ⊠ *2114 N. Halsted St., Lincoln Park* ☎ *773/327–1400* ⊕ *www.nookiesrestaurants.net.*

R.J. Grunt's. Just outside Lincoln Park, R.J. Grunts has been serving killer milk shakes and burgers since 1971. It is also known for its famous (and gargantuan) salad bar. ⊠ *2056 N. Lincoln Park West, Lincoln Park* ☎ *773/929–5363* ⊕ *www. leye.com/restaurants/directory/rj-grunts.*

Sightseeing ★★★★☆	In 1864 the vast park here—which extends from North
Dining ★★★★☆	Avenue to Foster Avenue—became the city's first public
Lodging ★★★★☆	playground. Its zoo is legendary. The area adjacent to it,
Shopping ★★☆☆☆	bordered by Armitage Avenue, Diversey Parkway, the lake,
Nightlife ★★★★☆	and the Chicago River, took the same name. To the west,

Sightseeing ★★★★☆
Dining ★★★★☆
Lodging ★★★★☆
Shopping ★★☆☆☆
Nightlife ★★★★☆

In 1864 the vast park here—which extends from North Avenue to Foster Avenue—became the city's first public playground. Its zoo is legendary. The area adjacent to it, bordered by Armitage Avenue, Diversey Parkway, the lake, and the Chicago River, took the same name. To the west, in Wicker Park and Bucktown, up-to-the-minute fashions mix with old-world memories and gorgeous Victorian-era architecture. Logan Square, just west of Wicker Park/Bucktown, is notable for its historic buildings and hip restaurants.

LINCOLN PARK

Updated by Roberta Sotonoff

Today Lincoln Park epitomizes all the things that people love—and love to hate—about yuppified urban areas: stratospheric housing prices, teeny boutiques with big-attitude salespeople, and plenty of fancy-schmancy coffee shops, wine bars, and cafés. It's also got some of the prettiest residential streets in the city, that gorgeous park, a great nature museum, a thriving arts scene, and the renowned Steppenwolf Theatre.

Old Town, bordered by Division Street, Armitage Avenue, Clark Street, and Larrabee Street, began in the 1850s as a modest German working-class neighborhood. Now its diverse population resides in some of the oldest (and most expensive) real estate in Chicago. Its best known tenants are the Second City and Zanies comedy clubs.

TOP ATTRACTIONS

FAMILY
Fodor's Choice ★

Chicago History Museum. Seeking to bring Chicago's often complicated history to life, this museum has several strong permanent exhibits, including "Chicago: Crossroads of America," which demystifies tragedies like the Great Chicago Fire and the Haymarket Affair, in which a bomb thrown during a labor rally in 1884 led to eight anarchists being convicted of conspiracy. In "Sensing Chicago," kids can feel what the city was once like—they can catch a fly ball at Comiskey Park (now U.S. Cellular Field), dress up like a Chicago-style hot dog, and "hear" the Great Chicago Fire. "Facing Freedom" takes a close look at what freedom means. Admission includes the audio tour. ⊠ *1601 N. Clark St., Lincoln Park* ☏ *312/642–4600* ⊕ *www.chicagohistory.org* ⊠ *$14* ☉ *Mon.–Sat. 9:30–4:30, Sun. noon–5.*

> **DID YOU KNOW?**
>
> Begun in 1868 with a pair of swans donated by New York's Central Park, the Lincoln Park Zoo grew through donations of animals from wealthy Chicago residents and the purchase of a collection from the Barnum & Bailey Circus.

FAMILY **Facets.** Film buffs shouldn't leave Lincoln Park without visiting this movie theater, which presents an eclectic selection of films from around the world on its two screens. Each year, Facets also hosts the Chicago International Children's Film Festival (*www.cicff.org*): one of the only Academy Award–qualifying children's film festivals in the world, it showcases the best in culturally diverse, value-affirming new cinema for kids. An on-site DVD store has more than 60,000 foreign, classic, and cult movies. ⊠ *1517 W. Fullerton Ave., Lincoln Park* ☏ *800/331–6197, 773/281–4114 for showtimes* ⊕ *www.facets.org* ⊠ *Nonmembers $10 for movies.*

FAMILY
Fodor's Choice
★
Lincoln Park Zoo. At this urban enclave near Lake Michigan, you can face off with a lion (separated by a window, of course) outside the Kovler Lion House; watch snow monkeys unwind in the hot springs of the Regenstein Macaque Forest; or ogle gorillas and chimpanzees in the sprawling Regenstein Center for African Apes, which has three separate habitats complete with bamboo stands, termite mounds, and 5,000 feet of swinging vines. Animals both slithery (pythons) and strange (sloths) reside in the glass-domed Regenstein Small Mammal and Reptile House, while the big guys (hippos, giraffes, and black rhinos) are in the Regenstein Animal Journey. More captivating critters will be on view when a new polar bear and penguin exhibit opens in late 2016.

Bird lovers should make a beeline to the McCormick Bird House, which contains extremely rare species—including the Bali mynah, Guam rail, and Guam Micronesian kingfisher, some of which are extinct in the wild. Families with little ones in tow will also want to see Farm-in-the-Zoo (with its barnyard animals and learning centers), and the LPZoo Children's Train Ride. Be sure to leave time for a ride (or two) on the Endangered Species Carousel, featuring a menagerie of 48 rare and endangered animals. ⊠ *2001 N. Clark St., Lincoln Park* ☏ *312/742–2000* ⊕ *www.lpzoo.org* ⊠ *Free; parking $20 for 30 minutes or more* ☉ *Animal houses Apr.–Memorial Day and Labor Day–Oct., daily 10–5 (gates open 7–6); Memorial Day–Labor Day, weekdays 10–5 (gates open 7–6), weekends 10–6:30 (gates open 7–7); Nov.–Mar., daily 10–4:30 (gates open 7–5).*

Old Town. A vibrant dining scene and lots of good bars and clubs (including the famed Second City) make Old Town a top nightlife destination.

A lioness broods atop a rock at the Lincoln Park Zoo.

✉ *Between Armitage Ave. and Division St., Clark and Larrabee Sts., Lincoln Park* ☎ *312/951–6106* ⊕ *www.oldtownchicago.org.*

WORTH NOTING

Green City Market. On Wednesday and Saturday mornings from May through October, the market takes over a large swath of grass at the south end of Lincoln Park. In addition to farmstands showcasing locally grown produce and sustainably raised meat, there are food booths and cooking demonstrations by local celebrity chefs. November through April, an indoor incarnation sets up two Saturdays a month between 8 am and 1 pm in the Peggy Notebaert Nature Museum's South Gallery, at 2430 North Cannon Drive. ✉ *1750 N. Clark St., near N. Lincoln Ave., Lincoln Park* ☎ *773/880–1266* ⊕ *www.chicagogreencitymarket. org* ✍ *Free* ☉ *May–Oct., Wed. and Sat. 7 am–1 pm.*

Lincoln Park Conservatory. The tranquillity and abundant greenery inside this 1892 conservatory offer a refreshing respite in the heart of a bustling neighborhood. Stroll through permanent displays in the Palm House, Fern Room, and Orchid House, or catch special events like the fragrant Spring Flower Show. ✉ *2391 N. Stockton Dr., Lincoln Park* ☎ *312/742–7736* ⊕ *www.chicagoparkdistrict.com/parks/lincoln-park-conservatory* ✍ *Free* ☉ *Daily 9–5.*

Louis Sullivan row houses. The love of geometric ornamentation that Sullivan eventually brought to such projects as the Carson, Pirie, Scott & Co. building (now the Sullivan Center) is already visible in these row houses, built in 1885. The terra-cotta cornices and decorative window tops are especially beautiful. ⊠ *1826–1834 N. Lincoln Park West, Lincoln Park.*

FAMILY **North Avenue Beach.** The beautiful people strut their stuff at this lakefront strand. The beachhouse, which has concession stands, a restaurant, showers, and bike and volleyball rentals, resembles a steamship. There are about 50 volleyball courts, an outdoor fitness center, and lots of sand. ⊠ *1600 N. Lake Shore Dr., Lincoln Park ⊕ www.chicagoparkdistrict.com/parks/north-avenue-beach ⊙ Late May–Labor Day.*

FAMILY **Oz Park.** Fans of *The Wizard of Oz* love getting up close with Dorothy, Toto, and all the other beloved characters assembled here in sculpture form. Author L. Frank Baum lived in Chicago at the turn of the 20th century. The park, located between Webster and Dickens avenues and Burling and Larrabee streets, also has a flowery Emerald Garden and play lot for pint-size visitors. ⊠ *2021 N. Burling St., Lincoln Park* ☎ *312/742–7898 ⊕ www.chicagoparkdistrict.com/parks/Oz-Park* ⊠ *Free ⊙ Daily 6 am–11 pm.*

FAMILY **Peggy Notebaert Nature Museum.** Walk among hundreds of species of tropical butterflies and learn about the impact of rivers and lakes on daily life at this modern, light-washed museum. Like Chicago's other science museums, this one is perfect for kids, but even jaded adults may be excited when bright yellow butterflies land on their shoulders. The idea is to connect with nature inside without forgetting graceful Lincoln Park outside. Interesting temporary exhibits round out the offerings. ⊠ *2430 N. Cannon Dr., Lincoln Park* ☎ *773/755–5100 ⊕ www. naturemuseum.org* ⊠ *$9 ⊙ Weekdays 9–5, weekends 10–5.*

St. Valentine's Day Massacre site. On Clark Street near Dickens, there's a rather inconspicuous landscaped nursing home parking lot where the SMC Cartage Company once stood. There's no marker, but it's the site of the infamous St. Valentine's Day Massacre, when seven men were killed on the orders of Al Capone on February 14, 1929. The massacre targeted Capone's main rival in the illegal liquor trade, Bugs Moran. Though Moran wasn't in the warehouse that day, he was finished as a bootlegger. The event shocked the city and came to epitomize the violence of the Prohibition era. ⊠ *2122 N. Clark St., Lincoln Park.*

WICKER PARK

Wicker Park, the area south of North Avenue to Division Street, is inhabited by creative types, young families, university students, and older but hip professionals. Art galleries, coffeehouses, nightclubs, and funky shops line its streets—it's a far cry from the Mag Mile. Along Hoyne and Pierce avenues, near the triangular park that gives the neighborhood its name, you'll find some of the biggest and best examples

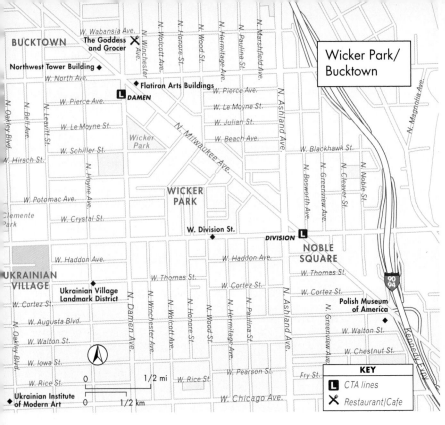

Wicker Park/Bucktown

of Chicago's Victorian-era architecture. So many brewery owners built homes in this area that it was once dubbed Beer Baron Row. Farther south is the Ukrainian Village.

TOP ATTRACTIONS

Division Street. At the southern border of Wicker Park, Division Street has become a shopping and dining destination in its own right. Bars, boutiques, and trendy restaurants line the once-gritty thoroughfare, which lent its name to journalist Studs Terkel's 1967 book about urban life. To start your exploration, head west on the stretch of Division between Wolcott and Western avenues. ⊠ *Ukrainian Village/Wicker Park.*

Polish Museum of America. The Chicago Metro area has the largest Polish population of any city outside Warsaw, and this museum celebrates that fact. Take a trip to the old country by strolling through exhibits of folk costumes, memorabilia from Pope John Paul II, American Revolutionary War heroes Tadeusz Kosciuszko and Casimir Pulaski, and pianist and composer Ignacy Paderewski. There's also Hussar armor and an 8-foot-long sleigh in the shape of a dolphin. It's a good place to catch up on your reading, too—the library has almost 100,000 volumes in Polish and English. ⊠ *984 N. Milwaukee Ave., Wicker Park*

☎ 773/384–3352 ⊕ www.polishmuseumofamerica.org ✉ $7 ⊙ Fri.– Tues. 11–4, Wed. 1–7.

Ukrainian Village Landmark District. For a glimpse of how the working class lived at the turn of the 20th century, head south of Wicker Park to the Ukrainian Village. In its center, on Haddon Avenue and on Thomas and Cortez streets between Damen Avenue and Leavitt Street, you'll find a well-preserved group of workers' cottages and apartments. (You can also see similar brick and wood-frame houses north of here on Homer Street between Leavitt Street and Oakley Avenue.) ⊠ *Between Division St. and Chicago Ave., Western and Damen Aves., Ukrainian Village.*

WORTH NOTING

Flatiron Arts Building. This distinctive three-story, terra-cotta structure sits opposite the Northwest Tower. Its upper floors have long served as a sort of informal arts colony, providing studio and gallery space for a number of visual artists. ⊠ *1579 N. Milwaukee Ave., Wicker Park* ☎ *312/335–3000 ⊕ www.flatiron.tv.*

Northwest Tower Building (*Coyote Building*). Erected in 1929, this triangular, 12-story art deco office building is the anchor of the North Milwaukee–Damen intersection and is used as a reference point from miles around. According to the *Chicago Tribune*, some artists dubbed it the Coyote Building in the 1980s, because they thought that the base attaching the flagpole to the rest of the tower "resembled a coyote howling at the moon." ⊠ *1600 N. Milwaukee Ave., Wicker Park.*

Ukrainian Institute of Modern Art. Modern and contemporary art fans head to this small museum at the far western edge of the Ukrainian Village. One of its two galleries is dedicated to changing exhibitions; the other features the museum's permanent collection of mixed media, sculpture, and painting from the 1950s to the present. Some of the most interesting works are kinetic steel-wire sculptures by Konstantin Milonadis, the constructed reliefs of Ron Kostyniuk, and painted wood structures by Mychajlo Urban. ⊠ *2320 W. Chicago Ave., Ukrainian Village* ☎ *773/227–5522 ⊕ www.uima-chicago.org ✉ Free ⊙ Wed.–Sun. noon–4.*

BUCKTOWN

North of Wicker Park, Bucktown got its name from the goats kept by the area's original Polish and German immigrants. These days it's mostly residential with a fairly wealthy population of professionals who can afford the rents, but evidence of its ethnic roots remains. For shopping—window or otherwise—with wares you won't likely find elsewhere, head to Damen Avenue between North and Fullerton. Fun restaurants and bars (some divey, others upscale) keep things busy at night, too.

LOGAN SQUARE

Logan Square sits just west of Wicker Park/Bucktown. Over the years, it has been a melting pot for immigrants—first European (primarily Scandinavian, English, Polish, and Jewish), then later Latino. Spacious tree-lined boulevards are the dominant aspect of the area, and many historic buildings still line the streets. But Logan Square's "cool quotient" has risen significantly in recent decades, leading some to compare it to Brooklyn.

5

LAKEVIEW AND THE FAR NORTH SIDE

GETTING ORIENTED

Lakeview and the
Far North Side

KEY

L CTA lines
M Metra lines
X Restaurant/Cafe

MAKING THE MOST OF YOUR TIME

A Wrigleyville and Lakeview stroll takes about 90 minutes; add another two hours to browse the Southport shops. To experience the *real* Chicago, take in a Cubs game from Wrigley Field's bleachers.

To see all of the Far North's neighborhoods, allow a day. Visit Graceland Cemetery for an hour or two. Leave three hours for Andersonville's shops and Swedish American Museum Center, then two more for shopping on Devon Avenue. Later peek at the boutiques and do dinner in Lincoln Square.

GETTING HERE BY PUBLIC TRANSPORTATION

You may need to take a combination of bus and El. Buses 22 and 36 go to Lakeview from downtown, as do the Brown Line (Southport) and the Purple and Red lines (Belmont). Take the El's Red Line north toward Howard to Lawrence for Uptown, Wilson for Andersonville, and Loyola for Devon. The 155 bus from Devon reaches the Far North. The Brown Line El north toward Kimball to Western takes you to Lincoln Square.

QUICK BITES

Ann Sather. This nominally Swedish mini-chain serves breakfast until midafternoon, including legendary lingonberry pancakes and giant cinnamon buns. Other locations include Granville at Broadway and Boystown. ⊠ *909 W. Belmont Ave., Lakeview* ☎ *773/348–2378* ⊕ *www.annsather.com.*

Bobtail Ice Cream Company. Head here for shakes, sundaes, and ice cream in flavors like Lakeview Barhopper, Cubby Crunch, and Daley Addiction. ⊠ *2951 N. Broadway St., Lakeview* ☎ *773/880–7372* ⊕ *www.bobtailicecream.com.*

Reza's. Outstanding Persian cuisine (think kebabs, dolma, and charbroiled ground beef with rice) is dished out at Reza's. On weekdays, its $10 lunch buffet is the best deal in town. ⊠ *5255 N. Clark St., Andersonville* ☎ *773/561–1898* ⊕ *www. rezasrestaurant.com.*

TOP REASONS TO GO

Take yourself out to the ball game: Sit in the bleachers with the locals at Wrigley Field, and be ready to throw the ball back onto the field if the opposing team hits a homer. When the Cubs are on the road, take a tour of the park.

Go to the movies: Catch a classic or indie flick at the vintage Music Box Theatre.

Tour Graceland Cemetery: Visit such famous "residents" as Marshall Field, George Pullman, and others at their final resting place.

Go Swedish: Check out the Swedish enclave Andersonville for authentic Swedish restaurants and bakeries.

GETTING HERE BY CAR

By car, take Lake Shore Drive north to Belmont (Lakeview), but keep in mind that parking can be scarce. When the Cubs play, take public transit. Head north up Western Avenue for between Montrose and Lawrence for Lincoln Square, Lawrence Avenue for Uptown, Foster Avenue for Andersonville, and Devon Avenue for the Far North.

Sightseeing
★★☆☆☆
Dining
★★★★☆
Lodging
★☆☆☆☆
Shopping
★★★★☆
Nightlife
★★★★☆

Stretching north in a rough row that runs parallel and close to the lake, the primarily residential neighborhoods in Lakeview and the Far North Side aren't the place for major museums or high-rises. Instead, they're best at giving you a feel for how local Chicagoans live. Whether you wander one of the many ethnic neighborhoods, contemplate the dignitaries (and scoundrels) buried in Graceland Cemetery, or celebrate a hard-won victory at Wrigley Field, this area is perfect for connecting with the sights and sounds that make Chicago the great city it is.

LAKEVIEW

Updated by Joseph Erbentraut

Initially a settlement and then a township independent of Chicago, Lakeview became part of the city in 1889. Today it is a massive neighborhood made up of small enclaves, each with its own distinct personality. There's Wrigley Field surrounded by the beer-swilling, Cubby-blue-'til-we-die sports-bar fanaticism of Wrigleyville; the gay bars, shops, and clubs along Halsted Street in Boystown; and an air of urban chic along Southport Avenue, where young families stroll amid the trendy boutiques and ice-cream shops.

TOP ATTRACTIONS

Fodor'sChoice
★

Boystown. Just beyond Wrigleyville lies this section of Lakeview; it's been a major "gayborhood" since the 1970s, which also makes it one of the country's first. Although the area has become much more mixed in recent years, distinctive rainbow pylons still delineate Boystown—most of its gay-oriented shops, bars, and restaurants are concentrated on and around Halsted. In June the street becomes a sea of people, when Chicago's gay pride parade floats down the block. Year-round, the neighborhood is home to the Legacy Walk, which celebrates the history and achievements of the LGBT community with plaques adorning the district's iconic pylons. ⊠ *Between Broadway, Belmont Ave., and Halsted St., Boystown.*

Fodor'sChoice
★
Graceland Cemetery. Near Irving Park Road, this graveyard has crypts that are almost as strikingly designed as the city skyline. A number of Chicago's most prominent citizens, including Daniel Burnham and Marshall Field, are spending

> **DID YOU KNOW?**
>
> The names on the grave sites at Graceland read like a who's who from a Chicago history book: Marshall Field, George Pullman, and Daniel Burnham are a few of the notables buried here. You can take a guided neighborhood tour or pick up a walking-tour map at the entrance Monday through Saturday to explore on your own.

eternity here. Architect Louis Sullivan (also a resident) designed some of its more elaborate mausoleums. Free maps, available at the cemetery office, will help you find your way around the pastoral 119-acre property. ⊠ *4001 N. Clark St., Lakeview* ☎ *773/525–1105* ⊕ *www. gracelandcemetery.org* ⊠ *Free* ☉ *Apr.–Oct., daily 8–6; Nov.–Mar., daily 8–4.*

Fodor'sChoice
★
Music Box Theatre. Southport's main claim to fame is this 1929 movie house, which shows independent and classic films on its two screens. Live organ music provides a retro preamble. Before the house lights dim, look up to admire twinkling stars and clouds on the ceiling. ⊠ *3733 N. Southport Ave., Wrigleyville* ☎ *773/871–6604* ⊕ *www. musicboxtheatre.com* ⊠ *$10; check website for specials.*

Southport Avenue. Southport and other streets that travel north to Irving Park Road are lined with independent shops, many of which cater to well-dressed young women with money to burn. ⊠ *Southport Ave., between Grace St. and Belmont Ave., Wrigleyville* ⊕ *www. southportneighbors.com.*

FAMILY
Fodor'sChoice
★
Wrigley Field. The nation's second-oldest major league ballpark—venerable, ivy-covered Wrigley Field—hosted its first major league game in 1914 and has been home to the Chicago Cubs since 1916. The original scoreboard is still used (score-by-innings, players' numbers, strikes, outs, hits, and errors are all posted manually); and though long-awaited renovations lie ahead, the character that makes this place so special will remain intact. On game day, diehard devotees opt for the bleachers, while the more gentrified prefer box seats along the first and third baselines. If you look up along Sheffield Avenue on the east side of the park, you can see the rooftop patios where baseball fans pay high prices to cheer for the home team; the less lucky sit in lawn chairs on Sheffield, waiting for foul balls to fly their way. While you're here, check out the **Harry Caray statue** commemorating the late Cubs announcer; in the bottom half of the seventh inning, fans sing "Take Me Out to the Ballgame" in his honor. Tours of the park and dugouts are given from April to October, when the Cubs are on the road. Note that big-name concerts by the likes of Elton John and Bruce Springsteen are also staged here when the team is out of town. ⊠ *1060 W. Addison*

Pay homage to the greats of Chicago's past at Graceland Cemetery.

St., at Sheffield St., Wrigleyville ☎ *773/404–2827* ⊕ *www.mlb.com/chc/ ballpark* 🎟 *Tours $25.*

WORTH NOTING

Lakeview Homes. Two- and three-story gray-stone houses and other residential buildings line the quiet, leafy side streets heading east and west of Boystown. Wandering along them, you might even feel transported back in time to 1920s or '30s Chicago. In 2008 a stretch of Newport Avenue between Clark and Halsted was temporarily transformed into a cobblestone thoroughfare for the John Dillinger flick *Public Enemies*, starring Johnny Depp. ✉ *Lakeview.*

FAR NORTH AND FAR NORTHWEST SIDES

The Far North and Far Northwest sides of Chicago are home to several of the city's most colorful neighborhoods. Just north of Lakeview, Uptown's beautiful architecture and striking old marquees are a testament to the time when it was a thriving entertainment district.

The area around Broadway and Argyle is known variously as Little Saigon, Little Chinatown, and North Chinatown. Andersonville was named for the Swedish community that settled near Foster Avenue and Clark Street in the 1960s, and it still maintains a huge concentration of Swedes.

Double street signs attest to Devon Avenue's diversity—in some places named for Gandhi, in others for Golda Meir, although much of the

Jewish population has moved to Skokie. Whatever the name, the area is best explored on foot.

South of Devon via Western Avenue is the former German enclave of Lincoln Square, now a happening dining and shopping destination. One of the best ways to discover all these neighborhoods' cultural diversity is by sampling the food.

TOP ATTRACTIONS

FAMILY
Fodor's Choice
★
Andersonville. Just north of Uptown there's a neighborhood that feels like a small town and still shows signs of the Swedish settlers who founded it. Andersonville has some great restaurants and bakeries, many of which pay tribute to its Scandinavian roots. In winter months, be sure to drop by **Simon's Tavern**, at 5210 North Clark, for a glass of *glögg* (mulled wine)—it's a traditional favorite. Helping anchor the area is the **Women & Children First** bookstore, at 5233 North Clark, which stocks an extensive selection of feminist tomes and children's lit. ⊠ *Between Glenwood, Foster, Ravenswood, and Bryn Mawr Aves., Andersonville* ☎ *773/728–2995* ⊕ *www.andersonville.org.*

Devon Avenue. Chicagoans flock here to satisfy cravings for Indian, Middle Eastern, and Asian fare, or, as the avenue moves west, a good Jewish challah. Indian restaurants and sari shops start popping up just west of Western Avenue. Though west of Talman Avenue was once an enclave for orthodox Jews and Russian immigrants, many of the people, along with the shops, have migrated to the northern suburbs. ⊠ *Devon Ave., between Kedzie and Ridge Aves., Far North.*

Lincoln Square. Long known for its Teutonic heritage, Lincoln Square is home to two annual German fests—Maifest in late May (held around a 30-foot-tall maypole) and German-American Fest in September—both featuring plenty of beer, brats, German-style pretzels, and folks dressed in lederhosen. Thursday evenings in summer bring free concerts and a farmers' market. Since the late 1990s this quiet North Side neighborhood, named for the Lincoln statue near Lawrence and Western avenues, has seen its currency with young professionals rise, and a spate of trendy new places is the result. Popular bars and restaurants line Lincoln Avenue between Montrose and Lawrence; shopping is a draw, too. Many credit Lincoln Square's renaissance to the relocation of the **Old Town School of Folk Music**, which moved to a long-vacant art deco building at 4544 North Lincoln Avenue in 1998. Each July, it sponsors the Square Roots festival. But those longing for a taste of Lincoln Square's ethnic roots shouldn't despair. You'll still find a handful of German restaurants and bars along the avenue. Also still here is the 1922 **Krause Music Store building** (*4611 N. Lincoln Avenue*), with its ornate green terra-cotta facade; it was the last work commissioned by architect Louis Sullivan. ⊠ *Between Foster, Montrose, and Damen Aves. and the Chicago River, Lincoln Square* ⊕ *www.LincolnSquare.org.*

OFF THE
BEATEN
PATH
National Veterans Art Museum. Located in Portage Park, this museum is dedicated to collecting, preserving, and exhibiting art inspired by combat and created by veterans. Founded in 1981, its goal is to serve as a space for civilians, veterans, and current military alike to share an open

The ornate details on Andersonville buildings speak to the neighborhood's Swedish roots.

dialogue on the lasting impacts of warfare. The museum features haunting works from all wars in which the United States has participated. ⊠ *4041 N. Milwaukee Ave., Far Northwest Side* ☎ *312/326–0270* ⊕ *www.nvam.org* ✉ *Free* ⊗ *Tues.–Sat. 10–5.*

FAMILY
Fodor'sChoice
★

Swedish American Museum Center. You don't have to be Swedish to find this tiny and welcoming museum interesting. Permanent displays include trunks immigrants brought with them to Chicago and a map showing where in the city different immigrant groups settled. On the third floor, in the only children's museum in the country dedicated to immigration, kids can climb aboard a colorful Viking ship. ⊠ *5211 N. Clark St., Andersonville* ☎ *773/728–8111* ⊕ *www.swedishamericanmuseum. org* ✉ *$4, free 2nd Tues. of month* ⊗ *Weekdays 10–4, weekends 11–4; children's section Mon.–Thurs. 1–4, Fri. 10–4, weekends 11–4.*

WORTH NOTING

Argyle Strip. Also known as Little Saigon (and Little Chinatown and North Chinatown), this area is anchored by the red pagoda of the El's Argyle Street stop. Home to many Vietnamese immigrants, the Strip teems with storefront noodle shops, bakeries, and pan-Asian grocery stores that are a huge draw for locals and tourists alike. Roasted ducks hang in shop windows and fish peer out from large tanks. ⊠ *Between Foster, Lawrence, Broadway and Lake Michigan, Uptown.*

PILSEN, LITTLE ITALY, AND CHINATOWN

with University Village and Prairie Avenue

GETTING ORIENTED

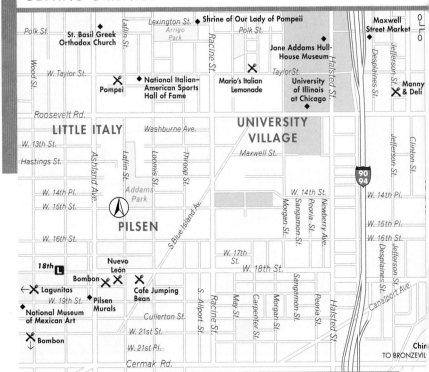

MAKING THE MOST OF YOUR TIME

Pilsen buzzes on weekends and during the Fiesta del Sol festival (at the end of July). On the second Friday of each month, neighborhood galleries stay open late for an art crawl. At night Little Italy's restaurants and bars bustle. On Sunday the Maxwell Street Market hums. Browse the shops and sample the goods along Wentworth Avenue or Chinatown Square. And don't forget to tour the nearby 19th-century Prairie Avenue homes, where many of the people who shaped Chicago lived.

GETTING HERE

If you're driving to Pilsen, take I–290 west to the Damen Avenue exit, and go south on Damen to 19th Street. There's parking at the National Museum of Mexican Art plus metered street parking. For Little Italy and University Village, take the Kennedy Expressway's Taylor Street exit and head west. Chinatown is west of Michigan Avenue via Cermak Road. There's a parking lot at Chinatown Gate, on Wentworth Avenue. Turn east off Michigan Avenue on East 21st Street to reach Prairie Avenue.

If you choose to use public transportation, the El's Pink Line stops at the 18th Street station in the Pilsen area. Check out the station's colorful murals. Take the Blue Line to UIC/Halsted for University Village and the No. 9 Ashland bus to Little Italy. For Chinatown, take the El's Red Line south to Cermak.

Pilsen, Little Italy, and Chinatown

KEY

L CTA Stations

✕ Restaurant/Cafe

TOP REASONS TO GO

Gallery-hop: On second Fridays in Pilsen the art galleries stay open late.

Shop: Haggle with the locals at the legendary Maxwell Street Market on Sunday.

Appreciate history: See where Chicago greats like Marshall Field and George Pullman lived in the Prairie Avenue Historic District.

SAFETY

The railway tracks and vacant lots between Pilsen and Little Italy make it unsafe to walk between the two neighborhoods. Drive if possible, or take the Blue Line to either UIC–Halsted or Racine to explore University Village and Little Italy; then take the Pink Line to 18th Street for Pilsen. Chinatown and Prairie Avenue are a bit removed from the heart of the city and bordered by slowly gentrifying neighborhoods, so be cautious and aware. Limit your visit to well-lighted and well-populated main streets after dark.

QUICK BITES

Cafe Jumping Bean. You'll find Mexican hot chocolate, focaccia pizzas, and fresh sandwiches at this cozy neighborhood coffee shop. ✉ 1439 W. 18th St., Pilsen ☎ 312/455–0019.

Joy Yee Noodles. From a massive menu, pan-Asian dishes arrive in a flash. The mouthwatering portions may be huge, but the prices aren't. ✉ Chinatown Square Mall, 2139 S. China Pl., Chinatown ☎ 312/328–0001 ⊕ www.joyyeechicago.com.

Manny's Coffee Shop & Deli. The corned-beef sandwich here is the one that other local delis aim to beat. Manny's has always been popular with Chicago politicians—so if these walls could talk, they'd spill a lot of secrets. ✉ 1141 S. Jefferson St., West Loop ☎ 312/939–2855 ⊕ www.mannysdeli.com.

Pompei. Head to this branch of a local restaurant empire for salads, house-made pasta, and its famous thick, bready squares of pizza. ✉ 1531 W. Taylor St., Little Italy ☎ 312/421–5179 ⊕ www.pompeiusa.com.

Sightseeing
★★★☆☆

Dining
★★★★☆

Lodging
★☆☆☆☆

Shopping
★★☆☆☆

Nightlife
★☆☆☆☆

A jumble of ethnic neighborhoods stretches west of the Loop and from the south branch of the Chicago River to the Eisenhower Expressway (I–290). Once home to myriad 20th-century immigrants, the area is now dominated by Pilsen's Mexican community, Little Italy, and the University of Illinois's Medical District and Circle Campus.

PILSEN

Updated
by Joseph
Erbentraut

Formerly full of Bohemian and Czech immigrants and now primarily Mexican, Pilsen is bounded on the east by 800 West Halsted Street, on the west by 2400 West Western Avenue, on the north by 16th Street, and on the south by the Chicago River. Keep an eye open for dramatic, colorful murals that showcase Mexican history, culture, and religion.

TOP ATTRACTIONS

Fodor'sChoice
★

National Museum of Mexican Art. The largest Latino museum in the country (and the only Latino one accredited by the American Alliance of Museums) is definitely worth a look. Its galleries house impressive displays of contemporary, traditional, and Mesoamerican art from both sides of the border, as well as vivid exhibits that trace immigration woes and political struggles. The 8,000-piece permanent collection includes pre-Cuauhtemoc artifacts, textiles, folk art, paintings, prints, and drawings. Every fall the giant "Day of the Dead" exhibit stuns Chicagoans with its altars from artists across the nation. ⊠ *1852 W. 19th St., Pilsen* ☎ *312/738–1503* ⊕ *www.nationalmuseumofmexicanart.org* ☎ *Free* ⊗ *Tues.–Sun. 10–5.*

Pilsen Murals. Murals give Pilsen its distinctive flair. You'll see their vibrant colors and bold images at many turns during a walk through the neighborhood. At Ashland Avenue and 19th Street, two large ones illustrate Latino family life and Latinos at work. More murals created by community youth groups and local artists brighten up the blocks

CLOSE UP

Bronzeville

Bronzeville lies between Douglas Boulevard (Cottage Grove Avenue) and Grand Boulevard (Martin Luther King Jr. Drive). History buffs can honor the neighborhood's numerous influential African-American inhabitants; architecture aficionados can head to the Illinois Institute of Technology (IIT) campus to check out the Mies van der Rohe creations; and sports fans can take in a White Sox game at nearby U.S. Cellular Field (aka "The Cell") in Bridgeport.

FOLLOW HISTORY'S TRAIL

After World War I, blacks began to move to Bronzeville to escape race restrictions prevalent in other parts of the city. Many famous African Americans are associated with the area, including Andrew "Rube" Foster, founder of the Negro National Baseball League; civil rights activist Ida B. Wells; Bessie Coleman, the first African American woman pilot; and jazz great Louis Armstrong. The symbolic entrance to the area is a tall statue at 26th Place and Martin Luther King Jr. Drive that depicts a new arrival from the South bearing a suitcase held together with string. A commemorative trail along Martin Luther King Jr. Drive between 25th and 35th streets has more than 90 sidewalk plaques honoring the best and brightest of the community, including the late Gwendolyn Brooks, whose first book of poetry was called *A Street in Bronzeville.*

ARCHITECTURE 101

"Less is more," claimed Mies van der Rohe, but for fans of the master's work, more is more at IIT. The campus has an array of the glass-and-steel structures for which he is most famous. Crown Hall, the jewel of the collection, has been designated a National Historic Landmark, but don't overlook the Robert F. Carr Memorial Chapel of St. Savior.

The McCormick Tribune Campus Center, designed by Dutch architect Rem Koolhaas, is fun to explore and pays homage to the Mies legacy. Its apparently opaque windows are actually see-through, as long as you stand head-on. Look at the glass walls near the entrance through a digital camera and you'll see depictions of IIT icons like Mies. In 2003 Helmut Jahn created the corrugated-steel, triple-glass student housing that runs alongside the El.

The campus is about 1 mile west of Lake Shore Drive on 31st Street. Both the El's Green and Red Line 35th Street stops are two blocks west of campus. S. State St. between 31st and 35th Sts. ☎ *312/567–3000* ⊕ *www. iit.edu.*

GO-GO, WHITE SOX!

The Chicago White Sox don't generate the same level of hype as their North Side rivals, the Cubs; however, taking in a game at U.S. Cellular Field (formerly Comiskey Park) is a great way to spend a summer afternoon. Tickets are typically much more reasonable than nine innings at Wrigley, too. Be sure to try the stadium's signature treat, helmet nachos (nachos served, just as the name implies, in a replica batting helmet.)

The ballpark is located immediately west of the Red Line's 35th Street stop and two blocks west of the Green Line's IIT/Bronzeville stop. 333 W. 35th St. ☎ *312/674–1000* ⊕ *www. chicago.whitesox.mlb.com/cws/ ballpark.*

6

centered at 16th and Ashland; Aztec sun-god inserts decorate the sidewalk stones. ⊠ *Pilsen.*

Thalia Hall. A few blocks east of 18th Street's hustle and bustle, you'll find this neighborhood landmark. Built in 1892, but shuttered for decades, it reopened as a stunning multipurpose space in 2013. The focal point is a concert hall, elegantly fashioned after a Prague opera house, which hosts a broad range of musical performances and artsy events. **Dusek's Board & Beer**, an upscale new American eatery with a brew-centric menu, and **Punch House**, a hip and moodily lit lounge for the cocktail crowd, are also on the premises. ⊠ *1807 S. Allport St., Pilsen* ☎ *312/526–3851* ⊕ *www.thaliahallchicago.com.*

WORTH NOTING

18th Street. Pilsen's main commercial strip is loaded with tempting restaurants, bakeries, and Mexican grocery stores. At 1515 West 18th, past the "Bienvenidos a Pilsen" sign, is **Nuevo León,** a brightly painted family restaurant that has been an anchor in the neighborhood since the Gutiérrez family set up shop in 1962. Inhale deeply if the doors to the tortilla factory next door are open. ⊠ *Chicago* ⊕ *www.eighteenth street.org.*

NEED A BREAK?

Bombon. If you like sweets or have kids in tow, keep an eye out for this bakery, which stocks a mind-boggling array of treats. ⊠ *1530 W. 18th St., Pilsen* ☎ *312/733–7788* ⊕ *www.chicagobestcakes.com.*

Halsted Street. Since the late 1960s, Halsted Street near 18th Street has lured a large number of artists, who live and work in the mixed-use community known as the Chicago Arts District. Its street-level galleries and studios have put Pilsen on the map as an art destination, and innovative spaces abound. The best time to visit them is on the second Friday of each month from 6 to 10 pm, when 30 artists open their doors to the public. Expect visual displays, interpretive dance, installations, music, and performance art. Most studios also have regular weekend hours or are open by appointment. ⊠ *Pilsen* ☎ *312/738–8000* ⊕ *www. chicagoartsdistrict.org.*

OFF THE BEATEN PATH

Lagunitas Brewing Company. Ever since California-based Lagunitas Brewing Company set up shop in industrial West Pilsen, it's been a must-see for beer lovers. The 300,000-square-foot facility offers free tours, no reservations necessary. Its tap room is regularly buzzing with live music—as you'd expect, there's great brew and good pub grub to go with it, too. ⊠ *1843 S. Washtenaw Ave., Pilsen* ☎ *773/522–2097* ⊕ *www.lagunitas.com.*

LITTLE ITALY

To the north of Pilsen is Little Italy, which, despite the encroachment by the University of Illinois at Chicago (UIC), still contains plenty of Italian restaurants, bakeries, groceries, and sandwich shops. The neighborhood is bordered by UIC (Morgan Street) on the east and Western

The Shrine of Our Lady of Pompeii keeps traditional Italian culture alive in Chicago.

Avenue on the west. Its north and south boundaries are Harrison and 12th streets (Roosevelt Road), respectively.

WORTH NOTING

National Italian American Sports Hall of Fame. The NIASHF was founded by George Randazzo in 1978 to honor Italian American athletes. Among the first inductee was baseball legend Joe DiMaggio; others include Rocky Marciano, Yogi Berra, Mary Lou Retton, and Phil Rizzuto. Originally housed in Elmwood Park, then Arlington Heights, the Hall of Fame came to Little Italy in 1994 with the help of Chicago native Jerry Colangelo, CEO of the Phoenix Suns. If you are interested in relics like the last coat worn by Vince Lombardi as the Green Bay Packers coach or Mario Andretti's Indy 500 race car, this is your kind of place. ⊠ *1431 W. Taylor St., Little Italy* ☎ *312/226–5566* ⊕ *www.niashf.org* ☉ *Mon.–Sat. noon–4.*

St. Basil Greek Orthodox Church. Located near Polk Street, this gorgeous Greek Revival building, erected in 1910, has an equally lavish interior. It was originally the Anshe Shalom Synagogue. ⊠ *733 S. Ashland Ave., Little Italy* ☎ *312/243–3738* ⊕ *www.stbasilchicago.org* ☑ *Free* ☉ *Weekdays 10–2.*

Shrine of Our Lady of Pompeii. Completed in 1923 and built to accommodate the area's growing number of Italian immigrants, this church is the oldest continuously operating Italian American church in Chicago. Its Romanesque Revival style was popular with the famous church architects Worthman and Steinbach, and its interior is filled with statues and striking stained-glass windows. The church sometimes serves as a venue for concerts and theatrical productions. ⊠ *1224 W. Lexington St., Little Italy* ☎ *312/421–3757* ⊕ *www.ourladyofpompeii.org* ▣ *Free* ⊙ *Weekdays 9–4:30, Sun. Mass at 8:30 and 11.*

> **DID YOU KNOW?**
>
> Clarke House Museum has been moved three times from its original location on Michigan Avenue between 16th and 17th streets. The last time, in 1977, it had to be hoisted above the nearby elevated train tracks.

Taylor Street. In the mid-19th century, when Italians started to migrate to Chicago, about one-third of them settled in and around Taylor Street, a 12-block stretch between Ashland and the University of Illinois at Chicago. It is best known for its Italian restaurants, though Thai food, tacos, and other ethnic options are here, too. ⊠ *Little Italy* ☎ *312/218–4044* ⊕ *www. taylorstreetarchives.com.*

NEED A BREAK?

Mario's Italian Lemonade. If you visit Taylor Street from May to mid-September, be sure to stop at Mario's Italian Lemonade, a neighborhood staple since the '50s. Everyone from politicians like Jesse Jackson to local families lines up for old-fashioned, slushy Italian ices here. ⊠ *1068 W. Taylor St., Little Italy* ⊙ *May–Sept. 15, daily 11–midnight.*

UNIVERSITY VILLAGE

Little Italy blends into University Village at its northeast corner. The Village, UIC's booming residential area, is centered on Halsted Street south to 14th Street.

TOP ATTRACTIONS

Fodor's Choice ★ **Jane Addams Hull-House Museum.** Hull House was the birthplace of social work. Social welfare pioneers and peace advocates Jane Addams and Ellen Gates Starr started the American settlement house movement in this redbrick Victorian in 1889. They wrought near-miracles in the surrounding community, which was then a slum for new immigrants. Pictures and letters add context to the two museum buildings, which re-create the homey setting the residents experienced. The museum, located on the UIC campus, also hosts a range of events typically geared toward progressive social movements. ⊠ *800 S. Halsted St., University Village* ☎ *312/413–5353* ⊕ *www.hullhousemuseum.org* ▣ *Suggested donation $5* ⊙ *Tues.–Fri. 10–4, Sun. noon–4.*

Maxwell Street Market. Until 1967 this famous Sunday flea market, begun in the 1880s by Jewish immigrants, was the place to barter for bargains. Then UIC took most of the property to build university housing. The market limped along and finally closed in the 1990s, but a public uproar led to its relocation to South Desplaines Street between West Polk Street and West Roosevelt Road, about ½ mile from the original site. Today more than 500 vendors sell clothing, power tools,

Go back in time to the late 1800s at the opulent Glessner House.

and household items; blues musicians often play; and some of the best Mexican food in town is available. ⊠ *800 S. Desplaines St., University Village* 🕾 *312/745–4676* ☉ *Sun. 7–3.*

PRAIRIE AVENUE

In the 1870s the **Prairie Avenue Historic District** served as Chicago's first Gold Coast. After the Chicago Fire of 1871, prominent Chicagoans, including George Pullman, Marshall Field, and the Armour family, had homes in the area two blocks east of Michigan Avenue, between 18th and 22nd streets. It's close to Chinatown, where Wentworth and Archer avenues are chockablock with Asian restaurants and shops.

TOP ATTRACTIONS

Clarke House Museum. This Greek Revival structure dates from 1836, making it Chicago's oldest surviving building. It's a clapboard house in a masonry city, built for Henry and Caroline Palmer Clarke to remind them of the East Coast they left behind. The Doric columns and pilasters were an attempt to civilize Chicago's frontier image. The everyday objects and furnishings inside evoke a typical 1850s–'60s middle-class home. Tours begin nearby at Glessner House. ⊠ *1827 S. Indiana Ave., Prairie Avenue* 🕾 *312/326–1480* ⊕ *www.clarkehousemuseum.org* 🎫 *$10, $15 combo ticket with Glessner House, free Wed.* ☉ *Tours Wed.–Sun. at noon and 2.*

Fodor's Choice ★ **Glessner House Museum.** This fortresslike residence is the only surviving building in Chicago by architect H.H. Richardson, who also designed Boston's Trinity Church. Completed in 1886, the L-shape mansion's stone construction and short towers are characteristic of the Richardsonian Romanesque Revival style. It's also one of the few great mansions left on Prairie Avenue, once home to such heavy hitters as retailer Marshall Field and meatpacking magnate Philip Armour. The area has lately seen the arrival of new, high-end construction, but nothing beats a tour of Glessner House, a remarkable relic of the days when merchant princes really lived like royalty. Enjoy the lavish interiors and the many artifacts, from silver pieces and art glass to antique ceramics and Isaac Scott carvings and furnishings. ⊠ *1800 S. Prairie Ave., Prairie Avenue* ☎ *312/326–1480* ⊕ *www.glessnerhouse.org* ☜ *$10, $15 combo ticket with Clarke House, free Wed.* ☉ *Tours Wed.– Sun. at 1 and 3.*

> **PRAIRIE AVENUE AND CHINATOWN TOURS**
>
> Guided tours of both the Clarke House and Glessner House museums run Wednesday through Sunday year-round. Wednesday tours are walk-in only and free of charge; these tend to fill up, so arrive early to guarantee a spot. In summer, the Chicago Chinese Cultural Institute (☎ *312/842–1988* ⊕ *www.chinatowntourchicago. com*) conducts 90-minute morning walks Friday through Sunday ($10); special food-oriented tours are available Saturday at 10:30 ($60), and dumpling-making tutorials are offered Sunday at 4:30 ($35). Reservations are necessary.

Quinn Chapel. One of Chicago's African American cornerstones, this church was founded in 1847 and served as an Underground Railroad stop. The present building, designed by Henry Starbuck, opened in 1891, and the rough-finished brick exterior is in keeping with the time. The interior has a tin ceiling and simple stained-glass windows. Many notable people have addressed the congregation, including President William B. McKinley, Booker T. Washington, and Dr. Martin Luther King Jr. ⊠ *2401 S. Wabash Ave., South Loop* ☎ *312/791–1846* ⊕ *www. quinnchicago.org* ☜ *Free* ☉ *Daily 9:30–5, services Sun. at 10.*

Second Presbyterian Church. Constructed in 1874, this handsome Gothic Revival church was designed by James Renwick, also the architect of the Smithsonian's Castle and New York City's St. Patrick's Cathedral. The National Historic Landmark features one of the largest collections of Tiffany stained-glass windows anywhere. ⊠ *1936 S. Michigan Ave., Prairie Avenue* ☎ *312/225–4951* ⊕ *www.2ndpresbyterian.org* ☜ *Free* ☉ *Tues.–Fri. 9–1, services Sun. at 11.*

Wheeler Mansion. At the intersection of Calumet Avenue and Cullerton Street is another of the area's great mansions, which was nearly replaced by a parking lot before it was saved and painstakingly restored in the late 1990s. Today it's a boutique hotel. ⊠ *2020 S. Calumet Ave., Prairie Avenue* ☎ *312/945–2020* ⊕ *www.wheelermansion.com.*

Performers participate in a festival in Chinatown.

Willie Dixon's Blues Heaven Foundation. A cadre of music legends, including Etta James, Bo Diddley, Aretha Franklin, Koko Taylor, and John Lee Hooker, recorded here in the former Chess Records building. Guides regale visitors with tales of the famous stars, and you can check out the old recording studios, office, rehearsal rooms, and memorabilia. Call ahead. ✉ *2120 S. Michigan Ave., Prairie Avenue* ☎ *312/808–1286* ⊕ *www.bluesheaven.com* 💲 *$10* ☯ *Weekdays 11–4.*

CHINATOWN

West of the Prairie Avenue district, this Chinese microcosm sits in the shadows of modern skyscrapers. The neighborhood is anchored by the **Chinatown Gate,** which spans West Cermak Road and South Wentworth Avenue. Referring to the tenacity of Chicago's first Chinese settlers, the gate's four gold characters proclaim, "The world belongs to the commonwealth." Also prominent are the enormous green-and-red pagoda towers of the **Pui Tak Center,** a church-based community center in the former On Leong Tong Building. Most visitors only come here to dine or to hunt for bargains in the gift and furniture shops on Wentworth Avenue. But Chinatown is more than that. So take some time to wander the streets and check out the local grocery stores, where English is rarely heard, live fish and crabs fill vats, and hard-to-identify canned and dried items bulge from shelves.

WORTH NOTING

Chinatown Square. Located on Princeton and Archer, this large square is punctuated by animal sculptures, each representing one of the 12 symbols of the Chinese zodiac. Below the sculptures is a plaque explaining the personalities of those born during each year. ⊠ *2133 S. China Pl., Chinatown.*

Nine Dragon Wall. Modeled after the one in Beijing's Beihai Park, this wall is graced by nine large and 500 smaller dragons, all signifying good fortune. It is right next to the El's Red Line Cermak-Chinatown stop. ⊠ *W. Cermak Rd., Chinatown.*

Ping Tom Memorial Park. Four pillars carved with dragon designs adorn the entrance of this beautifully landscaped park, which is named for Chinatown's most renowned civic leader. Wedged within the shadows of railroad tracks and highways, its 12 serene riverside acres include a children's playground, winding walking trails, a fieldhouse, and a boathouse (kayak rentals are available at the last of these in summer). A large yellow-and-red pagoda provides good views of the looming Chicago skyline to the north; April through September, you can also board a water taxi here for a scenic—and cost-effective—ride to the Loop. ⊠ *1700 S. Wentworth Ave., Chinatown* ⊕ *www.chicagoparkdistrict. com/parks/Ping-Tom-Memorial-Park* ⊡ *Free* ☉ *Daily 6 am–11 pm.*

HYDE PARK

7

Visit Fodors.com for advice, updates, and bookings

GETTING ORIENTED

KEY
- **M** Metra lines
- ✕ Restaurant/Cafe

Hyde Park

E. 46th St.

E. 47th St.

E. 48th St.

Burnham Park

Lake Michigan

E. 49th St.

E. 50th St.

HYDE PARK

Madison Park

E. Hyde Park Ave.

Model Yacht Basin

S. Cottage Grove Ave.

S. Drexel Ave.

S. Ingleside Ave.

S. Greenwood Ave.

S. University Ave.

S. Woodlawn Ave.

E. 52nd St.

S. Dorchester Ave.

S. Blackstone Ave.

S. Harper Ave.

S. Lake Park Ave.

◆ Heller House

E. 53rd St.

✕ Valois

E. 53rd St.

S. Cornell Dr.

S. Hyde Park Blvd.

Nichols Park

E. 54th St.

S. Kimbark Ave.

S. Kenwood Ave.

S. Ridgewood Ct.

E. 54th Ave.

E. 54th Ave.

Promontory Point ◆

S. Everett Ave.

Jimmy's: The Woodlawn Tap ✕

E. 55th St.

E. 55th St.

E. 55th Pl.

◆ Smart Museum of Art

Hyde Park Historical Society ◆

The Promontory ◆

E. 56th St.

DuSable Museum of African American ← ◆ History

E. 57th St.

Medici on 57th ✕

Museum of Science and Industry

Robie House ◆

E. 58th St.

S. Ellis Ave.

Oriental ◆ Institute

University of Chicago ◆

E. 59th St.

S. Dorchester Ave.

S. Blackstone Ave.

S. Harper Ave.

S. Stony Island Ave.

East Lagoon

Midway Plaisance

Midway Plaisance

Midway Plaisance

E. 60th St.

S. University Ave.

Jackson Park

E. 61st St.

West Lagoon

0   600 feet

0   200 meters

S. Dorchester Ave.

South Shore Cultural Center ◆

E. 62nd St.

S. Cornell Ave.

GETTING HERE

By car, take Lake Shore Drive south to the 57th Street exit and turn left into the parking lot of the Museum of Science and Industry. You can also take the Metra train from Randolph Street and Michigan Avenue; get off at the 55th Street stop and walk east through the underpass two blocks, then south two blocks. From Indiana, take the South Shore Line to the 57th Street station. CTA Buses 2, 6, 10, and 28 will also get you here from downtown.

MAKING THE MOST OF YOUR TIME

Visiting the Museum of Science and Industry will probably take most of a day. Go during the week to avoid crowds. Wind down by meandering through Jackson Park, the University of Chicago campus, or the Midway Plaisance, the main walkway for the 1893 World's Columbian Exposition.

QUICK BITES

Jimmy's: The Woodlawn Tap. At this favored tavern, locals and university students gather for beer, burgers, and Reuben sandwiches. On Sunday nights, jam sessions complement the pub grub. ⊠ 1172 E. 55th St., Hyde Park ☎ 773/643–5516 ⊕ www.josephsittler.org/jimmys/.

Medici on 57th. Known for its pizzas and burgers, Medici has served generations of University of Chicago students and faculty—many of whom carved their name on the tables and walls. Just to the east, the Medici deli and bakery serves mouthwatering croissants. ⊠ 1327 E. 57th St., Hyde Park ☎ 773/667–7394 ⊕ www.medici57.com.

Valois. This cash-only Hyde Park institution serves big portions of no-frills diner classics cafeteria-style. It's said that President Obama ate here daily during his University of Chicago days. ⊠ 1518 E. 53rd St., Hyde Park ☎ 773/667–0647 ⊕ www.valoisrestaurant.com ▭ No credit cards.

TOP REASONS TO GO

Get caught up in wonderment: Spend a few hours at the Museum of Science and Industry.

Enjoy Jackson Park: Revel in the tranquil mood and do some exotic-bird-watching.

Appreciate Frank Lloyd Wright: Take a tour of the fantastic Robie House.

Enjoy the views: Pack a picnic for Promontory Point.

SAFETY

Hyde Park is bordered to the west, south, and north by some poor, and at times dangerous, areas. Use caution, especially in the evening.

KENWOOD

The Kenwood area of Hyde Park was once home to the city's elite; after many of the residents moved to the suburbs, the neighborhood became run-down—it has since rebounded to a large degree. The Swifts of meatpacking fame lived not far from President Barack Obama's house, which is off-limits. **St. Gabriel Church** (4522 S. Wallace St. ☎ 773/268–9595), designed in 1887 by Daniel Burnham and John Root, is marked by a tower, arched doorways, and a large round window. The parish was organized to serve Irish workers at the Union Stock Yards, once in operation nearby.

7

HYDE PARK

Sightseeing
★★★★☆

Dining
★★☆☆☆

Lodging
★☆☆☆☆

Shopping
★☆☆☆☆

Nightlife
★★☆☆☆

Hyde Park is something of a trek from downtown Chicago, but it's worth the extra effort. Rich in academic and cultural life, it is also considered to be one of the country's most successfully integrated neighborhoods—a fact reflected in everything from the people you'll meet on the street to the diverse cuisine served in local eateries.

Updated by Joseph Erbentraut

Best known as the home of the University of Chicago, Hyde Park began to see significant growth only in the late 19th century, with the university opening in 1892 and the World's Columbian Exposition drawing an international influx a year later. The exposition spawned numerous Classical Revival buildings (including the behemoth Museum of Science and Industry) as well as the Midway Plaisance, which still runs along the southern edge of the University of Chicago's original campus. Sprawling residences were soon erected for school faculty in neighboring Kenwood, and the area began to attract well-to-do types who commissioned famous architects to build them spectacular homes.

Among the architecturally riveting buildings here are two by Frank Lloyd Wright, the Robie House and Heller House, as different as night and day. A thriving theater scene plus several art and history museums further add to the ambience. Most impressive, though, is the diverse population, with a strong sense of community pride and a fondness for the neighborhood's pretty tree-lined streets, proximity to the lake, and slightly off-the-beaten-path vibe.

TOP ATTRACTIONS

FAMILY
Fodor'sChoice
★

DuSable Museum of African American History. Sitting alongside the lagoons of Washington Park, the DuSable Museum offers an evocative exploration of the African American experience. The most moving display is about slavery—rusted shackles used on slave ships are among the poignant and disturbing artifacts. Other permanent exhibits include letters

WORLD'S COLUMBIAN EXPOSITION

In 1893 the city of Chicago hosted the **World's Columbian Exposition**. The fair's mix of green spaces and Beaux-Arts buildings offered the vision of a more pleasantly habitable metropolis than the crammed industrial center that rose from the ashes of the Great Fire. However, a ruffled Louis Sullivan prophesied that "the damage wrought to this country by the Chicago World's Fair will last half a century." He wasn't entirely wrong in his prediction—the neoclassical style vied sharply over the next decades with the native creations of the Chicago and Prairie schools, all the while incorporating their technical advances. One of Hyde Park's most popular destinations—the Museum of Science and Industry—was erected as the fair's Palace of Fine Arts. It's one of only three exposition buildings still standing; the others are the Art Institute of Chicago building and a small ladies' "comfort station" behind the MSI.

and memorabilia pertaining to scholar W.E.B. DuBois and poet Langston Hughes. The museum also has a significant art collection. Rotating exhibits showcase African American milestones, achievements, and contributions. ⊠ *740 E. 56th Pl., Hyde Park* ☎ *773/947–0600* ⊕ *www.dusablemuseum.org* ⊠ *$10* ☽ *Tues.–Sat. 10–5, Sun. noon–5.*

FAMILY
Fodor's Choice
★
Museum of Science and Industry.
See highlighted listing in this chapter.

Oriental Institute. This gem began with artifacts collected by University of Chicago archaeologists in the 1920s (one is rumored to have been the model for Indiana Jones) and has expanded into an interesting, informative museum with a jaw-dropping array of artifacts from the ancient Near East. In addition to the largest U.S. collection of Iraqi antiquities, you'll see amulets, mummies, limestone reliefs, gold jewelry, ivories, pottery, and bronzes from the 4th millennium BC through the 13th century AD. A 17-foot-tall statue of King Tut was excavated from the ruins of a temple in western Thebes in 1930. ⊠ *1155 E. 58th St., Hyde Park* ☎ *773/702–9250* ⊕ *www.oi.uchicago.edu* ⊠ *Suggested donation $10* ☽ *Tues. and Thurs.–Sun. 10–5, Wed. 10–8.*

Promontory Point. It's tough to top the view of Chicago's skyline from the Point—a scenic, man-made peninsula, which projects into Lake Michigan. Opened in 1937 as part of Burnham Park, it's entered via a tunnel underneath Lake Shore Drive at 55th Street or the Lakefront Trail. The fawn-shape David Wallach Memorial Fountain is located near the tunnel. The park's field house is a popular wedding venue, so you may catch a glimpse of a beaming bride during your visit. ⊠ *5491 S. Shore Dr., Hyde Park* ☎ *312/742–5369* ⊕ *www.chicagoparkdistrict.com/parks/Burnham-Park* ⊠ *Free* ☽ *Daily 6 am–11 pm.*

Fodor's Choice
★
Robie House. Named one of the 10 most significant buildings of the 20th century by the American Institute of Architects, the 9,000-square-foot Robie House (1910) is long and low. Massive overhangs shoot out from the low-pitched roof, and windows run along the facade in a glittering stretch. Inside, Wright's "open plan" echoes the great outdoors, as one

DID YOU KNOW?

The Laura Spelman Rocke-feller Memorial Carillon at the University of Chicago's Rockefeller Chapel is the largest instrument ever built, with 72 bells and 100 tons of bronze. Hear it ring each Sunday afternoon at 12:15 and on weekdays during the academic year at noon and 6 pm. Check the chapel's website (⊕ *rockefeller.uchicago.edu*) for information on special carillon recitals, concerts, and other notewor-thy events.

MUSEUM OF SCIENCE AND INDUSTRY

✉ 5700 S. Lake Shore Dr.,
Hyde Park ☎ 773/684–1414
🌐 www.msichicago.org
🎫 $18, $26 with Omnimax
🕙 Late May–early Sept., daily
9:30–5:30; early Sept.–late
May, daily 9:30–4.

7

TIPS

■ Use the museum map
to plan out your visit. Your
best bet is to hit a couple
of highlights (the onboard
U-boat tour will take about 20
minutes), and then see a few
quirky exhibits.

■ If the kids get grouchy,
bring them to the Idea
Factory, a giant playroom
where they can play with
water cannons, blocks, and
cranks. It's limited to ages 10
and younger.

■ Relax with some ice
cream in the old-fashioned
ice-cream parlor, tucked away
in a genteel re-creation of an
Illinois main street.

■ On nice days, hordes of
sunbathers and kite flyers
occupy the giant lawn out
front—it's almost as entertaining as the museum itself. Lake
Michigan is across the street.

■ The museum has free-
admission days, but the
schedule changes often. It is
also open for extended hours
during peak periods. Check
the website for details.

The MSI is one of the most-visited sites in Chicago, and
for good reason. The sprawling space has 2,000 exhib-
its on three floors, with new exhibits added constantly.
The museum's high-tech interior is hidden by a Classical
Revival exterior, designed in 1892 by D.H. Burnham
& Company to house the Palace of Fine Arts for the
World's Columbian Exposition. Beautifully landscaped
Jackson Park and its peaceful, Japanese-style Osaka
Garden are behind the museum.

Highlights

Descend into a simulated coal mine on a "miner"-led tour
that explores the technology behind digging energy out
of the ground.

Get swallowed up by the opulent Fairy Castle (really a giant
dollhouse), which has tiny chandeliers that flash with
real diamonds and floors that are laid with intricate
stone patterns.

Tour the cramped quarters of a U-505 German submarine—
the only one captured during World War II (additional
fee). Explore the free interactive exhibits surrounding
the sub, which give stunning insight into the strategy
behind the war at sea.

Discover how scientists can make frogs' eyes glow or watch
baby chicks emerge from their shells at the "Genetics–
Decoding Life" exhibit.

Find out how your body works at "You! The Experience,"
with 50 fascinating interactive stations.

See giant bolts of lightning, make a rainbow, and manipu-
late an indoor tornado at "Science Storms."

Navigate an 1,800-square-foot mirror maze and test your
face for symmetry as part of the museum's "Numbers
in Nature" exhibit.

The remarkable Robie House is a prime example of Frank Lloyd Wright's "open plan."

space flows into another, while sunlight streaming through decorative leaded windows bathes the rooms in patterns. The original dining room had a table with lanterns at each corner, giving the illusion that the table itself was a separate room. Other Wright innovations include a three-car garage (now the gift shop), an intercom, and a central vacuum-cleaner system. Check the website for tour options. It's a good idea to make reservations in advance. ⊠ *5757 S. Woodlawn Ave., Hyde Park* ☎ *312/994–4000* ⊕ *www.flwright.org* ✉ *$12–$55, depending on tour* ⊙ *Tours Thurs.–Mon. 10:30–3; museum shop Thurs.–Mon. 9:30–4:30.*

Fodor's Choice ★ **Smart Museum of Art.** If you want to see masterpieces but don't want to spend a long day wandering around one of the major art museums, the Smart may be just your speed. Its diverse permanent collection of more than 13,000 works includes paintings by old masters, furniture by Frank Lloyd Wright, and sculptures by Degas, Matisse, Rodin, and Henry Moore. Temporary exhibits are a great way to see startlingly good pieces in a smaller, intimate space. ⊠ *5550 S. Greenwood Ave., Hyde Park* ☎ *773/702–0200* ⊕ *www.smartmuseum.uchicago.edu* ✉ *Free* ⊙ *Tues., Wed., and Fri.–Sun. 10–5, Thurs. 10–8.*

Fodor's Choice ★ **University of Chicago.** Intellectuals come to the University of Chicago to breathe in the rarified air: after all, the faculty, former faculty, and alumni of this esteemed institution have won more Nobel prizes than any school in the country—89 in total, awarded in every field, including President Obama's 2009 Peace Prize. History buffs and art lovers are drawn by the Oriental Institute and Smart Museum of Art, while theater fans appreciate the campus-run Court Theatre, which stages new and classic works. Architecture aficionados won't be disappointed either.

MR. OBAMA'S NEIGHBORHOOD

Hyde Park's most famous family spends most of its time in Washington, D.C., these days, and the Secret Service prevents visitors from getting close to their Chicago home. Still, you can experience many of the First Family's favorite neighborhood haunts. Start at the **University of Chicago,** where Barack Obama taught law from 1992 to 2004. Make sure to look up: you'll see the university's iconic gargoyles on some buildings. From there, poke around at **57th Street Books** (57th and Kimbark 773/684–1300),

recommended by Michelle Obama for its extensive collection of fiction and nonfiction and its youth-oriented programs. The store bills itself as "the first stop for serious readers." With mind fed, it's time for some fresh air. Head east to Lake Shore Drive and walk to **Promontory Point** (5491 S. Lake Shore Dr.) for a stunning view of Lake Michigan. If you walk to the lake along East Hayes Drive, you'll pass by the basketball courts where President Obama likes to shoot hoops with his brother-in-law, Craig Robinson.

Much of the original campus was designed by Henry Ives Cobb, and its classic quadrangles were meant to mimic Oxford and Cambridge. The dominant building here, Rockefeller Memorial Chapel, is a neo-Gothic beauty complete with glorious stained-glass windows, a vaulted ceiling, 72-bell carillon, and 207-foot-high stone tower. In sharp contrast, the Booth School of Business is very modern looking; its horizontal accents imitate the Frank Lloyd Wright Robie House (1910), located directly across the street. Midcentury buildings designed by Ludwig Mies van der Rohe and Eero Saarinen, as well as contemporary ones by Helmut Jahn and husband-and-wife duo Tod Williams and Billie Tsien are also worth seeking out. A self-guided tour of UChicago architecture, *A Walking Guide to the Campus,* can be purchased at the campus bookstore or online at *architecture.uchicago.edu.* The university also highlights points of interest in a free mobile app that can be accessed through iTunes. ⊠ *Edward H. Levi Hall (Information Center), 5801 S. Ellis Ave., Hyde Park* ☏ *773/702–1234* ⊕ *www.visit.uchicago.edu* ⊙ *Weekdays 8:30–5.*

WORTH NOTING

Heller House. When he designed this house in 1897, Frank Lloyd Wright was still moving toward the mature Prairie style achieved in the Robie House 13 years later. As was common with Wright's designs, Heller House is entered from the side. But rather than being long and low, this one has three floors, the uppermost one of which comes complete with pillars and sculptured nymphs. The building is not open to the public. ⊠ *5132 S. Woodlawn Ave., Hyde Park.*

Hyde Park Historical Society. To get a good overview of the neighborhood, stop by the Hyde Park Historical Society, which sponsors lectures and tours. The society is housed in a building that once served as a waiting room for cable cars. ⊠ *5529 S. Lake Park Ave., Hyde Park* ☏ *773/493–1893* ⊕ *www.hydeparkhistory.org* ✉ *Free* ⊙ *Weekends 2–4.*

Jackson Park. This Hyde Park gem was designed by Frederick Law Olmsted (co-designer of New York City's Central Park) for the World's Columbian Exposition of 1893. It has lagoons, a Japanese garden with authentic Japanese statuary, and the Wooded Island, a nature retreat with wildlife and 300 species of birds. Its 63rd Street Beach is a popular summer destination, and the state-of-the-art fitness center means there's entertainment rain or shine. ✉ *Between E. 56th and 67th Sts., S. Stony Island Ave., and the lakefront, Hyde Park* ☎ *773/256–0903* ⊕ *www.chicagoparkdistrict.com/parks/jackson-park* ☉ *Daily 6 am–11 pm.*

> ## FOR THE BIRDS
>
> Harold Washington Park and Jackson Park have a notable parakeet population. Rumor has it they escaped from a cage at O'Hare Airport and settled in area parks. Somehow these natives of the tropics have been able to survive the harsh Chicago winter and have become neighborhood fixtures.

The Promontory. The tan brick building, designed by Mies van der Rohe in 1949, was named for nearby Promontory Point, which juts out into the lake. Mies's first Chicago high-rise, it exemplifies the postwar trend toward a clean, simple style. Even from street level, the Lake Michigan views here are breathtaking. Note the skylines and belching smokestacks of Gary and Hammond, Indiana, to the southeast. ✉ *5530–5532 S. Shore Dr., Hyde Park* ☎ *773/493–5599* ⊕ *www.miespromontory apartments.com.*

South Shore Cultural Center. Listed on the National Register of Historic Places, this opulent clubhouse on Lake Michigan is one of the last remaining Mediterranean resort–style buildings in the Midwest. The posh country club looks like something out of an F. Scott Fitzgerald novel. It boasts tennis courts, meeting rooms, horse stables, a 9-hole golf course, beach, and an art gallery. With magnificent crystal chandeliers, balconies, pillars, and a vaulted ceiling, its ballrooms and grand lobby wow visitors, including President Barack Obama and First Lady Michelle Obama, who chose the center for their wedding reception. Referred to by many as the "Gem of the Southside," it is also the home of the South Shore Cultural School of the Arts. ✉ *7059 S. Shore Dr., Hyde Park* ☎ *773/256–0149* ⊕ *www.hydepark.org/parks/southshore/ sscc1.html* ⊠ *Free* ☉ *Weekdays 9–6, Sat. 9–5.*

DAY TRIPS FROM
CHICAGO

GETTING ORIENTED

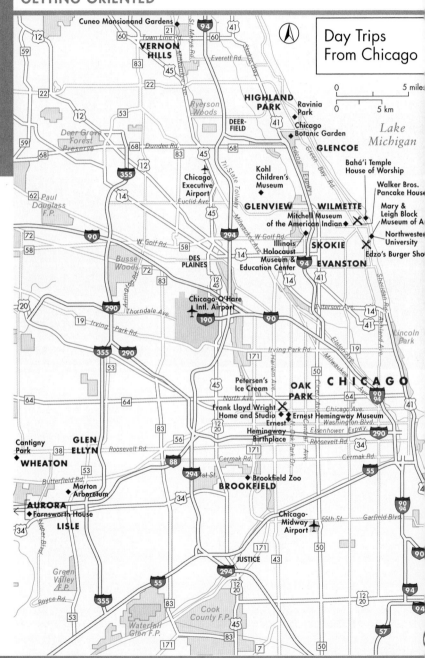

Day Trips
From Chicago

Cuneo Mansion and Gardens
VERNON HILLS
HIGHLAND PARK
Ravinia Park
Chicago Botanic Garden
GLENCOE
DEERFIELD
RYERSON WOODS
Deer Grove Forest Preserve
Paul Douglass F.P.
Chicago Executive Airport
Kohl Children's Museum
Bahá'i Temple House of Worship
Walker Bros. Pancake House
GLENVIEW
WILMETTE
Mary & Leigh Block Museum of A
Mitchell Museum of the American Indian
Northwestern University
Illinois Holocaust Museum & Education Center
SKOKIE
EVANSTON
Edzo's Burger Sho
Busse Woods
DES PLAINES
Lake Michigan
Lincoln Park
Chicago-O'Hare Intl. Airport
CHICAGO
Petersen's Ice Cream
OAK PARK
Frank Lloyd Wright Home and Studio
Ernest Hemingway Museum
Ernest Hemingway Birthplace
Cantigny Park
GLEN ELLYN
WHEATON
Morton Arboretum
AURORA
Farnsworth House
LISLE
Brookfield Zoo
BROOKFIELD
Chicago-Midway Airport
Green Valley F.P.
JUSTICE
Cook County F.P.
Waterfall Glen F.P.

0   5 miles
0   5 km

MAKING THE MOST OF YOUR TIME

A trip to Chicago shouldn't start and end within the city limits—after all, there's a lot worth seeing and doing in the suburbs. Spend at least half a day in historic Oak Park to learn about famous residents Ernest Hemingway and Frank Lloyd Wright. A second day devoted to points farther west can take you to the Brookfield Zoo or the Morton Arboretum. Chicago's picturesque North Shore won't disappoint either: enjoy a collegial day wandering Northwestern University's campus and downtown Evanston or take in a concert at Ravinia Park in Highland Park and the Chicago Botanic Garden in Glencoe.

QUICK BITES

Edzo's Burger Shop. Northwestern students and suits line up here for burgers (ground in-house), nine kinds of french fries (try the ones with truffle salt and Parmesan), and spicy Mexican-chocolate shakes. ⊠ *1571 Sherman Ave., Evanston* ☎ *847/864–3396* ⊕ *www.edzos.com* ☉ *Closed Mon.*

Petersen's Ice Cream. This old-fashioned parlor has been serving sundaes, shakes, malts, and cones of homemade ice cream for more than 90 years. ⊠ *1100 Chicago Ave., Oak Park* ⊕ *www.petersenicecream.com* ☉ *Closed Jan. and Feb.*

Walker Bros. Pancake House. Be prepared to stand in line for the mouthwatering apple cinnamon pancake, a massive disk loaded with apples, or the German pancake, a puffy oven-baked circle topped with powdered sugar. There are several branches, but the original Wilmette restaurant is where scenes from the 1980 movie *Ordinary People* were shot. ⊠ *153 Green Bay Rd., Wilmette* ☎ *847/251–6000* ⊕ *www.walkerbros.net.*

TOP REASONS TO GO

Expand your cultural knowledge: Take part in a tea ceremony or try your hand at calligraphy during weekend programs at the Mallott Japanese Garden inside the Chicago Botanic Garden.

See the animals: Get a fisheye view of polar bears swimming underwater from the belowground viewing area at the Brookfield Zoo's Great Bear Wilderness Habitat.

Get to know Frank Lloyd Wright: Take a trip back to 1909, the last year the famed architect lived and worked in his Oak Park home and studio.

Enjoy a picnic: Pack up a candelabra and some foie gras—or just a blanket and some bug spray—and head to the Ravinia Festival for a night of music under the summer stars.

Visit the Bahá'í Temple: Stroll the beautifully landscaped gardens, or watch the sunset from the peaceful grounds of this majestic temple in Wilmette.

GETTING HERE

Via the El, take the Purple Line to Evanston and Wilmette, the Green Line to Oak Park, and the Yellow Line to Skokie. Many suburbs can also be reached by the Metra commuter rail system (⊕ *www.metrarail.com*).

8

Updated
by Roberta
Sotonoff

Chicago's suburbs aren't just for commuters. The towns that lie to the north, west, and south of the city are rich in history, culture, and outdoor activities. So add a day or two to your itinerary and get out of town for a concert, architecture tour, or zoo visit; the journey to the 'burbs is well worth the additional vacation time.

The suburbs closest to the city limits have excellent theaters and museums that rival their urban cousins. The farther away you go, the more likely you are to find the wooded parks and wider streets that characterize towns outside just about any major city. But Chicago's bedroom communities aren't mirror images of others that dot the map. Far from ho-hum, they are destinations in their own right. Brookfield and Lisle, to the west, have top-notch zoos and exquisite gardens; along the North Shore, Highland Park and Evanston attract talented musicians and house internationally acclaimed art collections; and Oak Park is so rich in architectural history that you can't help but wish you had more time to simply stay put.

Forget strip-mall fast food, too—it's not uncommon to find decidedly urban types doing a reverse commute to visit a trendy new restaurant or ethnic eatery outside the city limits. With Chicago's bus and train system reaching some of the nearer ones, the trips are painless. In short, don't overlook the 'burbs when planning your Chicago trip. If you do, you'll miss out on some of the very best things the metropolitan area has to offer.

ERNEST HEMINGWAY: OAK PARK PROTÉGÉ

It seems rather ironic that, in 1899, rough-and-tumble Ernest Hemingway was born in the manicured suburb of Oak Park, Illinois—a town he described as having "wide lawns and narrow minds." Honing the skills that would last a lifetime, he excelled as a writer for the high-school paper. A volunteer stint as an ambulance driver introduced Hemingway to World War I and its visceral horrors;

he used that experience and the lessons he learned as a reporter for the *Kansas City Star* to craft emotionally complex novels built from deceptively simple sentences, like his masterwork, *A Farewell to Arms*. Though Hemingway's return visits to Oak Park were infrequent, residents celebrate him there to this day.

WEST OF CHICAGO

OAK PARK

9 miles west of downtown Chicago.

Oak Park is an architecture lover's dream, with many Frank Lloyd Wright–designed homes lining the streets, along with the birth home of Ernest Hemingway.

Ernest Hemingway Birthplace. Part of the literary legacy of Oak Park, this three-story, turreted Queen Anne Victorian, which stands in frilly contrast to the many streamlined Prairie-style homes elsewhere in the neighborhood, contains period-furnished rooms and many photos and artifacts pertaining to Hemingway's early life. Museum curators have restored rooms to faithfully depict the house as it looked at the turn of the 20th century. You can poke your head inside the one in which the author was born on July 21, 1899. ⊠ *339 N. Oak Park Ave., Oak Park* ☎ *708/848–2222* ⊕ *www.ehfop.org* ▨ *$15 joint ticket with Ernest Hemingway Museum* ☉ *Sun.–Fri. 1–5, Sat. 10–5; tours hourly.*

Ernest Hemingway Museum. How did the author's first 20 years in Oak Park affect his later work? Check out the exhibits and videos here to find out. Don't miss his first "book," a set of drawings with captions written by his mother, Grace. Holdings include reproduced manuscripts and letters. ⊠ *200 N. Oak Park Ave., Oak Park* ☎ *708/524–5383* ⊕ *www.ehfop.org* ▨ *$15 joint ticket with Ernest Hemingway Birthplace* ☉ *Sun.–Fri. 1–5, Sat. 10–5.*

Fodor's Choice ★ **Frank Lloyd Wright Home and Studio.** *For information, see the highlighted feature in this chapter.* ⊠ *951 Chicago Ave., Oak Park* ☎ *312/994–4000* ⊕ *www.flywright.org* ▨ *$17; area walking tour $15; optional pass for interior photography $5* ☉ *Daily 9–4; tour times vary by season.*

Continued on page 142

FRANK LLOYD WRIGHT

1867–1959

The most famous American architect of the 20th century led a life that was as zany and scandalous as his architectural legacy was great. Behind the photo-op appearance and lordly pronouncements was a rebel visionary who left an unforgettable imprint on the world's notion of architecture. Nowhere else in the country can you experience Frank Lloyd Wright's genius as you can in Chicago and its surroundings.

Born two years after the Civil War ended, Wright did not live to see the completion of his late masterpiece, the Guggenheim Museum. His father preached and played (the Gospel and music) and dragged the family from the Midwest to New England and back before he up and left for good. Wright's Welsh-born mother, Anna Lloyd Jones, grew up in Wisconsin, and her son's roots would run deep there, too. Although his career began in Chicago and his work took him as far away as Japan, the home Wright built in Spring Green, Wisconsin—Taliesin—was his true center.

Despite all his dramas and financial instability (Wright was notoriously bad with money), the architect certainly produced. He was always ready to try something new—as long as it fit his notion of architecture as an expression of the human spirit and of human relationship with nature. By the time he died in 1959, Wright had designed over 1,000 projects, more than half of which were constructed.

Robie House, Chicago

WELCOME TO OAK PARK!

★ Fodor's Choice

Oak Park is a leafy, quiet community just 10 miles west of downtown Chicago. When you arrive, head to the **Oak Park Visitors Center** and get oriented with a free map.

Next, wander to the **Frank Lloyd Wright Home and Studio**. From the outside, the shingle-clad structure may not appear all that innovative, but it's here that Wright developed the architectural language that still has the world talking.

Financed with a $5,000 loan from his mentor, Louis Sullivan, Wright designed the home when he was only 22. The residence manifests some of the spatial and stylistic characteristics that became hallmarks of Wright's work: there's a central fireplace from which other spaces seem to radiate and an enticing flow to the rooms. In 1974, the local Frank Lloyd Wright Home and Studio Foundation, together with the National Trust for Historic Preservation, embarked on a 13-year restoration that returned the building to its 1909 appearance.

STROLLING OAK PARK

A leisurely stroll around the neighborhood will introduce you to plenty of **Frank Lloyd Wright houses.** All are privately owned, so you'll have to be content with what you can see from the outside. Check out 1019, 1027, and 1031 Chicago Avenue. These are typical Victorians that

GETTING HERE

To get to the heart of Oak Park by car, take the Eisenhower Expressway (I-290) west to Harlem Avenue. Head north on Harlem and take a right on Lake Street to get to the Oak Park Visitors Center at Forest Avenue and Lake Street, where there's ample free parking. You can also take the Green Line of the El to the Harlem Avenue stop, or Metra's Union Pacific West Line from the Ogilvie Transportation Center in Citicorp Center downtown (500 W. Madison) to the Oak Park stop at Marion Street.

W. Augusta St.
Ernest Hemingway Boyhood Home
Frank Lloyd Wright Home and Studio
W. Iowa St.
Moore–Dugal Home
Ernest Hemingway Birthplace
W. Chicago Ave.
Superior St.
W. Superior St.
W. Erie St.
Oak Park Visitors Center
W. Ontario St.
Ernest Hemingway Museum
Scoville Park
W. Lake St.
Unity Temple
W. North Blvd.

WOMEN, FIRE, SCANDAL . . . AND OVER 1,000 DESIGNS

Dana Thomas House interior, 1904

1885 Wright briefly studies engineering at the University of Wisconsin.

1887 Wright strikes out for Chicago. He starts his career learning the basics with J. L. Silsbee, a residential architect.

1889 Wright marries Catherine Tobin; he builds her a home in suburban Oak Park, and they have six children together. In 1898 he adds a studio.

1893 Wright launches his own practice in downtown Chicago.

> "WHILE NEW YORK HAS REPRODUCED MUCH AND PRODUCED NOTHING, CHICAGO'S ACHIEVEMENTS IN ARCHITECTURE HAVE GAINED WORLD-WIDE RECOGNITION AS A DISTINCTIVELY AMERICAN ARCHITECTURE."

Wright designed on the sly while working for Sullivan.

For a look at the "real" Wright, don't miss the **Moore–Dugal Home** (1895) at 333 N. Forest Avenue, which reflects Wright's evolving architectural philosophy with its huge chimney and overhanging second story. Peek also at numbers 318, 313, 238, and 210, where you can follow his emerging modernism. Around the corner at 6 Elizabeth Court is the **Laura Gale House,** a 1909 project whose cantilevered profile foreshadows the thrusting planes Wright would create at Fallingwater decades later.

Between 1889 and 1913, Wright erected over two dozen buildings in Oak Park, so unless you're making an extended visit, don't expect to see everything. But don't leave town without a visit to his 1908 **Unity Temple**, a National Historic Landmark. Take a moment to appreciate Wright's fresh take on a place of worship; his bold strokes in creating a flowing interior; his unfailing attention to what was outside (note the skylights); and his dra-

A landmark profile: the eastern facade of the architect's home and studio, Oak Park.

matic use of concrete, which helps to protect the space from traffic noise.

Exterior, Unity Temple, Oak Park

1905 Wright begins designing the reinforced concrete Unity Temple.

1908 Construction begins on the Robie House in Chicago's Hyde Park neighborhood.

1909 Wright leaves for Europe with Mamah Cheney, the wife of a former client; Mrs. Wright does not consent to a divorce.

1911 Wright and Cheney settle at Taliesin, in Spring Green, Wisconsin.

GUIDED TOURS

A great way to get to know Oak Park is to take advantage of the guided tours. Well-informed local guides take small groups on tours throughout the day, discussing various architectural details, pointing out artifacts from the family's life, and often telling amusing stories of the rambunctious Wright clan. Reservations are required for groups of 10 or more for the home and studio tours. Note that you need to arrive as early as possible to be assured a spot. Tours begin at the **Home and Studio Museum Shop.** The shop carries architecture-related books and gifts. You can pick up a map ($3.95) to find other examples of Wright's work that are within easy walking or driving distance, or you can join a guided tour of the neighborhood led by volunteers.

THE HEMINGWAY CONNECTION

Frank Lloyd Wright wasn't the only creative giant to call Oak Park home. Ten years after Wright arrived, Ernest Hemingway was born here in 1899 in a proper Queen Anne, complete with turret. Wright was gone by the time Hemingway began to sow his literary oats. Good thing, too. It's doubtful the quiet village could have handled two such egos. ⇨ **See listings in this chapter for more information.**

Frank Lloyd Wright's distinctive take on a modern dining room.

TIPS

■ Tickets go on sale every October for the eagerly awaited annual **Wright Architectural Housewalk** in May, your chance to see the interiors of some of Oak Park's most architecturally notable homes. Check out ⊕ www.gowright.org for more details.

■ The Blue Line also stops in Oak Park, but we recommend sticking to the Green Line, as the Blue Line stop leaves you in a sketchy neighborhood.

Taliesin, Spring Green, Wisconsin

1914 Mrs. Cheney, her two children, and several other people are killed by a deranged employee, who also sets fire to Taliesin.

1915 With new mistress Miriam Noel in tow, the architect heads for Japan to oversee the building of the Imperial Hotel.

1922 Wright and his wife Catherine divorce.

1924 Wright marries Miriam Noel, but the marriage implodes three years later.

1928 Wright marries Olga (Olgivanna) Lazovich Milanoff. They have one daughter together.

PRAIRIE STYLE PRIMER

Primarily a residential mode, Wright's Prairie style is characterized by ground-hugging masses; low-pitched roofs with deep eaves; and ribbon windows. Generally, Prairie houses are two-story affairs, with single story wings and terraces that project into the landscape. Brick and stone, earth tones, and unpainted wood underscore the perception of a house as an extension of the natural world. Wright designed free-flowing living spaces defined by alternating ceiling heights, natural light, and architectural screens. Although a number of other Chicago architects pursued this emerging aesthetic, Wright became its

> "ALL FINE ARCHITECTURAL VALUES ARE HUMAN VALUES, ELSE NOT VALUABLE."

acknowledged master. Though Wright designed dozens of Prairie style homes, the most well-known is Robie House, in Chicago's Hyde Park neighborhood. A dynamic composition of overlapping planes, it seems both beautifully anchored to the ground and ready to sail off with the arrival of a sharp breeze.

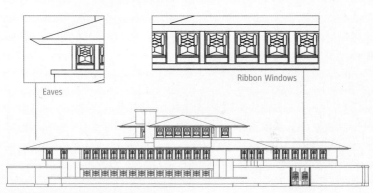

Eaves

Ribbon Windows

SOUTH ELEVATION, ROBIE HOUSE

Nathan G Moore-Dugal house, 1923

1930 The Taliesin Fellowship is launched; eager apprentices arrive to learn from the master.

1935 Fallingwater, the country home of Pittsburgh retailer Edgar J. Kaufmann, is completed at Bear Run, Pennsylvania.

1937 Wright begins construction of his winter getaway, Talesin West, in Scottsdale, Arizona.

1956 Wright designs the Guggenheim Museum in New York. It is completed in 1959.

1957 Wright joins preservationists in saving Robie House from demolition.

1959 Wright dies at the age of 91.

BROOKFIELD

10 miles west of downtown Chicago.

Brookfield makes a great day trip for families, thanks to the Brookfield Zoo.

FAMILY

Fodor's Choice

★

Brookfield Zoo. Spend the day among more than 2,000 animals at this gigantic zoo. The highlights? First, there's the 7½-acre **Great Bear Wilderness** exhibit, a sprawling replica of North American woodlands for the zoo's population of grizzlies, polar bears, bison, Mexican gray wolves, and bald eagles. It's the largest exhibit built in the zoo's history. Be sure to watch the polar bears from the popular underwater viewing area. Monkeys, otters, birds, and other rain-forest fauna cavort in a carefully constructed setting of rocks, trees, shrubs, pools, and waterfalls at **Tropic World.** At the **Living Coast** you can venture through passageways to see sharks, rays, and Humboldt penguins. Daily "Dolphins in Action"shows are a favorite even for adults. Harbor seals, gray seals, and sea lions inhabit a rocky seascape exhibit.

One of the best educational exhibits is **Habitat Africa,** where you can explore two very different environments. If you look closely in the dense forest section, you might be able to spot animals like the okapi; in the savannah section, which has a water hole, termite mounds, and characteristic rock formations, you can spy such tiny animals as the 22-inch-tall klipspringer antelope. Another winning option, **The Swamp,** is about as realistic as you would want an exhibit on swamps to be. It has a springy floor and open habitats with low-flying birds that vividly demonstrate the complex ecosystems of both Southern and Illinois wetlands. For hands-on family activities, visit the **Hamill Family Play Zoo** ($3.50), where kids can play zookeeper, gardener, or veterinarian. Special events—most notably **Holiday Magic,** which lights up the zoo on select December evenings—are also worth checking out. If you don't want to trek around the 216-acre property, don't worry. You can hop aboard a motorized safari tram ($5) in warm weather or the heated Snowball Express tram (free) in the colder months. ⊠ *1st Ave. and 31st St., Brookfield* ☎ *708/688–8000, 800/468–6966* ⊕ *www.czs. org* ☜ *$16.95; free Oct.–Dec. on Tues. and Thurs., and Jan. and Feb. on Sun., Tues., and Thurs.; parking $10* ☉ *Memorial Day–Labor Day, daily 9:30–6; Labor Day–Memorial Day, daily 10–5; indoor exhibits close 30 min before closing time.*

LISLE

25 miles southwest of downtown Chicago.

Visit Lisle to enjoy the natural beauty of woodlands, wetlands, and prairie at Morton Arboretum.

Morton Arboretum. At this 1,700-acre outdoor oasis, you can hike some of the 16 miles of manicured trails, or drive or bike along 9 miles of paved roads bordered by trees, shrubs, and vines. Every season is magnificent: spring's flowering trees, summer's canopy-covered trails, fall's dazzling foliage, and winter's serene beauty. Bike, snowshoe, and cross-country ski rentals are available. If you have kids, check out the award-winning 4-acre Children's Garden, which is stroller- (as well as wheelchair-) friendly. A 1-acre maze garden will delight as you wind your way to the lookout platform. ⊠ *4100 Illinois Rte. 53, Lisle* ☎ *630/968–0074* ⊕ *www.mortonarb.org* ✉ *Apr.–Nov., Thurs.–Tues., $14; Dec.–Mar. and Weds. year-round $9; 1-hr tram tours $6* ☉ *Jan. and Feb., daily 9–4; Mar., Apr., Nov., and Dec., daily 9–5; May–Oct., daily 9–6; grounds only daily 7 am–sunset.*

WHEATON

30 miles west of downtown Chicago.

Wheaton is home to Cantigny Park, which offers several different attractions, inlcuding a military history museum, walking trails, and the Robert R. McCormick Museum.

FAMILY **Cantigny Park.** The 500-acre estate of former *Chicago Tribune* editor and publisher Robert McCormick (1880–1955) has multiple attractions. For starters, there's the First Division Museum, an impressive military history museum with immersive exhibits that include touch-screen videos and re-created battle scenes. The sweeping landscape also incorporates formal gardens, picnic grounds, walking trails, and its own 27-hole public golf course with a separate 9-hole course for kids. The centerpiece, however, is the Beaux-Arts–style Robert R. McCormick Museum. This 35-room mansion contains the Joseph Medill Library, the stately wood-paneled Freedom Hall, and an art deco movie theater. The hidden Prohibition-era bar alone is worth a visit—we won't ruin the surprise by revealing where it is.

⊠ *1S151 Winfield Rd., Wheaton* ☎ *630/668–5161* ⊕ *www.cantigny. org* ✉ *$5 per car when museums are open, $2 when museums are closed* ☉ *Mar.–Dec., Tues.–Sun.; Feb., Fri.–Sun. (hrs vary by season, check website).*

AURORA AND VICINITY

41 miles west of downtown Chicago.

The Aurora vicinity has overcome lean times as a tourist destination and now offers something for everyone. Rent a kayak from **Paddle and Trail** (⊕ *paddleandtrail.com*) and float on the Fox River. Explore the sunken gardens, hiking paths, and zoo at **Phillips Park** (⊕ *www. phillipsparkaurora.com*). Or check out the plethora of art galleries in downtown Aurora.

Fodor's Choice **Farnsworth House.** This 1951 minimalist dwelling by Ludwig Mies Van
★ der Rohe sits just down the Fox River from Aurora. Constructed of steel, wood, and travertine marble, it appears to nearly float against a backdrop of serene river views and gardens. Now operated as a museum by the National Trust for Historic Preservation, Farnsworth House may only be seen by guided tour (reservations are highly recommended). Brad Pitt chose the site for a Japanese jeans commercial he shot in 2007, raising $60,000 for its upkeep. Note that the house is a ½ mile wooded walk from the visitor center. ⊠ *14520 River Rd., Plano*

☎ *630/552–0052* ⊕ *www.farnsworthhouse.org* ✉ *$20 in advance, $25 at door* ☉ *Apr.–Nov., Tues–Sun. 9–4.*

NORTH OF CHICAGO

EVANSTON

10 miles north of downtown Chicago.

The home of Northwestern University is a pretty-as-can-be town in its own right, perched along the lake and studded with some magnificent homes and charming shops. There are also a number of cultural offerings here worth checking out.

Mary & Leigh Block Museum of Art. Comprised of three galleries, this multipurpose space is among the most notable sights on the Northwestern University campus. The impressive permanent collection includes prints, photographs, and other works on paper spanning the 15th to 21st centuries. An outdoor sculpture garden features pieces by Joan Miró and Barbara Hepworth. Workshops, lectures, and symposia are also hosted here, and the museum's Block Cinema screens classic and contemporary films. ⊠ *Northwestern University, 40 Arts Circle Dr., Evanston* ☎ *847/491–4000* ⊕ *www.blockmuseum.northwestern.edu* ✉ *Free* ☉ *Tues. and Sat.–Sun. 10–5, Wed.–Fri. 10–8.*

FAMILY **Mitchell Museum of the American Indian.** Founded in 1977, the Mitchell Museum houses more than 10,000 Native American artifacts from the Paleo-Indian period through modern times. Permanent exhibits focus on tribes in the Plains, Southwest, Northwest Coast, Woodlands, and Arctic areas. Guided tours, lectures, and kids' craft mornings (weekends only) are a regular part of the programming here. ⊠ *3001 Central St., Evanston* ☎ *847/475–1030* ⊕ *www.mitchellmuseum.org* ✉ *$5, free 1st Fri. of month* ☉ *Tues., Wed., Fri., and Sat. 10–5, Thurs. 10–8, Sun. noon–4.*

Northwestern University. Studded with some magnificent homes and charming shops, Evanston is pretty as can be. But it's the private university founded here in 1851 by town namesake John Evans that puts it on the map. Northwestern's sprawling campus hugs Lake Michigan, and strolling around the ivy-covered walls while listening to the sounds of waves hitting the shore is delightful. The campus is home to highly regarded undergraduate and graduate schools (the Medill School of Journalism and Kellogg School of Management among them) as well as the Mary and Leigh Block Museum of Art, which has more than 4,000 works in its permanent collection. Northwestern's Big Ten athletics program draws a mix of students and locals to games, especially when the Wildcats football team play at Ryan Field. ⊠ *633 Clark St., Evanston* ☎ *847/491–3741* ⊕ *www.northwestern.edu.*

The three-island Japanese Garden at the Chicago Botanic Garden offers an oasis from the city.

SKOKIE

12 miles north of downtown Chicago.

Just north of Evanstan is Skokie, which is home to the powerful Illinois Holocaust Museum & Education Center.

Illinois Holocaust Museum & Education Center. In the 1970s a group of neo-Nazis planned a march in the predominantly Jewish suburb of Skokie, and local Holocaust survivors reacted by creating the Holocaust Memorial Foundation of Illinois, a group determined to educate the public about the atrocities of World War II. It took years of planning, but in 2009 the foundation finally unveiled a gem of a museum. The 65,000-square-foot building, designed by architect Stanley Tigerman, houses more than 11,000 Holocaust-related objects. An early 20th-century German railcar—of the type used by the Nazis during the Holocaust—serves as the central artifact. Permanent exhibits include the Legacy of Absence Gallery, which evokes other contemporary genocides and atrocities through art, and the Harvey L. Miller Family Youth Exhibition, which aims to teach kids about respecting differences. ⊠ *9603 Woods Dr., Skokie* 🕾 *847/967–4800* ⊕ *www.ilholocaustmuseum.org* 🎫 *$12* ⊘ *Mon.–Wed. and Fri. 10–5, Thurs. 10–8, weekends 10–5.*

WILMETTE

14 miles north of downtown Chicago.

The gorgeous Bahá'i Temple House of Worship is located in Wilmette.

Fodor'sChoice **Bahá'i Temple House of Worship.** Your mouth is sure to drop to the floor
★ the first time you lay eyes on this stunning structure, a nine-sided building that incorporates architectural styles and symbols from many of the
world's religions. With its delicate lacelike details and massive dome, the
Louis Bourgeois design emphasizes the 19th-century Persian origins of
the Bahá'i religion. The formal gardens are as symmetrical and harmo-
nious as the building they surround. The temple is the U.S. center of the
Baha'i faith, which advocates spiritual unity, world peace, racial unity,
and equality of the sexes. Stop by the visitor center to examine exhibits that explain it; you can also ask for a guide to show you around.
⊠ *100 Linden Ave., Wilmette* ☎ *847/853–2300* ⊕ *www.bahaitemple.
org* ☒ *Free* ⊙ *Visitor center mid-May–mid-Sept., daily 10–8; mid-Sept.–
mid-May, daily 10–5. Upstairs auditorium daily 6–10.*

GLENVIEW

17 miles north of downtown Chicago.

In Glenview, the Kohl Children's Museum will keep kids busy with its
interactive exhibits.

FAMILY **Kohl Children's Museum.** Adults are hard-pressed to get youngsters to
leave the 16 hands-on exhibits at this Glenview museum. Here toddlers to eight-year-olds can learn about solar power or how sounds
make music. They can don a white jacket and be pretend doctors in
a baby nursery or vets in an animal hospital. Kids can also get into
home construction in "Hands on House" or tire changing at "Car
Care," and, of course, there is a spot to put on raincoats and play
in the water. When weather permits, the 2-acre "Habitat Park," just
outside, is a great place for bug hunting, wall painting, and wandering
through a grass maze. ⊠ *2100 Patriot Blvd., Glenview* ☎ *847/832–6600*
⊕ *www.kohlchildrensmuseum.org* ☒ *$11* ⊙ *Mon.–Sat. 9:30–5 (Mon.
until noon only Sept.–May), Sun. noon–5.*

GLENCOE

19 miles north of downtown Chicago.

Glencoe is home to the Chicago Botanic Garden, the perfect place to
take a break from the big city and experience nature.

FAMILY **Chicago Botanic Garden.** Among the 26 different gardens here are the
Fodor'sChoice three-island Malott Japanese Garden, the 5-acre Evening Island, and the
★ Grunsfeld Children's Growing Garden. Three big greenhouses showcase desert, tropical, and semitropical climates with beautiful and fragrant flowers blooming year-round. Weather permitting, 35-minute
trams tours ($6) are offered daily from 10 to 4, April through Octo-
ber. Special summer exhibitions include the Model Railroad Garden, a
7,500-square-foot garden with 17 garden-scale trains traveling around
nearly 50 models of American landmarks, all made from natural materials, as well as Butterflies & Blooms, a 2,800-square-foot white mesh
enclosure filled with hundreds of colorful butterflies interacting with
plant life; a $6 admission fee applies for each. ⊠ *1000 Lake Cook Rd.,
Glencoe* ☎ *847/835–5440* ⊕ *www.chicagobotanic.org* ☒ *Free, special*

The Bahá'í Temple's symmetrical architecture represents harmony.

exhibits typically $6 per (combination tickets available). Parking $20 per car for Cook County residents, $25 for nonresidents ⏰ June–Aug., daily 7–9; Sept.–May, daily 8–sunset.

HIGHLAND PARK

26 miles north of downtown Chicago.

The town of Highland Park hosts the Ravina Festival every summer, showcasing several musical acts, including the Chicago Symphony Orchestra.

FAMILY **Ravinia Park.** If you enjoy music under the stars, the outdoor concerts at Ravinia are a stellar treat. The **Ravinia Festival**, a summerlong series of performances, is the hot-months' home of the Chicago Symphony Orchestra, but the festival also features popular jazz, chamber music, rock, pop, and dance acts. Pack a picnic (don't skimp, concertgoers do it up right with everything from fine china to candelabras), bring a blanket or chairs, and sit on the lawn for little more than the cost of a movie ($10 to $38). Large screens are placed on the lawn at some concerts so you won't miss anything. Seats are also available in the pavilion for a significantly higher price ($25 to $115). There are restaurants and snack bars on the park grounds, so if you forget your goodies you still won't go hungry. Concerts usually start at 7:30 or 8 pm; the park usually opens three to four hours ahead to let everyone score spots and get settled. Weekend-morning concerts are aimed at kids. They feature a "KidsLawn" before or after the concert with an interactive music experience, an "instrument petting zoo," and occasional live performances.

During the winter, check out the BGH Classics series; tickets for these indoor concerts at Bennett Gordon Hall cost only $10. ⊠ *200 Ravinia Rd., Highland Park* ☎ *847/266–5100 box office, 847/266–5000 administration* ⊕ *www.ravinia.org* ⊙ *Outdoor concerts June–early Sept.*

VERNON HILLS

40 miles northwest of downtown Chicago.

Head to Vernon Hills to explore the beautiful Cuneo Mansion and Gardens.

Loyola at Cuneo Mansion and Gardens. Samuel Insull, partner of Thomas Edison and founder of Commonwealth Edison, built this mansion as a country home in 1916. After Insull lost his fortune, John Cuneo Sr., the printing-press magnate, bought the estate and fashioned it into something far more spectacular. The skylighted great hall in the main house resembles the open central courtyard of an Italian palazzo, the private family chapel has stained-glass windows, and a gilded grand piano graces the ballroom. Tours highlight the antique furnishings, 17th-century Flemish tapestries, and Italian paintings that fill the interior. ⊠ *1350 N. Milwaukee Ave., Vernon Hills* ☎ *847/362–3042* ⊕ *www.luc.edu/cuneo* ⊠ *$10* ⊙ *Fri.–Sun. 11–4; tours at 11:30, 1, and 2:30.*

WHERE TO EAT

HOW TO EAT LIKE A LOCAL

Many travelers head to Chicago with an epicurean checklist in mind, a must-eat of Chicago foodstuff. The truth, of course, is that it's impossible to truly taste Chicago in just one visit; even locals are constantly learning about new chefs and stumbling upon old eateries they just didn't notice before. Here are some Chicago foods to place at the top of your list.

PIZZA

The undisputed deep-dish king of the country, Chicago-style pizza is often imitated, but there's nothing like tasting the thick crust, mountains of cheese, and chunky tomato sauce in its birthplace. You'll see tourists flock to the big-name places, but these aren't tourist traps—they're the real deal. And if deep-dish isn't your thing, there are many pizza joints that offer Chicago-style thin-crust pizza, with a firm, crunchy crust that some locals will claim is just as good, if not better, than its deep-dish cousin.

HOT DOGS

Most cities have plenty of indiscriminate hot dog vendors, but in Chicago, the hot dog is an art. For traditional Chicagoans the condiment list is set in stone: yellow mustard, white onions, sweet pickle relish, whole spicy peppers, and celery salt. Any requests for ketchup will not only mark you as a tourist, but might even garner a few scoffs. No need to get picky with a place—wander into any place with a proud "Vienna Beef" sign in the window and you'll be satisfied. Be on the lookout for places that offer both classic recipes and other rarer meat combinations (antelope hot dogs anyone?).

THE STEAK HOUSE

For a slightly more upscale Chicago dining experience, you'll find a huge number of steak houses, all ready for you to sit back and indulge in a classic porterhouse and a glass of red wine. You can hardly walk a block in River North or the Gold Coast without spotting a dark, classy steak house inviting you to kick-it old school. Midwestern farms from neighboring states mean a constant influx of fresh, local beef to the city, making a steak dinner a perfect way to begin and/or end any trip.

MEXICAN FOOD

If you're in Chicago, you're a long way from Mexico, but that doesn't mean you have to eat like it. Mexican immigrants have been making Chicago their home for decades and bringing their culinary traditions with them. Pilsen is the neighborhood for tortilla factories, Hispanic grocery stores, and plenty of soulful, inexpensive Mexican cooking. For a hip Chicago spin on south-of-the-border cuisine, head to Near North, where you'll find an array of eclectic eateries that offer a bold and unforgettable taste of Mexico.

ASIAN FUSION

For a cheap and classic Asian meal, head to Chinatown, but more adventurous eaters should travel north for a taste of Bill Kim's "belly" empire. The chef has set up shop in two trendy neighborhoods, each transforming standard Asian fare with unexpected and delicious twists. Belly Shack in Humboldt Park meshes Kim's Korean roots with his wife's Puerto Rican heritage, while Belly Q and Urban Belly in the West Loop go the Korean-BBQ route.

ITALIAN BEEF

Yep, more meat. These delicious sandwiches are found wherever hot dogs are sold, but they certainly deserve some attention of their own. Slices of seasoned roast beef are layered with sweet peppers and onions on a long roll with varying amounts of meat sauce, creating a messy and classic Chicago meal. There's heated debate over where to get the best sandwich (every local has their opinion), but don't fret—your options are virtually endless and you'd have to try hard to find a place that doesn't deliver the goods.

9

Updated by
Carly Fisher

Sure, this city has great architecture, museums, and sports venues. But at its heart, Chicago is really a food town. This is evident in the priority that good eating takes, no matter the occasion. Rain or shine, locals will wait in a line that snakes around the corner for dolled-up doughnuts at Doughnut Vault. They'll reserve part of their paychecks to dine at inventive Alinea. And they love to talk about their most recent meal—just ask.

It's no wonder that outdoor festivals are often centered on food, from Taste of Chicago in summer, which packs the grounds at Grant Park, to smaller celebrations, like the German-American fest in Lincoln Square, a mini-Oktoberfest in fall.

Although the city has always had options on the extreme ends of the spectrum—from the hole-in-the wall Italian beef sandwich shops to the special-occasion spots—it's now easier to find eateries in the middle that serve seasonal menus with a farm-to-table mantra. For the budget conscious, it's also a great time to dine: some talented chefs aren't bothering to wait for a liquor license, opening BYOB spots turning out polished fare (just try Ruxbin in West Town).

Expect to see more Chicago chefs open casual concepts—Rick Bayless, Paul Kahan, and Michael Kornick have a head start with their respective sandwich, taco, and burger spots. Yet the goal remains the same: to feed a populace that knows good food and isn't willing to accept anything less than the best. In the following pages, you'll find our top picks, from quick bites to multicourse meals, in the city's best dining neighborhoods.

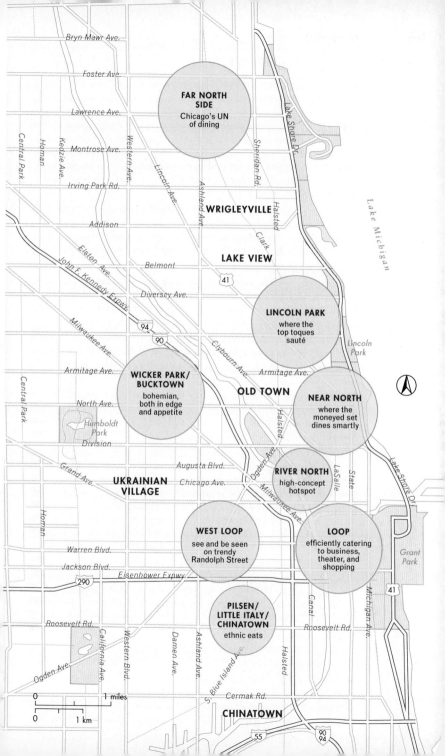

CHICAGO DINING PLANNER

EATING OUT STRATEGY

Where should we eat? With thousands of Chicago eateries competing for your attention, it may seem like a daunting question. But fret not— our expert writers and editors have done most of the legwork. The selections here represent the best this city has to offer—from hot dogs to haute cuisine. Search "Best Bets" for top recommendations by price, cuisine, and experience. Or find a review quickly in the listings, organized alphabetically within each neighborhood. Delve in, and enjoy!

WITH KIDS

Though it's unusual to see children in the dining rooms of Chicago's elite restaurants, dining with youngsters in the city does not have to mean culinary exile. Many of the restaurants in Chicago are excellent choices for families, and we've noted these in our reviews.

RESERVATIONS

Plan ahead if you're determined to snag a sought-after reservation. Some renowned restaurants are booked weeks or months in advance. If you're a large group, always call ahead, as even restaurants that don't take reservations often will make exceptions for groups of six or larger.

But you can get lucky at the last minute if you're flexible—and friendly. Most restaurants keep a few tables open for walk-ins and VIPs. Show up for dinner early (5:30 pm) or late (after 9 pm) and politely inquire about any last-minute vacancies or cancellations.

If you're calling a few days ahead of time, ask whether you can be put on a waiting list. Occasionally, an eatery may ask you to call the day before your scheduled meal to reconfirm: don't forget, or you could lose out.

WHAT TO WEAR

In general, Chicagoans are neat but casual dressers; only at the top-notch dining rooms do you see a more formal style. But the way you look can influence how you're treated—and where you're seated. Generally speaking, jeans will suffice at casual restaurants, although shorts, sweatpants, and sports jerseys are rarely appropriate. Moving up from there, a few pricier restaurants require jackets. In reviews, we mention dress only when men are required to wear a jacket or a jacket and tie.

TIPPING AND TAXES

In most restaurants, tip the waiter 18% to 20%. (To figure the amount quickly, just take 10% of the bill and double it.) Bills for parties of six or more sometimes include the tip already. The city's tax on restaurant food is 10.75%.

SMOKING

Smoking is prohibited in all enclosed public spaces in Chicago, including restaurants and bars.

WINE

Although some of the city's top restaurants still include historic French vintages, most sommeliers are now focusing on small-production, lesser-known new-world wineries. Some are even keeping their wine lists purposefully small, so that they can change them frequently to match the season and the menu. Half bottles are becoming more prevalent, and good wines by the glass are everywhere. Don't hesitate to ask for recommendations. Even restaurants without a sommelier on staff will appoint knowledgeable servers to lend a hand with wine selections.

PRICES

If you're watching your budget, be sure to ask the price of daily specials recited by the waiter or captain. The charge for specials at some restaurants is noticeably out of line with the other prices on the menu. Beware of the $10 bottle of water; ask for tap water instead. And always review your bill.

If you eat early or late, you may be able to take advantage of a prix-fixe deal not offered at peak hours. Most upscale restaurants offer great lunch deals, with special menus at cut-rate prices designed to give customers a true taste of the place.

Many restaurants (particularly smaller ones downtown) accept only cash. If you plan to use a credit card, it's a good idea to double-check its acceptability when making reservations or before sitting down to eat.

WHAT IT COSTS				
	$	**$$**	**$$$**	**$$$$**
AT DINNER	under $18	$18–$27	$28–$36	over $36

Prices are per person for a main course at dinner, or if dinner is not served, at lunch.

USING THE MAPS

Throughout the chapter, you'll see mapping symbols and coordinates after property reviews. To locate the property on a map, turn to the Chicago Dining and Lodging Atlas at the end of this chapter. The first number after the symbol indicates the map number. Following that is the property's coordinate on the map grid.

9

RESTAURANT REVIEWS

Listed alphabetically within neighborhood.

THE LOOP, INCLUDING SOUTH LOOP AND WEST LOOP

Business, theater, and shopping converge in the Loop, the downtown district south of the Chicago River distinguished by the elevated train that circles it. Long the city's financial center, the Loop is commuter central for inbound office workers. It's also Chicago's historic home of retail, where the flagship Marshall Field's (now Macy's) once made State Street a great shopping destination. As a theater district, the Loop hosts the Tony-awarded Goodman Theatre, which mounts its own productions, as well as the Oriental, Cadillac Palace, and Bank of America theaters, which generally run Broadway tours. In feeding these diverse audiences, Loop restaurants run the gamut from quick-service to high-volume and special-occasion. Beware noontime and precurtain surges

BEST BETS FOR CHICAGO DINING

With thousands of restaurants to choose from, how will you decide where to eat? Fodor's writers and editors have selected their favorite restaurants by price, cuisine, and experience in the Best Bets lists below. In the first column, Fodor's Choice properties represent the "best of the best" in every price category. You can also search by neighborhood for excellent eats—just peruse the following pages.

Fodor's Choice ★

Acadia, $$$
Alinea, $$$$
Au Cheval, $
Avec, $$
Big Star, $
Blackbird, $$$$
Boka, $$$
Bristol, The, $$
Chicago Cut Steakhouse, $$$$
Frontera Grill, $$
Gather, $$
Girl & the Goat, $$$$
Grace, $$$$
GT Fish & Oyster, $$
Hopleaf, $$
Little Goat, $$
Mindy's Hot Chocolate, $$
North Pond, $$$
Publican, The, $$$
Purple Pig, The $$
Slurping Turtle, $$
Spacca Napoli Pizzeria, $
Spiaggia, $$$$

Topolobampo, $$$$
Travelle, $$$
Trenchermen, $$
TRU, $$$$
Yusho, $$

Best by Price

$

Au Cheval
Belly Shack
Big Star
Dove's Luncheonette
Manny's Cafeteria and Delicatessen
Parson's Chicken and Fish
Smoque BBQ
Xoco

$$

Avec
Bristol, The
Frontera Grill
Gather
Hopleaf
Little Goat
Nightwood

Purple Pig, The
Slurping Turtle
Trenchermen
Yusho

$$$

Acadia
Arun's
Baffo
Balena
Boka
Mercat a la Planxa
Nico Osteria
NoMI Kitchen
North Pond
Publican, The
Tanta
Travelle

$$$$

Alinea
Blackbird
Girl & the Goat
Grace
mk
Sixteen
Spiaggia
TRU

Best by Cuisine

AMERICAN

DMK Burger Bar, $
Dove's Luncheontette, $
Parson's Chicken and Fish, $

BARBECUE

Green Street Smoked Meats, $
Honky Tonk Barbeque, $$
Smoke Daddy, $$
Smoque BBQ, $

CHINESE

Han 202, $$$
Lao Sze Chuan $
Phoenix Restaurant $

ITALIAN

Baffo, $$$
Coco Pazzo, $$$
Nico Osteria, $$$
Osteria via Stato, $$
Spiaggia, $$$$

JAPANESE

Japonais by Morimoto, $$$$
Kamehachi, $$
Slurping Turtle, $$
Yusho, $$

MEXICAN

Big Star, $
Frontera Grill, $$
Salpicón, $$
Xoco, $

MODERN AMERICAN

Bristol, The, $$
Lula Café, $$$
mk, $$$$

PIZZA

Bar Toma, $$
Piece, $
Spacca Napoli Pizzeria, $

SOUTHERN

Big Jones, $$
Heaven on Seven, $
Table Fifty-Two, $$$

SPANISH

Café Iberico, $
Mercat a la Planxa, $$$
Vera, $$

STEAKHOUSE

Chicago Cut Steakhouse, $$$$
David Burke's Primehouse, $$$$
Gibsons Bar & Steakhouse, $$$$

THAI

Arun's, $$$$

VEGETARIAN

Green Zebra, $$
MANA Food Bar, $
Native Foods Café, $

Best by Experience

BAR FOOD

Dusek's, $$
Hopleaf, $$
Publican, The, $$$

BEST BREAKFAST

Dove's Luncheonette, $
Lou Mitchell's, $
Manny's Cafeteria and Delicatessen, $

BEST BRUNCH

Lula Café, $$$
Mindy's Hot Chocolate, $$
Nightwood, $$
North Pond, $$$

BEST HOTEL DINING

Café des Architectes, $$$
Lobby at the Peninsula, The, $$$
Nico Osteria, $$$
Sixteen, $$$$
Travelle, $$$

BEST VIEWS

Chicago Cut Steakhouse, $$$$
Everest, $$$$
NoMI Kitchen, $$$
North Pond, $$$
Plaza, The, $
Signature Room at the 95th, $$$
Sixteen, $$$$
Spiaggia, $$$$

CAFÉ EATS

Café Selmarie, $
Julius Meinl Café, $
Milk & Honey Café, $
Pierrot Gourmet, $
Sweet Maple Café, $

CHICAGO CLASSICS

Billy Goat Tavern, $
Gene & Georgetti, $$$$
Mr. Beef, $
Pizzeria Uno, $
Twin Anchors Restaurant & Tavern, $$

CHILD-FRIENDLY

Ann Sather, $
Café Selmarie, $
Ed Debevic's, $
Eleven City Diner, $
Smoque BBQ, $

GOOD FOR GROUPS

Fogo de Chão, $$$$
Green Street Smoked Meats, $
Kinmont, $$
Plaza, The, $
Parthenon, The, $

HOT SPOTS

Au Cheval, $
Avec, $$
Big Star, $
Blackbird, $$$$
Girl & the Goat, $$$$
Paris Club Bistro & Bar, $$
Parson's Chicken and Fish, $
Tanta, $$$

Three Dots and a Dash, $$
Trenchermen, $$
Yusho, $$

LATE-NIGHT DINING

Au Cheval, $
Avec, $$
Big Star, $
Green Street Smoked Meats, $
Hopleaf, $$
Maude's Liquor Bar, $$$$
Parson's Chicken and Fish, $
Purple Pig, The, $$

MOST INNOVATIVE

Alinea, $$$$
Grace, $$$$
Moto Restaurant, $$$$

PRETHEATER MEAL

312 Chicago, $$
Boka, $$$
Petterino's, $$
Russian Tea Time, $

QUIET MEAL

Arun's, $$$$
Les Nomades, $$$$

SPECIAL OCCASION

Acadia, $$$
Everest, $$$$
North Pond, $$$
TRU, $$$$

9

(you'll need a reservation for the latter). It tends to clear out on weekends, and many restaurants close up shop.

A short trip to the West Loop—particularly Randolph Street—is where you'll find Chicago's restaurant row. Nearly every celebrity chef in town has set up post here, including Grant Achatz, Paul Kahan, and Stephanie Izard. Whether you're craving pizza and pasta or tapas and tacos, the flavors here are sure to satisfy any discerning foodie.

THE LOOP

$$ ✕ **312 Chicago.** Part handy hotel restaurant, part Loop power diner,
ITALIAN and all Italian down to its first-generation chef, Luca Corazzina, 312 Chicago earns its popularity with well-executed dishes that range from house-made pastas to *branzino* (Mediterranean sea bass) with cauliflower puree, Manila clams, zucchini, and sundried tomatoes. You'll be tempted to carbo-load on the house-baked bread alone, but make sure to save room for Italian-inspired desserts, including a spread of *baci di dama* (hazelnut cookies), biscotti, and cannoli. Note that upstairs tables are quieter. $ *Average main: $25* ⊠ *Hotel Allegro, 136 N. LaSalle St., Loop* ☎ *312/696–2420* ⊕ *www.312chicago.com* ✛ *1:C6.*

$$$ ✕ **Aria.** Can't decide between Japanese, Indian, or Mediterranean? Take
ASIAN FUSION your globe-trotting taste buds to Aria, which roams the world's larder with abandon: Asian-inspired tuna sashimi, Southern-inspired strip loin steak with house-cut fries and pickled okra, and braised Black Angus short ribs with star anise. Among generous freebies, tandoori-baked naan bread with Indian-inspired dipping sauces arrives before the meal, and a trio of exotically spiced potatoes comes with the entrées. In the convivial lounge, a full sushi bar also caters to adventurous appetites. $ *Average main: $31* ⊠ *Fairmont Chicago, 200 N. Columbus Dr., Loop* ☎ *312/444–9494* ⊕ *www.themillenniumparkhotel.com/dining/ aria-restaurant/cuisine* ✛ *1:F6.*

$$$$ ✕ **Everest.** No one expects romance at the top of the Chicago Stock
FRENCH Exchange, but Everest does its best to throw you a curve wherever and whenever. Consider the trip: two separate elevators whisk you 40 stories up, where there are sweeping views of the city's sprawl westward. Then there's the food. It's French, but with an Alsatian bent—a nod to chef Jean Joho's roots. He might just add Alsace Riesling to his risotto. And finally, there's the space, where modern sculpture melds with art nouveau. The whole experience, from the polished waiters to the massive wine list, screams "special occasion!" It's prix fixe only. $ *Average main: $165* ⊠ *440 S. LaSalle St., 40th fl., Loop* ☎ *312/663– 8920* ⊕ *www.everestrestaurant.com* ⊙ *Closed Sun. and Mon. No lunch* ⌒ *Reservations essential* ⌂ *Jacket required* ✛ *4:F2.*

$$ ✕ **The Grillroom Chophouse & Winebar.** If you're going to see a perfor-
STEAKHOUSE mance at the Bank of America Theatre across the street, you're close enough to dash over here for a drink at intermission (we love the lengthy by-the-glass wine selections). Pre- and postcurtain, the clubby confines fill with showgoers big on beef, though there are also ample raw bar, seafood, and pasta choices. For the most relaxing experience, plan to come after the theatergoers have left for Act I. $ *Average main: $25* ⊠ *33 W. Monroe St., Loop* ☎ *312/960–0000* ⊕ *www.grillroom-chicago. com* ⊙ *No lunch weekends* ✛ *4:F2.*

$ **✕Heaven on Seven.** Every day is Mardi Gras at Heaven on Seven, which
CREOLE pursues a good time all the time. The restaurant has a menu centered on a daring collection of hot sauces, and the food is plentiful and filling. Some guests find the menu too spicy for their kids, but would go back for the well-priced Mardi Gras jambalaya, fried oyster po'boy, cheese grits, and chicory coffee. Cheddar-jalapeño biscuits and chocolate peanut-butter pie are great menu bookends. $ *Average main: $12 ⊠ 111 N. Wabash Ave., 7th fl., Loop* ☎ *312/263–6443* ⊕ *www.heavenonseven. com* ⊘ *Closed Sun. No dinner except on 3rd Fri. of month* ✛ *1:E6.*

$$$$ **✕Morton's, The Steakhouse.** Morton's in the Gold Coast neighborhood
STEAKHOUSE can be more fun, but this location, a spin-off of the Gold Coast original, is one of Chicago's best steakhouses. Excellent service and a good wine list add to the principal attraction: beautiful, hefty steaks cooked to perfection. A kitschy tradition mandates that everything on the menu, from gargantuan Idahos to massive slabs of beef, is brought to the table for your approval before you order. White tablecloths create a classy feel. It's no place for the budget-conscious, but for steak lovers it's a 14-ounce (or more) taste of heaven. $ *Average main: $42 ⊠ 65 E. Wacker Pl., Loop* ☎ *312/201–0410* ⊕ *www.mortons.com* ⊘ *No lunch weekends* ✛ *1:E6.*

$ **✕The Plaza.** Location trumps service at The Plaza, where a seat outside
AMERICAN in summer, in full view of Millennium Park, is among the best in the
FAMILY city. The waitstaff is not always on top of things—grin and bear it with another drink from the outdoor bar. The menu includes small plates, soups and salads, and main courses, with a something-for-everyone selection. The burgers are first-rate, as is the more ambitious seasonal fare such as barbacoa tacos and pulled pork sliders. A grab-and-go window supplies park picnics. In winter, the restaurant shuts down to make way for the ice-skaters warming up in the rink right outside the picture windows. $ *Average main: $14 ⊠ Millennium Park, 11 N. Michigan Ave., Loop* ☎ *312/521–7275* ⊕ *www.parkgrillchicago.com* ⊘ *Closed Nov.–May* ✛ *4:G1.*

$$ **✕Petterino's.** Theatergoers to the Goodman, the Palace, and the Ori-
ITALIAN ental pack Petterino's (next door to the Goodman lobby) nightly. Not
FAMILY that the Italian supper club with framed caricatures of celebs past and present couldn't stand on its own merits. The deep, red-velvet booths make a cozy stage for old-school classics like steak Diane, chicken Parmesan, and tomato bisque, as well as prime steaks, seafood, and pastas. Although the show is usually next door, on Monday nights Petterino's hosts live open-mike cabaret. $ *Average main: $20 ⊠ 150 N. Dearborn St., Loop* ☎ *312/422–0150* ⊕ *www.petterinos.com* ✛ *1:D6.*

$ **✕Russian Tea Time.** Exotica is on the menu and in the air at this spot
RUSSIAN that's favored by visitors to the nearby Art Institute and the Symphony Center. Mahogany trim, samovars, and balalaika music set the stage for dishes from Russia and neighboring republics (the owners hail from Uzbekistan), including Ukrainian borscht, *blinis* (small, savory pancakes) with salmon caviar, Moldavian meatballs, and classic beef Stroganoff. Chilled vodka flights (three shots) certainly do help the herring go down. $ *Average main: $15 ⊠ 77 E. Adams St., Loop* ☎ *312/360– 0000* ⊕ *www.russianteatime.com* ✛ *4:G2.*

9

$$$

AMERICAN

✕ **Tavern at the Park.** Given its unique take on American classics and the splendid view of Chicago's Millennium Park, it would be a mistake to pass up this near–Michigan Avenue gem. Noise from the bar carries up to the second floor, giving this spacious restaurant a lively feel. The crab-stuffed artichokes and expertly fried calamari are perfect starters; mains run the gamut from Cajun-spiced grouper to butternut squash ravioli or the slow-roasted prime rib. Though many favor the warm blueberry-apple bread pudding for dessert, the towering carrot cake studded with pineapple and hazelnuts shouldn't be missed. Don't plan on a weekday lunch without a reservation—local businesspeople have made this their hangout. ⓢ *Average main: $32* ✉ *130 E. Randolph St., Loop* ☏ *312/552–0070* ⊕ *www.tavernatthepark.com* ☽ *Closed Sun.* ✛ *1:F6.*

$$$

ITALIAN

✕ **Trattoria No. 10.** It's hard to camouflage a basement location, but Trattoria No. 10 gives it a good go with terra-cotta colors, arched entryways, and quarry-tile floors, all of which evoke Italy. Pretheater diners crowd in for house specialties made with sustainable, locally sourced ingredients: classic antipasti selections like grilled treviso with mozzarella and hazelnuts, ravioli filled with seasonal stuffings like asparagus and provolone, and grass-fed New York strip steak with argula and shaved fennel. Meanwhile, cheap chowsters elbow into the bar for the $15 nibbles buffet served 5–7:30 pm Tuesday through Friday with a $6 drink minimum. ⓢ *Average main: $30* ✉ *10 N. Dearborn St., Loop* ☏ *312/984–1718* ⊕ *www.trattoriaten.com* ☽ *Closed Sun. No lunch Sat.* ✛ *4:F1.*

SOUTH LOOP

$$$

AMERICAN

Fodor'sChoice

★

✕ **Acadia.** The Northeast coast makes a splash in the South Loop with this elegant enclave from chef-owner Ryan McCaskey. Dishes are fresh, inventive, and often have a slight modernist touch, such as the vegetable ash and oxtail prune consommé or the Stonington lobster with maitake mushrooms, salsify, and lobster crumble. While many fine-dining destinations offer both à la carte and a tasting menu, Acadia is unique in that its bar menu has its own set of upscale bites like Korean-style fried Jidori Chicken and Maine lobster rolls. And if choosing among the decadent desserts proves problematic, there is always the three-course dessert tasting for $35. ⓢ *Average main: $35* ✉ *1639 S. Wabash Ave., South Loop* ☏ *312/360–9500* ⊕ *www.acadiachicago.com* ☽ *Closed Mon. and Tues.* ✛ *4:G5.*

$

AMERICAN

FAMILY

✕ **Eleven City Diner.** For all its great food, Chicago is not a big deli town, which endears Eleven City Diner, an old-school deli and family restaurant in the South Loop, to the locals. You can get breakfast all day (latkes and lox are popular, as is the "hoppel poppel" blending scrambled eggs with salami, potatoes, onions, and peppers) but deli staples like matzo-ball soup and pastrami and corned-beef sandwiches shouldn't be missed. There are also classic diner options including burgers, and soda-fountain floats and malts from the staff soda jerk. Breaking from the deli tradition, Eleven City also sells beer, wine, and cocktails. In keeping with its theme, there's an old-fashioned candy counter on your way out. ⓢ *Average main: $12* ✉ *1112 S. Wabash Ave., South Loop* ☏ *312/212–1112* ⊕ *www.elevencitydiner.com* ✛ *4:G3.*

$ ✕ **Epic Burger.** After walking through exhibits at the Art Institute, follow
BURGER the local college crowd to this order-at-the-counter eatery. While the
FAMILY ambience is kitschy (think bright orange walls and televisions broadcasting cartoons), the food is, as owner David Friedman describes it,
"more mindful." Friedman sources fresh, natural beef for the burgers,
which are shaped by hand, cooked to order, and served atop fresh
buns on nonpetroleum-based plates. Burger add-ons include Wisconsin
cheese, nitrate-free bacon, and an organic fried egg. While this might
mean the meal costs more than other counter-service spots, it all goes
back to Friedman's goal of building a greener burger joint—and it all
just seems to taste extra good. Ⓢ *Average main: $9* ✉ *517 S. State St.,
South Loop* ☎ *312/913–1373* ⊕ *www.epicburger.com* ✛ *4:G3.*

$$ ✕ **Gioco.** The name means "game" in Italian, and the restaurant ful-
ITALIAN fills the promise not with venison, but in the spirit of having fun. The
decor is distressed-urban, with brick walls and well-worn hardwood
floors—the space is said to have been used by the Chicago gangsters of
early 1900s as a gambling house. But the menu is comfort-Italian, with
dishes ranging from pizzas and homemade linguine with Manila clams
to rustic fare like grilled Colorado lamb chops, and roasted branzino
with puttanesca sauce. It's a cozy, neighborhoody spot that keeps the
regulars coming back. Ⓢ *Average main: $25* ✉ *1312 S. Wabash Ave.,
South Loop* ☎ *312/939–3870* ⊕ *www.giocorestaurant.com* ☾ *No lunch
weekends* ✛ *4:G4.*

$ ✕ **Manny's Cafeteria and Delicatessen.** Kibitzing counter cooks provide
DELI commentary as they sling chow—thick corned-beef and pastrami
FAMILY sandwiches, soul-nurturing matzo-ball soup, and piping-hot potato
pancakes—at this classic Near South Side cafeteria. Though they occa-
sionally bark at dawdlers, it's all in good fun—though looking for seat-
ing in two teeming, fluorescent-lighted rooms is not, so you're best off
coming at off hours. Don't try to pay the hash-slingers; settle up as
you leave. Ⓢ *Average main: $12* ✉ *1141 S. Jefferson St., South Loop*
☎ *312/939–2855* ⊕ *www.mannysdeli.com* ☾ *Closed Sun.* ⚭ *Reserva-
tions not accepted* ✛ *4:E4.*

$$$ ✕ **Mercat a la Planxa.** Inside the Blackstone Hotel, this Catalan-inspired
SPANISH restaurant offers a stylish respite from Michigan Avenue. Philadelphia-
based chef Jose Garces returned to his native Chicago for Mercat, where
he created a menu of small and midsize plates of Catalan *sopas* (soup),
cured meats, *fideos* (Spanish pasta), and a variety of vegetable sides, all
of which are great for sharing. Want to get more bang for your buck? Be
sure to try the chef's tasting menu, with prices starting at $65. Don't let
the small, cramped bar at the entrance fool you; once you walk up the
stairs, you'll encounter an airy dining room with a view of Grant Park.
Ⓢ *Average main: $29* ✉ *Blackstone Hotel, 638 S. Michigan Ave., South
Loop* ☎ *312/765–0524* ⊕ *www.mercatchicago.com* ✛ *4:G3.*

WEST LOOP

$$ ✕ **694 Wine & Spirits.** This smart wine bar is proof that you don't need
WINE BAR more than a minimal kitchen (limited to what will fit behind the bar's
counter) to thrill foodies. Simple snacks, such as a flight of various
butters accompanied by artisanal bread and slices of Benton's smoked
country bacon complement the real draw: hand-picked wines from

around the world. The two-story, cork-lined space really comes into its own later in the evening. For a more low-key experience, come on a weeknight as a precursor to dinner at a nearby West Loop restaurant. $ *Average main: $19* ⊠ *694 N. Milwaukee Ave., West Loop* 📞 *312/492–6620* ⊕ *www.694wineandspirits.com* ⊗ *No lunch.* ✛ *3:E6.*

$ ╳ **Au Cheval.** A menu packed with burgers, fries, and chopped liver might sound like your classic dive, but Au Cheval is no greasy spoon. Exposed brick, dim lighting, and antique-inspired fixtures give off a sultry feel, and rich takes on classic American diner dishes like crispy fries with Mornay sauce, garlic aioli, and fried farm egg, and griddled bratwurst with smashed potatoes and roasted-garlic gravy satisfy your cravings. Don't be fooled by the $11 price tag on the single cheeseburger—it's gigantic, and totally delicious. Like a good diner, the restaurant is open late, but with the added bonus of a solid craft beer and cocktail list to carry you through the night. $ *Average main: $16* ⊠ *800 W. Randolph St., West Loop* 📞 *312/929–4580* ⊕ *www.auchevalchicago.com* ▬ *No credit cards* ✎ *Reservations not accepted* ✛ *4:D1.*

DINER
Fodor'sChoice
★

$$ ╳ **Avec.** Go to this Euro-style wine bar when you're feeling gregarious; the rather stark space has seating for only 48 people, and it's a tight fit. The results are loud and lively, though happily the shareable fare—a mix of small and large Mediterranean plates, such as chorizo-stuffed dates and whole roasted fish from a wood-burning oven—is reasonably priced. Avec is as popular as its next-door neighbor Blackbird (and run by the same people), and only early birds are guaranteed tables. The doors open at 3:30 pm. $ *Average main: $20* ⊠ *615 W. Randolph St., West Loop* 📞 *312/377–2002* ⊕ *www.avecrestaurant.com* ⊗ *No lunch* ✎ *Reservations not accepted* ✛ *1:A6.*

MEDITERRANEAN
Fodor'sChoice
★

$$ ╳ **Belly Q and Urban Belly.** Chef-owner Bill Kim expands his Belly empire, moving his flagship ramen restaurant Urban Belly under the same roof as his trendy Korean barbecue house on the edge of Randolph's restaurant row. Secure a seat at one of the six grill tables—if you can—to engage in the authentic live fire action of DIY grilling over an open flame, with meats like short ribs and spicy lemongrass chicken. But bystanders can still order grilled meats safely on the sidelines, along with dishes like tea-smoked duck breast, pork and cilantro dumplings, and signature bowls of steaming soup. If you have the courage, warm up with a few drinks and head to the restaurant's karaoke lounge to belt out a few songs post-meal. $ *Average main: $25* ⊠ *1400 W. Randolph St., West Loop* 📞 *312/563–1010* ⊕ *www.bellyqchicago.com* ⊗ *No lunch Sat.* ✛ *4:B1.*

KOREAN
BARBECUE

$$$$ ╳ **Blackbird.** Being cramped next to your neighbor has never been as fun as it is at this hot spot run by award winning chef Paul Kahan. Celebs pepper the sleek see-and-be-seen crowd that comes for the creative dishes and exceptional cocktail list. While the menu changes constantly, you'll always find choices that highlight seasonal ingredients, such as rack of lamb with leeks and *spigarello* (wild broccoli) in spring, or aged duck breast with buttermilk spaetzle in winter. It all plays out against a minimalist backdrop of white walls, blue-gray banquettes, and aluminum chairs. Reservations aren't required, but they might as well be; the dining room is typically booked solid on Saturday night.

MODERN
AMERICAN
Fodor'sChoice
★

[$] *Average main: $40 ✉ 619 W. Randolph St., West Loop ☎ 312/715–0708 🌐 www.blackbirdrestaurant.com ⏲ Closed Sun. No lunch Sat. ✍ Reservations essential ✣ 1:A6.*

$ MEXICAN 🍴 **De Cero Taqueria.** Sometimes you want celebrity chef–made regional Mexican, and sometimes you just want a really good taco. For the latter, as well as zesty margaritas, a convivial setting, and lick-the-mortar-clean guacamole, grab a table at De Cero, the Mexican standout on Randolph Street's restaurant row. The highlight of the menu is the taco list. Each of 21 tacos is priced individually and made to order for a mix-and-match meal. Top choices include chipotle chicken, duck confit with corn salsa, and battered catfish with jalapeño jicama honey slaw, chipotle mayo, and cilantro. The restaurant is wood-tables-and-benches casual and can get loud; beat the crowds by phoning ahead for reservations, especially on weekends. [$] *Average main: $15 ✉ 814 W. Randolph St., West Loop ☎ 312/455–8114 🌐 hellotacos.com ⏲ Closed Sun. and Mon. ✣ 4:D1.*

$$$$ ECLECTIC Fodor's Choice ★ 🍴 **Girl & the Goat.** Bravo's *Top Chef* Season 4 champion Stephanie Izard's highly anticipated restaurant lives up to the hype, serving her personal brand of sharable, eclectic plates with seasonal flair. The antithesis of fussy, Girl & the Goat's rustic decor features communal butcher tables, dark antique fixtures, and an open kitchen. Dishes are grouped into straightforward categories—vegetable, fish, and meat—and range from pan-roasted skate cheeks with pecans and romesco sauce to roasted pig's face with tamarind and cilantro sauces. Not surprisingly, goat-centric plates take prominence, including a goat-liver mousse with apple butter, pickled mushroom relish, and crumpets. Desserts are also inventive, like the indulgent bittersweet chocolate cake served à la mode with shiitake-caramel gelato and drizzled toffee crème fraîche. [$] *Average main: $50 ✉ 809 W. Randolph St., West Loop ☎ 312/492–6262 🌐 www.girlandthegoat.com ⏲ No lunch ✍ Reservations essential ✣ 4:D1.*

$$$$ MODERN AMERICAN Fodor's Choice ★ 🍴 **Grace.** Breakout culinary star Curtis Duffy (veteran of Avenues and Alinea) makes a home for his inventive white-tablecloth cuisine at this West Loop stunner. Duffy artfully plates delicate, hyper-seasonal dishes on two tasting menus—flora and fauna themed—for $205 each. For a fine-dining institution, the menu is refreshingly vegetable heavy in dishes like winter squash with enoki mushrooms, pearl onions, and orange hyssop. If you can spare the extra cash, opt for the wine pairings—though the nonalcoholic pairings are just as exceptional. [$] *Average main: $205 ✉ 652 W. Randolph St., West Loop ☎ 312/234–9494 🌐 www.grace-restaurant.com 💳 No credit cards ⏲ Closed Sun. and Mon. ✣ 1:A6.*

$ BARBECUE 🍴 **Green Street Smoked Meats.** Taking a cue from the barbecue kings of Texas, this cool smoke joint is a little bit Southern, a little bit hipster. It's best to queue up immediately when you walk in—the counter service for food tends to draw a line that snakes through the hall. Black-gloved meat men carve up smoky brisket, savory pulled pork, and slathered ribs sold by the half-pound. Sides are about as American as you can get, including Frito pie, macaroni salad, and coleslaw. Head to a communal picnic table, but not before grabbing a few brews from the gigantic center bar. Beer flows freely here from the 16 crafts on draft and a bathtub of ice filled with plenty of cheap tallboys to keep you going late into the night. [$] *Average main: $15* ✉ *112 N. Green St., West Loop* ☎ *312/754–0431* 🌐 *www.greenstreetmeats.com* ⏲ *Closed Mon. No lunch Tues.-Fri.* ✍ *Reservations not accepted* ✥ *1:A6.*

$$ VEGETARIAN 🍴 **Green Zebra.** Chef Shawn McClain took the vegetable side dish and ran it up the marquee, earning raves nationwide for giving vegetables the gourmet treatment. But don't call it vegetarian, McClain says—it's "flexitarian," mostly veggie but not strictly so. The result gives good-for-you vegetables the starring role in a sleek shop suave enough to seduce the most ardent meat lovers. Chef de cuisine Jon DuBois changes the menu seasonally with dishes such as creamy white corn polenta cake with garlic scapes, Burrata cheese with pickled beets, or foraged maitake mushrooms with housemade kimchi. The occasional fish dish—like pan-seared trout—makes do for carnivores. [$] *Average main: $25* ✉ *1460 W. Chicago Ave., West Loop* ☎ *312/243–7100* 🌐 *www.greenzebrachicago.com* ⏲ *Closed Mon.* ✥ *3:C5.*

$$ ECLECTIC FAMILY Fodor's Choice ★ 🍴 **Little Goat.** Following the wild success of her flagship restaurant, the Girl & the Goat, *Top Chef* alum Stephanie Izard switches gears with this all-day counterpart. The diner/bakery/bar is open from early morning until late night, serving up comfort foods like fresh pastries, soups and sandwiches, burgers, and classic supper club entrées. Expect a rotating seasonal menu heavy on Americana nostalgia with a splash of Izard's eclectic touches, such as pork belly-topped scallion pancakes, and a sloppy joe made from goat with rosemary slaw on a squish squash roll. One of the bonuses of having an in-house bakery is a killer dessert menu, so save room for sweets. [$] *Average main: $20* ✉ *820 W. Randolph St., West Loop* ☎ *312/888–3455* 🌐 *www.littlegoatchicago.com* ✍ *Reservations not accepted* ✥ *4:D1.*

$ DINER 🍴 **Lou Mitchell's Restaurant.** Shelve your calorie and cholesterol concerns, because Lou Mitchell's heeds no modern health warnings. The diner, a destination close to Union Station since 1923, specializes in high-fat breakfasts and comfort-food lunches. You can start the day with eggs and homemade hash browns by the skillet; later in the day this is the place to take a break for meat loaf and mashed potatoes. Though you'll almost certainly have to have deal with out-the-door waits, staffers dole out doughnut holes and Milk Duds to pacify hunger pangs. [$] *Average main: $10* ✉ *565 W. Jackson Blvd., West Loop* ☎ *312/939–3111* 🌐 *www.loumitchellsrestaurant.com* ⏲ *No dinner* ✥ *4:E2.*

$$$$ BISTRO 🍴 **Maude's Liquor Bar.** A classic French menu of dishes like chicken liver mousse and French onion fondue is the only thing traditional about this sexy Randolph Street hot spot. Dim lighting, reclaimed vintage touches, and an indie soundtrack set the mood for sipping on cocktails like the Smokey Violet Smash and snacking on small plates like warm marinated mushrooms with swiss chard. If your table is feeling particularly indulgent, spoil yourselves with the towering Maude's Plateaux seafood platter for $175, filled with a ridiculous sampling of lobster, crab, mussels, oysters, shrimp, and ceviche large enough to share among a party of four. [$] *Average main: $36* ✉ *840 W. Randolph St., West Loop* ☎ *312/243–9712* 🌐 *www.maudesliquorbar.com* 💳 *No credit cards* ⏲ *No lunch* ✥ *4:D1.*

$$$$ ECLECTIC 🍴 **Moto Restaurant.** Mad-scientist chef Homaro Cantu has become a cult figure in the Windy City. His restaurant-cum-laboratory is sequestered in the city's still-working meatpacking district. Many of the techniques perfected in the basement kitchen have been put to use in the chef's work with NASA and corporate America. Inside the minimalist dining room patrons pay for the privilege of being guinea pigs. The spectacle begins with the menu—daily changing multicourse menus are available in 10- and 20-course options—which is printed on edible paper. Flavors are seared into wineglasses by an industrial laser, rigatoni is fashioned from lychee puree, and frozen flapjacks are "cooked" table-side on a liquid-nitrogen-filled box. The awe-factor is big but the portions are small. [$] *Average main: $175* ✉ *945 W. Fulton Market, West Loop* ☎ *312/491–0058* 🌐 *www.motorestaurant.com* ✍ *Reservations essential* 👔 *Jacket and tie* ✥ *4:D1.*

$$ MODERN EUROPEAN 🍴 **Nellcôte.** Inspired by the French Riviera mansion where the Rolling Stones recorded "Exile on Main Street," Nellcôte blends European opulence with raw bohemian chic. Most of the menu is driven by the restaurant's in-house flour mill, which is used to make everything from pizzas (topped with ingredients like fennel sausage, local ramps, and burrata) and pastas (hand-cut tagliatelli and agnolotti) to desserts (clementine pavlova and butterscotch budino). For a quieter dining experience, avoid Friday and Saturday nights, when the restaurant transforms into a sceney club with loud thumping music. [$] *Average main: $25* ✉ *833 W. Randolph St., West Loop* ☎ *312/432–0500* 🌐 *www.nellcoterestaurant.com* 💳 *No credit cards* ✥ *4:D1.*

$$$$ ECLECTIC 🍴 **Next Restaurant.** Grant Achatz's buzzworthy sophomore effort is big on concept: the restaurant completely transforms itself every three months to focus on a unique theme. The opening menu, Paris 1906, paid homage to famed chef Auguste Escoffier's tenure at the Ritz Paris. Subsequent incarnations have pulled favorite hits from iconic restaurants or explored the future of Chinese cuisine. The tasting menu ranges in price from $70 to $485, depending on the date and time you book; tickets are paid for in advance, nonrefundable, and available only online—or via resale markets at highly inflated prices against season ticket holders. Tables accommodate two to four guests, with the exception of the six-person kitchen table. [$] *Average main: $210* ✉ *953 W. Fulton Market, West Loop* ☎ *312/226–0858* 🌐 *www.nextrestaurant.com* 🕒 *Closed Mon. and Tues. No lunch* ✍ *Reservations essential* ✥ *4:D1.*

$ GREEK FAMILY 🍴 **The Parthenon.** The claim to fame here is the *saganaki*, the Greek flaming-cheese dish, which the Parthenon says it invented in 1968, thereby introducing "*opa!*" to the American vocabulary. So, ordering the flaming cheese here is a rite of passage for any first-time visitors, and it's delicious, but the regulars return to this Greektown hot spot for lamb and chicken preparations, often skewered on sticks. In fact, the restaurant also takes credit for being the first to serve gyros stateside. True or not, indulge the legends and stick to these classics. Be sure to ask for pita bread and a side of *tzatziki*, a yogurt-and-cucumber-based dipping sauce. The food is cheap and the atmosphere is festive and family-friendly. [$] *Average main: $13* ✉ *314 S. Halsted St., West Loop* ☎ *312/726–2407* 🌐 *www.theparthenon.com* ✥ *4:D2.*

$$$ AMERICAN Fodor's Choice ★ 🍴 **The Publican Restaurant.** Don't call this beer-focused hot spot a gastropub—Chef Paul Kahan (of Blackbird fame) prefers "beer hall" (though wine is available, too). Certainly the long communal tables, at which beer connoisseurs sample from a selection hovering around 100 brews, give the bustling space the air of an Oktoberfest celebration. The seafood- and pork-focused menu does give an elevated nod to pub fare, though, and diners share shucked oysters and just-fried pork rinds before tucking into grilled, smoky country ribs, fried perch, and beef-heart tartare. Brunch is just as popular as dinner here, so arrive early or call for a reservation—seating fills up fast. [$] *Average main: $35* ✉ *837 W. Fulton Market, West Loop* ☎ *312/733–9555* 🌐 *www.thepublicanrestaurant.com* ✥ *4:D1.*

$$$ MODERN AMERICAN 🍴 **Sepia.** The name may evoke nostalgia for the building's gritty past as a print shop, but Sepia is thoroughly forward-thinking in both its design (glassed-in chandeliers and leather-topped tables) and its simple, seasonal dishes created by chef Andrew Zimmerman. Order some country pâté for the table while you review the menu, which includes appetizers like potato gnocchi with pork and oxtail, and entrées such as smoked rainbow trout with swiss chard. A well-chosen, international wine list and thoughtfully prepared classic cocktails satisfy oenophiles and mixologists alike. Though reservations can be hard to come by for dinner, seats at the communal tables are first-come, first-served. [$] *Average main: $35* ✉ *123 N. Jefferson St., West Loop* ☎ *312/441–1920* 🌐 *www.sepiachicago.com* 🕓 *No lunch weekends* ✥ *4:E1.*

$$ SPANISH 🍴 **Vera.** Coffee bar by day, Spanish wine bar by night, this café run by husband-and-wife team Mark and Elizabeth Mendez is bound to have the fix you need. Swing by on weekdays to sip on brews from local coffee roasters. Roll in during the evening to take in Elizabeth's progressive wine list, including a flowing tap system that pours three rotating varietals to complement Mark's Latin-inspired cuisine. Naturally, a wine bar demands charcuterie and cheese, but Vera's personality truly shines in small plates like lamb and beef *albondigas* (meatballs) with whipped ricotta and the salt cod croquettes. Vegetarians will also feel at home with thoughtful dishes like roasted mushrooms with a thyme-and-garlic jus. [$] *Average main: $22* ✉ *1023 W. Lake St., West Loop* ☎ *312/243–9770* 🌐 *www.verachicago.com* 🕓 *No lunch weekends* ✥ *4:C1.*

$$ ITALIAN 🍴 **Vivo.** Vivo was trendy on this west-of-the-Loop stretch long before Randolph Street's restaurant row got hot, and it still draws a crowd. It may be slightly more about the scene—brick walls, black ceiling, open wine racks, and lots of pretty people—than the cuisine, but you'll find reliable Italian fare as well as a fun evening. You can't go wrong with bruschetta, beef tenderloin carpaccio, house-made tagliatelle, and wood-grilled Berkshire pork chops. [$] *Average main: $25* ✉ *838 W. Randolph St., West Loop* ☎ *312/733–3379* 🌐 *www.vivo-chicago.com* 💳 *No credit cards* 🕓 *No lunch weekends* ✥ *4:D1.*

NEAR NORTH AND RIVER NORTH

A couple of decades ago, when Rick Bayless and his wife, Deann, opened Frontera Grill, River North was still seen as a dicey part of town. In fact, anything west of Michigan Avenue was suspect. How times change. Now the mammoth Chicago Merchandise Mart anchors River North, where art and design trades patronize the area's hot spots, including Slurping Turtle, Gilt Bar, and Paris Club Bistro & Bar, as well as its refined restaurants, such as mk, Naha, and Topolobampo. Meanwhile the nearby Near North district, home to shopping's Magnificent Mile and the residential Gold Coast, specializes in upscale restaurants that suit the clientele like a bespoke suit. The Magnificent Mile is the land of posh hotels (Sofitel and Park Hyatt) and their sleek dining rooms (Café des Architectes and NoMI Kitchen, respectively), as well as stand-alone stars like TRU, Spiaggia, and Les Nomades. Head north on Wells Street to Old Town, or expect to spend a fair bit on dinner.

NEAR NORTH

$$$$ AMERICAN FAMILY 🍴 **Allium.** Believe it or not, one of Chicago's finest hot dogs is hiding at luxury hotel Four Seasons. The hotel is still all swank, but the restaurant has a much more relaxed attitude. Seasonal ingredients drive the comfort-heavy menu, which includes dishes like the grass-fed burger with smoked-onion remoulade, Buffalo rock shrimp, and the famed Chicago-style hot dog with "housemade everything." End with shareable sweets like bourbon *macarons* and brownie bites, or keep the larger-size s'mores with smoked marshmallow and graham cracker ice cream all to yourself. The white-tablecloth vibe may have dropped, but be wary of your wallet—prices tend to add up quickly here. [$] *Average main: $40* ✉ *The Four Seasons Hotel, 120 E. Delaware Pl., Near North* ☎ *312/799–4900* 🌐 *www.alliumchicago.com* ✥ *1:E2.*

$$ ITALIAN FAMILY 🍴 **Bar Toma.** Italian culinary master Tony Mantuano (of Spiaggia and Terzo Piano) has reclaimed the Water Tower tourist trap area as Chicago's landmark piazza with his neighborhood pizzeria, Bar Toma. Visitors stroll in throughout the day to snack on hand-rolled mozzarella, sip imported wines, and feast on artisanal wood-fired pizzas made with premium ingredients like house-made sausage and Calabrian chilis. If your schedule only allots for a grab-and-go bite, stop in for a quick gelato or *mamaluchi* (Italian doughnuts stuffed with lemon marmalade). [$] *Average main: $21* ✉ *110 E. Pearson St., Near North* ☎ *312/266–3110* 🌐 *www.bartomachicago.com* 💳 *No credit cards* ✥ *1:E2.*

$$ BISTRO 🍴 **Bistrot Margot.** We love this Old Town bistro for its faithfully executed menu, budget-friendly prices, and Parisian art-nouveau interior, even if it means sitting rather close to our neighbors. Chef-owner Joe Doppes whips up silky chicken-liver mousse, succulent *moules marinières* (mussels in white wine), escargots simmered in rich garlic butter, and expertly seared whitefish in amandine sauce. The additional seating on the second floor has more of an intimate French country-home feel. Bistrot Margot continues to draw the crowds, so come early or make a reservation. [$] *Average main: $25* ✉ *1437 N. Wells St., Near North* ☎ *312/587–3660* 🌐 *www.bistrotmargot.com* ✥ *3:G3.*

$$$ WINE BAR 🍴 **The Boarding House.** If the stunning 4,000-wine-bottle installation on the ceiling of the dining room isn't a dead giveaway, this Old Town newcomer belongs to master sommelier and former *Check, Please!* host Alpana Singh. Wine is obviously a big deal here; a 30-page catalog presents varietals from around the globe. Start in the first-floor wine bar, snacking on artisanal pizzas, charcuterie boards, and oysters

on the half shell, before heading to the second-floor dining room to feast on a sumptuous menu of hen eggs and polenta fries, lamb chops with red wine–braised cipollini onions, and seared sturgeon with lentils and bacon. $ *Average main: $32* ✉ *720 N. Wells St., Near North* ☎ *312/280–0720* ⊕ *www.boardinghousechicago.com* ▭ *No credit cards* ⊙ *Closed Sun. No lunch* ✛ *1:C3.*

$$$ ✕ **Café des Architectes.** French cuisine sometimes gets knocked for being
FRENCH   too rich, heavy, and expensive, but this is an image that Southern-born chef Greg Biggers is doing his best to prove wrong at this stylish restaurant on the ground floor of the Sofitel. Biggers serves house-cured charcuterie, robust cheeses, and seasonal dishes like Alaskan halibut with beet relish and mushrooms. Standout sweets, such as the chocolate Opera cake with coffee, ganache, and caramel, are worth the indulgence. Try the three-course executive lunch menu for $24; it's a steal. $ *Average main: $30* ✉ *Sofitel Chicago, 20 E. Chestnut St., Near North* ☎ *312/324–4000* ⊕ *www.cafedesarchitectes.com* ✛ *1:E2.*

$$$ ✕ **Ditka's.** NFL Hall-of-Famer Mike Ditka was one of only two coaches
STEAKHOUSE   to take the Bears to the Super Bowl. Sure, it was back in 1985, but Bears fans have long memories, and they still love "Da Coach" as well as his clubby, sports-themed restaurant where local performer John Vincent does dead-on impressions of Frank Sinatra, Thursday through Saturday. The dark-wood interior and sports memorabilia are predictable, but the menu clearly aims to please a large and diverse audience. Café staples (salads, fish) and bar food (burgers, pot roast) join steak-house fare (steaks, chops) and a few unexpected indulgences (sustainably sourced seafood dishes). $ *Average main: $31* ✉ *Tremont Hotel, 100 E. Chestnut St., Near North* ☎ *312/587–8989* ⊕ *www.mikeditkaschicago.com* ✛ *1:E2.*

$$$$ ✕ **Gibsons Bar & Steakhouse.** Chicago movers and shakers mingle with
STEAKHOUSE   conventioneers at Gibsons, a lively, homegrown, Gold Coast steak house renowned for overwhelming portions, good service, and celebrity spotting. Generous prime steaks and chops are the focus of the menu, but there are plenty of fish options, too, including planked whitefish and massive Australian lobster tails. Desserts are huge: the gargantuan slice of carrot cake could feed a table of four. $ *Average main: $45* ✉ *1028 N. Rush St., Near North* ☎ *312/266–8999* ⊕ *www.gibsonssteakhouse. com* ✛ *1:D1.*

$$ ✕ **Kamehachi.** It seems like there's a sushi spot on practically every cor-
JAPANESE   ner in Chicago, but when Kamehachi opened in Old Town in 1967 it was the first, though the restaurant has since moved down the block to a loftier space complete with sushi bar, upstairs lounge, and flowering garden (in season). Quality fish, updated decor, and eager-to-please hospitality keep fans returning. Behind the busy sushi bar, chefs manage both restaurant orders and the many take-out calls from neighbors. Combination sushi meals, which include maki rolls, nigiri sushi, and miso soup, are a relative bargain, running from $19 to $34. $ *Average main: $20* ✉ *1531 N. Wells St., Near North* ☎ *312/664–3663* ⊕ *www. kamehachi.com* ✛ *3:G3.*

$$ ✕ **Kinmont.** Who knew sustainability could be so sexy? Channeling the
SEAFOOD   rustic sportsman's clubs of the 19th century, this ethical fish restaurant

from the Element Collective (Old Town Social, Nellcote, RM Champagne Salon) can be summed up as rugged-meets-refined. Handsome dark leather and glowing chandeliers add character to this intimate space. Responsibly sourced seafood is the guiding ethos here, which makes up a menu filled with dishes like Skuna Bay salmon tartare, wild Gulf shrimp cocktail, and a selection of oysters that changes daily. Groups willing to throw down extra cash will be well-served here with large-format shareables like the towering seafood platters stacked with raw oysters, shrimp, mussels, Maine lobster, and Alaskan king crab. [$] *Average main: $25* ✉ *419 W. Superior St., Near North* ☎ *312/915–0011* 🌐 *www.kinmontrestaurant.com* ✥ *1:B3.*

$$$$ FRENCH 🍴 **Les Nomades.** Intimate and elegant doesn't make headlines, but Les Nomades holds a torch for tender refinements. Wood-burning fireplaces and original art warm the dining rooms of this Streeterville brownstone, and the carefully composed menu of French food includes the usual suspects, such as duck consommé, but also more contemporary fare, such as Arctic char with maitake mushrooms and forbidden rice, and earthy indulgences like veal sweetbreads with roasted venison loin. You can compose your own prix-fixe dinner from the menu; four courses cost $115; five courses cost $130. [$] *Average main: $115* ✉ *222 E. Ontario St., Near North* ☎ *312/649–9010* 🌐 *www.lesnomades.net* ⏲ *Closed Sun. and Mon. No lunch* ✍ *Reservations essential* 👔 *Jacket required* ✥ *1:F4.*

$$$ ITALIAN 🍴 **Nico Osteria.** The Thompson Hotel is one of Chicago's hottest hotel destinations, so it seems fitting to tap one of the city's finest chefs to make its restaurant a culinary destination. Another runaway hit from chef-owner Paul Kahan, he returns to his fine-dining roots with this elegant Italian seafood concept. Seasonally driven, regional Mediterranean staples are peppered with contemporary touches like dry-aged rib eye with Calabrian chili butter and hen-of-the-woods mushrooms, and scallops with fermented chilis, black lava salt, and Meyer lemons. Go à la carte or get the full tour with the $125 tasting menu. Either way, save room: the desserts here are notably innovative and not to be missed. [$] *Average main: $32* ✉ *Thompson Hotel, 1015 N. Rush St., Gold Coast* ☎ *312/994–7100* 🌐 *www.nicoosteria.com* ✥ *1:E1.*

$$$ MODERN AMERICAN 🍴 **NoMI Kitchen.** Suits and ties are no longer de rigueur at the Park Hyatt's NoMI Kitchen, a seventh-floor lifestyle-focused concept that goes along with NoMI Lounge, NoMI Garden, and NoMI Spa. Isamu Noguchi's *Wintry Branches* sculpture hangs above an airy dining room featuring wood tables with leather accents and floor-to-ceiling windows for breathtaking views of Michigan Avenue.The open kitchen churns out a locally sourced, approachable menu rooted in French techniques. Dessert is not to be missed, with seasonally changing sweets that range from house-made ice creams and sorbets to delectable cookies and tarts. [$] *Average main: $35* ✉ *Park Hyatt Hotel, 800 N. Michigan Ave., Near North* ☎ *312/239–4030* 🌐 *www.hyatt.com/gallery/nomi/kitchen.html* ✥ *3:G4.*

$ FRENCH FAMILY 🍴 **Pierrot Gourmet.** Despite the legions of shoppers on Michigan Avenue, there are few casual cafés to quell their collective hunger, making this bakery-patisserie-café a welcome neighbor. Breakfast leans upscale

European, with pastries, coffees, and breakfast sandwiches. Lunches center on quiche and *tarte flambé*—an Alsatian flatbread with bacon and onions—accompanied by a glass of Riesling. Solo diners are accommodated at the magazine-strewn communal table. Meals are served all day long. The upscale Peninsula Hotel runs Pierrot, accounting for both the high quality and the high cost. [$] *Average main: $15* ✉ *Peninsula Hotel, 108 E. Superior St., Near North* ☎ *312/573–6749* 🌐 *www.peninsula.com/chicago* ✥ *1:E3.*

$$ MODERN AMERICAN 🍴 **Pump Room.** Once famous for its star-studded clientele like Frank Sinatra and Humphrey Bogart, the iconic Pump Room was on the verge of extinction before world-class chef Jean-Georges Vongerichten and legendary hotelier Ian Schrager revived the Chicago landmark with a glitzy redesign and concept overhaul. The result is a sceney enclave mirroring Vongerichten's award-winning New York restaurant, ABC Kitchen. Diners can dig into wholewheat flatbreads and homemade pastas topped with seasonally driven ingredients like Meyer lemon cream and asparagus pesto, while keeping an eye out for the celebrities that are often spotted at the bar. [$] *Average main: $24* ✉ *Public Chicago, 1301 N. State Pkwy., Near North* ☎ *312/229–6740* 🌐 *www.pumproom.com* ✥ *3:H4.*

$$$ AMERICAN 🍴 **RL.** Power brokers, moneyed locals, and Michigan Avenue shoppers keep the revolving doors spinning at RL, the initials of designer Ralph Lauren who lent his name and signature *soigné* style to the eatery that adjoins his Polo/Ralph Lauren store. Inside, cozy leather banquettes are clustered under hunt-club-style art hung on wood-paneled walls. The menu of American classics, including crab Louis, Dover sole in lemon butter, and steak Diane flamed in the dining room, perfectly suits the country-club-in-the-city setting. [$] *Average main: $30* ✉ *115 E. Chicago Ave., Near North* ☎ *312/475–1100* 🌐 *www.rlrestaurant.com* ✥ *1:E3.*

$$ MODERN MEXICAN 🍴 **Salpicón.** Anyone who does authentic Mexican in Chicago operates in the shadow of Frontera Grill's Rick Bayless—which makes it easier for those in the know to snag a table at Salpicón. Chef Priscila Satkoff grew up in Mexico City, and her renditions of *mole poblano* and grilled fish with *salsa fresca* have unforced flair. Wash 'em down with a belt of one of 100 tequilas or choose from the extensive selection of vintage wines. Once you try the Mexican-style Sunday brunch, with dishes like the spicy *chilaquiles* with tomatillo-serrano sauce, you'll have a hard time going back to eggs Benedict. [$] *Average main: $27* ✉ *1252 N. Wells St., Near North* ☎ *312/988–7811* 🌐 *www.salpicon.com* 🕓 *No lunch* ✥ *3:G4.*

$$$ CANTONESE 🍴 **Shanghai Terrace.** As precious as a jewel box, and often as pricey, this red, lacquer-trimmed 70-seat restaurant hidden away in the Peninsula Hotel reveals the hotelier's Asian roots. Come for upscale dim sum, stylishly presented, and luxury-laden dishes such as Peking duck with Mandarin pancakes, wok-fried shredded beef, and braised giant tiger prawns. A patio that seats up to 60 during warmer months lets you revel in a relaxing meal four stories above the madding crowds of Michigan Avenue. Though fans admire the attentive, professional service, some warn that diners with larger appetites might leave feeling unsatisfied. [$] *Average main: $32* ✉ *Peninsula Hotel, 108 E. Superior St., 4th fl.,*

Near North ☎ 312/573–6744 🌐 www.peninsula.com/chicago ⏲ Closed Mon. ✥ 1:E3.

$$$ AMERICAN 🍴 **Signature Room at the 95th.** When you've got the best view in town and a lock on special-occasion dining, do you need to be daring with the food? The Signature Room keeps it simple, making a formal affair of dishes such as rack of lamb and sautéed salmon while everyone ogles the skyline views from the John Hancock's 95th floor. If you come at lunch, the daytime light lets you see Lake Michigan; the $20 lunch buffet is a steal, but only available on Friday and Saturday. Sunday brunch is lavish—and pricey. [$] *Average main: $34 ✉ John Hancock Center, 875 N. Michigan Ave., 95th fl., Near North ☎ 312/787–9596 🌐 www.signatureroom.com ✥ 1:E2.*

$$$$ ITALIAN Fodor's Choice ★ 🍴 **Spiaggia.** Refined Italian cooking dished alongside three-story picture-window views of Lake Michigan make Spiaggia one of the city's top eateries. The tiered dining room guarantees good sight lines from each table. Chef Tony Mantuano prepares elegant, seasonal dishes such as hand-cut spaghetti with fresh Umbrian black truffles, free-range veal chop, or Muscovy duck with sausage and blood oranges. Oenophiles consider the wine list to be scholarly. To really splurge, get the full treatment by opting for the chef's tasting menus for $130 or $235. Or if you want Spiaggia fare minus the luxury price tag, try lunch or dinner at the casual Cafe Spiaggia next door. [$] *Average main: $46 ✉ 980 N. Michigan Ave., Near North ☎ 312/280–2750 🌐 www.spiaggiarestaurant.com ⏲ No lunch ✍ Reservations essential 👔 Jacket and tie ✥ 1:E2.*

$$$ SOUTHERN 🍴 **Table Fifty-Two.** If it feels like everyone is a regular at chef Art Smith's Gold Coast restaurant, they very well might be. Oprah's former personal chef is not short on friends and admirers, yet newcomers who score a reservation feel just as welcome in the cozy, country-home environs, particularly when the complimentary cheese biscuits arrive. At its core is a formidable Southern lineup of dishes such as Lowcountry shrimp with white corn grits, fried catfish with maitake mushrooms, and a fried chicken worshipped by Lady Gaga (a Sunday- and Monday-only special). Save room for Smith's hummingbird cake, a homey banana-and-pineapple concoction topped with cream-cheese frosting. If you're in the neighborhood without a reservation, walk in and see whether the chef's counter is available: the restaurant keeps five seats open in front of the pizza oven. [$] *Average main: $29 ✉ 52 W. Elm St., Near North ☎ 312/573–4000 🌐 www.tablefifty-two.com ⏲ No lunch ✍ Reservations essential ✥ 1:D1.*

$$$$ FRENCH Fodor's Choice ★ 🍴 **TRU.** More than a decade after TRU opened under the direction of former chef/partners Rick Tramonto and Gale Gand, the award-winning progressive French restaurant still retains its critical acclaim under the helm of executive chef Anthony Martin. Expect stylish, contemporary dishes such as seared foie gras with quince, chestnut cream, and Alba white truffles, which complement the dining room's gallery-like feel (an Andy Warhol hangs on the wall). The caviar platter is served on a stunning coral display and the nine-course prix-fixe menu, priced at $158, is enough luxury to make anyone feel like royalty. Several of those courses are dessert, so save space. [$] *Average main: $158 ✉ 676 N. St. Clair St.,*

The Signature Room on the 95th floor in the John Hancock building offers unparalleled views.

Near North ☎ *312/202–0001* ⊕ *www.trurestaurant.com* ☯ *Closed Sun. No lunch* ⌁ *Reservations essential* 🏛 *Jacket required* ✛ *1:F3.*

$$
AMERICAN

✕ **Viand.** A Midwestern feel permeates Viand, a lively restaurant and bar that's a breath of fresh air after designer-centric Michigan Avenue, just a half block away. Expect local flavors prepared with contemporary flair, like free-range roasted chicken with creamy polenta and kale, and halibut with root vegetable hash. Don't miss the pork belly and grits, the five-cheese flatbread with golden raisin pesto, and a chat with the friendly chef. Adjacent to a Courtyard by Marriott, the restaurant serves breakfast, lunch, and dinner, and the bar is a busy meeting spot. $ *Average main: $22* ⊠ *155 E. Ontario St., Near North* ☎ *312/255–8505* ⊕ *www.viandchicago.com* ✛ *1:F4.*

RIVER NORTH

$$$
ITALIAN

✕ **Baffo.** Chicagoans are typically wary of outside chefs, but it seems that celebrity chef Mario Batali has received the local stamp of approval judging by the popularity of Baffo. Book early: tables fill up quickly at this fine-dining restaurant inside his upscale Italian grocery chain, Eataly. Hyper-regional dishes representing every corner of Italy make up the menu, from Piemontese beef tartare to charred rapini-stuffed pork jowl. There are also fresh-made pasta dishes like pork and veal-filled agnolotti, and garganelli with roasted tomato, ricotta, and fried eggplant. Wine geeks take note of the 600-label list, including a sizeable number of wines by the glass and tastings of rare vintages. $ *Average main: $35* ⊠ *44 E. Grand Ave., River North* ☎ *312/521–8701* ⊕ *www. bafforistorante.com* ⌁ *Reservations essential* ✛ *1:E4.*

$$ AMERICAN FAMILY 🍴 **Beatrix.** Finding it difficult to accommodate everyone's cravings? Beatrix is the ultimate crowd pleaser, pulling only the best menu items from the Lettuce Entertain You test kitchen. Which means a health-conscious vegetarian will be happy eating slow-roasted vegetables with pumpkin-seed pesto next to a diner who wants a simple burger and fries. Plus, there's a whole menu just for gluten-free folks. Open early until late, the bakery churns out fresh pastries and specialty coffees in the morning before the bar crowd swings in around happy hour to sip on fresh-squeezed-juice cocktails, wines, and craft beers. [$] *Average main: $20* ✉ *519 N. Clark St., River North* ☎ *312/284–1377* 🌐 *www.beatrixchicago.com* ✥ *1:D4.*

$ AMERICAN 🍴 **Billy Goat Tavern.** The late comedian John Belushi immortalized the Goat's short-order cooks on *Saturday Night Live* for barking, "No Pepsi! Coke!" and "No fries! Cheeps!" at customers. And you can still hear the shtick at this subterranean hole-in-the-wall favored by reporters from the nearby *Tribune* and the *Sun-Times*. Griddle-fried "cheezborgers" are the featured chow at this supercheap, friendly spot, and people-watching is a favorite sport. [$] *Average main: $4* ✉ *430 N. Michigan Ave., Lower Level, River North* ☎ *312/222–1525* 🌐 *www.billygoattavern.com* ✥ *1:E5.*

$ TAPAS 🍴 **Café Iberico.** A Spanish expat from Galicia runs this tapas restaurant hailed by visiting Spaniards and local families, dating couples, and cheap chowhounds. It's easy to build a meal from the selection of small plates, which range from baked goat cheese to Spanish ham, grilled squid, skewered beef, and the classic *pulpo a la plancha* (grilled octopus with potatoes and olive oil)—most for under $10. This is a loud and boisterous spot, so be prepared for conviviality—but on weekends waits can stretch to hours. [$] *Average main: $15* ✉ *737 N. LaSalle Blvd., River North* ☎ *312/573–1510* 🌐 *www.cafeiberico.com* ✥ *1:C3.*

$$$$ STEAKHOUSE Fodor's Choice ★ 🍴 **Chicago Cut Steakhouse.** As if steak houses didn't offer enough luxury already, Chicago Cut takes decadence to the next level. Sumptuous red banquettes and floor-to-ceiling windows with prime views of the Chicago River provide a romantic backdrop for the celebrities and A-listers who often make cameos here. Steak is clearly the star, and on offer are 15 cuts and 10 different preparations. But the rest of the menu is just as opulent, with dishes like seared foie gras with blackberry jam and Marcona almonds, Alaskan halibut with grilled cauliflower and chanterelle mushrooms in black truffle vinaigrette, along with a full raw bar. Seasoned drinkers willing to pony up can find an impressive selection of rare vintages and reserve spirits behind the bar. [$] *Average main: $50* ✉ *300 N. LaSalle St., River North* ☎ *312/329–1800* 🌐 *www.chicagocutsteakhouse.com* ✥ *1:C5.*

$$$ TUSCAN 🍴 **Coco Pazzo.** The spread of antipasti that greets you upon entrance into this Tuscan-inspired restaurant is a sign of good things to come. Coco Pazzo serves lusty, aggressively seasoned fare, such as homemade ricotta and spinach dumplings, grilled veal chop with a bone-marrow reduction, and wood-grilled Florentine steaks. Stop in at lunch for pizzas fresh from the wood-fired oven. The discreet but professional service goes far toward softening the open-loft setting of exposed-brick walls and wood floors, but the scene is rather formal. The well-rounded,

exclusively Italian wine list is impressive: *Wine Spectator* has lauded its selection ranging from popular to boutique producers. [$] *Average main: $35* ✉ *300 W. Hubbard St., River North* ☎ *312/836–0900* 🌐 *www.cocopazzochicago.com* 🕒 *No lunch weekends* ✥ *1:C5.*

$$$$ STEAKHOUSE ✕ **David Burke's Primehouse.** Though local reception was initially cautious about New York celebrity chef David Burke running Primehouse in the boutique James Hote—after all, what could a New Yorker teach a Chicagoan about steak?—the restaurant has been roundly embraced for its convivial setting and sense of playfulness. Cuts of meat include a 28-day, dry-aged rib eye and the bone-in filet mignon. Don't pass up the fill-your-own doughnuts and lollipop tree for dessert. The best seats are the red-leather booths along the walls. [$] *Average main: $50* ✉ *The James Hotel, 616 N. Rush St., River North* ☎ *312/660–6000* 🌐 *www.davidburke.com/restaurant_primehouse.html* ✥ *1:E4.*

$ AMERICAN FAMILY ✕ **Ed Debevic's.** Gum-snapping waiters in garish costumes trade quips and snide remarks with customers at this tongue-in-cheek re-creation of a 1950s diner, but it's all good, clean fun (except perhaps when they dance on the counter without removing their shoes). The menu is deep and cheap, with six unique chili preparations, five different hamburgers, four types of hot dogs, a large sandwich selection, and "deluxe plates" such as meat loaf, pot roast, and chicken-fried steak. Kids love it here, and for parents there's a selection of cocktails and wines. [$] *Average main: $10* ✉ *640 N. Wells St., River North* ☎ *312/664–1707* 🌐 *www.eddebevics.com* ✍ *Reservations not accepted* ✥ *1:C4.*

$$$$ BRAZILIAN ✕ **Fogo de Chão.** Gaucho-clad servers parade through the dining room brandishing carved-to-order skewered and grilled meats at this all-you-can-eat Brazilian churrascaria. First stop for diners is the lavish salad bar, then, using a plate-side chip, you signal green for "go" to bring on lamb, pork loin, ribs, and several beef cuts, stopped only by flipping your chip to red, for "stop." You can restart as often as you like. If that's not enough, there are starchy sides and desserts included in the $51.50 price as well; only drinks are extra. Compared to traditional steak houses, this carnivorous all-inclusive feast is somewhat of a bargain. Go on a busy night (Thursday, Friday, or Saturday) to ensure that the meat is tender and not dried out from reheating—this is also when the restaurant is the most fun and liveliest. [$] *Average main: $51* ✉ *661 N. LaSalle Blvd., River North* ☎ *312/932–9330* 🌐 *www.fogodechao.com* 🕒 *No lunch weekends* ✥ *1:C3.*

$$ MEXICAN Fodor's Choice ★ ✕ **Frontera Grill.** Devotees of chef-owner Rick Bayless queue up for the bold flavors of his distinct fare at this casual restaurant brightly trimmed in Mexican folk art. The menu changes monthly, but you can count on the freshest ingredients and options that include several varieties of guacamole, seafood, and ceviche, smaller "street food" options like soft or crispy tacos, and a variety of main courses typified by dishes like trout in cilantro sauce, red chili–marinated pork, and black-bean tamales filled with goat cheese. Bayless visits Mexico annually, updating his already extensive knowledge of regional food and cooking techniques, and he frequently takes his staff with him, ensuring that even the servers have an encyclopedic knowledge about the food. There are a limited number of reservations available, but most seats are first-come,

first-serve—expect a wait. $ *Average main: $24* ✉ *445 N. Clark St., River North* ☎ *312/661–1434* ⊕ *www.rickbayless.com/restaurants/ frontera-grill* ⊙ *Closed Sun. and Mon.* ✛ *1:D5.*

$$$$

STEAKHOUSE

✕ **Gene & Georgetti.** This old-school steak house, in business since 1941, is a Chicago institution. It thrives on the buddy network of high-powered regulars and celebrities who pop into the historic River North joint to carve up massive steaks, quality chops, and the famed "garbage salad"—a kitchen-sink creation of greens with vegetables and meats. The menu also includes Italian-American classics such as eggplant parmigiana and veal Vesuvio, along with simple seafood dishes like lobster tail, salmon, and whitefish. Service can be brusque if you're not connected, and prices can be steep, but the vibe is Chicago to the core. $ *Average main: $40* ✉ *500 N. Franklin St., River North* ☎ *312/527–3718* ⊕ *www.geneandgeorgetti.com* ⊙ *Closed Sun.* ✛ *1:C4.*

$$

SEAFOOD

Fodor'sChoice

★

✕ **GT Fish & Oyster.** The "GT" here stands for chef-partner Giuseppe Tentori, whose latest restaurant coup reinterprets the classic seafood shack as a refined, contemporary eatery, decorated with a few well-placed nautical details: think mounted shark jaws and rope buoy chandeliers. With an oyster bar spanning East and West coasts and dishes like smoked sunfish ceviche and a lobster roll stuffed with a full pound of chunky, sweet lobster, GT Fish & Oyster seems out to prove that this Chicago spot can tackle seafood as well as any coastal city. $ *Average main: $25* ✉ *531 N. Wells St., River North* ☎ *312/929–3501* ⊕ *www. gtoyster.com* ═ *No credit cards* ✛ *1:C4.*

$$$

STEAKHOUSE

✕ **Harry Caray's Italian Steakhouse.** Famed Cubs announcer Harry Caray died in 1998, but his legend lives on as fans continue to pour into the namesake restaurant where Harry frequently held court. Italian-American specialties including pastas and chicken Vesuvio share menu space with top-quality prime steaks and chops. The wine list has won a number of national awards. If you're looking for a classic Chicago spot to catch a game, the generally thronged bar serves items off the restaurant menu. Or follow the summer crowds to Navy Pier to the Harry Caray's outpost there. $ *Average main: $30* ✉ *33 W. Kinzie St., River North* ☎ *312/828–0966* ⊕ *www.harrycarays.com* ✛ *1:D5.*

$$$$

JAPANESE

✕ **Japonais by Morimoto.** As if this supersleek Japanese-fusion restaurant wasn't hot enough, Japonais got an added boost from the presense of internationally renowned chef Masaharu Morimoto of *Iron Chef America.* If the lengthy menu looks intimidating, you should feel free to trust the servers to direct you to savories such as sea urchin carbonara, foie gras oysters, and a raft of winning maki-roll combinations including shrimp tempura with asparagus. For a true taste of Morimoto's cuisine, adventurous diners should splurge on the chef's seven-course tasting menu. A traditional seating area with tables is supplemented by a couch-filled lounge, where you can also order from the entire menu, and the indoor-outdoor bar downstairs has seasonal seating along the Chicago River—the latter, not surprisingly, gets supercrowded on weekends. $ *Average main: $50* ✉ *600 W. Chicago Ave., River North* ☎ *312/822–9600* ⊕ *www.japonaismorimoto.com/chicago* ⊙ *No lunch weekends* ✛ *1:A3.*

9

$$$ SEAFOOD 🍴 **Joe's Seafood, Prime Steaks & Stone Crab.** Joe's may be far from the ocean, but the winning combination of stone crabs and other seafood, as well as prime steaks, has made this outpost of the original South Florida restaurant a continued success. The signature stone crabs are in season October to May, and the simple preparation—chilled with mustard sauce for dipping—suits the delicate meat best; they're served already cracked, but be prepared to get your hands dirty. There's plenty else on the menu all year-round, too, but the stone crabs are undeniably a star. The restaurant is almost as popular as the Miami original, so be sure to make reservations or expect a wait. [$] *Average main: $33* ✉ *60 E. Grand Ave., River North* ☎ *312/379–5637* 🌐 *www.joes.net/chicago* ✣ *1:E4.*

$$$ AMERICAN 🍴 **The Lobby at the Peninsula.** While most contemporary restaurants lean toward the avant garde, The Lobby continues the tradition of classic upscale hotel dining with all the frills. During the day, sunlight pours through the expansive floor-to-ceiling windows overlooking the terrace while diners take in elevated breakfast staples like brioche French toast with fresh berries and New York strip steak with poached farm eggs. Come afternoon, a string duo plays to the tea-service crowd enjoying finger sandwiches and pastries before transforming into a romantic dinner scene. Elegant seasonal takes on New American cuisine dominate the menu with dishes like roasted lamb loin with kale, sweet potato, cherries, and curried pistachio crumble, and slow-roasted sea trout with brussels sprouts. [$] *Average main: $35* ✉ *108 E. Superior St., River North* ☎ *312/573–6695* 🌐 *www.peninsula.com/chicago* ✣ *1:E3.*

$$$$ MODERN AMERICAN 🍴 **mk.** Foodies and fashionistas flock to owner-chef Michael Kornick's ultrahip spot for its sleek look and elegant menu. In a renovated former commercial paint facility, mk pairs its brick walls and soaring ceilings with fine linens, expensive flatware, and designer wine stems. Menus change with the season, and mains tend to hew to two or three dominant flavors—à la pan-seared Maryland striped bass with black garlic and sausage, and braised bison short ribs with potato gnocchi and manchego cheese—rather than getting overcomplicated. It's not cheap, but it is special. [$] *Average main: $38* ✉ *868 N. Franklin St., River North* ☎ *312/482–9179* 🌐 *www.mkchicago.com* ⏲ *No lunch* ✣ *1:C2.*

$ AMERICAN FAMILY 🍴 **Mr. Beef.** A Chicago institution for two-fisted Italian beef sandwiches piled with green peppers and provolone cheese, Mr. Beef garners citywide fans from area hard hats to restaurateurs and TV personalities. Service and setting—two indoor picnic tables and a dining rail—are fast-food no-nonsense, and the fare is inexpensive. This workingman's favorite is, go figure, located near River North's art galleries. [$] *Average main: $7* ✉ *666 N. Orleans St., River North* ☎ *312/337–8500* ⏲ *Closed Sun. No dinner* ✣ *1:B3.*

$$ LATIN AMERICAN 🍴 **Nacional 27.** Named after the 27 nations south of the U.S. border, this Pan-Latin restaurant serves a smattering of cross-cultural dishes from the Caribbean, Costa Rica, Mexico, Brazil, and Argentina. The menu is designed for sharing, with tapas like *tostones* (crispy plantains) and roasted corn *fundido* (melted cheese) alongside ceviches, tacos, and empanadas. It's best to come with a group if you want to order the slow-cooked pork Cubano with roasted plantains. The circular bar has

its own following, independent of the food, if you're looking for innovative cocktails, and after 11 pm on weekends, the floor in the middle of the dining room is cleared for salsa and merengue dancing. $ *Average main: $20* ⊠ *325 W. Huron St., River North* ☎ *312/664–2727* ⊕ *www.nacional27chicago.com* ☾ *Closed Sun. No lunch* ✛ *1:B3.*

$$$$ ✕ **Naha.** Cousins Carrie and Michael Nahabedian lend their name (well,
MEDITERRANEAN the first two syllables, anyway) and considerable culinary and hospitality skills to this upscale venture. The clean space is done in shades of cream and sage, and the menu focuses on sophisticated and eye-catching dishes such as wood-grilled beef rib eye, lacquered duck, or New Zealand venison glazed with mustard. Wine is treated with reverence, from the well-chosen selection of vintages to the high-quality stemware. Solos and social-seekers can sit at the convivial bar and order from the main menu. $ *Average main: $43* ⊠ *500 N. Clark St., River North* ☎ *312/321–6242* ⊕ *www.naha-chicago.com* ☾ *Closed Sun. No lunch Sat.* ✛ *1:D4.*

$$ ✕ **Osteria via Stato.** It's no-brainer Italian here, where the shtick is to
ITALIAN feed you without asking too many questions. If you opt for the $38.95 prix-fixe, you pick an entrée and waiters do the rest, working the room with several rounds of communal platters of antipasti, then pasta, followed by your entrée, and dessert. There's even a "just bring me wine" program for $30 that delivers preselected Italian vino to your table throughout your meal. The results are savory enough, but Osteria shines brightest at making you feel comfortable. For a faster meal, dine in the pizza bar, which is also open for lunch. $ *Average main: $18* ⊠ *620 N. State St., River North* ☎ *312/642–8450* ⊕ *www.osteriaviastato.com* ☾ *No lunch* ✛ *1:D4.*

$$ ✕ **Paris Club Bistro & Bar.** A stuffy French bistro this is not: lighting is
MODERN FRENCH low, music is loud, and space is usually tight, but that's what attracts the well-heeled diners to this see-and-be-seen restaurant, downstairs from the velvet-rope Studio Paris rooftop club. The restaurant feels clubby, too, but it takes food seriously, courtesy of chefs Doug Psaltis and Jean Joho. Parisian favorites like steak tartare, moules frites, and trout amandine pair up nicely with the exclusively French wine list and classic cocktails. $ *Average main: $22* ⊠ *59 W. Hubbard St., River North* ☎ *312/595–0800* ⊕ *www.parisclubchicago.com* ═ *No credit cards* ☾ *No lunch* ✛ *1:D5.*

$$ ✕ **Pizzeria Due.** Serving inch-thick pizzas in a comfortable, though well-
PIZZA worn dining room, Pizzeria Due is where everyone goes when they've
FAMILY found out that Uno, the original home of Chicago's deep-dish pizza up the street, has an hour-plus wait. Those in the know, though, say that Due is the place to order thin-crust pizza, while Uno is the traditional deep dish (both restaurants serve both styles). Regardless, Due quickly builds its own waiting list, and it's not unusual to wait for more than an hour here as well. The best strategy for dining out at either spot is to arrive early or opt to come at lunch. $ *Average main: $20* ⊠ *619 N. Wabash Ave., River North* ☎ *312/943–2400* ⊕ *762.unotogo.com* ✛ *1:E4.*

$ ✕ **Pizzeria Uno.** Chicago deep-dish pizza got its start here in 1943, and
PIZZA both local and out-of-town fans continue to pack this Victorian brown-
FAMILY stone for the filling pies—and the dim paneled rooms with reproduction

light fixtures make the setting a slice of Old Chicago. Spin-off Due down the street handles the overflow. Plan on two thick, cheesy slices or less as a full meal. This is no quick-to-your-table pie, so do order salads and be prepared to entertain the kids during the inevitable wait. [$] *Average main: $17* ✉ *29 E. Ohio St., River North* ☎ *312/321–1000* 🌐 *www.unos.com* ✥ *1:E4.*

$$ MEDITERRANEAN Fodor's Choice ★

🍴 **The Purple Pig.** The Magnificient Mile is known for many things—stunning architecture, historical landmarks, world-class shopping—but dining isn't usually one of them. An anomaly on the strip that both locals and tourists enjoy is Mediterranean wine bar the Purple Pig. Adventurous eaters will revel in the offal-centric dishes like pork sweetbreads with fennel and apricots, and roasted bone marrow with herbs, but vegetarians also get excited about dishes like salt-roasted beets with whipped goat cheeses and pistachio vinaigrette. This is a wine bar, and it's definitely worth exploring the hefty international wine list, which includes many affordable wines by the glass. [$] *Average main: $18* ✉ *500 N. Michigan Ave., River North* ☎ *312/464–1744* 🌐 *www.thepurplepigchicago.com* ⌚ *No breakfast.* ✍ *Reservations not accepted* ✥ *1:E4.*

$$ MODERN AMERICAN

🍴 **Sable Kitchen + Bar.** Sleek, stylish, and boasting one of the city's most accomplished mixology programs, it's almost hard to believe that Sable Kitchen + Bar is a hotel restaurant. This is definitely a dining destination in itself though, thanks to chef Heather Terhune—a "Top Chef: Texas" contestant—who serves contemporary American dishes like short rib sliders with root-beer glaze and crispy chicken thighs with duck fat–roasted cauliflower. These dishes complement an anthology of lovingly crafted cocktails. Can't wait for dinner to dig into pan-roasted venison or Spanish merguezsausage flatbread? The restaurant offers all-day dining, so you can order dinner for breakfast. [$] *Average main: $22* ✉ *Hotel Palomar, 505 N. State St., River North* ☎ *312/755–9704* 🌐 *www.sablechicago.com* ✥ *1:E4.*

$$$ SEAFOOD

🍴 **Shaw's Crab House.** Shaw's is, hands down, one of the city's best seafood spots, and though it's held an exalted position for years, the restaurant doesn't rest on its laurels. The kitchen stays on track, turning out famed classics like silky crab cakes and rich halibut from a menu that's been updated to also include sushi, maki, and fresh sashimi selections. The seafood salad served at lunch is big enough for two. Lunch, by the way, is rather a bargain, with well-priced entrées and $1 desserts. The restaurant does have something of a split personality, with a clubby main dining room in nautically themed loft digs as well as a lively exposed-brick bar where shell shuckers work extra hard. [$] *Average main: $29* ✉ *21 E. Hubbard St., River North* ☎ *312/527–2722* 🌐 *www.shawscrabhouse.com* ✥ *1:E5.*

$$$$ MODERN AMERICAN

🍴 **Sixteen.** Uninterrupted views of the landmark Wrigley Building, Lake Michigan, and the Chicago River make it easy to overlook the food at Sixteen—but you shouldn't. Located on the 16th floor (hence the name) of the sleek Trump International Hotel & Tower, the restaurant serves chef Thomas Lents's whimsically themed cuisine. Each tasting menu ($130 or $190) tells a seasonal tale with dishes like monkfish with endive, truffles, and blood orange served table-side. Desserts are just as inventive. Power lunching is still popular here, though if you have time for a leisurely lunch, the six-course tasting menu is more of a bargain than dinner for $78. Breakfast, with house-made crumpets, jumbo lump crab omelet, and freshly squeezed juices, are an indulgent accompaniment to early-morning views over the lake. [$] *Average main: $130* ✉ *Trump International Hotel & Tower, 401 N. Wabash Ave., River North* ☎ *312/588–8000* 🌐 *www.trumpchicagohotel.com* ✣ *3:H6.*

$$ RAMEN **Fodor's Choice** ★ 🍴 **Slurping Turtle.** Slurping is not only allowed at this casual River North noodle shop—it's encouraged. Chef Takashi Yagihashi's ramen gained a cult following at his eponymous Bucktown restaurant—but it was only available on weekends for lunch; now the all-star ramen has a permanent home at Slurping Turtle. Bursting with umami, the ramen is almost a religious experience here—particularly the Shoyu ramen with egg noodle, classic Tokyo-style soy broth, braised pork shoulder, naruto, and bamboo shoots. Ramen portions are extremely generous, but it's worth making room for the *bincho* (white charcoal) grilled meats and yakitori snacks like duck fat–fried chicken. [$] *Average main: $18* ✉ *116 W. Hubbard St., River North* ☎ *312/464–0466* 🌐 *www.slurpingturtle.com* 💳 *No credit cards* ✣ *1:C5.*

$$$ ASIAN 🍴 **Sunda.** Named for the Sunda Shelf, an ancient Southeast Asian landmass, this trendy spot scours Asia for riotously flavorful fare. There's a full sushi bar, of course, but we're more impressed by dishes such as the oxtail pot stickers, garlicky lump crab noodles, and Wagyu rib eye with yuzu-chili-stuffed bone marrow. Well-executed cocktails complement the sweet, sour, and spicy dishes. The buzzing and expansive space cobbles together communal tables, traditional and lounge seating, and Asian antiques. [$] *Average main: $30* ✉ *110 W. Illinois St., River North* ☎ *312/644–0500* 🌐 *www.sundachicago.com* 💳 *No credit cards* ✣ *1:D4.*

$$$ PERUVIAN 🍴 **Tanta.** World-renowned Peruvian chef Gastón Acurio makes his foray into the Chicago dining scene with this sexy homage to the cuisine of his homeland. Showcasing the cross-cultural influences of Peruvian cuisine from South America, Asia, and Europe, small format dishes make it easy to try everything from *chaufas* (Chinese rice) like pork fried rice with shrimp tortilla and spicy garlic to *cebiches* (raw seafood) like ahi tuna, avocado, cucumber, and tamarind. The pisco selection here is unmatched, with a rotating list of infusions like orange-clove and apple-cinnamon. Just be wary of your wallet: prices tend to add up quickly here. [$] *Average main: $28* ✉ *118 W. Grand Ave., River North* ☎ *312/222–9700* 🌐 *www.tantachicago.com* ⏲ *No lunch Mon.–Sat.* ✣ *1:D4.*

$$ HAWAIIAN 🍴 **Three Dots and a Dash.** Without the red-roped line of people waiting outside, it's pretty easy to walk past the alley entrance of this hip tiki bar. Climb down the glowing skull-lined stairs to reach the hip bungalow bar outfitted with an homage to the tiki craze of the '50s and '60s. Load up on Pan-Pacific nibbles like coconut shrimp, Polynesian short ribs, or pork belly buns with kimchi. You'll need it for all the incredibly strong tropical cocktails and punches served up with a garden of flora and fauna in ceramic coconuts, skulls, and tiki god mugs. Flashy groups would be wise to order the Treasure Chest, which arrives in a veritable

booze-filled chest with straws and a bottle of Dom Perignon. $ *Average main: $23* ⊠ *435 N. Clark St., River North* ☎ *312/610–4220* ⊕ *www. threedotschicago.com* ⚮ *Reservations essential* ✛ *1:D5.*

$$$$
MEXICAN
Fodor's Choice
★

✕ **Topolobampo.** Chef-owner Rick Bayless wrote the book on regional Mexican cuisine—several books, actually—and here he takes his faithfully prepared regional food upscale. Next door to the more casual Frontera Grill, Topolobampo is the higher-end room, with a more subdued mood and luxury menu, though it shares Frontera's address, phone, and dedication to quality. The ever-changing $120 seven-course tasting menu showcases game, seasonal fruits and vegetables, and exotic preparations like suckling pig braised with spicy red chili and tamales stuffed with chestnuts and turkey confit. For a taste of Topolobampo without the hefty price tag, try to nab a lunch reservation. $ *Average main: $120* ⊠ *445 N. Clark St., River North* ☎ *312/661–1434* ⊕ *www. rickbayless.com/restaurants/topolobampo/* ⊗ *Closed Sun. and Mon. No lunch Sat.* ⚮ *Reservations essential* ✛ *1:D5.*

$$$
MEDITERRANEAN
Fodor's Choice
★

✕ **Travelle.** The luxurious Langham Hotel doesn't disappoint with this swanky Mediterranean restaurant located on the second floor. Cushy white leather seats pamper guests gaping at the glittering city lights through the floor-to-ceiling windows. The business crowd often pops in during lunch for the three-course express menu for $29, while dim lights make the evening experience a bit more intimate. The menu here changes regularly, often focusing on a specific region of the Mediterranean. Look for favorites like whole roasted Provençal chicken, ocean trout crudo, and grilled lamb loin with hazelnuts and sunchokes. Groups should try to book the chef's table one week in advance, which features hand-selected shareables brought out by the chef himself. $ *Average main: $30* ⊠ *330 N. Wabash Ave., 2nd fl., River North* ☎ *312/923–7705* ⊕ *www.travellechicago.com* ✛ *1:E5.*

$$$
ECLECTIC

✕ **Vermilion.** Vermilion touts itself as a Latin–Indian fusion restaurant, but the best dishes here are the Eastern ones, such as artichoke pakoras and tamarind-glazed ribs. Lots of small-plate options—led by the lamb chops and scallops—encourage sampling. Despite cool fashion photography on the walls and techno music in the air, the welcome here is warm. Late-night dining hours on weekends draw a clubgoing crowd. $ *Average main: $28* ⊠ *10 W. Hubbard St., River North* ☎ *312/527–4060* ⊕ *www.thevermilionrestaurant.com* ⊗ *No lunch weekends* ✛ *1:D5.*

$$
AMERICAN

✕ **Wildfire.** This is as close as you can get to the grill without staying home and firing up the barbie, but the atmosphere here is a bit more refined than your backyard, and the menu isn't your average burgers and hot dogs. The Wildfire kitchen's wood-burning oven is visible from the dining room at this cozy supper club–style joint that plays a sound track of vintage jazz. No culinary innovations here, just exceptional chopped salad, roasted prime rib, and salmon roasted on a cedar plank, along with wood-fired, whole-wheat pizzas and fried calamari. Top taste: the roasted prime rib. $ *Average main: $26* ⊠ *159 W. Erie St., River North* ☎ *312/787–9000* ⊕ *www.wildfirerestaurant.com* ✛ *1:C4.*

$
MEXICAN

✕ **Xoco.** By opening a third restaurant next door to perennial favorites Frontera Grill and Topolobampo, celeb chef Rick Bayless has taken control of this River North block. With Xoco, he's given the city the ultimate place for *tortas* (Mexican sandwiches) filled with spiced-up fare such as *cochinita pibil* (suckling pig with pickled red onions, black beans, and searing habanero salsa) and *caldos*, generous bowls of pozole and other Latin-inspired soups. First timers shouldn't pass up the hot chocolate (available at breakfast, lunch, and dinner) made from cacao beans that are roasted and ground on the premises; a steaming cup is as rich as a chocolate bar and best consumed with a plate of hot churros. Enter around the corner on Illinois Street and join the (often long) line; orders are taken at the counter. [$] *Average main: $15* ✉ *449 N. Clark St., River North* ☎ *312/334–3688* 🌐 *www.rickbayless.com* 🕓 *Closed Sun. and Mon.* ✍ *Reservations not accepted* ✥ *1:D5.*

LINCOLN PARK AND WICKER PARK WITH BUCKTOWN AND LOGAN SQUARE

River North captures most of the expense-account diners, but the neighborhoods to the west of downtown—Bucktown, Wicker Park, and Logan Square—are where some of the city's most innovative dining occurs. With concepts like the vegetarian-friendly MANA, the pork-heavy Bristol, and dessert-focused Mindy's Hot Chocolate, West Side restaurateurs serve great food without looking like they're trying too hard. Pick a 'hood and wander on foot—good eating won't be hard to find.

To the east lies Lincoln Park, named for the lakefront park it borders. Often a first stop for recent Chicago transplants moving to the city as well as the permanent residence of families inhabiting pricey brownstones, the popular neighborhood is definitely worth exploring. From a food perspective, it's host to several of Chicago's best restaurants, including Alinea and Boka. On commercial thoroughfares such as Clark, Halsted, and Armitage, you can spend an afternoon bouncing back and forth from great restaurants and cafés to hip shops.

9

LINCOLN PARK

$$$$
MODERN AMERICAN
Fodor's Choice ★

🍴 **Alinea.** Believe the hype and secure tickets—yes, tickets—well in advance. Chicago's most exciting restaurant demands an adventurous spirit and a serious commitment of time and money. If you have four hours and $210 to $275 to spare, the 18-course tasting menu that showcases Grant Achatz's stunning, cutting-edge food is a fantastic experience. The gastronomic roller coaster takes you on a journey through intriguing aromas, visuals, flavors, and textures. The menu changes frequently, but you might find green beans perched on a pillow that emits nutmeg-scented air, sweetbreads served with burnt bread and toasted hay, and a helium balloon filled with green-apple air. Though some dishes—they range in size from one to four bites—may look like science projects, there's nothing gimmicky about the procession of bold and elegant tastes. The hours fly by in the windowless bi-level dining room, aided by the effortless service and muted decor. [$] *Average main: $265* ✉ *1723 N. Halsted St., Lincoln Park* ☎ *312/867–0110* 🌐 *www.alinea-restaurant.com* 🕓 *Closed Mon. and Tues. No lunch* ✍ *Reservations essential* 👔 *Jacket required* ✥ *3:E3.*

$$$ MODERN ITALIAN

🍴 **Balena.** This place burst onto the scene with a prime location across from Steppenwolf Theatre and a sexy Italian-inspired design that draws a respectable crowd. Be prepared to order plenty, from airy house-made pastas and crispy wood-fired pizzas to Mediterranean coastal fare like wild mussels and finger chilis, or black tagliolini with crab and sea urchin. Dessert is not to be missed, particularly elevated classics like tiramisu with chocolate sauce and coffee streusel, and the spiked *affogato* (vanilla gelato with a shot of espresso) served with apple fritters for dipping. [$] *Average main: $28* ✉ *1633 N. Halsted St., Lincoln Park* ☎ *312/867–3888* 🌐 *www.balenachicago.com* 💳 *No credit cards* 🕓 *No lunch* ✣ *3:E3.*

$$$ MODERN AMERICAN Fodor's Choice ★

🍴 **Boka.** If you're doing Steppenwolf pretheater dinner on North Halsted Street, this upscale spot gets the foodie stamp of approval, especially with executive chef Lee Wolenin in the kitchen. The seasonally driven menu is constantly changing, offering elegant fare such as seared scallops with cauliflower, apples, and radishes, and roasted chicken with boudin sausage, prunes, and burnt cabbage. Cocktails here are top shelf, often using house-made syrups and specialty, small-batch spirits. The slick lounge and outdoor patio both serve food, so this is a big draw even for those not watching curtain time. [$] *Average main: $35* ✉ *1729 N. Halsted St., Lincoln Park* ☎ *312/337–6070* 🌐 *www.bokachicago.com* 🕓 *No lunch* ✍ *Reservations essential* ✣ *3:E3.*

$$ SPANISH

🍴 **Cafe Ba-Ba-Reeba!** The name is kitschy cute, and it's jammed with partying Lincoln Parkers, so you might not think the food is a selling point—but you'd be wrong: expat Spaniards swear this is one of the best Spanish restaurants in town, and the colorful Mediterranean-style interiors encourage the fiesta feel. The large assortment of cold and warm tapas ranges from goat cheese *croquetas* to spicy potatoes with tomato aioli. It's worth checking out the entrée menu, too, for paella and skewered meats. In warm weather four different flavors of sangria flow freely on the outdoor patio. [$] *Average main: $20* ✉ *2024 N. Halsted St., Lincoln Park* ☎ *773/935–5000* 🌐 *www.cafebabareeba.com* 🕓 *No lunch Mon.–Thurs.* ✣ *3:E2.*

$$$ AMERICAN Fodor's Choice ★

🍴 **North Pond.** A former Arts and Crafts–style warming house for ice-skaters at Lincoln Park's North Pond, this gem in the woods fittingly champions an uncluttered culinary style. Talented chef Bruce Sherman emphasizes organic ingredients, wild-caught fish, and artisanal farm products. Menus change seasonally, but order the Midwestern favorite walleye pike if available. Like the food, the wine list seeks out boutique producers. The food remains top-notch at brunch but the scene, dense with strollers and high chairs, is far from serene. [$] *Average main: $36* ✉ *2610 N. Cannon Dr., Lincoln Park* ☎ *773/477–5845* 🌐 *www.northpondrestaurant.com* 🕓 *Closed Mon. and Tues.* ✣ *2:H6.*

$$$ ECLECTIC

🍴 **Perennial Virant.** Locavore obsessives should look no further than this farm-to-table gem facing Lincoln Park's seasonal farmers' market, the Green City Market. The fourth of Boka Restaurant Group's trendy restaurant empire (Boka, Girl & the Goat, GT Fish & Oyster) teams up with sustainability poster boy chef Paul Virant (also of the suburban restaurant Vie) to create a rotating menu of beautiful, locally driven dishes like braised venison meatballs and pan-seared diver scallops. The restaurant's motto is "eat what you can, and can what you can't"—hence the shelves of house-made preserves that grace the walls and are incorporated into the menu in everything from the maple-sherry aioli in the preserved pumpkin beignets to the jams and sauces and the bitters used in the cocktails. Ⓢ *Average main: $30* ⊠ *1800 N. Lincoln Ave., Lincoln Park* ☎ *312/981–7070* ⊕ *www.perennialchicago.com* ⊗ *No lunch* ✛ *3:G2.*

$$
AMERICAN

✕**Twin Anchors Restaurant & Tavern.** For a taste of classic Chicago, stop into Twin Anchors, which has been dishing out baby back ribs since 1932. The nautically themed brick tavern was a favorite of Frank Sinatra, who still croons nightly on the jukebox. If you're not in the mood for a messy slab of mild or zesty ribs—they're the main draw on the menu—order the battered codfish fry or the roasted chicken. In truth, dinner here is really less about cuisine and more about the scene—local and touring celebs often visit—but lovers of barrooms with personality don't mind the typically long waits during prime time. Ⓢ *Average main: $21* ⊠ *1655 N. Sedgwick St., Lincoln Park* ☎ *312/266–1616* ⊕ *www.twinanchorsribs.com* ⊗ *No lunch weekdays* ⌫ *Reservations not accepted* ✛ *3:G3.*

WICKER PARK

$
MEXICAN
Fodor's Choice
★

✕**Big Star.** It's cramped and noisy, and the service is often ambivalent, but most locals are willing to bear the substantial waits at Big Star because the tacos are some of the best in the city. Most of this honky-tonk taqueria's star power comes from chef Paul Kahan (of Blackbird, Avec, and the Publican), who serves up tasty tacos like spit-roasted pork shoulder with grilled pineapple and beer-battered tilapia with spicy chipotle slaw. If it's a taco emergency, skip the line for a table and head to the take-out window, taking your tacos to the spacious park across the street. Ⓢ *Average main: $12* ⊠ *1531 N. Damen Ave., Wicker Park* ☎ *773/235–4039* ⊕ *www.bigstarchicago.com* ⌫ *Reservations not accepted* ✛ *3:B3.*

$
DINER

✕**Dove's Luncheonette.** None of award-winning chef-owner Paul Kahan's restaurants are alike, so it's little surprise that his latest concept is another trendy original. Wood-paneled walls and a bluesy jukebox set the scene for this throwback '60s- and '70s-inspired diner featuring upscale takes on Southern and Mexican comfort foods like spicy fried chicken with chorizo-verde gravy and red-chili enchiladas. Seating is entirely counter space and very limited, but with much more elbow room than the shoulder-to-shoulder sister restaurant next door, Big Star. Ⓢ *Average main: $15* ⊠ *1545 N. Damen Ave., Wicker Park* ☎ *773/645–4060* ⊕ *www.doveschicago.com* ✛ *3:B3.*

$
VEGETARIAN

✕**MANA Food Bar.** It's easy to miss this slim, stylish restaurant amid the clothing boutiques and bars along Division Street, but those in the know squeeze in for globally inspired vegetarian, vegan, and gluten-free fare. Dishes are small, so plan to order a few to share. The health-conscious among you will delight in chef Jill Barron's dishes of red quinoa salad and curried cauliflower with brown rice, but carnivores won't miss their meat with mushroom sliders and hearty, sweet-potato pancakes served with chutney. Apart from the food, the list of sake-based cocktails fills the seats along the long wooden bar: try the refreshing

9

cucumber "sakerita" when it's available. [$] *Average main: $16* ✉ *1742 W. Division St., Wicker Park* ☎ *773/342–1742* 🌐 *www.manafoodbar.com* ⏲ *No lunch Sun.–Thurs.* ✍ *Reservations not accepted* ✥ *3:C4.*

$ CAFÉ 🍴 **Milk & Honey Café.** Division Street has long been a prowl of night owls but with the growing number of spas and boutiques in the area, not to mention the many work-from-home locals, this boho neighborhood needed a good breakfast and lunch spot. Milk & Honey exceeds expectations with hearty (eggs) and healthful (granola) breakfasts, and creative sandwiches (the avocado with smoked Gouda is delicious) at lunch. Choice seats change with the season: out on the sidewalk café in warm weather; in near the fireplace in cooler temperatures. [$] *Average main: $10* ✉ *1920 W. Division St., Wicker Park* ☎ *773/395–9434* 🌐 *www.milkandhoneycafe.com* ⏲ *No dinner* ✥ *3:B4.*

$ VEGETARIAN FAMILY 🍴 **Native Foods Café.** When Wicker Park's veggie-centric Earwax Café closed, vegans and vegetarians decamped to this new California transplant. Even devoted carnivores scarf down the café's satisfying vegan dishes featuring house-made tempeh, seiten, and other faux meats. Don't miss the decadent-tasting desserts, made without refined sugar. Additional locations in Lakeview and the Loop. [$] *Average main: $9* ✉ *1484 N. Milwaukee Ave., Wicker Park* ☎ *773/489–8480* 🌐 *www.nativefoods.com* 💳 *No credit cards* ✥ *3:B3.*

$ PIZZA FAMILY 🍴 **Piece.** The antithesis of Chicago-style deep-dish pizza, Piece's flat pies mimic those made famous in New Haven, Connecticut. The somewhat free-form, eat-off-the-baking-sheet pizzas come in plain (tomato sauce, Parmesan, and garlic), white (olive oil, garlic, and mozzarella), or traditional red, with lots of topping options. Salads like the greens with Gorgonzola and pears are more stylish than expected, and house-brewed beers pair perfectly with the chow. It's good enough that multipierced Wicker Parkers are willing to risk dining alongside local families (with kids in tow) in this former garage space. [$] *Average main: $15* ✉ *1927 W. North Ave., Wicker Park* ☎ *773/772–4422* 🌐 *www.piecechicago.com* ✥ *3:B3.*

$$ BARBECUE FAMILY 🍴 **Smoke Daddy.** A ribs-and-blues emporium in the gentrified though still funky Wicker Park neighborhood, Smoke Daddy serves up tangy barbecued ribs—with generously supplied napkins for swabbing stray sauce. Fans pack the bar and the booths for the chow, which includes richly flavored smoked pulled pork and homemade fries, as well as for the no-cover R&B and jazz bands that play nightly. It's a short walk from the Division Street El stop, making this barbecue spot an ideal point from which to explore the neighborhood's hipster scene. [$] *Average main: $19* ✉ *1804 W. Division St., Wicker Park* ☎ *773/772–6656* 🌐 *www.thesmokedaddy.com* ✥ *3:B4.*

$$ ECLECTIC Fodor'sChoice ★ 🍴 **Trenchermen.** When many people think of "adventurous dining," the first thought usually turns to offal. But this Wicker Park hot spot is full of unusual flavors beyond pork-centric dishes that are bound to be a first for most. Chef Pat Sheerin serves up original dishes with white-tablecloth interpretations like quail with chicken boudin, kale, wild chickpeas, and turnips, and scallops with carrots, crispy pig ear, kaffir lime, apricots, peanuts, and quinoa. The dining room is often booked, but seating in the sleek, antique-inspired bar is first come, first

served. Grab a stool and a drink, and order the pickle tots with red-onion yogurt and chicken bresaola as a dinner primer. [$] *Average main: $25* ✉ *2039 W. North Ave., Wicker Park* ☎ *773/661–1540* 🌐 *www.trenchermen.com* 🕒 *No lunch weekdays.* ✥ *3:B3.*

BUCKTOWN

$$ MODERN AMERICAN Fodor's Choice ★

🍴 **The Bristol.** While Bucktown isn't wanting for dining options, this self-proclaimed "eatery and bar" sets itself apart by focusing intently on the food. Chef Chris Pandel sources local produce and features meat from sustainably raised animals. As a consequence, it isn't rare to find slow-cooked beef brisket on the frequently changing menu. He also offers playful takes on more familiar fare, turning out popular small plates such as braised cabbage, smoked ham, and potato-stuffed pierogi, baked-to-order monkey bread, and the raviolo, a plate-size stuffed pasta filled with ricotta and egg yolk. Make reservations or plan to arrive early; the boisterous dining room gets busy. The upstairs lounge, though, is a pleasant place to wait for a table to free up. [$] *Average main: $25* ✉ *2152 N. Damen Ave., Bucktown* ☎ *773/862–5555* 🌐 *www.thebristolchicago.com* 🕒 *No lunch Mon.–Sat.* ✍ *Reservations essential* ✥ *3:B1.*

$$ AMERICAN

🍴 **Feast.** The cozy fireplace and sofa-filled lounge create a fittingly social, casual setting for the arty Bucktown locals who dine here regularly. If you can't find something to eat here, you're not hungry: hearty, comfort-driven dishes with a sophisticated New American angle offer something for everyone. Standouts include the sweet tea–glazed grilled pork chops, house-smoked pulled chicken sandwiches, and a mac 'n' cheese studded with bacon, roasted tomatoes, and Parmesan. Or snag a table at brunch for breakfast burritos and challah French toast. [$] *Average main: $20* ✉ *1616 N. Damen Ave., Bucktown* ☎ *773/772–7100* 🌐 *www.feastrestaurant.com* ✥ *3:B3.*

$$ BISTRO

🍴 **Le Bouchon.** The French comfort food at this charming-but-cramped bistro in Bucktown is in a league of its own. The onion tart has been a signature dish of owner Jean-Claude Poilevey for years; he also does a succulent sautéed rabbit and a definitive *salade Lyonnaise* (mixed greens topped with bacon croutons and a poached egg). On Tuesday the restaurant serves up a three-course prix-fixe menu for only $30. Save room for the fruit tarts. And don't attempt Le Bouchon on a Saturday night without a reservation. [$] *Average main: $25* ✉ *1958 N. Damen Ave., Bucktown* ☎ *773/862–6600* 🌐 *www.lebouchonofchicago.com* 🕒 *Closed Sun.* ✥ *3:B2.*

$$ AMERICAN Fodor's Choice ★

🍴 **Mindy's Hot Chocolate.** The city's most celebrated pastry chef, Mindy Segal, goes solo at Hot Chocolate, and as you might expect, it's a hit for a really great dessert selection ranging from a creative soufflé tart with salted caramel ice cream and homemade pretzels to warm brioche doughnuts and hot chocolate with homemade marshmallows. How sweet it is—and how busy it is. The savory menu is well crafted, too, with choices such as lobster spaghetti with sambal chilis. [$] *Average main: $23* ✉ *1747 N. Damen Ave., Bucktown* ☎ *773/489–1747* 🌐 *www.hotchocolatechicago.com* 🕒 *Closed Mon. No lunch Tues.* ✥ *3:B3.*

9

LOGAN SQUARE

$ ✕**Belly Shack.** Chef Bill Kim affectionately refers to Belly Shack as his
ECLECTIC   "love story," because the menu fuses his Korean roots and his wife's
Puerto Rican background. Not to be missed are the Belly Dog topped
with egg noodles, pickled green papaya, togarashi-spiced fries, and
the Boricua, a *jibarito* (fried plantain sandwich) with marinated tofu,
hoisin sauce, and brown rice. The space is tight at this casual-yet-hip
BYOB, so it's best to show up early to avoid a wait. $ *Average main:*
$10 ✉ *1912 N. Western Ave., Logan Square* ☎ *773/252–1414* ⊕ *www.*
bellyshack.com ⊘ *Closed Mon.* ⚞ *Reservations not accepted* ✛ *3:A2.*

$$ ✕**Longman & Eagle.** Chef Jared Wentworth adheres to a farm-to-table
MODERN   aesthetic, so the menu at this hip gastropub changes often. Look for
AMERICAN   gamey dishes such as fried goat ravioli, or a wild boar sloppy joe with
crispy sage and pickled jalapeños. Options range from bar snacks and
small plates to substantial entrées, so mix and match as you please—as
long as you chase your meal with one of nearly 150 whiskeys on offer.
Swing around back on weekends to catch the pop-up doughnut shop.
Wine and beer lovers won't go thirsty either; the beer selection is large
and well chosen, and the well-edited wine list leans toward biodynamic
and small-batch producers. $ *Average main: $24* ✉ *2657 N. Kedzie*
Ave., Logan Square ☎ *773/276–7110* ⊕ *www.longmanandeagle.com*
⊟ *No credit cards* ⚞ *Reservations not accepted* ✛ *3:A1.*

$$$ ✕**Lula Café.** Locals worship Lula Café, a neighborhood favorite that's a
MODERN   quick walk from the Logan Square El stop. A bohemian storefront splits
AMERICAN   a spacious café with counter seating and an intimate dining room with
closely set wooden tables and chairs. The food is stellar: expect modern
dishes like roasted duck breast with sunchokes and white truffles, or
rye cavatelli with pumpkin, pancetta, dates, and black walnuts. Menus
are seasonal, change frequently, and champion farm sources; in fact the
restaurant holds prix-fixe farm dinners every Monday. Lula is open for
breakfast and lunch, and diners come from far and wide for brunch,
when hour-long waits are common. $ *Average main: $32* ✉ *2537 N.*
Kedzie Blvd., Logan Square ☎ *773/489–9554* ⊕ *www.lulacafe.com*
⊘ *Closed Tues.* ✛ *3:A1.*

$ ✕**Parson's Chicken and Fish.** The crowd at this casual fried chicken and
AMERICAN   fish shack is decidedly hipster, but even if that's not your scene, the food
is worth the trek to this restaurant on the outskirts of Logan Square.
During the summer, the beer garden is usually packed with folks playing
table tennis, chowing down on baskets of crispy fried Amish chicken
and beer-battered fish sandwiches, and sipping on negroni slushies and
cheap beer. Come winter, the lot turns into an ice-skating rink with a
skate shack the serves up hot toddies and boozy hot chocolates. Linger
among the late-night crowd or take the party on the road with carry-out
food and six-packs of beer. $ *Average main: $15* ✉ *2952 W. Armitage*
Ave., Logan Square ☎ *773/384–3333* ⊕ *www.parsonschickenandfish.*
com ⚞ *Reservations not accepted* ✛ *3:A2.*

$$ ✕**Yusho.** Yes, it's Japanese, but a standard sushi-teriyaki spot this is not.
JAPANESE   Charlie Trotter's veteran Matthias Merges gives diners a cheffed-up
Fodor'sChoice   look at contemporary Japanese cuisine with this hip Avondale yakitori
★   joint. Most dishes are modestly priced and portioned to encourage

sharing, including the Logan Poser ramen with pig tail, fishball, and hen egg, and twice-fried chicken with *matcha* (green tea) and lime, along with plenty of vegetarian-friendly dishes. Score a deal on Sunday with the Sunday Noodles special for $20, which includes a ramen dish, soft-serve ice cream, and beverage. [$] *Average main: $20* ✉ *2853 N. Kedzie Ave., Logan Square* ☎ *773/904–8558* 🌐 *www.yusho-chicago.com* 🕓 *No lunch Mon.–Sat.* ✥ *3:A1.*

LAKEVIEW AND FAR NORTH SIDE

Some of Chicago's best ethnic food is found on the Far North Side, a vast catchall district north of Irving Park Road running all the way to suburban Evanston. Lakeview includes the subdistricts of Wrigleyville (buffering Wrigley Field) and Boystown. Restaurants that cluster around neighborhood hubs, like Lincoln Square and Andersonville, tend to take on similar characteristics—they're approachable, but also unique. Ethnic hole-in-the-wall restaurants such as German beer bars Chicago Brauhaus and Huettenbar share the same strip as romantic enclaves such as Bistro Campagne, so that every picky diner can find something to satisfy his or her craving. Both are pedestrian-friendly; Lincoln Square lies on the Brown Line El, though Andersonville is better reached via cab.

LAKEVIEW

$ SCANDINAVIAN FAMILY 🍴 **Ann Sather.** This Scandinavian mini-chain, open since 1945, is a Chicago institution for good reason: the aroma of fresh cinnamon rolls, Swedish pancakes with lingonberries, and waffles put this place on the map. It still draws a mob—at this location and at the handful of other spots on the city's North Side—where hungry diners line up along the block for weekend breakfasts. Sure, you can order a familiar brunch dish like eggs Benedict, but why not try the stellar potato pancakes with applesauce instead? There are a handful of Scandinavian specialties at lunch, as well as standard café sandwiches and salads. [$] *Average main: $10* ✉ *909 W. Belmont Ave., Lakeview* ☎ *773/348–2378* 🌐 *www.annsather.com* 🕓 *No dinner* ✍ *Reservations not accepted* ✥ *2:F4.*

$ BURGER FAMILY 🍴 **DMK Burger Bar.** Chef-owner Michael Kornick knows fine dining, but he is also a longtime fan of the simple burger. The two worlds commingle at DMK Burger Bar, where patties from grass-fed beef come topped with green chilis or caramelized onions and chipotle ketchup, and fries are adorned with truffle aioli. Yet the place is anything but fussy: the burgers, which are $9.50 each, are listed on the menu by number, and any of them can be made into a turkey burger on request. (There are also lamb and veggie options.) Diners used to thick burgers should consider ordering a double, since the patties here are purposely on the flat side. Come during the week to avoid the hour-long weekend waits, or be prepared to spend some time with a locally brewed beer at the bar. [$] *Average main: $10* ✉ *2954 N. Sheffield Ave., Lakeview* ☎ *773/360–8686* 🌐 *www.dmkburgerbar.com* ✍ *Reservations not accepted* ✥ *2:F5.*

$ CAFÉ FAMILY 🍴 **Julius Meinl Café.** Viennese coffee roaster Julius Meinl operates this very European café in an unexpected location at the intersection of Addison and Southport, just a few blocks from Wrigley Field. Comfortable

9

banquettes and a supply of international newspapers entice coffee sippers to stick around, and vegetable focaccia and pear-and-Brie sandwiches, hazelnut-and-blue-cheese salads, *Frittaten* (Austrian beef broth with crepe noodles), and loads of European pastries feed the peckish. The Austrian breakfast of soft-boiled egg, ham, and Emmentaler cheese is a gem. Classical and jazz combos entertain on Friday and Saturday. [$] *Average main: $8* ✉ *3601 N. Southport Ave., Lakeview* ☎ *773/868–1857* 🌐 *www.meinl.net* ✥ *2:D3.*

$ AMERICAN FAMILY 🍴 **Kitsch'n on Roscoe.** If you love all things '70s, you'll love Kitsch'n as much as the regulars. It's a diner in retro garb, with lava lamps and vintage appliances that have been turned into table lamps. The menu is full of fun options like pesto-dyed "green eggs and ham" and Twinkies tiramisu, but there are also straight shooters like a hefty tuna melt or chicken and waffles. Weekends are jammed; midweek is better for relaxing. [$] *Average main: $11* ✉ *2005 W. Roscoe St., Lakeview* ☎ *773/248–7372* 🌐 *www.kitschn.com* 🕒 *No dinner. Closed Wed.* ✥ *2:B4.*

$ ITALIAN 🍴 **Mia Francesca.** Moderate prices and a smart, urbane style drive ceaseless crowds to this Lakeview storefront. Enlightened Italian dishes like classic bruschetta, *quattro formaggi* (four-cheese) pizza, artichoke and prosciutto pasta, and roast chicken are made with fresh ingredients and avoid stereotypical heaviness. The limited meat options keep the menu prices low. While you wait for one of the small, tightly spaced tables—and you *will* wait—you can have a drink at the bar. There are more than 20 other Francesca's locations around town, including Francesca's Forno in Wicker Park, Francesca's on Taylor in Little Italy, and Francesca's on Chestnut in the Gold Coast. [$] *Average main: $15* ✉ *3311 N. Clark St., Lakeview* ☎ *773/281–3310* 🌐 *www.miafrancesca.com* 🕒 *No lunch weekdays* ✥ *2:F4.*

$$ TURKISH 🍴 **Turquoise Restaurant and Café.** This bustling Turkish-owned café attempts to please every palate with a mixed menu of Continental and Turkish foods, but it's the latter that star here. Don't-miss items include lamb *begendi* (braised lamb shoulder with cherry tomatoes, red bell peppers, and eggplant), *sogurme* (a smoked eggplant, yogurt, and walnut dip) , and homemade *lahmacun* (flatbread topped with ground beef). Vested waiters, white tablecloths, and wood-trimmed surroundings outclass the neighborhood lot. [$] *Average main: $20* ✉ *2147 W. Roscoe St., Lakeview* ☎ *773/549–3523* 🌐 *www.turquoisedining.com* ✥ *2:B4.*

$$ ASIAN 🍴 **Yoshi's Café.** Decades ago Yoshi's was launched as a pricey fine-dining restaurant in the Lakeview neighborhood. We offer this history lesson to say that while the atmosphere went jeans-casual and the prices became more reasonable, the cooking quality remained, and remains, high. Yoshi Katsumura turns out informal French-Asian cuisine, like duck breast with black currant sauce or roasted Japanese pumpkin filled with tofu (it's good enough to convert a carnivore). Sunday brunch includes the expected eggs along with a Japanese-inspired breakfast (fish, miso soup, vegetables, and steamed rice). [$] *Average main: $19* ✉ *3257 N. Halsted St., Lakeview* ☎ *773/248–6160* 🌐 *www.yoshiscafe.com* 🕒 *Closed Mon. No lunch Tues.–Thurs. and Sun.* ✥ *2:F4.*

FAR NORTH SIDE

$$$$ THAI 🍴 **Arun's.** One of the finest Thai restaurants in Chicago—some say in the country—is also one of the most expensive, featuring only seven-course tasting menus for a flat $65. The kitchen artfully composes four appetizers, two entrées, and one dessert nightly, using the freshest ingredients. Results might include shrimp-filled golden pastry baskets, rice noodles in an aromatic coconut-tamarind sauce, and seared sea scallops in a kabocha-chili sauce. Arun's out-of-the-way location in a residential neighborhood on the Northwest Side doesn't discourage a strong following among locals and visiting foodies. [$] *Average main: $85* ✉ *4156 N. Kedzie Ave., Irving Park* ☎ *773/539–1909* 🌐 *www.arunsthai.com* 🕒 *Closed Mon. No lunch* ✍ *Reservations essential* ✥ *2:A1.*

$$ SOUTHERN 🍴 **Big Jones.** Even if you weren't raised by a Southern grandmother, the heirloom cooking at this Andersonville restaurant will make you feel right at home. A parlor-like backdrop sets the scene for chef-owner Paul Fehribach's contemporary American takes on classic Southern dishes. The menu revives century-old recipes scrupulously sourced from historical cookbooks from New Orleans to Appalachia and re-creates them with high-quality, sustainable ingredients. Brunch is particularly special here, served with complimentary beignets for an extra touch of Southern hospitality. [$] *Average main: $20* ✉ *5347 N. Clark St., Far North Side* ☎ *773/275–5725* 🌐 *www.bigjoneschicago.com* ✥ *2:D1.*

$$ FRENCH 🍴 **Bistro Campagne.** If you're looking for rustic French fare on the North Side, this is the place to come: crispy roast chicken with mushroom ragout, steak piled with frites, goat cheese salad, and ale-steamed mussels are top-notch, while the lovely, wood-trimmed Arts and Crafts interior is the perfect complement to a relaxing meal. In warmer weather, ask for a table in the torch-lighted garden. Prices are reasonable, including those for the French-centric wine list. [$] *Average main: $25* ✉ *4518 N. Lincoln Ave., Lincoln Square* ☎ *773/271–6100* 🌐 *www.bistrocampagne.com* 🕒 *No lunch Mon.–Sat.* ✥ *2:B1.*

$ CAFÉ 🍴 **Café Selmarie.** For a light meal in Lincoln Square, line up at this bakery-turned-café, a long-standing favorite among locals—especially during warmer months, when the outdoor patio beckons. Breakfast means brioche French toast and vegetarian breakfast sandwiches; lunch ranges from goat cheese salads to turkey-and-Brie sandwiches; and dinner runs to pan-seared salmon and herb-roasted chicken. Don't miss the fabulous pastries (you can also buy them to go at the front counter). Pass summer waits pleasantly in the neighboring plaza; other seasons, you're out in the cold. [$] *Average main: $16* ✉ *4729 N. Lincoln Ave., Lincoln Square* ☎ *773/989–5595* 🌐 *www.cafeselmarie.com* 🕒 *No breakfast or dinner Mon.* ✥ *2:B1.*

$ GERMAN FAMILY 🍴 **Chicago Brauhaus.** The German immigrants who settled in Lincoln Square have mostly moved on, but they left behind the Brauhaus, an Oktoberfest of a restaurant featuring a live band playing nightly polkas and waltzes that bring old-timers and new converts to the dance floor. Though the atmosphere is the draw over the food, you can't go wrong with the bratwurst and sauerkraut or the schnitzel. Large tables add to the convivial atmosphere: you may make some new friends. As expected, there is a good selection of German beer. [$] *Average main: $17* ✉ *4732 N. Lincoln Ave., Lincoln Square* ☎ *773/784–4444* 🌐 *www.chicagobrauhaus.com* 🕒 *Closed Tues.* ✥ *2:B1.*

$$ AMERICAN Fodor's Choice ★ 🍴 **Gather.** Class meets comfort in this upscale neighborhood eatery. The service is top-notch and everything on your plate is made in-house from scratch—right down to the fresh breads and condiments—at prices that feel like a steal. The seasonally driven menu features farm-fresh ingredients applied to inventive riffs on classic dishes like diver scallops with sunflower risotto and bacon-sage gremolata, and egg raviolo with ricotta, sweet jalapeños, house-cured pancetta, and white truffle butter. Score a deal on Sunday nights with the three-course family-style dinner for $26. [$] *Average main: $20* ✉ *4539 N. Lincoln Ave., Lincoln Square* ☎ *773/506–9300* 🌐 *www.gatherchicago.com* ⏲ *No lunch Mon.–Sat.* ✣ *2:B1.*

$$ AMERICAN Fodor's Choice ★ 🍴 **Hopleaf.** When hops devotee Michael Roper added a dining room onto the back of his beloved tavern, swillers were thrilled with the opportunity to sop their suds with delectable specialties such as Belgian-style mussels steamed in white ale with herbs, Montreal-style brisket (it's slow roasted and briefly smoked, and less sweet than New York–style brisket), and porter-braised beef cheek stew. Even with the expansion of a second full dining room and upstairs space, it's still best to arrive early to avoid waiting in the bar for a table. But don't bring the kids; Roper insists that only those of legal drinking age can eat here. [$] *Average main: $25* ✉ *5148 N. Clark St., Far North Side* ☎ *773/334–9851* 🌐 *www.hopleaf.com* ✍ *Reservations not accepted* ✣ *2:D1.*

$ BARBECUE FAMILY 🍴 **Smoque BBQ.** The sweet smoky aroma wafting out of this casual barbecue spot always attracts a crowd, and while the line to order at the counter extends out the door on weekends, it moves quickly. If you can't make up your mind between brisket or shredded pork shoulder (both are tender and cooked for about 14 hours), order the half-and-half—a sandwich with half of each. Or try a slab of ribs. Sides of vinegar-spiked slaw, rich baked beans, and corn bread round out the meal, and kids love the creamy mac and cheese. Smoque is BYOB, so pick up a beer or two before arriving if desired. [$] *Average main: $14* ✉ *3800 N. Pulaski Rd., Irving Park* ☎ *773/545–7427* 🌐 *www.smoquebbq.com* ⏲ *Closed Mon.* ✍ *Reservations not accepted* ✣ *2:A2.*

$ PIZZA FAMILY Fodor's Choice ★ 🍴 **Spacca Napoli Pizzeria.** Despite Chicago's renown for deep-dish pizza, locals are swept away by the thin-crust Neapolitan pies at this bright Ravenswood gem. Finely ground Italian flour, imported buffalo mozzarella, hand-stretched dough, and a brick, wood-fired oven built by Italian craftsmen are credited for producing the bubbling, chewy crusts of these pies, which diners eat with a fork. Antipasti, a well-priced Italian wine and beer selection, and desserts like tiramisu round out the menu. The proprietors shun takeout and turn up the lights a little too high, but the food wins out, accounting for out-the-door waits, even on weekdays. In summer, angle for a table on the large pleasant sidewalk patio. [$] *Average main: $16* ✉ *1769 W. Sunnyside Ave., Ravenswood* ☎ *773/878–2420* 🌐 *www.spaccanapolipizzeria.com* ⏲ *Closed Mon.* ✣ *2:C1.*

$ SCANDINAVIAN FAMILY 🍴 **Svea.** The North Side's Andersonville neighborhood, once a haven for Swedes, plays host to the humble Svea, a Swedish version of an American diner. There are Swedish pancakes with lingonberries and Swedish rye *limpa* bread with eggs in the morning; lunch means Swedish meatballs and open-face sandwiches. The digs are no-frills, but the service is almost unvariably friendly. The locals love it. $ *Average main: $10* ⊠ *5236 N. Clark St., Andersonville* ☎ *773/275–7738* ⊗ *No dinner* ✛ *2:D1.*

PILSEN, LITTLE ITALY, AND CHINATOWN

If there ever were a need to convince someone of Chicago's culinary diversity, a progressive dinner through Chinatown, Little Italy, and Pilsen would be the way to go. Pilsen, Chicago's vibrant Mexican neighborhood; Chinatown, a confluence of tea shops, dim-sum spots, and hardware stores; and Little Italy, which runs through Chicago's medical district, make for a fun day's adventure that's off the beaten tourist path. Expect to eat cheaply and well in both Pilsen and Chinatown. And although Little Italy is no longer a truly living and breathing Italian neighborhood, the main drag, Taylor Street, makes for pleasant strolling and casual grazing (and stay tuned for new Italian restaurants on their way).

PILSEN

$$
ECLECTIC
✕ **Dusek's.** Pilsen is primarily known for its Mexican food, but more recently the neighborhood has been attracting high-end names, including this next-level concept from the folks at Longman & Eagle. Chef Jared Wentworth's brand of innovative cuisine breaks all the rules with dishes like General Tso's sweetbreads with charred shishito peppers, a Moroccan spiced vegetable tagine, and octopus confit with black-olive risotto. Craft beer fans will feel right at home with the 24 drafts pouring specialty suds from all over the world. Make an evening of it by heading upstairs to the music venue at Thalia Hall or downstairs to the basement cocktail bar, Punch House. $ *Average main: $21* ⊠ *1227 W. 18th St., Pilsen* ☎ *312/526–3851* ⊕ *www.dusekschicago.com* ⊗ *No lunch weekdays* ✛ *4:C5.*

$$
BARBECUE
✕ **Honky Tonk Barbeque.** The twang of country meets the tang of barbecue sauce at this Pilsen spot known for award-winning barbecue. There's definitely plenty of meat on the menu—from ribs and brisket to whole-smoked chicken—but the tender pulled pork might be the standout; try it first with a dab of regular sauce, then try the spicy. Setting the scene for the down-home meal are dining rooms decked out in vintage Americana (including a pink fridge) accompanied by live honky-tonk music on weekends and the occasional weekday evening. As for the address, it's easy to spot the restaurant: look for the flames painted alongside the entrance. $ *Average main: $20* ⊠ *1800 S. Racine Ave., Pilsen* ☎ *312/226–7427* ⊕ *www.honkytonkbbqchicago.com* ⊗ *Closed Mon.* ⚐ *Reservations not accepted* ✛ *4:C5.*

$$
MODERN
AMERICAN
✕ **Nightwood.** It's almost as if a piece of Brooklyn touched down here on the southern border of the Pilsen neighborhood. Everyone who works here appears to double as an artist or musician, which seems appropriate given the artful, understated dishes. Like its sister restaurant, Lula Café in Logan Square, local and seasonal rule the menu. There is usually at least one spit-roasted entrée, perhaps chicken, pork loin, or duck leg, along with a vegetarian main and a fish option, as well as house-made

pastas, and appetizers that make use of the freshest produce. You can see the open kitchen from the bar, but to be close to the flames, snag a seat next to the fireplace on the enclosed patio, complete with a living wall. Nightwood draws a crowd at brunch, and the butterscotch-bacon doughnut is unforgettable. $ *Average main: $26* ✉ *2119 S. Halsted St., Pilsen* 🕾 *312/526–3385* ⊕ *www.nightwoodrestaurant.com* ☾ *No lunch Mon.–Sat. No dinner Sun.* ✛ *4:D6.*

$ ✕ **Nuevo León.** Fill up on the exotic (tripe soup) or the familiar (tacos)
MEXICAN at this bustling, family-run restaurant in the heart of Pilsen, Chicago's Mexican neighborhood. Big tables are often filled with large groups, lending a fiesta feel to the scene. Fans love the authentic food, including *chilaquiles* (tortillas with salsa and scrambled eggs) for breakfast and dinners of shrimp fajitas, chiles rellenos, and *barbacoa* (braised beef served with refried beans). Brush up your Spanglish; not all servers are fluent in English, though all are welcoming to newcomers. To wash it all down, order a tall glass of *horchata*, a milky, cinnamon-flecked rice beverage, or bring a couple of beers; Nuevo León is cash-only and BYOB. $ *Average main: $12* ✉ *1515 W. 18th St., Pilsen* 🕾 *312/421–1517* ⊕ *www.nuevoleonrestaurant.com* ▭ *No credit cards* ⌚ *Reservations not accepted* ✛ *4:B5.*

LITTLE ITALY

$$ ✕ **Chez Joël Bistro Français.** Unlike the rest of Taylor Street, which is pre-
FRENCH dominantly Italian in allegiance, Chez Joël waves the flag for France. The sunny, cozy bistro, run by brothers Joël and Amed Kazouini, serves well-prepared classics like steak frites, coq au vin, escargots, and bouillabaisse. It's a favorite with the locals thanks to its authentic bistro feel. There is a full bar and a reasonably priced wine list favoring French and Californian selections. On a warm Chicago day, ask for a seat outside on the patio. $ *Average main: $25* ✉ *1119 W. Taylor St., Little Italy* 🕾 *312/226–6479* ⊕ *www.chezjoelbistro.com* ☾ *Closed Mon. No lunch Sun.* ✛ *4:C3.*

$ ✕ **Pompei Little Italy.** Cheap, cheerful, and fast—what's not to love about
PIZZA Pompei? Little Italy's only casual café with a strong kitchen specializes
FAMILY in square slices of pizza, each under $4, with toppings ranging from shredded onions and sausage to basil and tomato. One to two easily makes a meal. Between the University of Illinois Chicago students and the Rush University Medical Center workers, Pompei is jammed at lunch. If you can tolerate the self-serve system at dinner, the evening hours are more relaxing. If pizza's not your thing, salad, generous sandwiches, and handmade pastas are also on the menu. And keep your eye out for Pompei's Near North and Lakeview locations. $ *Average main: $10* ✉ *1531 W. Taylor St., Little Italy* 🕾 *312/421–5179* ⊕ *www. pompeiusa.com* ✛ *4:B4.*

$ ✕ **Sweet Maple Café.** On a Sunday morning, this breakfast-all-day spot is
AMERICAN easy to find on Taylor Street: just look for the line out the door. In fact,
FAMILY expect a line on most days as customers ranging from students to police officers and politicians wait for a table in anticipation of warm, buttery biscuits and a side of generous hospitality. Laurene Hynson's menu has something for everyone: buttermilk pancakes and hefty omelets for those who prefer American classics, as well as dishes such as the Dias

y Noches Scramble—eggs cooked with grilled chicken and jalapeños and served with a side of freshly made salsa. Not to be overlooked are the home fries, which come in any combination of peppers, cheese, and bacon. For non-breakfast eaters, well-executed salads and soups are available after 11:30 on weekdays. $ *Average main: $10* ✉ *1339 W. Taylor St., Little Italy* ☎ *312/243–8908* ⊕ *www.sweetmaplecafe.com* ☽ *No dinner* 🗇 *Reservations not accepted* ✛ *4:B4.*

$ ✕ **Three Aces.** The rustic menu here, heavy on pasta and pizza, fits nicely
MODERN ITALIAN among the Little Italy neighbors, but the grittier rock and roll vibe and free-flowing craft beer makes Three Aces stand out among the other classic mom-and-pop restaurants. Expect less eggplant Parm and more farmhouse Italian: there's short-rib pizza with garlic cream and confit mushrooms, and pappardelle with seasoned mascarpone, mint, and Parmesan. Don't pass up the spicy Bolognese fries, an Italian take on Canadian poutine featuring sauced-slathered fries with Parmesan. $ *Average main: $15* ✉ *1321 W. Taylor St., Little Italy* ☎ *312/243–1577* ⊕ *www. threeaceschicago.com* ✛ *4:C4.*

CHINATOWN

$ ✕ **Emperor's Choice.** This sophisticated restaurant sets out to prove that
CHINESE Chinese specialties can get beyond deep-fried prawns and Kung Pao chicken, and it succeeds with strong seafood offerings, such as baked clams, Peking-style lobster, or Dungeness crab, fried and served whole, and seasoned with salt. There is also a separate menu of "delicacies," which includes items like shark's fin soup and pork belly. Diners come for the good food, decent prices, and friendly service—not for the atmosphere, which is cramped and bustling. $ *Average main: $10* ✉ *2238 S. Wentworth Ave., Chinatown* ☎ *312/225–8800* ⊕ *www.emperorschoice chicago.com* ✛ *4:F6.*

$$$ ✕ **Han 202.** Tasting menus tend to come with sky-high prices, but that's
CHINESE not the case at this BYOB spot in Chicago's Bridgeport neighborhood, just south of Chinatown. For $35 you get four courses, which can progress from lobster tail with beetroot and honey mustard dressing to Shanghai dumplings, sweet walnut shrimp, and spicy Sichuan duck breast, ending with a small sweet bite, like crème brûlée. While portions aren't overwhelming, they are satisfying. Compared with the low-key entrance, the dining room is sleeker—and more comfortable—than you'd expect, making the southward trek all the more worthwhile. $ *Average main: $35* ✉ *605 W. 31st St., Chinatown* ☎ *312/949–1314* ⊕ *www.han202.com* ☽ *No lunch* ✛ *4:F6.*

$ ✕ **Lao Sze Chuan.** If you're looking for spicy, filling food and great prices
CHINESE in Chinatown, check out this Szechuan kitchen from Tony Hu, the neighborhood's most prolific restaurateur. Chilis, garlic, and ginger seem to go into every dish, whether it's chicken, green beans, eggplant, or dumplings. The digs are nothing to write home about, but you'll feel smug for choosing it once the feast is finished and you're sipping your tea with a happy tummy. $ *Average main: $14* ✉ *2172 S. Archer Ave., Chinatown* ☎ *312/326–5040* ⊕ *www.chicagolaoszechuan.com* ✛ *4:F6.*

$ ✕ **Phoenix Restaurant.** This bustling dim-sum house can feel overwhelm-
CHINESE ing with the hordes of diners who flock here on weekends, and service can be brusque, but even so, it delivers. First Phoenix softens you up

9

with second-floor picture-window views that frame the Loop skyline. Then, just when you're most vulnerable, it develops the food punch—and it's a pretty good one, too. The dim sum, dispensed from rolling carts all day long on weekends, is a big draw; don't miss the barbecue pork buns (*char siu bao*) or the shrimp dumplings (*shumai*). Arrive before noon on weekends or stew as you wait—and wait. [$] *Average main: $15* ✉ *2131 S. Archer Ave., Chinatown* ☎ *312/328–0848* 🌐 *www.phoenixchinatownchicago.com* ⊕ *4:F6.*

HYDE PARK

A 20-minute drive from downtown is historic Hyde Park, one of the city's most self-contained enclaves, and where residents are steadfastly loyal to their local businesses. Restaurants in intellectual Hyde Park have a welcoming "come as you are" air about them that's a pleasant surprise for a neighborhood that houses a top-tier university and the country's highest-profile couple. Perhaps the area's proximity to downtown has made flashy eateries and big-name chefs unnecessary. It might be for the best, since visitors tend to feel comfortable in any restaurant, regardless of how much foodie cred they bring to the table. In the compact heart of the area, expect to find a little of everything, from Thai eats to pizza spots, bakeries, and coffee shops.

$$ EUROPEAN

🍴 **A10.** Hyde Park is experiencing a bit of a culinary renaissance thanks to a few new faces in the crowd. Take chef-owner Matthias Merges, who does a 180 from his Japanese-centric menu at Logan Square restaurant Yusho with this hip Alpine concept in Hyde Park. Expect contemporary American interpretations of cuisines from France, Italy, and Germany in dishes like smoked-cheddar bratwurst with broccoli spaetzle, house-made lobster orecchiette with gruyere and garlic, and Roman-style pizza topped with Genoa salami and pepperoncini. Tipples are just as innovative here as they are at sister Logan Square cocktail bar, Billy Sunday. [$] *Average main: $20* ✉ *1462 E. 53rd St., Hyde Park* ☎ *773/288–1010* 🌐 *a10hydepark.com* 🕒 *No lunch Mon.–Sat.* ⊕ *4:H5.*

$$ ASIAN FAMILY

🍴 **Chant.** Asian-cuisine purists might raise their eyebrows at dishes such as Peking duck tacos or Thai hummus, but Chant's Asian-inspired global cuisine has plenty of fans. Those who crave familiar Thai takeout can order the pleasantly chewy wide-egg noodle *pad see ew* while nonmeat eaters appreciate the broad selection available (several dishes, even the pad Thai, can be prepared vegan). There's even a kids' menu. A full bar, with cocktails, wine, and several bottled Asian beers, distinguishes this pan-Asian eatery from restaurants with similar menus, making it a hangout on weekend nights and at Sunday brunch when live music draws a crowd ready to groove. [$] *Average main: $20* ✉ *1509 E. 53rd St., Hyde Park* ☎ *773/324–1999* 🌐 *www.chantchicago.com* ⊕ *4:H5.*

CHICAGO DINING MAP ATLAS

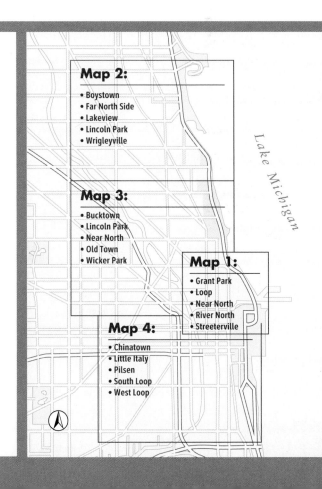

Map 2:
- Boystown
- Far North Side
- Lakeview
- Lincoln Park
- Wrigleyville

Map 3:
- Bucktown
- Lincoln Park
- Near North
- Old Town
- Wicker Park

Map 1:
- Grant Park
- Loop
- Near North
- River North
- Streeterville

Map 4:
- Chinatown
- Little Italy
- Pilsen
- South Loop
- West Loop

Lake Michigan

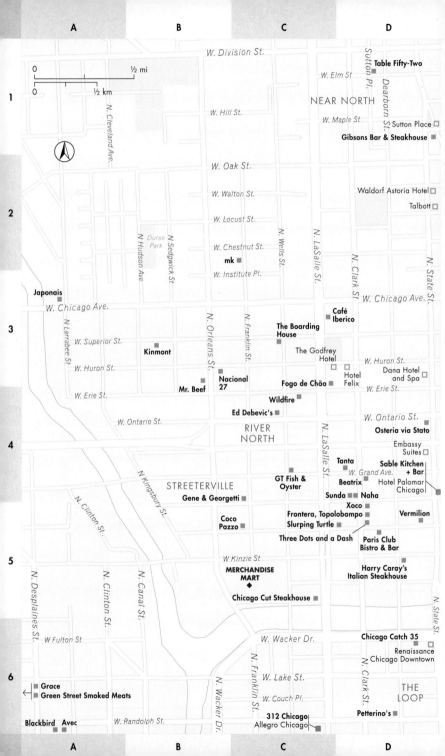

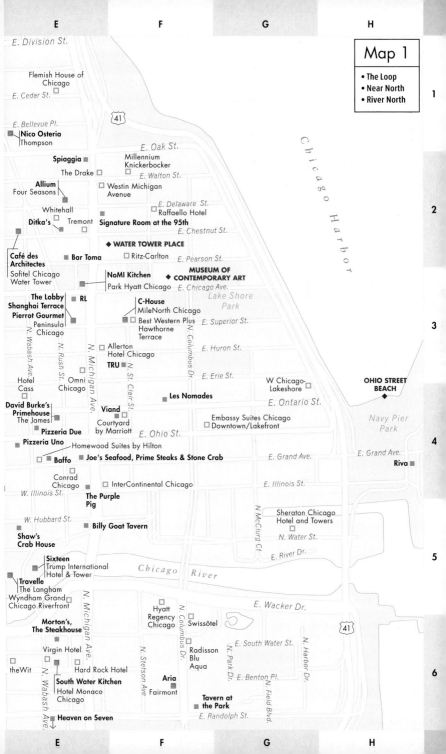

Map 1

- The Loop
- Near North
- River North

E

E. Division St.

Flemish House of Chicago

E. Cedar St.

E. Bellevue Pl.

〔41〕

Nico Osteria
Thompson

Spiaggia
The Drake

Allium
Four Seasons

Whitehall

Ditka's Tremont

Café des
Architectes

Sofitel Chicago
Water Tower

The Lobby
Shanghai Terrace
Pierrot Gourmet

Peninsula
Chicago

N. Wabash Ave.

N. Rush St.

RL

Hotel
Cass

Omni
Chicago

David Burke's
Primehouse
The James

Pizzeria Due

Pizzeria Uno

Baffo

Conrad
Chicago

W. Illinois St.

W. Hubbard St.

Shaw's
Crab House

Sixteen
Trump International
Hotel & Tower

Travelle
The Langham
Wyndham Grand
Chicago Riverfront

Morton's,
The Steakhouse

Virgin Hotel

theWit

Hard Rock Hotel

South Water Kitchen
Hotel Monaco
Chicago

Heaven on Seven

N. Wabash Ave.

F

Millennium
Knickerbocker

E. Oak St.

E. Walton St.

Westin Michigan
Avenue

E. Delaware St.
Raffaello Hotel

Signature Room at the 95th

E. Chestnut St.

◆ WATER TOWER PLACE

Bar Toma Ritz-Carlton E. Pearson St.

NoMI Kitchen ◆ CONTEMPORARY ART

Park Hyatt Chicago E. Chicago Ave.

C-House
MileNorth Chicago
Best Western Plus
Hawthorne
Terrace

N. Michigan Ave.

Allerton
Hotel Chicago

TRU

N. St. Clair St.

Les Nomades

Viand

Courtyard
by Marriott

E. Ohio St.

Homewood Suites by Hilton

Joe's Seafood, Prime Steaks & Stone Crab

InterContinental Chicago

The Purple
Pig

Billy Goat Tavern

Chicago

N. Michigan Ave.

Hyatt
Regency
Chicago

N. Columbus Dr.

Swissôtel

N. Stetson Ave.

Radisson
Blu
Aqua

Aria
Fairmont

Tavern at
the Park

E. Randolph St.

G

MUSEUM OF

E. Superior St.

E. Huron St.

E. Erie St.

W Chicago-
Lakeshore

E. Ontario St.

Embassy Suites Chicago
Downtown/Lakefront

E. Grand Ave.

E. Illinois St.

N. McClurg Ct.

Sheraton Chicago
Hotel and Towers

N. Water St.

E. River Dr.

River

E. Wacker Dr.

E. South Water St.

N. Park Dr.

E. Benton Pl.

N. Field Blvd.

〔41〕

H

Chicago Harbor

1

2

Lake Shore
Park

3

OHIO STREET
BEACH ◆

Navy Pier
Park

E. Grand Ave.

Riva

4

5

N. Harbor Dr.

6

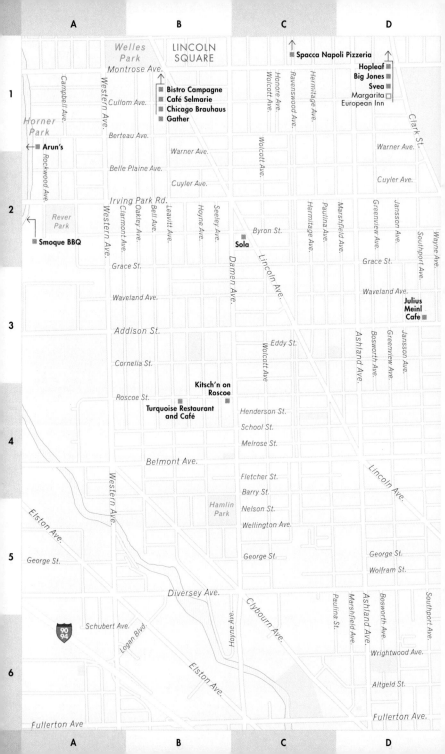

A

Welles Park

Campbell Ave.

Horner Park

Western Ave.

Rockwood Ave.

Cullom Ave.

Berteau Ave.

Belle Plaine Ave.

← ■ Arun's

Rever Park

■ Smoque BBQ

Western Ave.

Clarmont Ave.

Oakley Ave.

Grace St.

Waveland Ave.

Addison St.

Cornelia St.

Roscoe St.

Elston Ave.

Western Ave.

George St.

Schubert Ave.

90 94

Logan Blvd.

Fullerton Ave

B

LINCOLN SQUARE

Montrose Ave.

↑ ■ Spacca Napoli Pizzeria

■ Bistro Campagne
■ Café Selmarie
■ Chicago Brauhaus
■ Gather

Warner Ave.

Cuyler Ave.

Irving Park Rd.

Bell Ave.

Leavitt Ave.

Hoyne Ave.

Seeley Ave.

Damen Ave.

Byron St.

■ Sola

Eddy St.

Kitsch'n on Roscoe

Turquoise Restaurant and Café

Henderson St.

School St.

Melrose St.

Belmont Ave.

Fletcher St.

Barry St.

Hamlin Park   Nelson St.

Wellington Ave.

George St.

Diversey Ave.

Hoyne Ave.

Clybourn Ave.

Elston Ave.

C

Wolcott Ave.

Honore Ave.

Ravenswood Ave.

Hermitage Ave.

Wolcott Ave.

Lincoln Ave.

Hermitage Ave.

Paulina Ave.

Marshfield Ave.

Wolcott Ave.

Ashland Ave.

Paulina St.

Marshfield Ave.

Ashland Ave.

D

Hopleaf ■
Big Jones ■
Svea ■
Margarita □
European Inn

Clark St.

Warner Ave.

Cuyler Ave.

Greenview Ave.

Jansson Ave.

Southport Ave.

Wayne Ave.

Grace St.

Waveland Ave.

Julius Meinl Cafe ■

Bosworth Ave.

Greenview Ave.

Jansson Ave.

Lincoln Ave.

George St.

Wolfram St.

Bosworth Ave.

Southport Ave.

Wrightwood Ave.

Altgeld St.

Fullerton Ave.

1
2
3
4
5
6

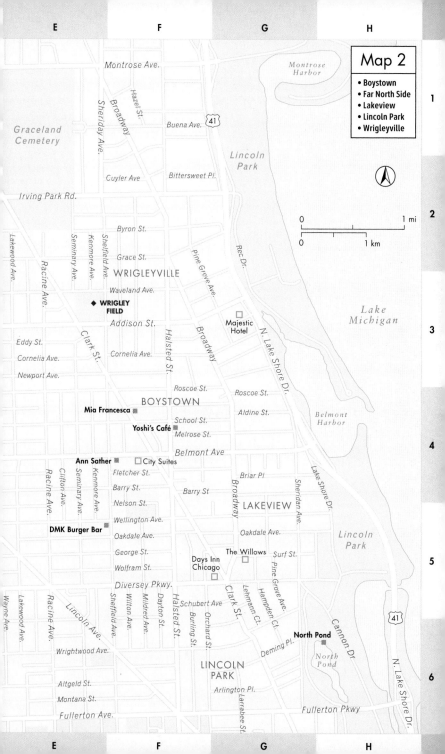

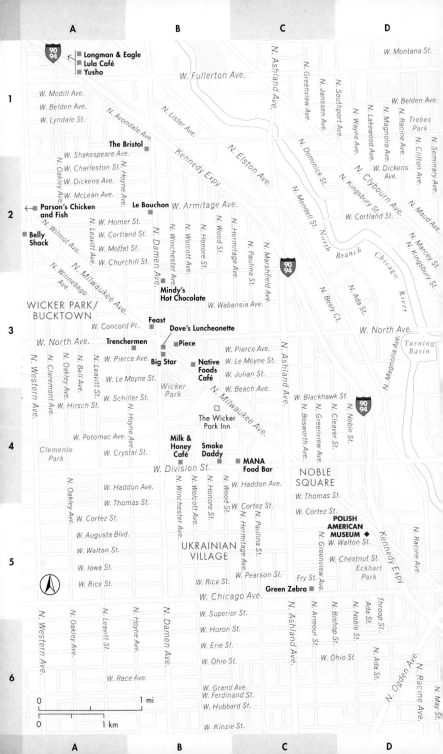

A

90 94
← ■ Longman & Eagle
■ Lula Café
■ Yusho

W. Montana St.

W. Fullerton Ave.

W. Belden Ave.

Trebes Park

1
W. Medill Ave.
W. Belden Ave.
W. Lyndale St.

N. Avondale Ave.
N. Lister Ave.
N. Elston Ave.

W. Dickens Ave.

W. Shakespeare Ave.
■ The Bristol
N. Hoyne Ave.
W. Charleston St.
W. Dickens Ave.
W. McLean Ave.

Kennedy Expy.

W. Armitage Ave.
■ Le Bouchon

2
←■ Parson's Chicken and Fish
N. Leavitt Ave.
W. Homer St.
W. Cortland St.
W. Moffat St.
W. Churchill St.
N. Winchester Ave.
N. Wolcott Ave.
N. Honore St.
N. Wood St.
N. Hermitage Ave.
N. Paulina St.
N. Marshfield Ave.

W. Cortland St.

North Branch Chicago River

■ Belly Shack
N. Wilmot Ave.
N. Milwaukee Ave.
N. Winnebago Ave.
N. Damen Ave.

■ Mindy's Hot Chocolate
W. Wabansia Ave.

WICKER PARK/ BUCKTOWN

W. North Ave.

Turning Basin

3
■ Feast
W. Concord Pl.
Dove's Luncheonette
W. North Ave.
■ Trenchermen ■ Piece
W. Pierce Ave.
W. Pierce Ave.
N. Western Ave.
N. Claremont Ave.
N. Oakley Ave.
N. Bell Ave.
N. Leavitt St.
■ Big Star ■ Native Foods Café
W. Le Moyne St.
W. Julian St.
W. Le Moyne St.
W. Schiller St.
Wicker Park
W. Beach Ave.
W. Hirsch St.
N. Hoyne Ave.
N. Milwaukee Ave.

W. Blackhawk St.

N. Ashland Ave.

90 94

The Wicker Park Inn

4
Clemente Park
W. Potomac Ave.
Milk & Honey Café
Smoke Daddy
W. Crystal St.
W. Division St.
■ MANA Food Bar
N. Oakley Ave.
W. Haddon Ave.
W. Thomas St.
W. Cortez St.
N. Winchester Ave.
N. Wolcott Ave.
N. Honore St.
N. Wood St.
W. Haddon Ave.
W. Cortez St.
N. Hermitage Ave.
N. Paulina St.

NOBLE SQUARE
W. Thomas St.
W. Cortez St.

POLISH AMERICAN MUSEUM ◆

5
W. Augusta Blvd.
W. Walton St.
W. Iowa St.
UKRAINIAN VILLAGE
W. Walton St.
W. Chestnut St.
Eckhart Park
N. Greenview Ave.
Fry St.
W. Rice St.
W. Rice St.
W. Pearson St.
W. Chicago Ave.
Green Zebra ■
N. Ashland Ave.
N. Armour St.
N. Bishop St.
N. Noble St.
Ada St.
N. Throop St.
Kennedy Expy.
N. Racine Ave.

W. Superior St.
W. Huron St.
W. Erie St.
W. Ohio St.

W. Ohio St.

6
N. Western Ave.
N. Oakley Ave.
N. Leavitt St.
N. Hoyne Ave.
W. Race Ave.
N. Damen Ave.

W. Grand Ave.
W. Ferdinand St.
W. Hubbard St.

N. Ogden Ave.
N. May St.
N. Racine Ave.

W. Kinzie St.

0 _____ 1 mi
0 _____ 1 km

A   **B**   **C**   **D**

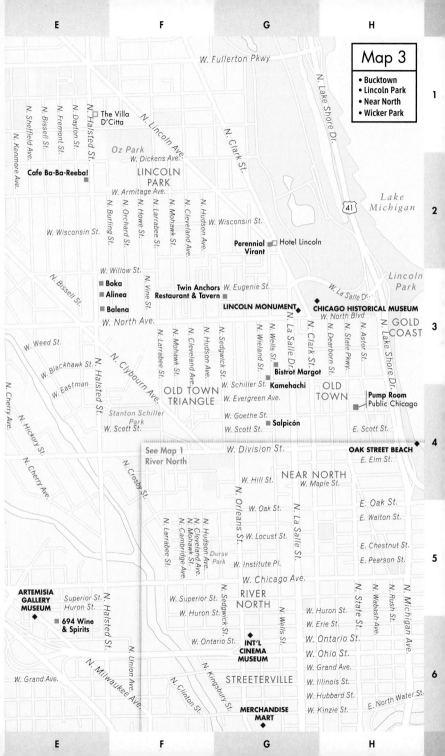

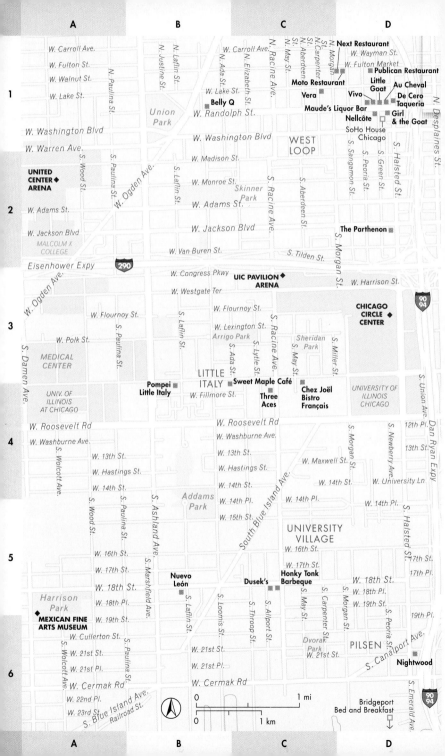

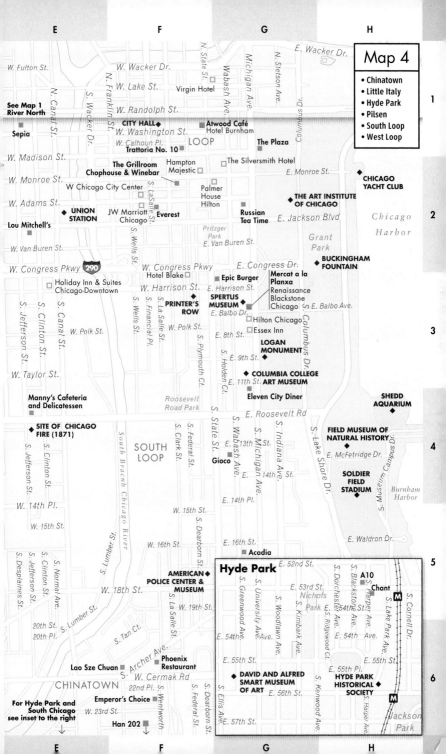

WHERE TO STAY

Updated by
Jenny Berg

Chicago hotel rates are as temperamental as the city's climate. And just as snow in April and balmy weather in November are not uncommon, it is widely accepted that a hotel's room rates may drop $50 to $100 overnight—and rise again the next day. It all depends on the season and what festivals, conferences, and other events are happening around town.

Even so, it's wise to shop around. Focus on a neighborhood of interest, like the Near North Side, and you'll find budget chains such as Embassy Suites and luxury properties such as the Four Seasons Hotel Chicago within a few blocks of each other.

Ask yourself whether you'd rather be surrounded by the sedately dressed—think Trump International Hotel—or tattooed hipsters, à la the James Chicago. Is it romance you're seeking (try the Drake) or a quick weekend escape with the kids in tow (they can splash around the pool at the Radisson Blu Aqua, then walk a block to Millennium Park)?

On the lower end, expect well-maintained, but often boxy and sparsely decorated rooms. The good news is that free Wi-Fi is now a feature of most budget-friendly hotels, such as the Best Western or Holiday Inn chains, and local outfits like the Essex Inn.

Top-tier hotels have no problem filling their rooms: in some cases, this has little to do with amenities. Instead, their vibrant bar scenes are the draw, as is the case at the W Chicago–Lakeshore, W Chicago–City Center, the Wit, and the James Hotel. Rooms at these hot spots usually don't go for less than $250, but the "it" factor is huge. That said, between 2013 and 2015 the city saw a building boom that introduced some 2,700 new hotel rooms; the added competition may help lower prices and increase overall quality.

WHERE SHOULD I STAY?

Neighborhood	Vibe	Pros	Cons
The Loop	Mostly historic hotels of architectural interest in an area filled with business-people on weekdays and shoppers on weekends. The scene has become increasingly hip over the years.	Accessible public transportation and abundant cabs; a business district with decent nightlife.	El train noise; construction common; streets can sometimes be bare in late evening. It draws an older, more established crowd.
West Loop and South Loop	Mixed residential and business neighborhoods that are gentrifying, although empty buildings and storefronts are not uncommon.	Hotels are cheaper; streets are quieter; Museum Campus and McCormick Place are within easy reach; family-friendly; lots of new lounges and restaurants.	Sometimes long walks to public transportation; minimal shopping; quiet at night with many darkened streets. If you're looking for entertainment, it might require a quick drive or a long walk.
Near North	The pulse of the city, on and around North Michigan Avenue, has ritzy high-rise hotels and plenty of shopping and restaurants. As you go farther north, streets become residential.	Many lodging options, including some of the city's most luxurious hotels. Lively streets abuzz until late night; safe. The shopping couldn't be better for those with deep pockets.	Some hotels on the pricey side; crowded sidewalks; lots of tourists. And don't expect to find many bargains here.
River North	Lots of chains, from hotels to restaurants to shops, patronized mostly by travelers. Though this is a tourist haven, the area also has many art galleries and antiques stores.	Affordable lodging; easy access to public transportation; attractions nearby are family-friendly, especially during the day; high concentration of nightclubs.	Area might be too touristy for some. This is Chicago's home for chain restaurants; parking is a drag.
Lincoln Park and Wicker Park	Small, boutique hotels tucked on quiet, tree-lined streets with many independent shops and restaurants. Pedestrian-friendly area; you don't need a car to find a restaurant, bar, or bank.	Low crime; great paths for walks; lots of parkland. Eclectic collection of shops and restaurants, ranging from superaffordable to ultrapricey; from hot dogs to sushi, this place has it all.	Limited hotel selection; long walks to El train. Parking is almost impossible in some spots, and garages don't come cheap; very young and trendy crowd.
Lakeview and Far North Side	Especially busy around Wrigley Field, where both Chicagoans and travelers congregate in summertime; the area's lodging is midsize boutique hotels and B&Bs.	Low crime; moderately priced hotels; dining and shopping options (include many vintage-clothing boutiques) for all budgets; a plethora of sports-themed bars.	Congested traffic; panhandlers common, especially around El stations and Wrigley Field. Parking is a nightmare when the Cubs are playing in town.

10

CHICAGO LODGING PLANNER

LODGING STRATEGY

Where should we stay? With hundreds of Chicago hotels, it may seem like a daunting question. But don't worry—our expert writers and editors have done most of the legwork. The selections here represent the best this city has to offer—from the best budget motels to the sleekest designer hotels. Scan "Best Bets" on the following pages for top recommendations by price and experience. Or find a review quickly in the listings. Search by neighborhood, then alphabetically.

FACILITIES

Unless otherwise noted in the individual descriptions, all the hotels listed have private baths, central heating, and private phones. Almost all have Internet capability and Wi-Fi access as well as valet service.

RESERVATIONS

Reservations are an absolute necessity when planning your trip to Chicago—hotels often fill up with convention traffic, so book your room in advance.

WITH KIDS

In the listings, look for the word "family," which indicates the property is particularly good for kids.

PRICES

Prices in the reviews are the lowest cost of a standard double room in high season; they do not take into account discounts or package deals you may find on consolidator websites.

WHAT IT COSTS			
$	**$$**	**$$$**	**$$$$**
For two people under $220	$220–$319	$320–$420	over $420

Prices are the lowest cost of a standard double room in high season.

USING THE MAPS

Throughout the chapter, you'll see mapping symbols and coordinates (3:F2) after property names or reviews. To locate the property on a map, turn to the Chicago Dining and Lodging Atlas at the end of the Where to Eat chapter. The first number after the symbol indicates the map number. Following that is the property's coordinate on the map grid.

HOTEL REVIEWS

Listed alphabetically within neighborhood. Reviews have been shortened. For full information, visit Fodors.com.

THE LOOP, INCLUDING SOUTH LOOP AND WEST LOOP

Chicago's business district, laced with the overhead train tracks of the El, is a desirable—if slightly noisy—place to stay. Hotels here tend to be fairly priced, and many are housed in historic buildings, giving them

BEST BETS FOR CHICAGO LODGING

Fodor's offers a selective listing of high-quality lodging experiences at every price point, from the city's best budget motel to its most sophisticated luxury hotel. Here we've compiled our top recommendations by price and experience. The best properties—those that provide a remarkable experience in their price range—are designated in the listings with the Fodor's Choice logo.

Fodor's Choice ★

Essex Inn, $

Flemish House of Chicago, $

Four Seasons Hotel Chicago, $$$

Hotel Lincoln, $$

InterContinental Chicago Magnificent Mile, $$

The James Chicago, $

The Langham Chicago, $$$

Park Hyatt Chicago, $$$

The Peninsula Chicago, $$$$

Public Chicago, $

Radisson Blu Aqua, $$

The Ritz-Carlton Chicago, $$$

Sofitel Chicago Water Tower, $$

Trump International Hotel & Tower Chicago, $$$$

Waldorf Astoria Chicago, $$$

Best by Price

$

City Suites Hotel

Essex Inn

Flemish House of Chicago

Hampton Majestic

Hilton Chicago

The James Chicago

Margarita European Inn

Public Chicago

theWit

$$

The Drake

Hotel Blake

Hotel Lincoln

Hotel Monaco Chicago

InterContinental Chicago Magnificent Mile

Radisson Blu Aqua

The Silversmith Hotel

Sofitel Chicago Water Tower

$$$

Four Seasons Hotel Chicago

JW Marriott Chicago

The Langham Chicago

Park Hyatt Chicago

Renaissance Blackstone Chicago Hotel

The Ritz-Carlton Chicago

W Chicago-City Center

Waldorf Astoria Chicago

Wyndham Grand Chicago Riverfront

$$$$

The Peninsula Chicago

Trump International Hotel & Tower Chicago

Best by Experience

BEST CONCIERGE

Fairmont Chicago, $$

Hotel Monaco Chicago, $$

BEST POOL

Essex Inn, $

Hilton Chicago, $

InterContinental Chicago Magnificent Mile, $$

The Peninsula Chicago, $$$$

Trump International Hotel & Tower Chicago, $$$$

BEST SPA

Four Seasons Hotel Chicago, $$$

The James Chicago, $

The Langham Chicago, $$$

Trump International Hotel & Tower Chicago, $$$$

MOST KID-FRIENDLY

Essex Inn, $

Holiday Inn & Suites Chicago-Downtown, $

Hotel Allegro Chicago, $

Hotel Monaco Chicago, $$

Public Chicago, $

Radisson Blu Aqua, $$

The Ritz-Carlton Chicago, $$$

10

a charm you won't find along glitzier North Michigan Avenue. Easy access to the Art Institute and Millennium Park is a plus.

In the South Loop, the spots of gentrification—most apparent in the new restaurants popping up along South Michigan Avenue—have made this area increasingly popular. A hotel boom has not occurred here yet, so lodging choices are limited to a few old reliables. Many hotels offer package deals with the nearby Museum Campus.

THE LOOP

$$
HOTEL
Fairmont Chicago. On a quiet block near both Michigan Avenue and Lake Michigan, this 45-story pink-granite building has suites with stunning views of Millennium Park. **Pros:** short walk from the heart of the city; soothing spa facilities; spacious rooms. **Cons:** no swimming pool; not child-friendly. $ *Rooms from: $289* ✉ *200 N. Columbus Dr., Loop* ☎ *312/565–8000* ⊕ *www.fairmont.com* ➷ *622 guest rooms, 65 suites* ⏹ *No meals* ✣ *1:F6.*

$
HOTEL
Hampton Majestic Chicago Theatre District. The Hampton Majestic is in one of the most high-traffic areas of town; it offers stunning, quiet guest rooms done up in designer tones. **Pros:** steps from the Art Institute and downtown theaters; unique style; great complimentary breakfast. **Cons:** a hike to the Magnificent Mile; the lobby can seem too crowded with furniture. $ *Rooms from: $199* ✉ *22 W. Monroe, Loop* ☎ *312/332–5052, 800/548–8690* ⊕ *www.hamptonmajestic.com* ➷ *135 rooms* ⏹ *Breakfast* ✣ *4:F2.*

$$
HOTEL
Hard Rock Hotel Chicago. Flashy, loud, and packed with plasma TVs, this hotel in the 40-story, art deco Carbide and Carbon Building has modern rooms adorned with rock-and-roll paraphernalia. **Pros:** well-appointed rooms with great views; good location; Aveda bath products. **Cons:** the dim lighting can get old. $ *Rooms from: $289* ✉ *230 N. Michigan Ave., Loop* ☎ *312/345–1000, 866/966–5166* ⊕ *www.hardrockhotelchicago.com* ➷ *361 rooms, 20 suites* ⏹ *No meals* ✣ *1:E6.*

$
HOTEL
FAMILY
Hotel Allegro Chicago. Theater lovers will relish an opportunity to stay at this art deco–themed hot spot; the eclectic decor—including ornate chandeliers, cobalt-blue sofas, and ethereal painted feathers on the ceiling of the private dining room—is a hit. **Pros:** C.O. Bigelow products in the bathrooms; yoga equipment available on request; complimentary 24/7 fitness center. **Cons:** small bathrooms and closets. $ *Rooms from: $209* ✉ *171 W. Randolph St., Loop* ☎ *312/236–0123, 800/643–1500* ⊕ *www.allegrochicago.com* ➷ *452 rooms, 31 suites* ⏹ *No meals* ✣ *1:C6.*

$$
HOTEL
FAMILY
Hotel Monaco Chicago. A renovated lobby featuring pops of color and texture (check out the high-gloss red alligator fabric on the registration desk) as well as redesigned meeting rooms named for international destinations inspire wanderlust here; guest rooms reflect the hotel's global-chic aesthetic, with steamer-trunk nightstands and Moroccan lamps. **Pros:** hip and happening aesthetic; no extra charge for pets; comfortable beds. **Cons:** small gym for a hotel of this size. $ *Rooms from: $239* ✉ *225 N. Wabash Ave., Loop* ☎ *312/960–8500, 866/610–0081* ⊕ *www.monaco-chicago.com* ➷ *171 rooms, 20 suites* ⏹ *No meals* ✣ *1:E6.*

$$ **Hyatt Regency Chicago.** A massive, light-filled lobby—part of a
HOTEL $168-million renovation—is the centerpiece of the Hyatt Regency Chicago, the city's largest hotel with 2,018 rooms in a prime downtown locale. **Pros:** looks spiffy after redesign; excellent location; great winter rates. **Cons:** there's always a lot of activity; not designed for families. *$ Rooms from: $289 ⊠ 151 E. Wacker Dr., Loop ☎ 312/565–8000 ⊕ www.chicagoregency.hyatt.com ⤢ 2,018 rooms ⦿ No meals ✛ 1:F5.*

$$$ **JW Marriott Chicago.** Mixing architectural elegance with a sleek modern style, this historic property has lots of gorgeous areas, from a bright and welcoming lobby bar to spacious guestrooms with high ceilings and marble baths. **Pros:** blocks from Art Institute and Millennium Park; use of 24-hour fitness center and pool; very friendly staff. **Cons:** lackluster views; not a good option for families. *$ Rooms from: $329 ⊠ 151 W. Adams St., Loop ☎ 312/660–8200, 888/238–2427 ⊕ www.jwmarriottchicago.com ▭ No credit cards ⤢ 581 rooms, 29 suites ⦿ No meals ✛ 4:F2.*

$ **The Palmer House Hilton.** The epitome of a grande dame, this massive
HOTEL property in the center of the Loop underwent a $215-million renovation in 2014, but the lobby—with its wow-worthy ceiling mural and lots of gold, marble, and tapestry—preserves the original splendor. **Pros:** within walking distance of almost everything most visitors want to do. **Cons:** some rooms are quite small; steep parking fees and daily charges for fitness center; you can hear the El train from some rooms. *$ Rooms from: $199 ⊠ 17 E. Monroe St., Loop ☎ 312/726–7500, 800/445–8667 ⊕ www.palmerhousehiltonhotel.com ⤢ 1,588 rooms, 53 suites ⦿ No meals ✛ 4:F2.*

$$ **Radisson Blu Aqua.** With design savvy inside as well as out, this gem
HOTEL has generously sized rooms and so many amenities and so much out-
FAMILY door space that it feels like an upscale resort in the heart of downtown.
Fodor'sChoice **Pros:** great location; unique design; friendly. **Cons:** room keycards need
★ to be swiped quickly in the elevator, or you're sent off to the lobby. *$ Rooms from: $249 ⊠ 221 N. Columbus Dr., Loop ☎ 312/565–5258, 800/333–3333 ⊕ www.radissonblu.com/ ▭ No credit cards ⤢ 334 rooms, 18 suites ⦿ No meals ✛ 1:F6.*

$$ **Renaissance Chicago Downtown Hotel.** The cosmopolitan Renaissance
HOTEL Chicago, situated on the south bank of the Chicago River, puts a premium on a good night's sleep: there's no missing the seven—yep, seven—fluffy white pillows on each bed. **Pros:** excellent service, even when the hotel is packed to capacity; spacious rooms are a good value. **Cons:** can get pricey during high season. *$ Rooms from: $289 ⊠ 1 W. Wacker Dr., Loop ☎ 312/372–7200 ⊕ www.renaissancechicagodowntown.com ⤢ 513 rooms, 40 suites ⦿ No meals ✛ 1:D6.*

$$ **The Silversmith Hotel.** Don't be fooled by the tiny front entrance under
HOTEL the El; the Silversmith's oak-covered lobby is enormous and houses a sleek, chandelier-decked restaurant and lounge. **Pros:** convenient to public transportation; bathrooms are stocked with Molton Brown products. **Cons:** entrance can be hard to find; some guests complain about outside noise. *$ Rooms from: $249 ⊠ 10 S. Wabash Ave., Loop ☎ 312/795–6500, 800/979–0084 ⊕ www.silversmithchicagohotel.com ⤢ 144 rooms ⦿ No meals ✛ 4:G2.*

10

$$$ HOTEL **Swissôtel Chicago.** The Swissôtel's triangular Harry Weese design allows for panoramic vistas of the city, lake, or river—and the comfortable, contemporary rooms feel like condos. **Pros:** guests love the view, the pool, and the location; marble bathrooms. **Cons:** pricey parking. [$] *Rooms from: $389* ✉ *323 E. Wacker Dr., Loop* ☎ *312/565–0565, 888/737–9477* 🌐 *www.swissotelchicago.com* 🛏 *621 rooms, 40 suites* 🍴 *No meals* ✥ *1:F6.*

$$$ HOTEL **The Virgin Hotel.** The world's first Virgin Hotel offers loads of techage amenities: a custom app called "Lucy" lets guests check in or out remotely, order room service, control the thermostat, and more, plus there is free Wi-Fi at unlimited bandwidth, and outlets are everywhere—including in front of each stool at the sleek lobby bar. **Pros:** in the heart of downtown, close to major attractions; free Wi-Fi and lots of outlets; no delivery charge for room service. **Cons:** no pool; pricey parking. [$] *Rooms from: $399* ✉ *203 N. Wabash Ave., Loop* ☎ *312/940–4400, 855/946–6600* 🌐 *virginhotels.com* 🛏 *208 rooms, 42 suites* 🍴 *No meals* ✥ *1:E6.*

$$$ HOTEL **W Chicago–City Center.** With a club-like lobby and spacious high-tech rooms done up in graphite and cream, this financial district hotel attracts both business travelers and tourists. **Pros:** sleek, modern design; great location. **Cons:** no free in-room Wi-Fi; you can hear the El from some rooms. [$] *Rooms from: $399* ✉ *172 W. Adams St., Loop* ☎ *312/332–1200, 877/822–0000* 🌐 *www.whotels.com/citycenter* 🛏 *358 rooms, 12 suites* 🍴 *No meals* ✥ *4:F2.*

$ HOTEL **theWit.** The atmosphere at this sleek spot, topped by ROOF, one of the Loop's most happening bars, is fun and youthful; the same can be said of the guest rooms, which are moderately sized and modern, with hanging wall art meant to resemble puckered lips. **Pros:** bold, bright modern decor; excellent dining and drinking options; close to theaters, shopping, and public transportation. **Cons:** may be too hip for some. [$] *Rooms from: $189* ✉ *201 N. State St., Loop* ☎ *312/467–0200, 866/318–1514* 🌐 *www.thewithotel.com* 🛏 *310 room, 36 suites* 🍴 *No meals* ✥ *1:E6.*

WEST LOOP

$$ HOTEL **Soho House Chicago.** Occupying a former belt factory in the West Loop, this private members club feels like a bohemian artist's loft; it's not uncommon to find artists, architects, and musicians lounging in the chandelier-decked lobby, which slings cold-pressed juices by day and craft cocktails at night. **Pros:** great on-site spa; rooftop pool; impressive art collection. **Cons:** air of exclusivity may be disarming to some; better suited to adults than kids. [$] *Rooms from: $300* ✉ *113–125 North Green St., West Loop* ☎ *312/521–8000* 🌐 *www.sohohousechicago.com* 🛏 *31 rooms, 9 suites* 🍴 *No meals* ✥ *4:D1.*

SOUTH LOOP

$ HOTEL FAMILY Fodor's Choice ★ **Essex Inn.** Don't judge this place on appearance alone: the nondescript tower is actually one of the city's most family-friendly hotels, and its location—just five minutes by foot from the Museum Campus—is one reason why. **Pros:** good value; big pool. **Cons:** bathrooms on the small side; the Wi-Fi is free but slow. [$] *Rooms from: $149* ✉ *800 S. Michigan*

Ave., South Loop ☎*312/939–2800, 800/621–6909* ⊕*www.essexinn.
com* ⮎*231 rooms, 23 suites* ⎮○⎮*No meals* ✢ *4:G3.*

$ **Hilton Chicago.** On a busy day the lobby of this Hilton might be mis-
HOTEL   taken for a terminal at O'Hare Airport; it's a bustling convention hotel,
but one that retains its distinguished 1920s heritage in a Renaissance-
inspired entrance hall and gold-and-gilt grand ballroom. **Pros:** close to
the museum district; well-appointed public spaces. **Cons:** a fee for use
of the fitness area; steep parking fees. $ *Rooms from: $199* ⊠ *720 S.
Michigan Ave., South Loop* ☎ *312/922–4400, 877/865–5320* ⊕ *www.
hiltonchicagohotel.com* ⮎*1,544 rooms, 49 suites* ⎮○⎮*Some meals*
✢ *4:G3.*

$ **Holiday Inn & Suites Chicago-Downtown.** Not only is this Holiday Inn
HOTEL   close to Chicago's main attractions, it's also within steps of CTA trains
FAMILY   that go directly to either O'Hare or Midway airports. **Pros:** staff goes
out of their way to be helpful; convenient on-site washing machines and
dryers. **Cons:** the lobby can get quite crowded; bathrooms are on the
small side. $ *Rooms from: $179* ⊠ *506 W. Harrison St., South Loop*
☎ *312/957–9100, 800/465–4329* ⊕ *www.hidowntown.com* ⮎*145
rooms, 27 suites* ⎮○⎮*No meals* ✢ *4:E3.*

$$ **Hotel Blake.** A multimillion-dollar renovation a few years back
HOTEL   updated this spacious landmark in Chicago's historic Printers Row
neighborhood; the lobby is dark but welcoming, and the rooms, in a
mix of browns, reds, and creams, are very large considering the loca-
tion. **Pros:** good South Loop location. **Cons:** the hotel spans three con-
nected buildings, so the layout can be tricky. $ *Rooms from: $309*
⊠ *500 S. Dearborn, South Loop* ☎ *312/986–1234, 888/999–3223*
⊕ *www.hotelblake.com* ⮎*168 rooms, 4 suites* ⎮○⎮*No meals* ✢ *4:F3.*

$$$ **Renaissance Blackstone Chicago Hotel.** The lobby of this classic hotel
HOTEL   has gold-trimmed walls, a gold sofa, and modern flower arrangements
that make it an unusual mix of old and new; the guest rooms are simple
and elegant, with enough flair to feel updated yet still give a sense of the
past. **Pros:** great location; close to Museum Campus and theater district.
Cons: lobby can be a bit dark, and its decor a bit too ornate. $ *Rooms
from: $329* ⊠ *636 S. Michigan Ave., South Loop* ☎ *312/447–0955,
888/236–2427* ⊕ *www.blackstonerenaissance.com* ⮎*328 rooms, 4
suites* ⎮○⎮*Some meals* ✢ *4:G3.*

NEAR NORTH AND RIVER NORTH

With a cluster of accommodations around North Michigan Avenue (the
"Magnificent Mile"), the Near North neighborhood is where many new
hotels are springing up—or reinventing themselves, thanks to multimil-
lion-dollar makeovers. Prices are at the high end, but there are a few
deals to be found if you're willing to forgo a pool or concierge service.
Consider the area's proximity to great shopping part of the bargain.

In River North, aside from the concentration of independently owned
galleries, it's national chains that lead most of the commerce, including
some surprising boutique hotels that may be part of a chain but have
nevertheless carved out a personality all their own.

NEAR NORTH

$ HOTEL 🏨 **The Allerton Hotel Chicago.** Named a National Historic Landmark in 1999, the Allerton was a residential "club hotel" for men when it opened in 1924; a renovation restored the limestone facade and left it with a more contemporary feel. **Pros:** lovely neighborhood; close to Mag Mile shopping, Rush Street nightlife, and Navy Pier; delightful concierge and doormen. **Cons:** guest rooms and bathrooms can be small. [$] *Rooms from: $199* ✉ *701 N. Michigan Ave., Near North* ☎ *312/440–1500* 🌐 *www.theallertonhotel.com* 🛏 *443 rooms, 54 suites* 🍴 *No meals* ✥ *1:E3.*

$$ HOTEL 🏨 **Conrad Chicago.** This hotel's art deco–inspired lobby avoids feeling like a period piece through its clean-line furniture and creative floral arrangements, and the rooms here—featuring European duvets, oversize pillows, plush bathrobes, and slippers—aim to pamper. **Pros:** beautifully appointed lobby; free Wi-Fi in guest rooms. **Cons:** antiquated heating and cooling systems; it takes two elevators to reach some rooms. [$] *Rooms from: $279* ✉ *521 N. Rush St., Near North* ☎ *312/645–1500, 800/266–7237* 🌐 *www.conradchicago.com* 🛏 *278 rooms, 33 suites* 🍴 *No meals* ✥ *1:E4.*

$ HOTEL 🏨 **Courtyard by Marriott Chicago/Magnificent Mile.** This modern hotel has a convenient location and a bustling lobby that visitors will love; the modest accommodations, with their art deco–inspired decor, white linens, and splashes of red, are also appealing. **Pros:** great location in the heart of the shopping district. **Cons:** pool is small; some guests complain of noise problems. [$] *Rooms from: $199* ✉ *165 E. Ontario St., Near North* ☎ *312/573–0800, 800/321–2211* 🌐 *www.courtyardchicago.com* 🛏 *283 rooms, 23 suites* 🍴 *No meals* ✥ *1:F4.*

$$ HOTEL 🏨 **The Drake.** Built in 1920, the grande dame of Chicago hotels stands tall where Michigan Avenue and Lake Shore Drive intersect in the city's swanky Gold Coast. **Pros:** lovely, walkable neighborhood; steps from Oak Street Beach and high-end boutiques. **Cons:** no swimming pool; some rooms are tiny. [$] *Rooms from: $289* ✉ *140 E. Walton Pl., Gold Coast* ☎ *312/787–2200, 800/553–7253* 🌐 *www.thedrakehotel.com* 🛏 *535 rooms, 74 suites* 🍴 *No meals* ✥ *1:E2.*

$$ HOTEL FAMILY 🏨 **Embassy Suites Chicago-Downtown/Lakefront.** Every room is spacious here, with a separate bedroom and living area, as well as a view of either Lake Michigan or the Chicago skyline. **Pros:** fitness center with a view of the city; heated indoor pool. **Cons:** long line for free wine. [$] *Rooms from: $259* ✉ *511 N. Columbus Dr., Near North* ☎ *312/836–5900, 800/362–2779* 🌐 *www.chicagolakefront.embassysuites.com* 🛏 *455 suites* 🍴 *Breakfast* ✥ *1:F4.*

$ B&B/INN Fodor's Choice ★ 🏨 **Flemish House of Chicago.** This classic, four-story bed-and-breakfast is a good value considering the posh zip code; each of its eight suites has a slightly different decor, but all are roomy and well appointed, with an impressive collection of antique desks, lamp, and armoires. **Pros:** refrigerators stocked with healthy breakfast foods; complimentary use of laptops. **Cons:** the owners don't always rent rooms for a single night, though they try to be flexible. [$] *Rooms from: $200* ✉ *68 E. Cedar St., Near North* ☎ *312/664–9981* 🌐 *www.innchicago.com* 🛏 *8 suites* 🍴 *Breakfast* ✥ *1:E1.*

CLOSE UP

Chicago Conventions

Travelers to Chicago take note: more than 1,000 conventions and trade shows are scheduled throughout the year. The International Home and Housewares show in March, the National Restaurant Association show in May, the Manufacturing Technology show in September, and the Radiological Society of America show in late November are among the biggest. Hotel rooms may be hard to come by—and snagging tables at popular restaurants is even harder.

Proximity to McCormick Place, where most of Chicago's huge trade shows hunker down, is often a conventioneer's top priority, so most wind up staying in the Loop or South Loop, where hotels are just a five-minute cab ride away from the mammoth venue. In these neighborhoods accommodations tend to be older and somewhat less expensive—although there are certainly a few exceptions.

Expect somewhat quiet nights in these parts; the Loop boasts a revitalized theater district, but come sundown there's a lot more revelry north of the Chicago River in the neighborhoods surrounding the Mag Mile. Vibrant Near North has many bars, and River North has a high concentration of restaurants and nightclubs.

A meeting or convention in Rosemont or a tight flight schedule should be the only reasons to consider an airport hotel. Prices at these properties are a bit lower, but the O'Hare area is drab. Plus, trips from there to downtown may take an hour during rush hour, bad weather, or periods of heavy construction on the Kennedy Expressway.

Contact the Chicago Convention and Tourism Bureau at *877/244–2246* for information on conventions, trade shows, and other travel concerns before you book your trip.

$$$ HOTEL Fodor's Choice ★ 🏨 **Four Seasons Hotel Chicago.** At the refined Four Seasons, guest rooms begin on the 30th floor (the hotel sits atop the tony 900 North Michigan Shops), so there's a distinct feeling of seclusion—and there are great views to boot. **Pros:** in the middle of high-end shopping; well-appointed, generously sized rooms; outstanding room service and housekeeping. **Cons:** very expensive; being so high up means that rooms can get a little noisy on windy days. [$] *Rooms from: $405* ✉ *120 E. Delaware Pl., Near North* ☎ *312/280–8800, 800/332–3442* 🌐 *www.fourseasons.com/chicagofs* 🛏 *175 rooms, 168 suites* 🍴 *No meals* ⊕ *1:E2.*

$ HOTEL FAMILY 🏨 **Homewood Suites by Hilton Chicago Downtown.** The suites here seem custom-designed for families, with sleeper sofas, separate bedrooms, and fully equipped kitchens that feature full-size refrigerators and granite countertops. **Pros:** great view of skyline; heated pool; free, hot breakfast. **Cons:** bathrooms feel cramped. [$] *Rooms from: $159* ✉ *40 E. Grand Ave., Near North* ☎ *312/644–2222, 800/225–5466* 🌐 *www.homewoodsuiteschicago.com* 🛏 *233 suites* 🍴 *Some meals* ⊕ *1:E4.*

$$ HOTEL 🏨 **Hotel Palomar Chicago.** In the middle of one of Chicago's most vibrant neighborhoods and close to Rush Street nightlife, this trendy hot spot delivers solid rooms and excellent cuisine. **Pros:** hotel's bustling vibe matches its surroundings; great for the young and hip; Sable, the on-site

restaurant, is worth a visit. **Cons:** lobby is on the small side. [$] *Rooms from: $249* ✉ *505 N. State, Near North* ☎ *312/755–9703, 877/731–0505* 🌐 *www.hotelpalomar-chicago.com* ↪ *242 rooms, 19 suites* 🍴 *No meals* ⊕ *1:D4.*

$$ HOTEL Fodor's Choice ★ 🏨 **InterContinental Chicago Magnificent Mile.** Renovations completed in 2013 made this historic hotel even more equipped to address the evolving needs of today's traveler—from the contemporary air of the guest rooms to the enormous swimming pool and well-stocked fitness center. **Pros:** historic feel; jaw-dropping pool; view of the Magnificent Mile. **Cons:** concierge service is spotty; staff can be less than friendly. [$] *Rooms from: $299* ✉ *505 N. Michigan Ave., Near North* ☎ *312/944–4100, 800/628–2112* 🌐 *www.icchicagohotel.com* ↪ *720 rooms, 72 suites* 🍴 *No meals* ⊕ *1:E4.*

$ HOTEL Fodor's Choice ★ 🏨 **The James Chicago.** This trendy boutique hotel has a prime location and comfortable, contemporary rooms, many of them large, with platform beds and dark woods. **Pros:** free Wi-Fi; steps from nightlife and close to many attractions. **Cons:** some guests complain of noise; steep parking fees. [$] *Rooms from: $209* ✉ *55 E. Ontario St., Near North* ☎ *312/337–1000, 888/526–3778* 🌐 *www.jameshotels.com* ↪ *297 rooms, 106 suites* 🍴 *No meals* ⊕ *1:E4.*

$$ HOTEL 🏨 **Millennium Knickerbocker Hotel.** This 1927 hotel has had a number of identities—including a 1970s stint as the Playboy Hotel and Towers under owner Hugh Hefner; these days the guest rooms sport a gold, beige, plum, and espresso color palette. **Pros:** location can't be beat; generously sized rooms. **Cons:** quality of rooms is inconsistent. [$] *Rooms from: $249* ✉ *163 E. Walton Pl., Near North* ☎ *312/751–8100, 800/621–8140* 🌐 *www.knickerbockerchicago.com* ↪ *306 rooms, 26 suites* 🍴 *No meals* ⊕ *1:F2.*

$$ HOTEL FAMILY 🏨 **Omni Chicago Hotel.** The only all-suites hotel on Michigan Avenue has a lot going for it: every room is good-sized, and French doors separate the living room from the bedroom, making them feel more like apartments. **Pros:** modern, comfortable rooms with spacious sitting area, desk, and bar. **Cons:** hotel can be too noisy for some. [$] *Rooms from: $225* ✉ *676 N. Michigan Ave., Near North* ☎ *312/944–6664, 800/843–6664* 🌐 *www.omnichicago.com* ↪ *347 suites* 🍴 *No meals* ⊕ *1:E3.*

$$$ HOTEL Fodor's Choice ★ 🏨 **Park Hyatt Chicago.** This Gold Coast star dominates the skyline high above the old Water Tower, and the views are understandably spectacular from many of its oversize rooms; done up in tasteful, understated tones, they include touches like the signature Eames chairs that emphasize quiet luxury. **Pros:** marble bath and soaking tub; free in-room Wi-Fi. **Cons:** some people complain of street noise and slow elevators. [$] *Rooms from: $375* ✉ *800 N. Michigan Ave., Near North* ☎ *312/335–1234, 800/633–7313* 🌐 *www.parkchicago.hyatt.com* ↪ *198 rooms, 13 suites* 🍴 *No meals* ⊕ *1:E3.*

$$$$ HOTEL Fodor's Choice ★ 🏨 **The Peninsula Chicago.** On weekend nights the Peninsula's soaring lobby-level restaurant—aptly named the Lobby—becomes a sweet fantasia, centered on an overflowing chocolate buffet; guest rooms are pretty sweet, too, with plush pillow-top beds and bedside consoles that control both the TV and the "do-not-disturb" light. **Pros:** top-notch bath products; separate shower and bath. **Cons:** in-house dining options

aren't the best for families; rates are sky-high. $ *Rooms from: $625* ⊠ *108 E. Superior St., Near North* ☎ *312/337–2888, 866/288–8889* ⊕ *www.peninsula.com* ⤴ *339 rooms, 83 suites* ⦿*No meals* ✛ *1:E3.*

$ ▦ **Public Chicago.** With iMacs in the lobby, free Wi-Fi throughout, bikes
HOTEL   for borrowing at the front door, and generously sized, minimalist cream-
FAMILY   and-white guest rooms, what was once the slightly faded Ambassador
Fodor's Choice   East is now hip and sleek. **Pros:** close to North Avenue Beach, nightlife,
★   and downtown; friendly, jeans-clad staff; hotelier Ian Schrager's trademark glamour. **Cons:** smallish bathrooms; mocha-colored walls and
ceilings and subtle lighting make the hallways dark. $ *Rooms from:*
$175 ⊠ *1301 N. State Pkwy., Near North* ☎ *312/787–3700* ⊕ *www.*
publichotels.com ▭ *No credit cards* ⤴ *250 rooms, 35 suites* ⦿*No*
meals ✛ *3:H4.*

$ ▦ **Raffaello Hotel.** Location is a big draw for visitors to this hotel near
HOTEL   the Magnificent Mile; inside you'll find spacious, comfortable rooms
in neutral shades, with modern-looking bathrooms and superlative city
views (request a west-facing one for a close-up look at the John Hancock Center). **Pros:** rooms are comfortable and elegant; bathrooms with
rain showers. **Cons:** some guests have complained of long waits for
elevators. $ *Rooms from: $199* ⊠ *201 E. Delaware Pl., Near North*
☎ *312/943–5000, 800/898–7198* ⊕ *www.chicagoraffaello.com* ⤴ *170*
rooms, 72 suites ⦿*No meals* ✛ *1:F2.*

$$$ ▦ **The Ritz-Carlton Chicago.** Shoppers, get ready: the sophisticated yet
HOTEL   comfortable Ritz-Carlton has indoor access to the Water Tower Place
FAMILY   shopping mall and is close to many high-end boutiques. **Pros:** guests feel
Fodor's Choice   pampered; great stay for families with children. **Cons:** expensive; some
★   guests miss having in-room tea/coffeemakers. $ *Rooms from: $395*
⊠ *160 E. Pearson St., Near North* ☎ *312/266–1000, 800/332–3442*
outside Illinois ⊕ *www.fourseasons.com/chicagorc* ⤴ *344 rooms, 91*
suites ⦿*No meals* ✛ *1:F2.*

$$ ▦ **Sheraton Chicago Hotel and Towers.** Enormous and ideally situated,
HOTEL   this hotel calls out to families with its generously sized rooms and
FAMILY   large pool. **Pros:** a short walk from Michigan Avenue, Navy Pier, and
Millennium Park; a reasonable cab ride away from major museums.
Cons: best for families and businesspeople, not those seeking a romantic
escape. $ *Rooms from: $229* ⊠ *301 E. North Water St., Near North*
☎ *312/464–1000* ⊕ *www.sheratonchicago.com* ⤴ *1214 rooms* ⦿*No*
meals ✛ *1:G5.*

$$ ▦ **Sofitel Chicago Water Tower.** A wonder of modern architecture, this
HOTEL   French-owned gem is a prism-shape structure that juts over the street
Fodor's Choice   and widens as it rises; design sensibility also shines in the guest rooms,
★   thanks to honey maple–wood furnishings, Barcelona chairs, and marble
bathrooms. **Pros:** modern decor; great ambience. **Cons:** the place is
so sleek that some guests have a hard time finding the light switches.
$ *Rooms from: $285* ⊠ *20 E. Chestnut St., Near North* ☎ *312/324–*
4000, 877/813–7700 ⊕ *www.sofitel.com/Chicago* ⤴ *415 rooms, 33*
suites ⦿*No meals* ✛ *1:E2.*

$$ ▦ **The Talbott Hotel.** Built in 1927, this European-style boutique hotel
HOTEL   has a lobby that calls to mind an English manor house and elegant
accommodations that mix the classic and contemporary. **Pros:** a hotel

10

where the guest comes first; pet-friendly property. **Cons:** a hike from Millennium Park and Museum Campus. [$] *Rooms from: $225* ✉ *20 E. Delaware Pl., Gold Coast* ☎ *312/944–4970* 🌐 *www.talbotthotel.com* 🛏 *149 rooms, 29 suites* 🍴 *No meals* ✥ *1:D2.*

$$$ HOTEL 🏨 **Thompson Chicago.** In the heart of the Gold Coast, this design-focused property has the feel of a posh urbanite's home—its walls are lined with a slightly edgy art collection (no corporate-looking sailboats here), while the jewel-hued lobby has stacks of books and velvety seating. **Pros:** centrally located; great for weddings and meetings; C.O. Bigelow products in the bathrooms. **Cons:** better suited to business travelers than families; no pool; pricey parking. [$] *Rooms from: $379* ✉ *21 E. Bellevue Pl., Gold Coast* ☎ *312/266–2100* 🌐 *www.thompsonhotels.com* 🛏 *223 rooms, 24 suites* 🍴 *No meals* ✥ *1:E1.*

$ HOTEL 🏨 **The Tremont Hotel Chicago at Magnificent Mile.** Just off North Michigan Avenue, this hotel's restaurant, Mike Ditka's, gets infinitely more attention than the rooms do, although its standard options offer all the essential amenities, including work desks and iHome docking stations. **Pros:** great location; good value. **Cons:** some guests have complained of small rooms and slow elevators. [$] *Rooms from: $209* ✉ *100 E. Chestnut St., Near North* ☎ *312/751–1900, 800/621–8133* 🌐 *www.tremontchicago.com* 🛏 *130 rooms, 5 suites* 🍴 *No meals* ✥ *1:E2.*

$$$ HOTEL 🏨 **W Chicago–Lakeshore.** Overlooking Lake Michigan and Navy Pier, this high-energy hotel emerged from a $38-million makeover in 2014; now its sleek, contemporary guest rooms feature a neutral palette with pops of primary color. **Pros:** cool, hip vibe; business center; right on the lake. **Cons:** service isn't as high as the price would lead you to expect. [$] *Rooms from: $369* ✉ *644 N. Lake Shore Dr., Near North* ☎ *312/943–9200, 877/946–8357* 🌐 *www.whotels.com/lakeshore* 🛏 *490 rooms, 30 suites* 🍴 *No meals* ✥ *1:G4.*

$$$$ HOTEL Fodor's Choice ★ 🏨 **Waldorf Astoria Chicago.** Two large, Greek-inspired sculptures greet guests as they walk through the entrance of this exquisitely designed hotel, where rooms start at 632 square feet and double in size if you're willing to spend even more. **Pros:** you don't have to leave the hotel to enjoy a fabulous bar—theirs is packed on weekends. **Cons:** the high room bill; most guests say the staff is eager to please, but a few have complained about subpar service and long waits at the very popular bar/restaurant. [$] *Rooms from: $335* ✉ *11 E. Walton St., Near North* ☎ *312/646–1300, 888/370–1938* 🌐 *www.waldorfastoriachicagohotel.com* 🛏 *35 rooms, 154 suites* 🍴 *No meals* ✥ *1:D2.*

$$ HOTEL 🏨 **The Westin Michigan Avenue Chicago.** Location-wise, this hotel scores big because major malls and flagship shops are steps from the front door; once inside, the lobby seems a bit like an airport terminal—long, narrow, and full of folks tapping away on laptops—but the rooms are restful. **Pros:**"heavenly" beds; proximity to area attractions; ever-present cabs. **Cons:** guests have complained of poor water pressure; steep parking fees. [$] *Rooms from: $279* ✉ *909 N. Michigan Ave., Near North* ☎ *312/943–7200, 800/937–8461* 🌐 *www.westin.com/michiganavenue* 🛏 *752 rooms, 23 suites* 🍴 *No meals* ✥ *1:E2.*

$$$ HOTEL 🏨 **The Whitehall Hotel.** Built in the late 1920s and originally filled with luxury apartments, this Gold Coast boutique hotel has hosted the

likes of Katharine Hepburn and Mick Jagger. **Pros:** terrific location; updated rooms; remarkably comfortable mattresses. **Cons:** small elevators and fitness center; expensive parking. $ *Rooms from: $329* ✉ *105 E. Delaware Pl., Gold Coast* ☎ *312/944–6300, 800/948–4255* ⊕ *www. thewhitehallhotel.com* ⇨ *214 rooms, 8 suites* ⦿ *No meals* ✛ *1:E2.*

$$$ 🖥 **Wyndham Grand Chicago Riverfront.** This property (formerly the Hotel
HOTEL 71) was renovated and rebranded in 2013; just blocks from the Wrigley Building and Tribune Tower, it offers impressive views of the Chicago River and the heart of downtown. **Pros:** prime location that's steps away from excellent restaurants and bars. **Cons:** no pool. $ *Rooms from: $369* ✉ *71 E. Wacker Dr., Near North* ☎ *312/346–7100, 800/621–4005* ⊕ *www.wyndham.com* ⇨ *300 rooms, 34 suites* ⦿ *No meals* ✛ *1:E5.*

RIVER NORTH

$$$ 🖥 **Dana Hotel and Spa.** Chic yet comfy, the newly renovated guest rooms
HOTEL in this hot boutique hotel have an earthy palette, clean-lined wood furnishings, patterned rugs, and ambient lighting that guests can control themselves; many also have floor-to-ceiling windows. **Pros:** the honor bar offers reasonably priced snacks and bottles of wine for less than $20; soothing on-site spa. **Cons:** rooms can be on the small side; some say the bathrooms don't allow for enough privacy. $ *Rooms from: $359* ✉ *660 N. State St., River North* ☎ *312/202–6000, 888/301–3262* ⊕ *www.danahotelandspa.com* ⇨ *216 rooms, 22 suites* ⦿ *No meals* ✛ *1:D3.*

$$$ 🖥 **Embassy Suites Chicago Downtown.** Suites here are arranged around an
HOTEL 11-story, plant-filled atrium lobby where bubbling fountains keep noise levels relatively high; making efficient use of space, all have separate living rooms with a pullout sofa, four-person dining table, and extra TV. **Pros:** great cocktail hour; hotel is just three blocks away from the Magnificent Mile. **Cons:** paid Internet ($9.95 a day or $44.95 for five days). $ *Rooms from: $399* ✉ *600 N. State St., River North* ☎ *312/943–3800* ⊕ *www.embassysuiteschicago.com* ⇨ *368 suites* ⦿ *Breakfast* ✛ *1:D4.*

$$ 🖥 **The Godfrey Hotel Chicago.** The big draw at this modern hotel is its
HOTEL popular bar, IO Godfrey, a swanky "urban roofscape" that has indoor seating on plush banquettes and a patio with glittering city views. **Pros:** windows open in rooms; great bar; small on-site spa. **Cons:** not ideal for kids; no pool; may be too hip for some. $ *Rooms from: $309* ✉ *127 West Huron St., River North* ☎ *312/649–2000* ⊕ *www.godfreyhotel chicago.com* ⇨ *194 rooms, 27 suites* ⦿ *No meals* ✛ *1:C3.*

$ 🖥 **Hotel Cass, Holiday Inn Express.** With cheerful rooms and nicely
HOTEL designed public spaces, the Hotel Cass is a true boutique property that bears little resemblance to more generic branches in the Holiday Inn chain. **Pros:** stellar location; good value. **Cons:** some guests have complained of small rooms; crowded elevators. $ *Rooms from: $169* ✉ *640 N. Wabash Ave., River North* ☎ *312/787–4030* ⊕ *www.hotelcass.com* ⇨ *172 rooms, 3 suites* ⦿ *Breakfast* ✛ *1:E4.*

$ 🖥 **Hotel Felix.** Hip but cozy, the Hotel Felix uses a mixture of soft browns
HOTEL and grays throughout; the rooms are stylish, and the lobby, decorated with glass sculptures hanging from the ceiling, is small and inviting. **Pros:** eco-friendly (recycled products show up everywhere); free Wi-Fi.

10

Cons: the rooms might be too small for some; some say the rooms let in too much hallway noise. $ *Rooms from: $179* ✉ *111 W. Huron, River North* ☎ *312/447–3440* ⊕ *www.hotelfelixchicago.com* ⤳ *225 rooms* ‖○‖ *No meals* ✛ *1:D3.*

$$$ 🛉 **The Langham Chicago.** A Mies van der Rohe-designed skyscraper is
HOTEL   now home to the city's hottest stay: opened in 2013, the Langham
Fodor'sChoice   stands out for its winning mix of impeccable service, sleek style, and
★   outstanding location. **Pros:** attentive and friendly service; gorgeous facilities; location can't be beat. **Cons:** street noise may be heard on lower floors. $ *Rooms from: $395* ✉ *330 N. Wabash Ave., River North* ☎ *312/923–9988* ⊕ *chicago.langhamhotels.com* ⤳ *316 rooms* ‖○‖ *No meals* ✛ *1:E5.*

$$ 🛉 **MileNorth, a Chicago Hotel.** In an often overlooked section of Chicago
HOTEL   just east of Michigan Avenue, this hotel has a sublime 29th-floor indoor/
FAMILY   outdoor bar with an enviable view of the city; its stylish guest rooms are contemporary and comfy. **Pros:** bars and restaurants steps away; excellent customer service. **Cons:** steep parking fees; might be a little too far to walk to Millennium Park and the theater district. $ *Rooms from: $299* ✉ *166 E. Superior St., River North* ☎ *312/787–6000* ⊕ *www. milenorthhotel.com* ⤳ *124 rooms, 91 suites* ‖○‖ *No meals* ✛ *1:F3.*

$$$$ 🛉 **Trump International Hotel & Tower Chicago.** With some of the best views
HOTEL   in Chicago, the Trump International Hotel & Tower attracts power
Fodor'sChoice   brokers, women in fur coats, and anyone else who is prepared to pay
★   for top-of-the-line luxury. **Pros:** impeccable service; lavish amenities. **Cons:** the rates (and everything else) may be way too much; expensive drinks at the bar. $ *Rooms from: $445* ✉ *401 N. Wabash Ave., River North* ☎ *312/588–8000, 866/891–2125* ⊕ *www.trumphotelcollection. com/chicago* ⤳ *218 rooms, 121 suites* ‖○‖ *No meals* ✛ *1:E5.*

LINCOLN PARK AND WICKER PARK

Three miles of lakefront parkland draw people to the Lincoln Park neighborhood—and most hotels here are just blocks away. Room rates are decidedly lower than those downtown, the downside being that you'll invest more in transportation to hit top sites. Parking is easier, but never a snap; plan on using the valet. Wicker Park attracts an artsy mix of young couples and singles who can't walk more than a yard without stumbling into a mom-and-pop-owned fast-food joint or a four-star restaurant.

LINCOLN PARK

$ 🛉 **Days Inn Chicago.** This Days Inn branch is one of the more luxuri-
HOTEL   ous in the sometimes so-so chain: it's an affordable stay in a good location. **Pros:** recently renovated; knowledgeable staff makes it a good value for the price. **Cons:** the location—bustling even very late at night—can make it a little noisy for some guests. $ *Rooms from: $131* ✉ *644 W. Diversey Pkwy., Lincoln Park* ☎ *773/831–4289, 888/419–1603* ⊕ *www.daysinnchicago.net* ⤳ *131 rooms, 2 suites* ‖○‖ *Breakfast* ✛ *2:G5.*

$$ 🏨 **Hotel Lincoln.** Directly across from Lincoln Park, this historic property
HOTEL has a cool, kitschy vibe but still feels authentic, thanks to details like the
FAMILY original Hotel Lincoln sign in the lobby. **Pros:** pet-friendly; great resi-
Fodor's Choice dential neighborhood; authentic Chicago feel. **Cons:** a/c units are noisy;
★ historic hotel means small bathrooms. [$] *Rooms from: $249* ✉ *1816 N. Clark St., Lincoln Park* ☎ *312/254–4700, 888/378–7994* 🌐 *www.hotellincolnchicago.com* 🛏 *127 rooms, 57 suites* 🍴 *No meals* ✥ *3:G2.*

$$ 🏨 **Villa D'Citta Boutique Mansion.** This Tuscan-themed bed-and-
B&B/INN breakfast—complete with a (shared) fully stocked gourmet kitchen—allows guests all the comforts of a top-notch hotel in a residential neighborhood where such rooms can be hard to find. **Pros:** meticulous innkeeper keeps the rooms well cared for; bustling neighborhood; steps away from dozens of boutiques. **Cons:** some guests have complained of noise. [$] *Rooms from: $299* ✉ *2230 N. Halsted St., Lincoln Park* ☎ *312/771–0696, 800/228–6070* 🌐 *www.villadcitta.com* 🛏 *1 room, 5 suites* 🍴 *Breakfast* ✥ *3:E1.*

WICKER PARK

$ 🏨 **Wicker Park Inn.** One of the condo-like rooms in this small B&B is a
B&B/INN great choice for anyone who wants to venture outside downtown Chicago and sample two of its most popular neighborhoods—Wicker Park and Bucktown. **Pros:** rooms are spacious, very well maintained, and homey; top-notch service; dozens of restaurants and bars just blocks away. **Cons:** some complain of noise problems from the El or other guests. [$] *Rooms from: $149* ✉ *1329 N. Wicker Park Ave., Wicker Park* ☎ *773/486–2743* 🌐 *www.wickerparkinn.com* 🛏 *4 rooms, 3 suites* 🍴 *Breakfast* ✥ *3:B4.*

LAKEVIEW AND FAR NORTH SIDE

Seemingly light-years away from downtown, Lakeview hotels entice with their proximity to Wrigley Field and the summertime street festivals for which this neighborhood is known. As you venture farther north, accommodations tend to be quainter and spaces more intimate. But you'd be hard-pressed to find a better or more eclectic collection of shops and eateries. This is a vibrant neighborhood that buzzes well into the night; you're never too far from a cold Goose Island, a hole-in-the-wall sushi joint, or Lake Michigan itself.

LAKEVIEW

$$ 🏨 **Best Western Plus Hawthorne Terrace Hotel.** Centrally located in the
HOTEL Lakeview neighborhood, this Best Western offers all essential amenities at a reasonable price: the rate includes a free Continental breakfast plus use of the business facilities and fitness center. **Pros:** close to Wrigley Field and popular bars and restaurants; helpful staff. **Cons:** parking is not ideal. [$] *Rooms from: $269* ✉ *3434 N. Broadway, Lakeview* ☎ *773/244–3434, 888/675–2378* 🌐 *www.hawthorneterrace.com* 🛏 *59 rooms, 24 suites* 🍴 *Breakfast* ✥ *1:F3.*

$ 🏨 **City Suites Hotel.** European travelers love this hotel for its residential
HOTEL feel; redecorated in 2014, the rooms now boast black-and-white linens plus midcentury-inspired accents, and two-thirds of them have separate sitting areas with pull-out couches. **Pros:** flat-screen TVs in all rooms;

LODGING ALTERNATIVES

APARTMENT RENTALS

When you want a little more space than a hotel room provides, consider staying in an apartment. If you decide to book one online, choose a reputable provider of short-term rentals—like **Vacation Rental By Owner** (🌐 *www.vrbo.com*), which offers a money-back guarantee.

Other top choices include **HomeAway** (🌐 *www.homeaway.com*). Owned by the folks behind VRBO, it lists rental properties from one to six-plus bedrooms. **Airbnb** (🌐 *www.airbnb.com*) is also popular, but beware: it began charging customers the Chicago Hotel Accommodations Tax in early 2015.

BED-AND-BREAKFASTS

For an intimate look at the city, some visitors like to stay at bed-and-breakfasts. For additional options, try the **Chicago Bed & Breakfast Association** (*773/394–2000,800/375–7084* 🌐 *www.chicago-bed-breakfast.com*).

great neighborhood. **Cons:** rooms are on the small side; an underwhelming breakfast; possible El noise. [$] *Rooms from: $209* ✉ *933 W. Belmont Ave., Lakeview* ☎ *773/404–3400, 800/248–9108* 🌐 *www.chicagocitysuites.com* 🛏 *16 rooms, 29 suites* 🍴 *Breakfast* ✣ *2:F4.*

$$$ HOTEL 🏨 **The Majestic Hotel.** Everything at this charming boutique hotel says homey—from the quiet, side-street location to the roaring fireplace in the lobby and the complimentary cookies served each afternoon; guest rooms, renovated in 2014, are contemporary yet cozy, and plush bathrobes hang in the bathrooms. **Pros:** friendly staff; some rooms have pull-out couches; free Wi-Fi and Continental breakfast. **Cons:** you'll have to walk a block for a cab; some have complained of issues with the heating. [$] *Rooms from: $329* ✉ *528 W. Brompton Ave., Lakeview* ☎ *773/404–3499, 800/727–5108* 🌐 *www.majestic-chicago.com* 🛏 *28 rooms, 24 suites* 🍴 *Breakfast* ✣ *2:G3.*

$$ HOTEL 🏨 **The Willows Hotel Chicago.** Designed in French Provincial style, the lobby of this 1920s hotel opens onto a tree-lined street in Lakeview, just three blocks from the lake and central to stores, restaurants, and movie theaters. **Pros:** just steps away from bars, restaurants, and public transit. **Cons:** modestly decorated rooms; no on-site fitness center, but guests have access to a nearby gym. [$] *Rooms from: $279* ✉ *555 W. Surf St., Lakeview* ☎ *773/528–8400, 800/787–3108* 🌐 *www.willowshotelchicago.com* 🛏 *51 rooms, 4 suites* 🍴 *Breakfast* ✣ *2:G5.*

EVANSTON

$ B&B/INN 🏨 **Margarita European Inn.** While the varied room sizes and narrow corridors may bring to mind a college dormitory, you won't find a more charming place to stay in Chicago's Near North suburbs. **Pros:** a fun, off-the-beaten-path place; close to Northwestern University; small but helpful staff. **Cons:** breakfast is merely adequate. [$] *Rooms from: $119* ✉ *1566 Oak Ave., Evanston* ☎ *847/869–2273* 🌐 *www.margaritainn.com* 🛏 *46 rooms* 🍴 *Breakfast* ✣ *2:D1.*

SHOPPING

Updated
by Joseph
Erbentraut

A potent concentration of famous retailers around Michigan Avenue and neighborhoods bursting with one-of-a-kind stores combine to make Chicago a shopper's paradise. Michigan Avenue's legendary Magnificent Mile lures thousands of avid shoppers every week. How often can you find Neiman Marcus, Macy's, Nordstrom, Saks Fifth Avenue, and Barneys New York within walking distance of one another? In recent years State Street has regained some of its former glory as well, with discount department stores sharing prime real estate with trendier clothing boutiques and the Block 37 retail development.

Neighborhood shopping areas, like fun-but-sophisticated Lincoln Park, eclectic Lakeview, and the hipster haven of Wicker Park/Bucktown, offer countless independent stores that cater to every desire, whether Prairie tyle furniture, cowboy boots, or outsider art. And there are countless smaller shopping enclaves within these neighborhoods that have concentrated clusters of antiques stores, home-furnishings shops, high-end boutiques, and other specialty stores. Those averse to paying retail won't have to venture far to unearth bargains on everything from fine jewelry to business attire. When it comes to shopping, this is one city that has it all.

Be forewarned that a steep 9.5% sales tax is added to all purchases in the city except groceries and prescription drugs. Neighborhood shops on the North Side, especially those in Wicker Park and Bucktown, tend to open late—around 11 or noon. Most stores, particularly those on North Michigan Avenue and the North Side, are open on Sunday, although this varies by type of business (galleries, for example, are often closed on Monday); where applicable, more information is provided at the beginning of each category.

SHOPPING BY NEIGHBORHOOD

THE LOOP

Named for the elevated train tracks encircling it, the Loop is the city's business and financial hub as well as a thriving shopping destination.

The Loop's main thoroughfare, State Street, has had its share of ups and downs. After serving as Chicago's retail corridor for much of the 20th century, the street lost its stature for a time, but these days "that great street" is once again on the ascent, with a number of discount retailers like Old Navy and New York & Company dotted around the lone remaining department store, Macy's (formerly Marshall Field's). Branches of Urban Outfitters and the cosmetics store Sephora add to the mix. The opening of Block 37 in 2009 injected fresh excitement into the area. The glass-enclosed mall features major retail chains like Anthropologie and Zara alongside local independent shops. One block east, Wabash Street's "Jewelers Row" is a series of high-rises and street-level shops hawking serious bling.

ANTIQUES

Harlan J. Berk. Travel back to antiquity amid this wondrous trove of classical Greek, Roman, and Byzantine coins and artifacts. Don't miss the gallery rooms in the back. ⊠ *31 N. Clark St., Loop* ☎ *312/609–0016.*

ART GALLERIES

Douglas Dawson Gallery. Douglas Dawson showcases ancient and historic art from Africa, Oceania, and the Americas in his beautiful new space in the Loop. ⊠ *224 S. Michigan Ave., Suite 266, Loop* ☎ *312/226–7975* ⊕ *www.douglasdawson.com.*

BOOKS, MUSIC, AND GIFTS

Coulsons Music Matters. Musicians come here to find sheet music that suits their style—whether it's jazz, classical, pop, or just about anything else. You can also pick up accessories like piano lights and metronomes. ⊠ *71 E. Van Buren St., Loop* ☎ *312/461–1989.*

Selected Works Bookstore. This charming used-book store relocated from a warren-like basement in Wrigleyville to a bright, sunny shop on the second floor of the Fine Arts Building. Inside you'll discover an intriguing, though somewhat chaotic, assortment of used books and sheet music watched over by the proprietor's friendly cat. ⊠ *410 S. Michigan Ave., Suite 210, Loop* ☎ *312/447–0068* ⊕ *www.selworkschicago.com.*

CAMERAS AND ELECTRONICS

Fodor's Choice ★ **Central Camera.** This century-old store is a Loop institution. It's stacked to the rafters with cameras and darkroom equipment at competitive prices. ⊠ *230 S. Wabash Ave., Loop* ☎ *312/427–5580* ⊕ *www.central camera.com.*

CLOTHING

Florodora. This boutique's location in the historic Monadnock Building complements the vintage-inspired clothing and accessories it carries. Just down the hall, at 348 South Dearborn, you can browse the well-edited selection of footwear at sister shop Florodora Shoes; it stocks brands like Coclico and Chie Mihara. ⊠ *330 S. Dearborn St., Loop* 🕾 *312/212–8860* ⊕ *florodora.com.*

Optimo Fine Hats. One of the last establishments of its kind, Optimo makes high-end custom straw and felt hats for men in an atmosphere that evokes 1930s and '40s haberdashery. It also offers a complete line of related services, including cleaning, blocking, and repairs. Hat connoisseurs can visit Optimo's original store on the Far Southwest Side (*10215 S. Western Avenue*). ⊠ *320 S. Dearborn St., Loop* 🕾 *312/922–2999* ⊕ *www.optimohats.com.*

Syd Jerome. Board of Trade types who like special attention and snazzy designers come to this legendary clothier for brands like Giorgio Armani and Ermenegildo Zegna. Home and office consultations are available. ⊠ *2 N. LaSalle St., Loop* 🕾 *312/346–0333* ⊕ *www.sydjerome.com.*

FOOD AND TREATS

Iwan Ries and Co. Iwan Ries didn't just jump on the cigar bandwagon; the family-owned store has been around since 1857. Cigar smokers are welcome to light up in a designated area, which also displays antique pipes. ■TIP➡ **Almost 100 brands of cigars are available, along with 15,000 or so pipes, deluxe Elie Bleu humidors, and many other smoking accessories.** ⊠ *19 S. Wabash Ave., 2nd fl., Loop* 🕾 *312/372–1306* ⊕ *www.iwanries.com.*

JEWELRY AND ACCESSORIES

Jewelers Center. The largest concentration of wholesale and retail jewelers in the Midwest has been housed in this building since 1921, and it's open to the general public. Roughly 190 retailers span 13 floors, offering all kinds of jewelry, watches, and related repairs and services. ⊠ *5 S. Wabash Ave., Loop* 🕾 *312/424–2664* ⊕ *www.jewelerscenter.com.*

Legend of Time. This family-owned business, the former Chicago Watch Center, has one of the city's most outstanding inventories of used luxury watches. ⊠ *3 S. Wabash Ave., Loop* 🕾 *312/609–0003* ⊕ *www.legend oftime.com.*

Wabash Jewelers Mall. Compare prices on engagement rings or tennis bracelets at the Wabash Jewelers Mall, which houses more than a dozen vendors under one roof. This is also one of the best places in the city to shop for loose diamonds. ⊠ *21 N. Wabash Ave., at Washington St.* 🕾 *312/263–1757.*

MUSEUM STORES

Fodor's Choice ★ **Chicago Architecture Foundation ArchiCenter Shop & Tour Center.** Daniel Burnham's 1904 Santa Fe Building is a fitting home for the Chicago Architecture Foundation. Chock-full of architecture-related books, home accessories, and everything and anything related to Frank Lloyd Wright, its gift shop is also the place to sign up for one of the foundation's acclaimed tours, which are conducted on foot or by bus, bicycle, and boat. ⊠ *224 S. Michigan Ave., Loop* 🕾 *312/922–3432* ⊕ *www. architecture.org.*

Illinois Artisans Shop. Run by the Illinois State Museum, this shop culls the best jewelry, ceramics, glass, and dolls from craftspeople around the state and sells them at very reasonable prices. There are also exhibits on anything from quilting to Celtic design. ⊠ *James R. Thompson Center, 100 W. Randolph St., Suite 2-200, Loop* ☎ *312/814–5321* ⊕ *www. museum.state.il.us/programs/illinois-artisans/.*

Museum Shop at the Art Institute of Chicago. Museum reproductions in the form of jewelry, posters, and Frank Lloyd Wright–inspired decorative accessories, as well as books and toys, fill the Art Institute's gift shop. If you're keen on one of the museum's current big exhibits, chances are you'll find some nifty souvenirs to take away. ⊠ *111 S. Michigan Ave., Loop* ☎ *855/301–9612* ⊕ *www.artinstituteshop.org.*

Spertus Shop. Come here for modern Jewish must-haves, like Moses action figures and Jonathan Adler yarmulkes. There's also more traditional holiday ware, books, and music. The shop's inside the Spertus Institute for Jewish Learning and Leadership. ⊠ *610 S. Michigan Ave., South Loop* ☎ *312/322–1740* ⊕ *www.spertusshop.org.*

SHOES, HANDBAGS, AND LEATHER GOODS

Altman's Men's Shoes and Boots. Price tags are still written by hand at this family-owned institution that's been around since 1932. Its 27 stockrooms hold 50,000 pairs of men's shoes in sizes from 5 to 20 and in widths from AAA to EEEEEE. You can find anything from Timberland and Tony Lama boots to Allen Edmonds and Alden oxfords. ⊠ *120 W. Monroe St., Loop* ☎ *312/332–0667* ⊕ *www.altmansshoesandboots.com.*

SPAS

Valeo Spa. This isn't your typical spa, although you can get typical treatments if you like. Focused on wellness, the sprawling, newly renovated space includes a fitness center, pool, and elegant, understated locker and transition rooms, where you're offered a glass of wine at the end of your treatment. Men and women will feel comfortable in their separate areas, but there's also a couples suite for those so inclined. In Valeo's "clarity chambers"—based on Turkish or Moroccan hammams—guests are warmed by a fireplace and heated stone benches and floors. At the center is an oval-shape "belly stone"—a slab of heated marble used for body treatments or just for relaxation. ⊠ *JW Marriott, 151 W. Adams St., Loop* ☎ *312/660–8250* ⊕ *www.valeochicago.com* ⊗ *Daily 8–8* ☞ *$150 60-min massage, $125 40-min facial. Pool, sauna, steam room. Gym with: cardiovascular machines, free weights, weight-training equipment. Services: baths, body wraps, facials, massages, nail treatments, scrubs, waxing. Classes and programs: body sculpting, personal training, weight training.*

SOUTH LOOP

ANTIQUES

Susanin's Auctions. Live, usually themed, auctions occur on Saturday mornings about once a month. Preview items are also displayed on the floor for immediate sale at a set price. Preview hours are typically Monday through Saturday 10–5 the week before the auction. ⊠ *900 S. Clinton St., University Village* ☎ *312/832–9800* ⊕ *www.susanins.com.*

WEST LOOP

ANTIQUES

Salvage One. An enormous warehouse chock-full of leaded glass, garden ornaments, fireplace mantels, bathtubs, bars, and other architectural artifacts draws creative home remodelers and restaurant designers from around the country. ⊠ *1840 W. Hubbard St., West Loop* ☎ *312/733–0098* ⊕ *www.salvageone.com.*

ART GALLERIES

Mars Gallery. A neighborhood pioneer that showcases contemporary pop and outsider artwork, Mars Gallery displays work by Peter Mars and other well-known locals like Kevin Luthardt. ⊠ *1139 W. Fulton Market, West Loop* ☎ *312/226–7808* ⊕ *www.marsgallery.com.*

Packer Schopf Gallery. Browse through an extensive collection of contemporary art with a special emphasis on folk and outsider pieces at this gallery, which is run by well-known local owners Aron Packer and William Schopf. ⊠ *942 W. Lake St., West Loop* ☎ *312/226–8984* ⊕ *www.packergallery.com.*

Primitive. Find ethnic and tribal art, including textiles, furniture, and jewelry, at this longtime Chicago favorite. ⊠ *130 N. Jefferson St., West Loop* ☎ *312/575–9600* ⊕ *www.beprimitive.com.*

Robert Wayner/Black Walnut Gallery. The gallery has a selection of beautiful handcrafted wood furniture and sculpture as well as stunning and affordable contemporary art. ⊠ *220 N. Aberdeen St., West Loop* ☎ *312/286–2307* ⊕ *www.blackwalnutgallery.com.*

FOOD AND TREATS

Terry's Toffee. This local fave hit the big time by becoming a staple in Academy Awards gift bags. Try exotic chai-infused, peppermint pistachio, and lavender-vanilla toffee—or stick with the irresistible almond-and-pecan McCall's Classic, named for owner Terry Opalek's grandmother, whose recipe inspired the entire operation. There's a second location on the first floor of the Galleria (*5247 N. Clark Street*). ⊠ *1117 W. Grand Ave., West Loop* ☎ *312/733–2700* ⊕ *www.terrystoffee.com.*

MARKETS

Fodor'sChoice ★ **Chicago Antique Market.** March through December, usually on the last weekend of the month, 200-odd stalls selling clothing, furniture, jewelry, books, and more fill the Plumbers' Hall building and parking lot. Their wares (picture funky finds and vintage treasures rather than tattered paperbacks and refurbished vacuums) appeal to trendy types. The top-rated event also includes an Indie Designer Fashion Market, showcasing one-of-a-kind wearables by up-and-coming local designers. Weekend admission is $10 at the gate ($8 in advance), and children under 12 get in free. ⊠ *Plumbers Hall, 1340 W. Washington St., West Loop* ☎ *312/666–1200* ⊕ *www.randolphstreetmarket.com/chicago antiquemarket* ⚏ *$10.*

Maxwell Street Market. This legendary outdoor bazaar, which operates on Sunday from 7 to 3, is part of Chicago's cultural landscape. Closed by the city amid much controversy in the 1990s, it reopened soon after in its current location and remains a popular spot, particularly for Latino immigrants, to buy and sell wares year-round. The finds aren't so fabulous, but the atmosphere sure is fun, with live blues and stalls peddling Mexican street food. ⊠ *800 S. Desplaines St., West Loop* ☎ *312/745–4676* ⊕ *www.cityofchicago.org/city/en/depts/dca/supp_info/maxwell_street_market.html* 🖘 *Free.*

SPAS

Spa Space. The warm, inviting spa is a favorite of stressed-out type A's who work nearby at the Chicago Board of Trade and other Loop office buildings. Serious pampering includes massages specifically geared to runners and golfers and a pedicure suite where bottles of wine are welcome. All facials are dermatologist approved, and body treatments include grapeseed scrubs, seaweed wraps, and waxing. Packages include the Space Stressbuster Express, with a 60-minute massage, facial, aromatherapy manicure, and peppermint pedicure. ⊠ *161 N. Canal St., West Loop* ☎ *312/466–9585* ⊕ *www.spaspace.com* ☺ *Mon., Wed., Thurs. 10–8, Tues. 11–8, Fri. 9–7, Sat. 9–6, Sun. 11–5* ☞ *$95 60-min facial, $160 3-treatment package. Steam room. Services: aromatherapy, body wraps, facials, massages, nail treatments, scrubs, waxing.*

NEAR NORTH AND THE MAGNIFICENT MILE

We've got news for shopaholics who consider the Midwest flyover country: if you haven't done Chicago's Magnificent Mile, you simply haven't shopped. With more than 450 stores along the stretch of Michigan Avenue that runs from the Chicago River to Oak Street, the Mag Mile is one of the best retail strips the world over. Chanel, Hermès, and Gucci are just a few of the fashion houses with fabulous boutiques here. Other notables such as Anne Fontaine, Kate Spade, and Prada also have Mag Mile outposts, recognizing the everybody-who's-anybody importance of the address. Shoppers with down-to-earth budgets will find there's plenty on the Mag Mile as well, with national chains making an extra effort at their multilevel megastores here. Cozying up against the Magnificent Mile is the Gold Coast, an area that's as moneyed as it sounds. The streets teem with luxury hotels, upscale restaurants, and snazzy boutiques, mainly concentrated on Oak and Rush streets. There's also a huge new Barneys New York on East Oak Street just off Rush. (Many consider swanky Oak Street part of the Mag Mile, though neighboring streets technically are not.)

ART GALLERIES

Colletti Gallery. Fine antique posters, a serious collection of European ceramics and glass, and an eclectic selection of furniture transport you to the late 19th century. ⊠ *49 E. Oak St., Near North* ☎ *312/664–6767* ⊕ *www.collettigallery.com.*

Joel Oppenheimer, Inc. Established in 1969, this gallery in the Wrigley Building has an amazing collection of Audubon prints and specializes in antique natural-history pieces. ⊠ *410 N. Michigan Ave., Near North* ☎ *312/642–5300* ⊕ *audubonart.com.*

Richard Gray Gallery. This gallery in the John Hancock Center lures serious collectors with modern masters such as David Hockney and Roy Lichtenstein. ⊠ *875 N. Michigan Ave., Suite 2503, Near North* ☎ *312/642–8877* ⊕ *www. richardgraygallery.com.*

R.S. Johnson Fine Art. More than 50 museums are among the clients of R. S. Johnson, a Mag Mile resident for almost 60 years. The family-run gallery sells old masters along with art by Picasso, Degas, and Goya to the public and to private collectors. ⊠ *645 N. Michigan Ave., 9th fl., entrance on Erie St., Near North* ☎ *312/943–1661* ⊕ *www. rsjohnsonfineart.com.*

BEAUTY

Bravco Beauty Centre. Need a hard-to-find shampoo, an ionic hair dryer, or simply a jar of Vaseline? Bravco is the place for all this and more, with an expert staff and a huge inventory. Also check out B-Too upstairs for makeup and accessories. Cash or check only. ⊠ *43 E. Oak St., Near North* ☎ *312/943–4305* ⊕ *www.bravco.com.*

BOOKS, MUSIC, AND GIFTS

Accent Chicago. Pop into Accent Chicago for locally inspired gifts that range from prints of vintage Chicago Transit Authority posters to mugs adorned with the city's iconic skyline. In addition to the John Hancock Center store, this mini-chain also has branches in the Water Tower Building (*835 N. Michigan Avenue*) and in the Loop (*150 N. Michigan Avenue*). ⊠ *John Hancock Center, 875 N. Michigan Ave., Near North* ☎ *312/654–8125* ⊕ *www.lovefromchicago.com.*

Jazz Record Mart. Billing itself as the world's largest jazz record store, this "mart" sells tens of thousands of new and used titles on CD, vinyl, and cassette. Along with the vast, in-depth selection of jazz and blues, you'll also find a broad range of world music. ⊠ *27 E. Illinois St., Near North* ☎ *312/222–1467* ⊕ *jazzmart.com.*

Space 519. Looking for a last-minute gift? This style-conscious Mag Mile general store has anything and everything you need—clothing, accessories, perfume and makeup, coffee-table books, vintage watches, and even vintage furniture. ⊠ *900 N. Michigan Shops, 900 N. Michigan Ave., Level 5, Near North* ☎ *312/751–1519* ⊕ *www.space519.com.*

CAMERAS AND ELECTRONICS

Apple Store. A multilevel fantasyland for fans of Apple's iPad, computers, and related accessories, this store also has an Internet café where PC fans can get a glimpse of life on the other side. There's a second location in Lincoln Park (*801 W. North Avenue*). ⊠ *679 N. Michigan Ave., Near North* ☎ *312/529–9500* ⊕ *apple.com.*

SPOTLIGHT: NAVY PIER

Extending more than a half mile onto Lake Michigan from 600 East Grand Avenue, Navy Pier treats you to spectacular views of the skyline, especially from a jumbo Ferris wheel set in slow motion. Stores and carts gear their wares to families and tourists, and most don't merit a special trip. But if you're out there, check out **Oh Yes Chicago!** (*312/321–0557*) for souvenirs and the **Chicago Children's Museum Store** (*312/527–4276*) for educational kids' toys. Many stores are open late into the evening, especially in summer.

11

CLOTHING

Anne Fontaine. The French designer's famous takes on the classic white shirt sport hefty price tags, though they also show a careful attention to detail. ✉ *909 N. Michigan Ave., Near North* ☎ *312/943–0401* ⊕ *www.annefontaine.com.*

Brooks Brothers. This bastion of conservative ready-to-wear fashion still sells boatloads of their classic 1837 navy blazer. But this one-stop shop for Oxfords and khakis also sneaks in bold colors. ✉ *713 N. Michigan Ave., Near North* ☎ *312/915–0060* ⊕ *www.brooksbrothers.com.*

Burberry. The label once favored by the conservatively well dressed is now hot with lots of other people who can't get enough of its signature plaid on everything from bikinis to baby gear. Even the exterior of this stunning Mag Mile flagship features that tan-and-black plaid. ✉ *633 N. Michigan Ave., Near North* ☎ *312/787–2500* ⊕ *us.burberry.com.*

Chanel Boutique. Ensconced in the Drake Hotel, this shop carries the complete line of Chanel products, including ready-to-wear, fragrances, and cosmetics. ✉ *935 N. Michigan Ave., Near North* ☎ *312/787–5500* ⊕ *www.chanel.com.*

Ermenegildo Zegna. The sportswear, softly tailored business attire, and dress clothes of this Italian great are gathered all under one roof. ✉ *645 N. Michigan Ave., Near North* ☎ *312/587–9660* ⊕ *www.zegna.com/ us/home.html.*

Giorgio Armani. An airy, two-floor space displays Armani's discreetly luxurious clothes and accessories. The store includes the top-priced Black Label line, considered a cut above the department store line. ✉ *800 N. Michigan Ave., Near North* ☎ *312/573–4220* ⊕ *www.armani.com.*

Gucci. Though the prices aren't for the faint of heart, there are some pieces here that will last a lifetime. ✉ *900 North Michigan Shops, 900 N. Michigan Ave., Near North* ☎ *312/664–5504* ⊕ *www.gucci.com.*

Haberdash. Tailored clothes from designers like Barbour and Gitman Bros., plus Wolverine boots, and wood shelving make Adam Beltzman's men's shop decidedly masculine. An in-shop barber will even cut your hair, which further adds to the ambience. Haberdash's sister—or, rather, brother—store, EDC (for "everyday carry"), focuses on apothecary items, accessories, and footwear; you'll find it at 607 North State Street. ✉ *611 N. State St., Near North* ☎ *312/624–8551* ⊕ *www.haberdashmen.com.*

FESTIVAL OF LIGHTS

Chicago's holiday season officially gets under way every year at the end of November with the Magnificent Mile Lights Festival, a weekend-long event consisting of family-friendly activities that pack the shopping strip to the gills. Music, ice-carving contests, and stage shows kick off the celebration, which culminates in a parade and the illumination of more than a million lights along Michigan Avenue. Neighborhood stores keep late hours to accommodate the crowds. For more information, check out ⊕ *www. themagnificentmile.com.*

Hermès of Paris. The well-heeled shop the Chicago flagship for suits, signature scarves, and leather accessories. ✉ *25 E. Oak St., Near North* ☎ *312/787–8175* ⊕ *www.hermes.com.*

Hugo BOSS. Men will find modern, well-cut suits with attention to tailoring, as well as other signature Boss clothing and accessories here. ✉ *The Shops at North Bridge, 520 N. Michigan Ave., Near North* ☎ *312/321–0700* ⊕ *www.hugoboss.com.*

Ikram. Best known for her role as informal stylist to Michelle Obama, fashion maven Ikram Goldman moved her eponymous boutique to a 16,000-square-foot mini–department store in 2011, effectively quadrupling her inventory—and her influence. The shop carries an assortment of new and old fashion icons, from Alexander McQueen and Jean Paul Gaultier to Narciso Rodriguez and Zac Posen, along with home furnishings and art. ✉ *15 E. Huron St., Near North* ☎ *312/587–1000* ⊕ *ikram.com.*

Jil Sander. This line has captured the devotion of the fashion crowd for its minimalist look and impeccable tailoring. Prices are at the upper end of the designer range. ✉ *48 E. Oak St., Near North* ☎ *312/335–0006* ⊕ *www.jilsander.com.*

Karen Millen. The U.K. designer's first shop in the Midwest takes you from day to night; pieces range from tailored skirts and cardigans to drapey tanks, skinny jeans, and leather jackets. There is a selection of sky-high heels featuring bold patterns and embellishments, too. ✉ *900 N. Michigan Ave., Near North* ☎ *312/867–1760* ⊕ *us.karenmillen.com.*

L.K. Bennett. A favorite of Kate Middleton, this London fashion house turns out tailored pieces for work and play. If your look leans toward modern but practical basics, sophisticated handbags, and chic wear-with-everything shoes (like the kitten heels the line is known for), you'll find plenty to fancy here. ✉ *900 North Michigan Shops, 900 N. Michigan Ave., Near North* ☎ *312/374–0958* ⊕ *www.lkbennett.com.*

Londo Mondo. A great selection of swimwear for buff beach-ready bodies is available at Londo Mondo. You can also find workout and yoga gear and men's and women's in-line skates. If you're in Lincoln Park, drop by the branch at 2148 North Halsted Street. ✉ *1100 N. Dearborn St., Near North* ☎ *312/751–2794* ⊕ *www.londomondo.com.*

Marc Jacobs. Jacobs's high-end runway line is showcased in this glamorous boutique in the swanky Elysian Hotel. ✉ *11 E. Walton St., Near North* ☎ *312/649–7260.*

Palazzo Bridal. Chic urban brides trust Jane and Saeed Hamidi for their clean-lined bridal collection. ✉ *1872 N Damen Ave., Near North* ☎ *312/337–6940* ⊕ *www.palazzobridal.com.*

Polo/Ralph Lauren. Manor house meets mass marketing—the upper-crust chic covers men's, women's, and children's clothing as well as housewares. Fabrics are often enticing (suede, silk organza, cashmere), but expect to pay a pretty penny. ✉ *750 N. Michigan Ave., Near North* ☎ *312/266–9581* ⊕ *www.ralphlauren.com.*

Prada. This store has a spare, cool look that matches its modern inventory of clothing, shoes, and bags. In fact, unless you're a Miuccia devotee, the three-story shop can seem almost bare. ⊠ *30 E. Oak St., Near North* ☎ *312/951–1113* ⊕ *www.prada.com.*

Topshop. In 2011 this beloved British brand invaded a 30,000-square-foot space on the corner of Michigan Avenue and Pearson Street, bringing the latest U.K. fashions to the Mag Mile. Notable among the three floors of clothes, shoes, lingerie, and accessories are collections from Topman, the men's clothing branch, and cosmetics exclusive to Chicago. ⊠ *830 N. Michigan Ave., Near North* ☎ *312/280–6834* ⊕ *us.topshop.com.*

Zara. The Spanish chain's original Chicago outpost has 34,000-square feet of cute, trendy clothing that usually won't bust your wallet. A second location opened in retail hub Block 37 (*1 W. Randolph Street*). ⊠ *700 N. Michigan Ave., Near North* ☎ *312/255–8123* ⊕ *www.zara.com.*

DEPARTMENT STORES

Barneys New York. Covering 90,000-square feet, the massive six-level store boasts ample space for women's high-end designer threads, shoes, an expansive menswear department with on-site tailoring, and an in-house Co-Op, which carries clothes for young adults. After dropping a dime (or two) on fashion-forward finds, head up to the bright and airy sixth-floor eatery Fred's at Barneys for a chopped salad. ⊠ *15 E. Oak St., Near North* ☎ *312/587–1700* ⊕ *www.barneys.com.*

Bloomingdale's. Chicago's Bloomie's is built in a clean, airy style that is part Prairie School, part postmodern (and quite unlike its New York City sibling), giving you plenty of elbow room to sift through its selection of designer labels. ⊠ *900 North Michigan Shops, 900 N. Michigan Ave., Near North* ☎ *312/440–4460* ⊕ *bloomingdales.com.*

Macy's. In the fall of 2006 Marshall Field's, Chicago's most famous—and perpetually struggling—department store, became a Macy's. Some of the higher-end designers Field's carried are gone from the racks, but overall the store is the same, standing as a glorious reminder of how grand department stores used to be. Founder Marshall Field's motto was "Give the lady what she wants!" And for many years both ladies and gentlemen had been able to find everything from furs to personalized stationery on one of the store's nine levels. You can still buy Field's famous Frango mints, and the seventh-floor Walnut Room restaurant remains a magical place to dine at Christmas. Note that the famous Tiffany Dome—designed in 1907 by Louis Comfort Tiffany—is visible from the fifth floor. ⊠ *111 N. State St., Loop* ☎ *312/781–1000* ⊕ *macys.com.*

Neiman Marcus. Prices are high here, but they're usually matched by the outstanding and tasteful selection of designer clothing and accessories for men and women. The gourmet food area on the top floor tempts with hard-to-find delicacies and impeccable hostess gifts. ⊠ *737 N. Michigan Ave., Near North* ☎ *312/642–5900* ⊕ *www.neimanmarcus.com.*

Nordstrom. This is a lovely department store with a killer shoe department, a vast BP juniors' section, great petites and menswear

MIGHTY VERTICAL MALLS

Forget all your preconceived notions about malls being suburban wastelands. Three decidedly posh urban ones dot the Mag Mile, and another holds court on State Street. The toniest of the four is 900 North Michigan Shops, which promises a dazzling list of tenants plus live weekend piano serenades. A more casual but no less entertaining shopping mecca is just blocks away at Water Tower Place. The newer kids on the block are The Shops at North Bridge, which debuted in 2000, and Block 37, which opened on State Street in late 2009 after much anticipation.

The elegant deco design of **900 North Michigan Shops** (*900 N. Michigan Ave. 312/915–3916*) matches the upscale ambience of the stores it houses. Inside you'll find the Chicago branches of Bloomingdale's and L.K. Bennett as well as dozens of boutiques, including Gucci, L'Occitane, and Karen Millen.

Water Tower Place (*835 N. Michigan Ave. 312/440–3165*) has seven floors of retail, and spots like the flagship American Girl store, the Art of Dr. Seuss Gallery, and the Chicago Sports Museum gift shop make it popular with the younger set. Foodlife, a step above the usual food court, is a fantastic place for a quick bite.

The big draw at **The Shops at North Bridge** (*520 N. Michigan Ave. 312/327–2300*) is Nordstrom. Sephora, CHICO'S, A|X Armani Exchange, and other chains are found alongside specialty stores such as Vosges Haut-Chocolat, a city chocolatier with an international following.

The modern glass-enclosed **Block 37** (*108 N. State St. 312/220–0037*) occupies a full city block—bordered by Randolph, Washington, Dearborn, and State streets (number 37 of the city's original 58 blocks). Big-name retailers like Zara and Puma share space with local favorites such as Akira.

departments, and outstanding customer service. Leave yourself time to linger at the Nordstrom Spa on the third floor (accessible via the main mall entrance) and Café Nordstrom on the fourth floor. ⊠ *The Shops at North Bridge, 520 N. Michigan Ave., Near North* ☎ *312/327–2300* ⊕ *shop.nordstrom.com.*

Saks Fifth Avenue. The smaller, less-crowded cousin of the New York flagship doesn't scrimp on its selection of designer clothes, though the primary draw might be the store's noteworthy first-floor makeup and fragrance department. A men's specialty store is across the street. ⊠ *700 N. Michigan Ave., Near North* ☎ *312/799-5211* ⊕ *saksfifthavenue.com.*

FOOD AND TREATS

FAMILY **Dylan's Candy Bar.** Taking up two floors of the historic Tribune Tower, Dylan's Candy Bar is filled with imaginative sweets that will delight kids—and kids at heart. ⊠ *445 N. Michigan Ave., Near North* ☎ *312/702–2247* ⊕ *www.dylanscandybar.com.*

Fodor's Choice ★ **Eataly Chicago.** Celebrity chef Mario Batali's sprawling Eataly has a little bit of everything. Part grocery store, part food court, part craft

Floor upon floor upon floor of goodies at Macy's, in the former Marshall Field's department store building.

brewery, with a Nutella bar, multiple cafés, and a gelato shop thrown in for good measure, it is a foodie's paradise. ⊠ *43 E. Ohio St., Near North* ☎ *312/521–8700* ⊕ *www.eataly.com/eataly-chicago/.*

Garrett Popcorn. Bring home a tub of Chicago's famous popcorn instead of a giant pencil or T-shirt, and you'll score major points. Lines can be long, but trust us—this stuff is worth the wait. The Magnificent Mile flagship store is one of a dozen locations citywide. Check Garrett's website for details. ⊠ *625 N. Michigan Ave., Near North* ☎ *888/476–7267* ⊕ *www.garrettpopcorn.com.*

HOME DECOR

Jonathan Adler. Design guru Adler's store is chock-full of his signature fun, funky pottery and home furnishings, all arranged in a series of small living spaces. ⊠ *676 N. Wabash Ave., Near North* ☎ *312/274–9920* ⊕ *www.jonathanadler.com.*

Quatrine. The washable upholstered and slipcovered furniture for dining rooms, living rooms, and bedrooms here looks decidedly chic and not at all what you'd consider typically child- or pet-friendly. ⊠ *670 N. Wabash Ave., Near North* ☎ *312/649–1700* ⊕ *www.quatrine.com.*

Room & Board. Straightforward yet stylish pieces with a modern sensibility blend quality craftsmanship and materials with relatively affordable pricing. ⊠ *The Shops at North Bridge, 55 E. Ohio St., Near North* ☎ *312/222–0970* ⊕ *www.roomandboard.com.*

LINGERIE

Intimacy. These bra-fit gurus specialize in a "holistic" fitting process that results in a more flattering shape; that's enough to make any customer, well, perk up. Schedule your fitting ahead of time if possible. ⊠ *900 North Michigan Shops, 900 N. Michigan Ave., Near North* ☎ *312/337–8366* ⊕ *myintimacy.com.*

MUSEUM STORES

Museum of Contemporary Art Chicago Store. This outstanding museum gift shop has out-of-the-ordinary decorative accessories, tableware, and jewelry, as well as a superb collection of books on modern and contemporary art. It has its own street-level entrance. ⊠ *220 E. Chicago Ave., Near North* ☎ *312/397–4000* ⊕ *www.mcachicagostore.org.*

SHOES, HANDBAGS, AND LEATHER GOODS

adidas Originals Chicago. The main attractions here are old-school sneakers and hip urban fashions for a fresh generation of fans. ⊠ *900 North Michigan Shops, 923 N. Rush St., Near North* ☎ *312/932–0651* ⊕ *www.adidas.com.*

Allen Edmonds. Men's footwear essentials range from classic Italian leather wing-tips and slip-ons to casual moccasins and rugged boots. You'll find a second store in the Loop at 122 South LaSalle Street. ⊠ *541 N. Michigan Ave., Near North* ☎ *312/755–9306* ⊕ *www.allen edmonds.com.*

AllSaints. AllSaints' immaculate Chicago outpost is a required stop for edgy, dark-hearted fashionistas and fashionistos alike—especially those looking for a killer leather jacket or a head-turning pair of boots. ⊠ *700 N. Michigan Ave., Near North* ☎ *312/283–0400* ⊕ *www. us.allsaints.com.*

Coach. Well-designed leather goods, in the form of purses, briefcases, and cell phone holders, are Coach's specialty. Smart shoes and other accessories have joined the inventory as well. Embossing is available on-site at this impressive location. There's a Water Tower Place shop (*835 N. Michigan Avenue*), too. ⊠ *625 N. Michigan Ave., Near North* ☎ *312/587–3167* ⊕ *www.coach.com.*

Hanig's Footwear. This family-owned store in the John Hancock Center stocks a well-chosen selection of stylish and comfortable European and U.S. brands, including Camper, Dansko, and Hunter. There's also a Lincoln Park location (*1000 W. North Ave.*). ⊠ *875 N. Michigan Ave., Near North* ☎ *312/787–6800* ⊕ *www.hanigs.com.*

Jimmy Choo. These are the extremely expensive heels that keep celebs and stylish women the world over drooling. ⊠ *63 E. Oak St., Near North* ☎ *312/255–1170* ⊕ *www.jimmychoo.com.*

Kate Spade. The goddess of handbags has filled her two-floor boutique in the heart of Oak Street with adorable shoes, small leather goods and, of course, her to-die-for purses and totes. (If you're after men's clothing and accessories, head across the street to Jack Spade.) Ladies will find more to fall in love with at the Kate Spade store in 900 North Michigan Shops. ⊠ *56 E. Oak St., Near North* ☎ *312/654–8853* ⊕ *www. katespade.com.*

Louis Vuitton. Louis Vuitton has it all under one roof—the coveted purses, leather goods, and luggage bearing the beloved logo, plus the designer's men's and women's shoes and jewelry lines. There's also a Louis Vuitton boutique in Nordstrom (*55 E. Grand Avenue*). ⊠ *919 N. Michigan Ave., Near North* ☎ *312/944–2010* ⊕ *www.louisvuitton.com.*

Fodor'sChoice
★
Nike Chicago. This is one of Chicago's top tourist attractions. Many visitors—including professional athletes—stop here to take in the sports memorabilia, road test a pair of sneakers, or watch the inspirational videos. The shop includes a Nike iD lab, where you can design your own kicks. ⊠ *669 N. Michigan Ave., Near North* ☎ *312/642–6363* ⊕ *store.nike.com.*

Salvatore Ferragamo. The shoes have been the classic choice of the well-heeled for generations, but it's the designer's handbags, with a fresh, contemporary sensibility, that are generating excitement of late. ⊠ *645 N. Michigan Ave., Near North* ☎ *312/397–0464* ⊕ *www.ferragamo. com.*

Tod's. Choose from a wide selection of the practical bags and driving moccasins that made Tod's famous, as well as newer additions to the line, including high heels. ⊠ *121 E. Oak St., Near North* ☎ *312/943–0070, 800/457–8637* ⊕ *www.tods.com.*

SPAS

NoMi Spa at Park Hyatt. This simple, elegant spa offers big-time customer satisfaction by operating with the mantra "Eat well, live well, be well." NoMi, whose name is derived from its North Michigan location, has just two treatment rooms; one comes with its own steam shower and bathroom, so there's no need for traipsing through the locker room to extend your indulgence. Spagoers also have access to the hotel's swimming pool and fitness center, both with cityscape views. The products used include seasonal ingredients, French sunflower seeds, ground olive pits, and citrus. ⊠ *Park Hyatt, 800 N. Michigan Ave., Near North* ☎ *312/335–1234* ⊕ *www.nomispa.com* ☉ *Daily 8–8* ☞ *$160 60-min massage, $180 45-min facial. Hair salon, steam room. Gym with: cardiovascular machines, free weights, weight-training equipment. Services: aromatherapy, facials, light therapy, massages, nail treatments, waxing.*

Spa at Four Seasons Hotel Chicago. Comfort and relaxation are taken seriously at this spa, where private treatment rooms are soundproofed for maximum serenity. Opt for a tempting wrap that uses cane sugar and honey from Hawaii or an intoxicating massage that begins with a bourbon–brown sugar scrub in the spa and ends with a drink of single-barrel bourbon in the bar. If you're ready to splurge, go for the mini-spa escape package, which includes a manicure, mini-pedicure, 55-minute massage, and 55-minute facial. In the lounge, guests are welcome to stretch out on daybeds and snack on fresh fruit for as long as they like before and after treatments. ⊠ *Four Seasons Hotel, 120 E. Delaware Pl., Near North* ☎ *312/280–8800* ⊕ *www.fourseasons.com/ chicagofs* ☉ *Daily 8–9* ☞ *$150 55-min massage, $150 50-min facial, $290 4-treatment package. Pool, sauna, steam room. Gym with: cardiovascular machines, free weights, weight-lifting equipment. Services:*

body wraps, facials, massages, nail treatments, scrubs, waxing. Classes and programs: personal training.

The Spa by Asha. It pays to be early at this spa on the lower level of the James Hotel so that you have time to take advantage of the complimentary preservice aromatherapy foot bath in the darkened lounge; a therapist will also tuck a heated pillow behind your neck and massage your feet and calves with a scrub of walnut, lavender, and herbal extracts. It may feel like a shame to leave for the actual treatments, but services that include Aveda plant-based facials, body wraps, and massages will only up your relaxation factor. Special services catering to moms-to-be include a hydrating belly treatment. There are massages and facials designed exclusively for men, too, plus a Himalayan rejuvenation treatment that claims to boost your immune system during the change of seasons. ⊠ *James Hotel, 55 E. Ontario St., Near North* ☎ *312/664–0200* ⊕ *www.ashasalonspa.com* ⊗ *Weekdays 9–9, Sat. 8–7, Sun. 10–6* ☞ *$105 60-min massage, $115 60-min facial. Services: body wraps, facials, hair, makeup, massages, nail treatments, scrubs, waxing.*

TOYS

American Girl Place. Little girls from just about everywhere arrive here with their signature dolls in tow. There's easily a day's worth of activities offered at American Girl Place—shop at the boutique, take in a live musical revue, and have lunch or afternoon tea at the café, where dolls can partake in the meal from their own "sassy seats." Brace yourself for long lines just to get into the store during high shopping seasons. ⊠ *Water Tower Place, 835 N. Michigan Ave., Near North* ☎ *877/247–5223* ⊕ *www.americangirl.com.*

The Disney Store. At this Mouse emporium, there's everything little Disney disciples need for a fix: a plethora of plush toys, DVDs, games, and other goodies. You'll find a second store in Block 37 (*108 N. State Street*). ⊠ *717 N. Michigan Ave., Near North* ☎ *312/654–9208* ⊕ *www. disneystore.com.*

WINE

The House of Glunz. Don't let the upper-crust vibe dissuade you from setting foot inside. The folks at this family-owned wineshop know their stuff but aren't in the least snobbish or pretentious about helping you find a bottle that suits your needs, whether you're building your cellar with rare vintages or in the market for a $15 bottle for dinner. ⊠ *1206 N. Wells St., Near North* ☎ *312/642–3000* ⊕ *www.thehouse ofglunz.com.*

RIVER NORTH

In the area between the buzzy Gold Coast and the Chicago River, the vibe is less frenetic and the retail is more focused on art galleries, antiques shops, and home-furnishings stores. Some of these are housed in historic buildings—most notably Bloomingdale's Home & Furniture Store, which occupies the Moorish Revival–style Medinah Temple. Shoppers who work up an appetite needn't worry. Somewhat surprisingly, there are also a number of touristy megarestaurants here, including Ed Debevic's, Rainforest Café, and a humongous flagship McDonald's.

ANTIQUES

The Golden Triangle. In a block-long, 23,000-square-foot space, Asian furnishings and artifacts are arranged in vignettes depicting various eras and regions, from a British Colonial reception hall to a Chinese scholar's courtyard. The vast collection includes a line of custom-designed modern furnishings made from reclaimed wood. ⊠ *330 N. Clark St., River North* ☎ *312/755–1266* ⊕ *www.goldentriangle.biz.*

JRoberts Antiques. The sprawling, 50,000-square-foot showroom once known as Jay Robert's Antique Warehouse holds 17th- to 21st-century European furniture—ranging from French Empire to art deco—as well as objets d'art. ⊠ *149 W. Kinzie St., River North* ☎ *312/222–0167* ⊕ *www.1stdibs.com/dealers/j-roberts-antiques/.*

P.O.S.H. It's hard to resist the charming, piled-up displays of vintage hotel and restaurant china here. There's also an impressive selection of silver gravy boats, creamers, and flatware that bear the marks of ocean liners and private clubs. ⊠ *613 N. State St., River North* ☎ *312/280–1602* ⊕ *poshchicago.com.*

Rita Bucheit, Ltd. Devoted to the streamlined Biedermeier aesthetic, this shop carries choice furniture and accessories from the period along with art deco and modern pieces that are perfect complements to the style. ⊠ *449 N. Wells St., River North* ☎ *312/527–4080* ⊕ *www.rita bucheit.com.*

ART GALLERIES

Alan Koppel Gallery. An eclectic mix of works by modern masters and contemporary artists is balanced by a selection of French and Italian Modernist furniture from the 1920s to 1950s. ⊠ *806 N. Dearborn Ave., River North* ☎ *312/640–0730* ⊕ *www.alankoppel.com.*

Ann Nathan Gallery. The specialty here is contemporary paintings, but the gallery also showcases sculpture and singular artist-made furniture. ⊠ *212 W. Superior St., River North* ☎ *312/664–6622* ⊕ *www. annnathangallery.com.*

Carl Hammer Gallery. Lee Godie and Henry Darger are among the outsider and self-taught artists whose work is shown at this gallery. ⊠ *740 N. Wells St., River North* ☎ *312/266–8512* ⊕ *www.carlhammer gallery.com.*

Catherine Edelman Gallery. This gallery of contemporary photography explores the work of emerging, mixed-media, photo-based artists such as Carlos Diaz, Sandro Miller, and Jack Spencer. ⊠ *300 W. Superior St., River North* ☎ *312/266–2350* ⊕ *www.edelmangallery.com.*

Echt Gallery. Collectors of fine studio art glass are drawn here by such luminaries as Dale Chihuly. ⊠ *222 W. Superior St., River North* ☎ *312/440–0288* ⊕ *www.echtgallery.com.*

Stephen Daiter Gallery. This space showcases stunning 20th-century European and American photography, particularly avant-garde photojournalism. ⊠ *230 W. Superior St., 4th fl., River North* ☎ *312/787–3350* ⊕ *www.stephendaitergallery.com.*

BOOKS, MUSIC, AND GIFTS

Abraham Lincoln Book Shop. The shop owner here buys, sells, and appraises books, paintings, documents, and other paraphernalia associated with American military and political history. It's been around since 1938. ⊠ *357 W. Chicago Ave., River North* ☎ *312/944–3085* ⊕ *www. alincolnbookshop.com.*

Paper Source. Reams and reams of different types of paper are sold here; much of it is unusual and expensive. Check out the custom-invitation department and good selection of rubber stamps and bookbinding supplies. Paper Source also has stores in Lincoln Park (*919 W. Armitage Avenue*) and Southport (*3543 N. Southport Avenue*). ⊠ *232 W. Chicago Ave., River North* ☎ *312/337–0798* ⊕ *www. papersource.com.*

> ### GALLERY TOURS
>
> Every Saturday morning at 11, Chicago Gallery News offers complimentary gallery tours. Groups meet at the Starbucks at 750 North Franklin Street and are guided each week by a different gallery owner or director from the River North area. For more information (and holiday weekend schedules) call *312/649-0064* or click ⊕ *www.chicagogallerynews. com.*

CLOTHING

Blake. A no-nonsense boutique without pomp, circumstance, or even signage, Blake displays clean-lined clothes in a pristine setting. You'll find designers like Dries van Noten and Balenciaga as well as shoes and accessories of a similar subtle elegance. ⊠ *212 W. Chicago Ave., River North* ☎ *312/202–0047.*

FOOD AND TREATS

Fodor's Choice
★
Blommer Chocolate Outlet Store. "Why do parts of River North smell like freshly baked brownies?" is a question you hear fairly often. The oh-so-sweet reason: it's downwind from the Blommer Chocolate Factory, which has been making wholesale chocolates since 1939. More important, the retail outlet store is also here, so you can snap up your Blommer chocolates and candies at a discount—a handy tip to know when those smells give you a case of the munchies. ⊠ *600 W. Kinzie St., at N. Desplaines St., River North* ☎ *312/492–1336* ⊕ *www.blommer.com.*

HOME DECOR

Fodor's Choice
★
Bloomingdale's Home Store. This former meeting space and concert hall, known as the Medinah Temple, was built for the Shriners in 1912. After it took over, Bloomie's kept the historically significant exterior intact but gutted the inside to create its first stand-alone furnishings store in Chicago. It's stocked to the rafters with everything you need to eat, sleep, and relax in your home in high style. ⊠ *600 N. Wabash Ave., River North* ☎ *312/324–7500* ⊕ *bloomingdales.com.*

The Chopping Block. New and seasoned chefs appreciate the expertly chosen selection of pots and pans, bakeware, gadgets, and ingredients here. Intimate cooking classes are hugely popular and taught by a fun, knowledgeable staff. (Students get 10% off store merchandise.) The Chopping Block's second location on Lincoln Square (*4747 N. Lincoln Avenue*) includes a wineshop. ⊠ *The Merchandise Mart, 222*

Merchandise Mart Plaza, Suite 107, River North ☎ *312/644–6360* ⊕ *www.thechoppingblock.net.*

Lightology. Dedicated to modern lighting, this 20,000-square-foot showroom is an essential stop for designers and architects, not to mention passersby drawn to the striking designs visible from the windows. It's the brainchild of Greg Kay, who started out as a roller-disco lighting designer in the 1970s and made a name for himself in Chicago with Tech Lighting, a contemporary design gallery. ⊠ *215 W. Chicago Ave., River North* ☎ *312/944–1000* ⊕ *www.lightology.com.*

Luminaire. The international contemporary furniture in this 21,000-square-foot showroom includes pieces by Philippe Starck, Antonio Citterio, and Jeffrey Bernett. Sleek kitchen designs and tabletop pieces are from Zaha Hadid, Joseph Joseph, Damian Evans, KnIndustrie, and other edgy designers from around the globe. ⊠ *301 W. Superior St., River North* ☎ *312/664–9582* ⊕ *luminaire.com.*

Manifesto. One of the largest design ateliers in the city occupies this huge, street-level space; look for work by furniture designer (and owner) Richard Gorman plus a smattering of home accessories. ⊠ *755 N. Wells St., River North* ☎ *312/664–0733* ⊕ *www.manifestofurniture.com.*

Merchandise Mart. This massive marketplace between Wells and North Orleans streets just north of the Chicago River is more notable for its art deco design than its shopping. Many of the stores inside are only for the design trade, meaning that you have to be an interior designer to access their wares. However, the first two floors have been turned into retail with the unveiling of LuxeHome, the world's largest collection of high-end kitchen, bath, and building showrooms open to the public. ⊠ *222 W. Merchandise Mart Plaza, River North* ☎ *800/677–6278* ⊕ *www.mmart.com.*

Orange Skin. The go-to resource for modern furniture, lighting, and accessories in Chicago carries pieces by Minotti, Philippe Starck, and Piero Lissoni in a bi-level industrial space. ⊠ *223 W. Erie St., Suite 1NW, River North* ☎ *312/335–1033* ⊕ *www.orangeskin.com.*

SPAS

Chuan Spa. You could easily spend a day at this 22,000-square-foot relaxation den, which offers lush amenities and treatments rooted in traditional Chinese medicine. Start by drinking in views from the tranquil lobby, where staffers rarely speak above a whisper; then let a personal attendant guide you through a changing room (complete with salt-stone sauna and herbal steam shower) into a dimly lighted treatment space, appointed with Asian-inspired furnishings. You can linger after your soothing session, reclining in a heated lounge chair as you gaze out onto the Chicago River. ⊠ *Langham Hotel, 330 N. Wabash Ave., River North* ☎ *312/923–9988* ⊕ *www.chuanspa.com* ☞ *$115 30-min massage, $125 50-min facial, $340 4-treatment package. Pool, sauna. Gym with: cardiovascular machines, strength machines. Services: body wraps, facials, massages, nail treatments, scrubs, traditional Chinese medicine treatments. Classes and programs: personal training.*

Spa at Trump. The one thing most Trump hotel spas have in common is that they're likely the swankiest places in their respective towns to relax and rejuvenate, with luxe locker rooms tricked out with multijet showers, signature gemstone massages with the essences of rubies, diamonds, emeralds, and sapphires (you can see the tiny stones in the oil bottles), and your every need addressed. What makes each location unique, though, are seasonal offerings, such as a hot-chocolate pedicure or body scrub, very welcome in the middle of a brutal Chicago winter. ☒ *Trump International Hotel & Tower Chicago, 401 N. Wabash Ave., River North* ☎ *312/588–8020* ⊕ *www.trumpchicagohotel.com* ☉ *Daily 8–9* ☞ *$165 60-min massage, $195 60-min facial. Lap pool, sauna, steam room. Gym with: cardiovasular machines, free weights, weight-lifting equipment. Services: body wraps, facials, massages, nail treatments, scrubs, waxing. Classes and programs: body sculpting, kickboxing, personal training, Pilates, Spinning, weight training, yoga.*

WINE

Pops for Champagne. Stock up on bubbly and assorted accoutrements at the retail shop of a popular champagne bar. ☒ *601 N. State St., River North* ☎ *312/266–7676* ⊕ *popsforchampagne.com.*

LINCOLN PARK

Upscale Lincoln Park features a mix of distinctive boutiques and national chain stores. It was an established shopping destination way back when rents were low and the vibe was still gritty in nearby Bucktown and Wicker Park. Start your visit on Armitage Avenue, where you'll find boutiques selling everything from of-the-moment clothing and shoes to bath products and goods for pampered pooches. Around the corner on Halsted Street, independent shops are dotted in among big-name clothing stores. Hit North and Clybourn avenues for housewares from the flagship Crate&Barrel, Restoration Hardware, and other chains.

BEAUTY

Aroma Workshop. Customize lotions, massage oils, and bath salts with more than 150 essential and fragrance oils in this beauty boutique. The workshop makes its own line of facial-care products, too. ☒ *2050 N. Halsted St., Lincoln Park* ☎ *773/871–1985* ⊕ *www.aromaworkshop.com.*

BOOKS, STATIONERY, AND MUSIC

Greer. Quality products—all beautifully displayed—make it hard to leave this Lincoln Park favorite without a smile on your face. Come here to stock up on unique greeting cards, stationery, journals, and more. ☒ *1657 N. Wells St., Lincoln Park* ☎ *312/337–8000* ⊕ *www.greerchicago.com.*

Old Town School of Music Store. This spot within the Old Town School of Folk Music has a good selection of kids' instruments, plus all manner of instruments for rent. There's a sibling store in Lincoln Square (*4544 N. Lincoln Avenue*). ☒ *909 W. Armitage Ave., Lincoln Park* ☎ *773/525–1506* ⊕ *www.oldtownschool.org/musicstore.*

CHILDREN'S CLOTHING

FAMILY **Camelot Children's Kingdom.** This brightly colored boutique carries American and European clothing lines for babies and children up to age 12. Some of the brands you'll find are Little Mass and IKKS. Also on offer are cute Room Seven diaper bags and gifts. ⊠ *2203 N. Halsted St., Lincoln Park* ☎ *773/525–3310.*

Giggle. This style-focused children's boutique proves that having a baby doesn't have to mean sacrificing your modern aesthetic. Contemporary nursery furniture, strollers, and gear share space with well-designed activity mats, clothes, and keepsakes. ⊠ *2116 N. Halsted St., Lincoln Park* ☎ *773/296–6228* ⊕ *www.giggle.com.*

FAMILY **Monica+Andy.** In addition to a wide array of stylish duds made from high-quality fabrics, this children's boutique features a milk-and-cookie bar. The hip infants and toddlers in your life will be seriously impressed. ⊠ *2038 N. Halsted St., Lincoln Park* ☎ *312/600–8530* ⊕ *www.monicaandandy.com.*

CLOTHING

Art Effect. This modern-day general store stocks trendy clothes and accessories at approachable prices. Ella Moss tanks, Rich and Skinny jeans, and Alexis Bittar necklaces share space with gifts and home furnishings, ranging from candles and bath products to mortar-and-pestle sets and juicers. ⊠ *934 W. Armitage Ave., Lincoln Park* ☎ *773/929–3600* ⊕ *www.shoparteffect.com.*

Fox's. Snap up canceled and overstocked designer clothes from the likes of Tahari and ABS at 40% to 70% discounts. Shipments come in several times a week, so there's always something new to try on. (Modest shoppers take note: The dressing room is communal.) ⊠ *2150 N. Halsted St., Lincoln Park* ☎ *773/281–0700* ⊕ *foxs.com.*

The Green Goddess Boutique. This expansive boutique, whose motto is "sustainably chic," sells "upcycled," cruelty-free, and fair-trade clothing, jewelry, and home accessories from around the globe—think vintage jewelry, handmade knits, and more. There are unique products at every price point. ⊠ *1009 W. Armitage Ave., Lincoln Park* ☎ *773/281–5600* ⊕ *thegreengoddessboutique.com.*

Luxury Garage Sale. Thanks to its ever-changing selection of gently used designer clothes and accessories, this high-end consignment shop is a favorite of locals. ⊠ *1658 N. Wells St., Lincoln Park* ☎ *312/291–9126* ⊕ *www.luxurygaragesale.com.*

FOOD AND TREATS

Vosges Haut-Chocolat. Local chocolatier Katrina Markoff's exotic truffles, flavored with spices like curry and ancho chili, have fans across the globe. Her ever-expanding line of goodies now includes caramels, ice cream, chocolate tortilla chips, and even yoga wear and dresses. You can also satisfy your sweet tooth at Vosges Haut-Chocolat in the Shops at North Bridge (*520 N. Michigan Avenue*) or make a quick airport pit stop at one of the three outposts in O'Hare. ⊠ *951 W. Armitage Ave., Lincoln Park* ☎ *773/296–9866* ⊕ *www.vosgeschocolate.com.*

HOME DECOR

Bedside Manor. Dreamland is even more inviting with these handcrafted beds and lush designer linens, many of which come in interesting jacquard weaves or are nicely trimmed and finished. ✉ *2056 N. Halsted St., Lincoln Park* ☏ *773/404–2020* ⊕ *www.shopbedside.com.*

Fodor's Choice ★ **CB2.** A concept store by furniture giant Crate&Barrel, CB2 got its start right here in Chicago. Expect bold basics for trendy urban abodes, all sans big-ticket price tags. ✉ *800 W. North Ave., Lincoln Park* ☏ *312/787–8329* ⊕ *www.cb2.com.*

Crate&Barrel. There are plenty of "oohs" and "aahs" throughout the three floors of stylish home furnishings and kitchenware at Crate&Barrel's flagship location. There's plenty of free parking as well. If you're on the Magnificent Mile, you can drop into the store at 646 North Michigan Avenue. ✉ *850 W. North Ave., Lincoln Park* ☏ *312/573–9800* ⊕ *www.crateandbarrel.com.*

Fodor's Choice ★ **Jayson Home.** Loaded with new and vintage European and American furnishings, this decor store carries the Mitchell Gold + Bob Williams line. Look for oversize cupboards and armoires, decorative accessories, stylish garden furniture, and a bevy of beautiful floral arrangements. ✉ *1885 N. Clybourn Ave., Lincoln Park* ☏ *800/472–1885* ⊕ *www.jaysonhome.com.*

The Land of Nod. Crate&Barrel is a next-door neighbor (and business partner) of this quirky-cool children's furniture store. It carries lots of parent-pleasing designs, plus loads of fun accessories and toys, and has a great music section, too. ✉ *900 W. North Ave., Lincoln Park* ☏ *312/475–9903* ⊕ *www.landofnod.com.*

A New Leaf. You'll find one of Chicago's best selections of fresh flowers here. Designed by architect Cynthia Weese, the breathtaking Wells Street store (one of three in the city) also carries singular antique and vintage furnishings and accessories as well as a mind-boggling selection of candles, vases, tiles, and pots. ✉ *1818 N. Wells St., Lincoln Park* ☏ *312/642–8553* ⊕ *www.anewleafchicago.com.*

Tabula Tua. The colorful, contemporary, mix-and-match dishes and tabletop accessories at Tabula Tua are worlds away from standard formal china. Other offerings include gorgeous mosaic tables handmade to order, rustic furniture crafted from old barn wood, and sleek, polished pewter pieces. ✉ *1015 W. Armitage Ave., Lincoln Park* ☏ *773/525–3500* ⊕ *www.tabulatua.com.*

JEWELRY AND ACCESSORIES

The Left Bank. An eclectic mix of antique-style French jewelry brings a touch of Paris chic to Chicago. There's also a beautiful selection of French-themed jewelry boxes, perfume bottles, and other accessories. Owner Susan Jablonski (who is also a wedding planner) has become known for her large assortment of bridal headpieces and tiaras. ✉ *1155 W. Webster Ave., Lincoln Park* ☏ *773/929–7422* ⊕ *www.leftbankjewelry.com.*

The Tie Bar. If you're in need of a new necktie, the Tie Bar's flagship store is the place for you. It stocks everything from funky bow ties to more traditional styles, with pocket squares to match—all bargain-priced, considering the quality. ⊠ *918 W. Armitage Ave., Lincoln Park* ☎ *312/241–1299* ⊕ *www.thetiebar.com.*

Warby Parker. You can try on endless types of trendy eyewear at Warby Parker's Chicago frame studio. It's the company's first brick-and-mortar store in the Midwest. ⊠ *851 W. Armitage Ave., Lincoln Park* ☎ *773/341–1890* ⊕ *www.warbyparker.com.*

LINGERIE

Underthings. At this small but well-stocked shop, you can augment your collection of everyday bras, panties, and pajamas or splurge on sexy lingerie. Lines range from Hanky Panky to high-end designers such as Dolce & Gabbana. ⊠ *804 W. Webster Ave., Lincoln Park* ☎ *773/472–9291.*

PET STORES

Barker & Meowsky. This "paw firm" carries great gifts for dogs, cats, and humans. There are beautiful bowls, plush beds, picture frames, treats, and even pet massage and grooming services—just the things to get tails wagging. ⊠ *1003 W. Armitage Ave., Lincoln Park* ☎ *773/868–0200* ⊕ *www.barkerandmeowsky.com.*

SHOES, HANDBAGS, AND LEATHER GOODS

Fleet Feet Sports. Serious runners rely on Fleet Feet Sports for expert running shoe fittings, which entail foot measurement and a thorough gait analysis. Athletic wear and sports gear round out the offerings at its six Chicago area stores. ⊠ *1620 N. Wells St., Lincoln Park* ☎ *312/587–3338* ⊕ *www.fleetfeetchicago.com.*

Fodor's Choice ★ **Lori's Designer Shoes.** Owner Lori Andre's obsession with shoes takes her on biannual trips to Europe to scour for styles you won't likely see at department stores. The result is an inventory that many fine-footed women consider to be the best in Chicago. Shoes by designers like Jeffrey Campbell, Frye, and Sam Edelman are sold in a self-serve atmosphere. Terrific handbags, jewelry, bridal shoes, and other accessories are also available. ⊠ *824 W. Armitage Ave., Lincoln Park* ☎ *773/281–5655* ⊕ *www.lorisshoes.com.*

Running Away Multisport. Whatever sports gear you need, this expansive store likely has it in stock: wet suits, running shoes and apparel, sunglasses, hydration gear, and more. ⊠ *2219 N. Clybourn Ave., Lincoln Park* ☎ *773/395–2929* ⊕ *www.runningawaymultisport.com.*

TOYS

Rotofugi. A toy store for grown-up kids, Rotofugi specializes in artist-created, limited-edition playthings. You'll find dozens of specialty lines from the United States, China, and Japan, like Shawnimals and Tinder Toys. The store also hosts revolving gallery exhibitions. ⊠ *2780 N. Lincoln Ave., Lincoln Park* ☎ *773/868–3308* ⊕ *rotofugi.com.*

WICKER PARK

Former artists' enclaves Wicker Park and Bucktown were long ago taken over by style-conscious businesses and the hip-seekers who support them. Today the ever-more-gentrified areas are clogged with cool clothing stores, trendy restaurants, and galleries, mostly centered on the intersection of North, Damen, and Milwaukee avenues and along Division Street; however, large retailers such as Urban Outfitters, American Apparel, and Marc by Marc Jacobs have also moved into the area, much to the chagrin of indie-loving locals.

BEAUTY

RR#1 Chicago. A wood-paneled 1930s pharmacy is the setting for this charming gift shop, which stocks eclectic wares for everyone on your list, plus a tempting selection of bath and beauty products. ⊠ *814 N. Ashland Ave., West Town* ☎ *312/421–9079* ⊕ *www.rr1chicago.com.*

Ruby Room. This Wicker Park spa–boutique sells a mix of bath, body, and beauty products from brands like Weleda Bare Escentuals and Arcona. The spa services are an interesting mix, too, with everything from intuitive astrology to brow waxing and facials. Too relaxed to leave? You don't have to—the Ruby Room doubles as a boutique hotel. ⊠ *1743–45 W. Division St., Wicker Park* ☎ *773/235–2323* ⊕ *www. rubyroom.com.*

BOOKS, MUSIC, AND GIFTS

Dusty Groove. The retail outlet of a massive online business, Dusty Groove stocks an enormous collection of older jazz, funk, soul, and blues in both LP and CD formats. It also buys used records. ⊠ *1120 N. Ashland Ave., Wicker Park* ☎ *773/342–5800* ⊕ *www.dustygroove.com.*

Fodor'sChoice ★ **Myopic Books.** One of Chicago's largest used-book dealers carries more than 80,000 titles and buys books from the public on Friday evenings and all-day Saturday. ■TIP→ This community mainstay also hosts regular music and poetry events. ⊠ *1564 N. Milwaukee Ave., Wicker Park* ☎ *773/862–4882* ⊕ *www.myopicbookstore.com.*

Paper Doll. Doll up your gift with an unusual card and handmade wrapping paper from this Wicker Park shop. Finger puppets, candles, and other gift items are also available. ⊠ *2027 W. Division St., Wicker Park* ☎ *773/227–6950* ⊕ *paperdollchicago.com.*

Quimby's Bookstore. This indie bookstore offers one of the city's most diverse selections of reading material. You'll find everything from fancy coffee-table art books and flashy comics to hand-drawn zines created by obscure local artists here. ⊠ *1854 W. North Ave., Wicker Park* ☎ *773/342–0910* ⊕ *www.quimbys.com.*

CHILDREN'S CLOTHING

FAMILY **The Boring Store.** Outfit your aspiring sleuth with the necessary spy paraphernalia and secret agent supplies—such as mirror glasses, fake mustaches, and voice amplifiers—at this shop run by writer Dave Eggers's nonprofit group 826CHI. Proceeds help fund the group's after-school tutoring and writing programs for kids. ⊠ *1331 N. Milwaukee Ave., Wicker Park* ☎ *773/772–8108* ⊕ *www.826chi.org/shop.*

CLOTHING

Akira. Young trendsetters flock to this mini-empire for fashion-forward threads at easy-to-swallow prices. The flagship women's boutique shares a stretch of North Avenue with offshoot men's clothing and women's shoe stores. Check the website for other locations. ✉ *1814 W. North Ave., Wicker Park* ☎ *773/489–0818* ⊕ *www.shopakira.com.*

Alcala's Western Wear. Alcala stocks more than 10,000 pairs of cowboy boots—many in exotic skins—for men, women, and children. Since it's in Ukrainian Village, it's a bit out of the way if you're staying downtown, but the amazing array of Stetson hats and rodeo gear makes this a must-see for cowboys, caballeros, and country-and-western dancers. ✉ *1733 W. Chicago Ave., Ukrainian Village* ☎ *312/226–0152* ⊕ *www.alcalas.com.*

Eskell. Although this women's boutique can be a bit on the pricey side, Eskell's selection of clothing, jewelry, fragrances, and assorted home goods is ever-evolving and truly one-of-a-kind. ✉ *1509 N. Milwaukee Ave., Wicker Park* ☎ *773/486–0830* ⊕ *www.eskell.com.*

Kokorokoko. This unusual vintage shop specializes in loud, bold clothing, shoes, and accessories from the '80s and '90s. ✉ *1323 N. Milwaukee Ave., Wicker Park* ☎ *773/252–6996* ⊕ *www.kokorokokovintage.com.*

Moon Voyage. A new kid on the block in Wicker Park, Moon Voyage has quickly become one of the neighborhood's most exciting women's boutiques. Expect a hip selection of clothing, jewelry, and accessories with a breezy, Los Angeles vibe. ✉ *2010 W. Pierce Ave., Wicker Park* ☎ *773/423–8853* ⊕ *www.shopmoonvoyage.com.*

Mulberry & Me. Snag work-appropriate blouses, cute dresses, glitzy jackets, and accessories in this boutique with a New York feel. ✉ *2019 W. Division St., Wicker Park* ☎ *773/952–7551* ⊕ *mulberryandme.com.*

Penelope's. Step inside this spacious shop for flirty dresses from Sessun, Mink Pink, and Dolce Vita, as well as funky accessories such as Cheap Monday sunglasses. Menswear by the likes of APC and Gitman Bros. plus a selection of housewares and gift items round out the collection. ✉ *1913 W. Division St., Wicker Park* ☎ *773/395–2351* ⊕ *shoppenelopes.com.*

Una Mae's. This Wicker Park favorite is bursting at the seams with affordable styles for guys and girls. The accessories here, often even more fun than the clothing, may include vintage bow ties, Mexican blankets, backpacks, and incredibly colorful jewelry. ✉ *1528 N. Milwaukee Ave., Wicker Park* ☎ *773/276–7002* ⊕ *www.unamaeschicago.com.*

HOME DECOR

Asrai Garden. Although you'd be hard-pressed to find fresher blooms or more carefully constructed bouquets, this quirky boutique is more than a flower shop. It also contains a thoughtful, visually stunning collection of terrariums, jewelry, soaps, scented candles, ornate tableware, scrimshaw, stationery, and other gifts. ✉ *1935 W. North Ave., Wicker Park* ☎ *773/782–0680* ⊕ *www.asraigarden.com.*

Sprout Home. If your taste runs toward the modern, you'll drool over every nook and cranny of this home-furnishings store, which sells items like terrariums, planters, and bud vases for your indoor life, plus unusual plants and gardening products for your outdoor one. Sprout Home also offers regular classes in terrarium-building and *kokedama,* a Japanese gardening art. ⊠ *745 N. Damen Ave., Ukrainian Village, Wicker Park* ☎ *312/226–5950* ⊕ *www.sprouthome.com.*

JEWELRY AND ACCESSORIES

Labrabbit Optics. In the market for unique eyewear? Labrabbit Optics, a favorite of in-the-know locals, sells unusual new and vintage designs. Quality and attention to detail make them worth the price. ⊠ *1104 N. Ashland Ave., Wicker Park* ☎ *773/957–4733* ⊕ *www.labrabbit.org.*

Red Eye. This boutique stocks a wide array of specs from the likes of Anne Klein alongside stylish newcomers such as Jai Kudo and Gant. There's also an in-house optometrist to make sure your glasses not only look good but help you look better. ⊠ *2158 N. Damen Ave., Wicker Park* ☎ *773/782–1660* ⊕ *www.redeyeoptical.com.*

SHOES, HANDBAGS, AND LEATHER GOODS

John Fluevog Boots & Shoes. Canadian designer Fluevog's chunky platforms and bold designs have graced the famous feet of Madonna and throngs of other loyal devotees. If you shop here, they can house your toes, too. ⊠ *1539 N. Milwaukee Ave., Wicker Park* ☎ *773/772–1983* ⊕ *www.fluevog.com.*

BUCKTOWN

ANTIQUES

Pavilion. The specialty here is French, Italian, and Scandinavian antiques, but you'll be lured in by the altogether uncommon mix of industrial and decorative furnishings, accessories, and fixtures. The selection reflects the collecting acumen of its two idiosyncratic owners, who scour Europe and the Midwest for items in the perfect state of intriguing decay. ⊠ *2055 N. Damen Ave., Bucktown* ☎ *773/645–0924* ⊕ *www.1stdibs.com/dealers/pavilion-antiques/.*

CHILDREN'S CLOTHING

FAMILY   **Psychobaby.** The best-dressed urban tykes send their parents to this shop to spend a pretty penny on funky duds by lines like Sourpuss and Appaman. There's also a great selection of shoes, toys, and books, plus a story hour every Wednesday for parents brave enough to tote their wee ones along. ⊠ *1657 W. Divison St., Wicker Park* ☎ *773/772–2815* ⊕ *www.psychobabyonline.com.*

FAMILY   **The Red Balloon.** A good selection of children's clothing, books, and toys are on offer at the Red Balloon. It also has stores in Andersonville (*5407 N. Clark Street*) and Southport (*3651 N. Southport Avenue*). ⊠ *1940 N. Damen Ave., Bucktown* ☎ *773/489–9800* ⊕ *www.theredballoon.com.*

CLOTHING

apartment number 9. Siblings Amy and Sarah Blessing offer sisterly advice to guys on what styles best suit them. Their store, named for the Tammy Wynette song, carries classic lines like Paul Smith and Jack Spade as well as a wall full of Warby Parker specs. ⊠ *1804 N. Damen Ave., Bucktown* ☎ *773/395–2999* ⊕ *www.apartmentnumber9.com.*

Cynthia Rowley. Chicago-area native Cynthia Rowley fills her Bucktown store with the exuberant, well-priced dresses, separates, and accessories that have made her so popular. ✉ *1653 N. Damen Ave., Bucktown* ☎ *773/276–9209* ⊕ *www.cynthiarowley.com.*

Helen Yi. This loftlike, minimalist boutique stocks sophisticated styles from up-and-coming designers. ✉ *1725 N. Damen Ave., Bucktown* ☎ *773/252–3838* ⊕ *www.helenyi.com.*

Intermix. Label hunters were thrilled when branches of this New York boutique opened in Chicago, offering designer lines like Rag & Bone, Elizabeth & James, Helmut Lang, and Missoni. In addition to the Bucktown outpost, there are stores in Lincoln Park (*841 W. Armitage Avenue*) and the Gold Coast (*40 E. Delaware Place*). ✉ *1633 N. Damen Ave., Bucktown* ☎ *773/292–0894* ⊕ *www.intermixonline.com.*

Marc by Marc Jacobs. Bucktown is a fitting locale for Marc Jacobs, a fashion icon whose whimsical, slightly offbeat designs make trend-followers drool. ✉ *1714 N. Damen Ave., Bucktown* ☎ *773/276–2998* ⊕ *www. marcjacobs.com.*

Michelle Tan. Local indie design star Michelle Tan's shop doubles as a working studio where she creates clothes with an emphasis on interesting textures. You'll also find pieces by other area designers here. ✉ *1920 N. Damen Ave., Bucktown* ☎ *773/252–1888* ⊕ *michelletan.com.*

p.45. This store is a must-hit for its fashion-forward collection by a cadre of hip women's designers like MiH, Rachel Comey, and Ulla Johnson. Customers from all over the city and well beyond come for adventurous to elegant styles at prices that don't get out of hand. ✉ *1643 N. Damen Ave., Bucktown* ☎ *773/862–4523* ⊕ *p45.com.*

Robin Richman. Robin Richman showcases her famous knitwear alongside pieces from lesser-known European labels and local clothes designers. The eclectic displays never disappoint. ✉ *2108 N. Damen Ave., Bucktown* ☎ *773/278–6150* ⊕ *www.robinrichman-shop.com.*

Silver Moon Chicago. Vintage wedding gowns and tuxedos are a specialty here, but you can also find less-formal vintage clothing and even Vivienne Westwood accessories. ✉ *1721 W. North Ave., No. 101, Bucktown* ☎ *773/235–5797* ⊕ *www.silvermoonvintage.com.*

Sir and Madame. Displayed among the leather suitcases and vintage furniture are of-the-moment denim, tops, Ts, and dresses from the likes of Cheap Monday, Boxing Kitten, and Funktional, along with the equally hip in-house label—for men and women, naturally. The aesthetic? "Classic with a twist." Vintage eyewear keeps you looking just as sharp from the neck up. ✉ *938 N. Damen Ave., Bucktown* ☎ *773/489–6660* ⊕ *www.sirandmadame.com.*

The T-Shirt Deli. Order up a customized T-shirt with iron-on letters or throwback '70s decals. Your creation will be served to you on the spot, wrapped in paper like a sandwich, and packed with a bag of chips for good measure. There's also an Andersonville location at 1482 West Berwyn Avenue. ✉ *1739 N. Damen Ave., Bucktown* ☎ *773/276–6266* ⊕ *www.tshirtdeli.com.*

HOME DECOR

Alan Design Studio. The offerings at this design atelier, owned by a former feature-film set decorator, range from Victorian to mid-20th-century modern. There's always a healthy assortment of sofas and chairs recovered in eclectic fabrics, plus pillows made of unusual textiles and refurbished vintage lamps with marvelous shades. ✉ *2134 N. Damen Ave., Bucktown* ☎ *773/278–2345* ⊕ *www.alandesignstudio.com.*

JEWELRY AND ACCESSORIES

Soutache. French for "braid," Soutache is all about the extras that make life so much more interesting. High-end trimmings and embellishments; tortoise shell–and–bamboo belt buckles; exotic ostrich plumes; suede tassels; and reams and reams of ribbon—it's up to you how to get creative with this fun stuff. ✉ *2130 N. Damen Ave., Bucktown* ☎ *773/292–9110* ⊕ *www.soutacheribbons.com.*

LINGERIE

G Boutique. Here's an all-in-one stop for women planning on a little romance. G Boutique sells beautiful lingerie from brands such as Eberjey and Cosabella, plus massage oils, books, videos, and toys. Looking for some education? Check out the workshops, which are listed online. ✉ *2131 N. Damen Ave., Bucktown* ☎ *773/235–1234* ⊕ *www. boutiqueg.com.*

SHOES, HANDBAGS, AND LEATHER GOODS

City Soles. This on-trend shop is a mecca for shoe lovers. There's a vast selection of edgy men's and women's footwear from Coclico, Chie Mihara, Sorel, and more. ✉ *1514 N. Milwaukee Ave., Bucktown* ☎ *773/489–2001* ⊕ *www.citysoles.com.*

Shinola. A Detroit-based purveyor of American-made goods, Shinola has a new Chicago location that is a perfect fit for the bustling Bucktown shopping district. It specializes in high-quality watches, bicycles, and leather goods. ✉ *1619 N. Damen Ave., Bucktown* ☎ *773/904–2417* ⊕ *www.shinola.com.*

Stitch. Leather goods of every ilk—purses, travel bags, desk accessories—are the main attraction here, but you'll also find minimalist furniture, tabletop goods, and jewelry. ✉ *1937 N. Damen Ave., Bucktown* ☎ *773/782–1570* ⊕ *www.stitchchicago.com.*

LAKEVIEW

Home to Wrigley Field, this North Side neighborhood is broken into several smaller shopping areas, each with a distinct flavor and each making for a fun afternoon out. Clark Street, between Diversey Avenue and Addison Street, is Cubs central, with shops hawking sports-centric paraphernalia. A slew of upscale boutiques draws trend seekers to Southport Avenue between Belmont Avenue and Grace Street. Antiquers and bargain hunters should head straight for the intersection of Lincoln Avenue and Diversey Parkway and meander north on Lincoln.

ANTIQUES

Antique Resources. Choice antiques from Europe and elsewhere are sold at fair prices here. This is an excellent source for stately desks and dignified dining sets, but the true find is a huge trove of antique crystal and gilt chandeliers from France. ⊠ *1741 W. Belmont Ave., Lakeview* ☎ *773/871–4242* ⊕ *www.antiqueresourcesinc.com.*

Father Time Antiques. Father Time bills itself as the Midwest's largest retailer of vintage timepieces. In addition to pocket watches and clocks, it carries accessories like watch holders and display cases. ⊠ *2108 W. Belmont Ave., Lakeview* ☎ *773/880–5599* ⊕ *www.fathertimeantiques. com.*

Modlife. The emphasis here is on mid-20th-century furniture, accessories, and lighting from well-known designers like Paul McCobb, Eames, and Eero Saarinen. You'll also find original paintings and sculptures at overall affordable price points. ⊠ *3061 N. Lincoln Ave., Lakeview* ☎ *773/868–0844* ⊕ *modlifehome.com.*

Smythson Yeats Antiques. The always-changing selection here includes plenty of art deco and art nouveau treasures, with a particularly impressive assortment of lamps, chandeliers, and ceramics. There are fabulous larger pieces, too, including sideboards, bookcases, and plush leather chairs. ⊠ *3851 N. Lincoln Ave., Lakeview* ☎ *773/244–6365.*

Urban Artifacts. This store's superb collection of furniture, lighting, and decorative accessories from the 1940s to the '70s emphasizes industrial designs. ⊠ *2928 N. Lincoln Ave., No. 1, Lakeview* ☎ *773/404–1008.*

BOOKS, MUSIC, AND GIFTS

Bookworks. The stock here includes thousands of titles, many of them used or rare. There's an emphasis on sports (for Cubs fans strolling by from nearby Wrigley Field) and contemporary fiction. Music lovers can check out the vinyl-record section, too. ⊠ *3444 N. Clark St., Lakeview* ☎ *773/871–5318* ⊕ *www.thebookworks.com.*

Gramaphone Records. Local DJs and club kids go to Gramaphone to find vintage and cutting-edge dance, house, and hip-hop releases. You can hear them on the spot at one of the store's listening stations. It also stocks DJ gear. ⊠ *2843 N. Clark St., Lakeview* ☎ *773/472–3683* ⊕ *www.gramaphonerecords.com.*

Inkling. This quirky hole-in-the-wall specializes in locally made cards, art prints, jewelry, and other hipster-friendly gifts. Every first Friday, Inkling hosts a reception showcasing whichever artist's work is featured on the shop's gallery wall that month. ⊠ *2917 ½ N. Broadway, Lakeview* ☎ *773/248–8004* ⊕ *www.theinklingshop.com.*

Fodor's Choice ★ Reckless Records. Reckless Records ranks as one of the city's leading alternative and secondhand record stores. Besides the indie offerings, you can flip through jazz, classical, and soul recordings, or catch a live appearance by an up-and-comer passing through town. Look for other locations in the Loop (*26 E. Madison Street*) and Wicker Park (*1379 N. Milwaukee Avenue*). ⊠ *3126 N. Broadway St., Lakeview* ☎ *773/404–5080* ⊕ *www.reckless.com.*

Combine holiday shopping with fantastic eye candy at the Magnificent Mile Lights Festival.

Transistor. A favorite of music fans, Transistor is part record shop, part art gallery, and part electronics store. As a bonus, it hosts regular live music and film events. ⊠ *3441 N. Broadway, Lakeview* ☎ *312/631–9408* ⊕ *www.transistorchicago.com.*

Unabridged Bookstore. Since 1980 this independent bookshop has maintained a loyal clientele who love its vast selection and dedicated staff. Known for having one of the most extensive gay and lesbian sections in the city, it also has an impressive array of children's books. ⊠ *3251 N. Broadway St., Lakeview* ☎ *773/883–9119* ⊕ *www.unabridgedbookstore.com.*

CHILDREN'S CLOTHING

FAMILY **Little Threads.** Trumpette, Wes & Willy, and Petunia Picklebottom are just some of the funky kids' labels at this cute neighborhood shop. There's also a fun selection of children's reading material. ⊠ *2033 W. Roscoe St., Lakeview* ☎ *773/327–9310* ⊕ *www.shoplittlethreads.com.*

CLOTHING

Belmont Army. Converse, Dr. Martens, and other familiar brands get mixed in with fatigues, flak jackets, skate gear, and faux-fur coats at Belmont Army. The Lakeview veteran—open since 1975—occupies an entire building just down the street from its original home adjacent to the Belmont El station. The top floor, devoted to vintage goods, makes for an always entertaining shopping adventure. ⊠ *855 W. Belmont Ave., Lakeview* ☎ *773/549–1038* ⊕ *www.belmontarmy.wordpress.com.*

Hubba-Hubba. You will feel like you're rummaging through your best friend's closet at this packed-to-the-gills shop. It carries flowy, feminine clothes with a retro flavor as well as vintage and modern accessories.

✉ *2040 W. Roscoe St., Lakeview* ☎ *773/477–1414* ⊕ *hubbahubba chicago.com.*

Kickin'. Hip, urban women snap up their maternity wear at this shop. There's an emphasis on workout and yoga gear. ✉ *2118 W. Roscoe St., Lakeview* ☎ *773/281–6577* ⊕ *www.kickinmaternity.com.*

Krista K Boutique. An inventory of must-haves for women from designers like Citizens of Humanity, Theory, and Splendid reflects the style of this neighborhood. The boutique has become a go-to spot for the latest denim, too. ✉ *3458 N. Southport Ave., Lakeview* ☎ *773/248–1967* ⊕ *www.kristak.com.*

Mint Julep. This Southport store is not afraid of color. Find a cheery selection of statement necklaces, pastel denims, bright printed dresses, and much more for reasonable prices. ✉ *3432 N. Southport Ave., Lakeview* ☎ *773/472–6717.*

Uncle Dan's. This is the place for camping, skiing, and general outdoorsy gear by brands like Marmot and North Face. There's a good kids' selection here as well. ✉ *3551 N. Southport Ave., Lakeview* ☎ *773/348–5800* ⊕ *www.udans.com.*

She One. A plentiful assortment of bright T-shirts, oh-so-pretty dresses, and trendy jewelry appeals to young urban women. ✉ *3544 N. Southport Ave., Lakeview* ☎ *773/549–9698* ⊕ *www.sheonechicago.com.*

HOME DECOR

Waxman Candles. The candles sold here are made on the premises and come in countless shapes, colors, and scents. There's an incredible selection of candle holders and incense, too. ✉ *3044 N. Lincoln Ave., Lakeview* ☎ *773/929–3000* ⊕ *www.waxmancandles.com.*

JEWELRY AND ACCESSORIES

Bourdage Pearls. Sherry Bourdage sells Chinese freshwater pearls in a staggering array of colors and styles that range from simple and inexpensive to elaborate custom designs. ✉ *4039A N. Ravenswood Ave., North Center* ☎ *773/244–1126* ⊕ *www.bourdagepearls.com.*

Glam to Go. The lotions and potions sold at Glam to Go will help you stay soft and smelling good. There's also clothing by Language, Talla, Scrapbook, and others for getting glammed up, along with handbags, accessories, toys, and baby clothes. ✉ *2002 W. Roscoe St., Lakeview* ☎ *773/525–7004* ⊕ *glamtogo.com.*

PET STORES

Dog-a-Holics. Catering to pampered pooches and their devoted owners, Dog-a-Holics sells treats, bedding, collars, carriers, and clothes. There's even a selection of birthday items for Fido, such as party hats, pup-themed balloons, and canine cakes. ✉ *3657 N. Southport Ave., Lakeview* ☎ *773/857–7600* ⊕ *www.dog-a-holics.com.*

Wigglyville. Everything you need for your furry friend (leashes, collars, bedding, carriers, shampoo, and more), along with pet-themed artwork, is carefully arranged in this inviting pet boutique. Another branch is at 1137 West Madison Street, in the West Loop. ✉ *3337 N. Broadway Ave., Lakeview* ☎ *773/528–3337* ⊕ *www.wigglyville.com.*

SHOES, HANDBAGS, AND LEATHER GOODS

Spare Parts. The selection of fine leather goods here draws from many sources, including Village Tannery, Jack Spade, and Brynn Capella. Jewelry, baby gear, and home accessories round out the selection. ⊠ *2949 N. Broadway St., Lakeview* ☎ *773/525–4242* ⊕ *www.shop spareparts.com.*

TOYS

Building Blocks. From cars and train sets to puzzles and musical instruments, Building Blocks carries classic toys designed to appeal to kids' natural curiosity and imagination—and they'll gift wrap them for you at no charge. In Wicker Park, stop by the store at 2130 West Division Street. ⊠ *3306 N. Lincoln Ave., Lakeview* ☎ *773/525–6200* ⊕ *www. buildingblockstoys.com.*

Robot City Workshop. Wander east of Southport to Sheffield to find Robot City Workshop; it's the place for all things robotic, including kits to help kids and inquisitive adults build their own. ⊠ *3226 N. Sheffield Ave., Wrigleyville* ☎ *773/281–1008* ⊕ *www.robotcityworkshop.com.*

WINE

Lush Wine and Spirits. This full-service liquor store specializes in wine, microbrews, and obscure spirits from small-batch distilleries. Attend one of the frequently held wine tastings to try before you buy. There are also branches in West Town (*1412 W. Chicago Avenue*) and University Village (*1257 S. Halsted Street*). ⊠ *2232 W. Roscoe St., Lakeview* ☎ *773/281–8888* ⊕ *www.lushwineandspirits.com.*

FAR NORTH AND FAR NORTHWEST SIDES

In the Far North, Swedish-settled Andersonville specializes in antiques and home furnishings. If you need a break while perusing the stores, many funky coffee shops and casual restaurants await.

ANTIQUES

Fodor'sChoice ★ **Architectural Artifacts.** The selection here matches the warehouse proportions. A mammoth two-story space contains oversize garden ornaments, statuary, iron grills, fixtures, and decorative tiles. Architectural fragments—marble, metal, wood, terra-cotta—hail from historic American and European buildings. ⊠ *4325 N. Ravenswood Ave., Far Northwest Side* ☎ *773/348–0622* ⊕ *www.architecturalartifacts.com.*

Broadway Antique Market. More than 75 hand-picked dealers make it worth the trek to the Broadway Antique Market (known as BAM by its loyal fans). Mid-20th century is the primary emphasis, but items range from Arts and Crafts and art deco to Heywood-Wakefield. All are wonderfully presented, and the building itself is a prime example of deco architecture. ⊠ *6130 N. Broadway St., Far North* ☎ *773/743–5444* ⊕ *www.bamchicago.com.*

Edgewater Antique Mall. A couple of blocks north of the Broadway Antique Market, this mall specializes in 20th-century goods. ⊠ *6314 N. Broadway St., Far North* ☎ *773/262–2525* ⊕ *www.edgewaterantiquemall.com.*

Evanstonia Antiques and Restoration. Dealer Ziggy Osak has a rich collection of fine 19th-century English and Continental antiques that are prized for being as functional as they are striking. ✉ *4555 N. Raven-swood Ave., Lincoln Square* ☎ *773/907–0101* ⊕ *evanstoniaantiques. com.*

Lincoln Antique Mall. Dozens of dealers carrying antiques and collectibles share this large space. There's a good selection of French and mid-20th-century modern furniture, plus estate jewelry, oil paintings, and photographs, but you can find virtually anything here. ✉ *3115 W. Irving Park Rd., Far Northwest Side* ☎ *773/604–4700* ⊕ *www. lincolnantiquemall.com.*

Fodor'sChoice ★ **Woolly Mammoth Antiques, Oddities & Resale.** In the market for a stuffed giraffe head? How about a bracelet made of human hair or some vintage medical supplies? Woolly Mammoth has an ever-evolving selection of strange, unusual, and sometimes disturbing items. For those who are so inspired, the shop also hosts its own taxidermy classes. ✉ *1513 W. Foster Ave., Far North* ☎ *773/989–3294* ⊕ *www.woollymammoth chicago.com.*

BEAUTY

Fodor'sChoice ★ **Merz Apothecary.** In addition to being a normal pharmacy, this old-fashioned druggist also stocks all manner of homeopathic and herbal remedies, as well as hard-to-find European toiletries, cosmetics, candles, and natural laundry products. There is a second store (called Merz Downtown) in the Palmer House Hilton at 17 East Monroe Street. ✉ *4716 N. Lincoln Ave., Lincoln Square* ☎ *773/989–0900* ⊕ *merz apothecary.com.*

BOOKS, MUSIC, AND GIFTS

The Book Cellar. The bright, inviting Book Cellar has a well-edited selection of works ranging from local interest to popular fiction. There's also a small wine bar/coffee shop on the premises, where customers can linger over their purchases. Readings and other literary events are held here frequently. ✉ *4736 N. Lincoln Ave., Far Northwest Side* ☎ *773/293–2665* ⊕ *www.bookcellarinc.com.*

Enjoy. Calling itself an "urban general store," this welcoming Lincoln Square shop stocks a wide selection of greeting cards, cute kids' clothes, toys, and fun gift items. ✉ *4723 N. Lincoln Ave., Far Northwest Side* ☎ *773/334–8626* ⊕ *www.urbangeneralstore.com.*

Gallimaufry Gallery. Browse the tightly packed selection of greeting cards, wood carvings, jewelry, and incense in this eclectic little shop. ✉ *4712 N. Lincoln Ave., Lincoln Square* ☎ *773/728–3600* ⊕ *www. gallimaufry.net.*

Women & Children First. This feminist bookstore stocks fiction and nonfiction, periodicals, journals, small-press publications, and a strong selection of gay and lesbian titles. The children's section also has a great array of books, all politically correct. Authors, both local and world-famous, often give readings here. ✉ *5233 N. Clark St., Andersonville* ☎ *773/769–9299* ⊕ *www.womenandchildrenfirst.com.*

FOOD AND TREATS

City Olive. This cute shop in Andersonville sells olive oil in every imaginable form, from bottles of the extra-virgin variety to bath and body products made with the stuff. Other gourmet foods from around the globe also fill the shelves. ✉ *5644 N. Clark St., Andersonville* ☎ *773/942–6424* ⊕ *www.cityolive.com.*

HOME DECOR

Brimfield. Brimfield is brimming with blankets, pillows, and more made from the popular plaid fabric for which this store was named. A range of vintage furniture and home accessories is available as well. ✉ *5219 N. Clark St., Andersonville* ☎ *773/271–3501* ⊕ *www.brimfieldus.com.*

Neighborly. Living up to its name, Neighborly focuses on ethically sourced, independently made home goods and gifts with a local vibe. ✉ *2003 W. Montrose Ave., Far North* ☎ *773/840–2456* ⊕ *www.neighborlyshop.com.*

MARKETS

Vintage Garage. On the third Sunday of the month, from April through October, dozens of Chicago area vintage and antiques vendors descend on an empty parking garage for one of the city's finest markets. A local DJ typically spins records while shoppers browse through clothes, furniture, housewares, music, and the like. Admission is $5. ✉ *5051 N. Broadway St., Far North* ✛ *On the east side of Broadway between Foster and Argyle* ☎ *847/607–1087* ⊕ *www.vintagegaragechicago.com.*

SPAS

Sir Spa. There's nothing pretty or poufy about this men's spa, and that's the way clients like it. The space—awash in black leather, exposed brick, and marble—is well appointed, and it includes a Grooming Club Lounge with armchairs, a plasma TV, and beer-stocked fridge. With services like a back buff and detoxifying mud wrap, treatments are just as focused on cleaning and revitalizing as they are on purely relaxing. ✉ *5151 N. Clark St., Andersonville* ☎ *773/271–7000* ⊕ *www.sirspa.com* ☞ *$100 60-min massage, $200 3-treatment packages, $175 couple packages. Hair salon, steam room. Services: Botox, facials, massages, reflexology, tanning.*

TOYS

Timeless Toys. This old-timey toy shop has a Santa's-workshop feel. Inside you'll find plenty of classic wooden toys alongside fanciful dress-up costumes, plush puppets, cuddly stuffed animals, board games, puzzles, and books. ✉ *4749 N. Lincoln Ave., Lincoln Square* ☎ *773/334–4445* ⊕ *www.timelesstoyschicago.com.*

NIGHTLIFE AND PERFORMING ARTS

Updated
by Joseph
Erbentraut

Despite their hardworking Midwestern image, Chicagoans know how to let loose. And, unlike that big city on the East Coast (ahem), the city that plays as hard as it works is refreshingly devoid of attitude. Sure, some nightclubs trot out the velvet ropes or feature exclusive, members-only VIP rooms, but for the most part Chicago's nightlife scene reflects the same qualities that make the city itself great: it's lively, diverse, and completely unpretentious.

Entertainment options abound every night of the week. The challenge won't be finding something that suits your mood and budget, but rather narrowing down the seemingly endless array of choices. Should you hit the theater for a Broadway-in-Chicago spectacle followed by a post-performance cocktail? Or explore the city's dynamic fringe theater scene? Catch some first-rate improv? Or get your dance on at a trendy nightclub?

Music lovers will find much to adore in Chicago. The city is justifiably famous for its blues scene, which still thrives in clubs from the South Side to the North Side, but it's equally fertile ground for classical, folk, rock, alt-country, or whatever genre captures your fancy. The summer's free concert series in Grant Park and Millennium Park—from the jam-packed blues and jazz festivals to low-key weeknight concerts—consistently draw top-tier performers.

If your idea of the perfect evening means kicking back with a local brew or a glass of wine, there are bars and lounges catering to every taste—from neighborhood dives to sports bars to swanky spots where patrons dress to the nines. Some of these locales also feature entertainment in the form of karaoke, trivia competitions, readings, and poetry slams.

In the summer, Chicagoans thankful for an end to the long winter head out in droves to the city's many rooftop bars and patios. The hotel bar scene has exploded, and now features some of the city's trendiest nightspots, including a number of rooftop lounges with bird's-eye views of the city.

There's only one thing you won't find in Chicago: the urge to hole up in your hotel room at night.

12

PLANNING

FESTIVALS

FodorśChoice
★
Chicago Blues Festival. The Chicago Blues Festival leaves no doubt about it: Chicago still loves to sing the blues. Each June, the city pulses with sounds from the largest free blues festival in the world, which takes place over three days and on five stages in both Grant Park and Millennium Park. The always-packed open-air festival has been headlined by blues legends such as B.B. King, Koko Taylor, and Buddy Guy. ☎ 312/744–3315 ⊕ www.cityofchicago.org/city/en/depts/dca/supp_ info/chicago_blues_festival.html.

Chicago Improv Festival. The springtime Chicago Improv Festival, the nation's largest festival for improvisers, has stages devoted to group, pair, and single improv; sketch comedy; and more. ☎ 773/875–6616 ⊕ www.chicagoimprovfestival.org.

Lollapalooza. The current incarnation of Perry Farrell's famed festival takes over Grant Park for three days in August. Lollapalooza boasts a packed slate of big-name musicians (past editions have included the Red Hot Chili Peppers, Kanye West, Lady Gaga, and Pearl Jam). Tickets typically sell out before the lineup is even announced, but many turn up on Craigslist and third-party websites in the days leading up to the event. ☎ 888/512–7469 ⊕ www.lollapalooza.com.

Pitchfork Music Festival. This three-day indie-oriented festival brings a diverse array of top and emerging talent to Union Park each July. Although smaller than Lollapalooza (it has three stages compared to eight-plus), devotees say the acts are more eclectic and the environment more comfortable. Artists including Beck, Kendrick Lamar, The National, and St. Vincent have played Pitchfork. ☎ 312/746–5494 ⊕ www.pitchforkmusicfestival.com.

GET TICKETS

You can save money on seats at **Hot Tix** (⊕ www.hottix.org), where unsold tickets are available, usually at half price (plus a service charge) on the day of the performance; if you go on Friday you can buy tickets for Saturday and Sunday, too. Hot Tix booths are located across from the Chicago Cultural Center at 72 East Randolph Street, in the Chicago Water Works building at the southeast corner of Michigan Avenue and Pearson Street, and in the Block 37 shopping complex at 108 North State Street. Only the last of these is open on Monday. Full-price tickets can be purchased by phone or online through **Ticketmaster** (☎ 800/745–3000 ⊕ www.ticketmaster.com).

For a cheaper, more intimate, and—arguably—equally rewarding theater experience, Chicago has a lively fringe theater scene. You'll find smaller storefront theater spaces scattered across the city (but concentrated on the North Side), where you can catch everything from dramatic classics mounted on tiny stages to edgy works by emerging writers. Best of all, tickets often go for $20 or less and are usually available at the box office on the day of performance.

For hot, sold-out shows, such as performances by the Chicago Symphony Orchestra or the Lyric Opera of Chicago, call a day or two before the performance to see if there are any subscriber returns. Another option is to show up at the box office on concert day—a surprising number of people strike it lucky with on-the-spot tickets because of cancellations.

Small fees can have big payoffs! Many of the smaller neighborhood street festivals (there are hundreds in summer) request $5 to $10 donations upon entry, but it's often worth the expense: big-name bands are known to take the stage of even the most under-publicized festivals. For moment-to-moment festival coverage, check out ⊕ *chicago.metromix. com*, ⊕ *do312.com*, or ⊕ *timeoutchicago.com*.

RESOURCES

To find out what's happening in the Windy City, the *Chicago Tribune*'s Metromix Chicago (⊕ *chicago.metromix.com*) is a good resource. Head to ⊕ *www.timeout.com/chicago* or ⊕ *do312.com* for club listings, rotating parties, and DJ appearances. *The Chicago Reader* and Metromix also dish on the hottest bars and clubs. (You'll find theater and music listings in these publications as well.) Centerstage Chicago (⊕ *www. centerstagechicago.com*) has a calendar of music and theater events.

TIMING

Live music begins around 9 pm at bars around town. If you want to guarantee a seat, arrive well before the band's scheduled start and stake out a spot. Most bars close at 2 am Sunday through Friday and 3 am Saturday. A few dance clubs and late-night bars remain open until 4 am or 5 am (Berlin and Transit are very popular). Outdoor beer gardens such as Sheffield's are the exception; these close at 11 pm on weeknights and midnight on weekends. Some bars are not open seven days a week, so call before you go. Curtain calls for performances are usually at 7:30 or 8 pm.

GETTING HERE

Parking in North Side neighborhoods—particularly Lincoln Park, Lakeview, and Wicker Park/Bucktown—is increasingly scarce, even on weeknights. If you're going out in these areas, take a cab or the El. The Red, Brown, and Blue lines will get you within a few blocks of most major entertainment destinations downtown and on the North and Near Northwest sides. If you do decide to drive, use the curbside valet service available at many restaurants and clubs for about $7 to $10. If you're headed to the South Side, be cautious about public transportation late at night. It's best to drive or cab it here.

NIGHTLIFE

Chicago's entertainment varies from loud and loose to sophisticated and sedate. You'll find classic Chicago corner bars in most neighborhoods, along with trendier alternatives like wine bars and lounges. The strains of blues and jazz provide much of the backbeat to the city's groove, and an alternative country scene is flourishing. As far as dancing is concerned, take your pick from cavernous clubs to smaller spots with DJs spinning dance tunes; there's everything from hip-hop to swing. Wicker Park/Bucktown and River North have the hottest nightlife, but prime spots are spread throughout the city.

Shows usually begin at 9 pm; cover charges generally range from $3 to $20, depending on the day of the week (Friday and Saturday nights are the most expensive). The list of blues and jazz clubs includes several South Side locations: be cautious about transportation here late at night, because some of these neighborhoods can be unsafe. Drive your own car or ask the bartender to call you a cab.

THE LOOP, SOUTH LOOP, AND WEST LOOP

Sleek and sexy wine bars and lounges like ROOF on the Wit Hotel light up Chicago's core business district after work. On weekends and late nights the action shifts to the West Loop—centered on Fulton, Lake, and Randolph streets—which is home to a diverse array of nightspots, from megaclubs like Transit to of-the-minute drinking establishments like the Aviary. ■ TIP→ If you're sticking to downtown and North Side bars, it's relatively safe to rely on public transportation. But if you're planning on staying out past midnight, we suggest taking a cab home.

BARS

The Aviary. Wednesday through Sunday, Chef Grant Achatz applies his cutting-edge culinary style to cocktails at this West Loop bar, adjacent to his high-concept restaurant Next. Your newfangled old-fashioned might arrive injected into an egg of ice, or your drink's flavor might change subtly as its flavored ice melts. Inventive bar bites are on offer as well. Be prepared for a wait. ⊠ *955 W Fulton Market, West Loop* ☏ *312/226–0868* ⊕ *www.theaviary.com.*

Kitty O'Shea's. This handsome spot in the Chicago Hilton and Towers is an authentic Emerald Isle pub with all things Irish, including live music seven nights a week, beer, food, and bar staff. ⊠ *Chicago Hilton and Towers, 720 S. Michigan Ave., South Loop* ☏ *312/294–6860.*

Red Kiva. Red Kiva serves up cocktails, martinis, and draft beers—along with house-made flat-bread pizzas—in a cozy, candlelit lounge centered on a sunken circular area (the titular kiva). DJs spin tunes, or musical guests heat up the grand piano. ⊠ *1108 W. Randolph St., West Loop* ☏ *312/226–5577* ⊕ *www.redkiva.com.*

ROOF on the Wit. One of the city's hottest perches, ROOF occupies the 27th floor of the Wit Hotel. The outdoor space entices with fire pits and panoramic city views; floor-to-ceiling glass windows make the indoor area equally breathtaking. DJs spinning eclectic beats and a menu of pricey cocktails and small plates complete the scene. ⊠ *201 N. State St., Loop* ☎ *312/239–9502* ⊕ *www.roofonthewit.com.*

DANCE CLUBS

Transit. Despite being hidden away underneath the El tracks in a spooky stretch west of downtown, Transit is wildly popular with young club-goers. Inside, the multiroom space has a crisp design and sumptuous VIP area. Don't miss the glowing black-and-white bar between the oval and chandelier rooms, or the mezzanine with its minimalist furniture and oversize mahogany table. ⊠ *1431 W. Lake St., West Loop* ☎ *312/491–8600* ⊕ *www.transitnightlife.com.*

MUSIC VENUES

BLUES

Blues Heaven Foundation. For a walk into history, stop by the Blues Heaven Foundation, which occupies the former home of the legendary Chess Records. Breathe the same rarefied air as blues (and rock-and-roll) legends Muddy Waters, Howlin' Wolf, Chuck Berry, and the Rolling Stones, all of whom recorded here. Check out the Chess brothers' private offices, the recording studio, and the back stairway used only by signed musicians. Be sure to see the eerie "Life Cast Portraits" wall showcasing the plaster heads of the Chess recording artists. Tour hours are 11 to 4 Monday through Saturday. ⊠ *2120 S. Michigan Ave., South Loop* ☎ *312/808–1286* ⊕ *www.bluesheaven.com.*

Fodor's Choice ★ **Buddy Guy's Legends.** Relocated from its original location a few doors down, Buddy Guy's Legends has a superb sound system, excellent sightlines, and more space to showcase Grammy Award–winning blues performer/owner Buddy Guy's collection of blues memorabilia. Look for local blues acts during the week and larger-scale touring acts on weekends. Don't miss Buddy Guy in January, when he performs a monthlong home stand of shows (tickets go on sale one month in advance). There's also a substantial menu of Cajun and Creole favorites. ⊠ *700 S. Wabash Ave., South Loop* ☎ *312/427–1190* ⊕ *www.buddyguy.com.*

NEAR NORTH AND RIVER NORTH

Rush Street may have lost its former glory, but the bars along Division Street still attract rowdy singles. Reprieve from the bustling Division Street scene is only a few blocks south, in the Near North and River North neighborhoods. Hunker down in a low-key lounge or sip a hearty pint of Guinness at an authentic Irish pub. At the southern edge of River North, waterfront lounges popular with the after-work crowd line the Chicago Riverwalk.

BARS

3rd Coast Cafe & Wine Bar. The oldest coffeehouse in the Gold Coast pleases just about everyone with a full menu served until midnight seven nights a week. The inviting space combines warm woods, etched glass, and funky local art. A diverse clientele—from students and twentysomethings to retirees living nearby—comes for coffee, Sunday brunch, or late-night jazz sessions. ⊠ *1260 N. Dearborn St., Near North* ☎ *312/649–0730* ⊕ *www.3rdcoastcafe.com.*

Continued on page 269

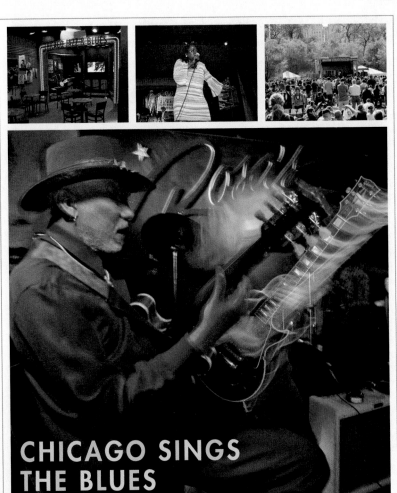

CHICAGO SINGS THE BLUES

Cool, electric, urban blues are the soundtrack of the Windy City. The blues traveled up the Mississippi River with the Delta sharecroppers during the Great Migration, settled down on Maxwell Street and South Side clubs, and gave birth to such big-name talent as Muddy Waters, Howlin' Wolf, Willie Dixon, and, later, Koko Taylor. Today, you can still hear the blues in a few South Side clubs where it all began, or check out the current scene on the North Side. *Check the listings in the chapter for specifics.*

Clockwise from top left: Chicago Jazz & Blues at the Chicago History Museum; Chicago Blues Festival; Chicago Blues Festival; Carlos Johnson performing at Rosa's Lounge

THE BIRTH OF THE CHICAGO BLUES

CHESS RECORDS

Founded by Philip and Leonard Chess, Polish immigrant brothers, in 1947. For the first two years, the label was called Aristocrat. Its famous address, 2120 S. Michigan Avenue, was the nucleus of the blues scene. Up-and-comers performed on the sidewalk out front in hopes of being discovered. Even today, locals and visitors peek through the windows of the restored studio (now the Blues Heaven Foundation) looking for glimpses of past glory.

The label's first hit record was Muddy Waters' *I Can't Be Satisfied.*

The brothers were criticized for having a paternalistic relationship with their artists. They reportedly bought Muddy Waters a car off the lot when he wasn't able to finance it himself.

The company was immortalized in the excellent 2008 film *Cadillac Records,* which starred Adrian Brody.

Did you know? When the Rolling Stones recorded the track "2120 South Michigan Avenue" (off the *12 x 5* album) at the Chess Records studio in June 1964, the young Brits were reportedly so nervous about singing in front of Willie Dixon (Buddy Guy and Muddy Waters were also hanging around the studio that day) that they literally became tongue-tied. As a result, the song is purely instrumental.

WILLIE DIXON (July 1, 1915–Jan. 29, 1992) Chess Records' leading A & R (artist and repertoire) man, bass player, and composer. Founded the Blues Heaven Foundation, Chess Records' restored office and studio. *See Blues Heaven Foundation review next page.*

Famous compositions: "Hoochie Coochie Man" (recorded by Muddy Waters), "My Babe" (recorded by Little Walter), and "Wang Dang Doodle" (recorded by Koko Taylor)

MUDDY WATERS: KING OF ELECTRIC BLUES (4/1915–4/1983)

When Muddy Waters gave his guitar an electric jolt, he didn't just revolutionize the blues. His electric guitar became a magic wand: Its jive talk (and cry) turned country-blues into city-blues, and it gave birth to rock and roll. Waters's signature sound has been firmly imprinted on nearly all subsequent musical genres.

Best known for: Riveting vocals, a swooping pompadour, and, of course, plugging in the guitar

Biggest break: Leonard Chess, one of the Chess brothers of Chess Records, let Waters record two of his own songs. The record sold out in two days, and stores issued a dictum of "one per customer."

Biggest song: "Hoochie Coochie Man"

Lyrics: *Y'know I'm here / Everybody knows I'm here / And I'm the hoochie-coochie man*

Awards: 3 Grammies, Lifetime Achievement induction into the Rock and Roll Hall of Fame

Local honor: A strip of 43rd Street in Chicago is renamed Muddy Waters Drive.

HOWLIN' WOLF (June 10, 1910–Jan. 10, 1976)

In 1951, at the age of 41, Wolf recorded with Sun Studios in Memphis, TN. Shortly thereafter, Sun sold Wolf's only two songs, "Moanin' At Midnight" and "How Many More Years," to Chess Records, kicking off his prolific recording career with Chess.

Most popular songs: "Backdoor Man" and "Little Red Rooster"

Instruments: Electric guitar and harmonica

Dedication to his craft: Wolf was still taking guitar lessons even a year before his death, even though he was long recognized as one of the two greatest blues musicians in the world.

DON'T MISS ACTS

Classic slide-guitar and hard-driving blues beats mixed with jazz and even rock 'n' roll influences makes **Melvin Taylor & The Slack Band** a must-see. Call Rosa's Lounge for details. **Billy Branch and the Sons of Blues** frequently bring their forward-thinking sounds (steeped in blues tradition) to Rosa's Lounge and Kingston Mines, though they have been known to make rousing onstage appearances at the Chicago Blues Festival.

Bridge House Tavern. With an enormous patio overlooking the Chicago River, this bar attracts both the after-work crowd and tourists searching for the quintessential city view. Order a burger or bratwurst and watch the boats docking barside. Off-season visitors can take refuge inside the cozy lounge with stone walls and wood paneling. ⊠ *321 N. Clark St., River North* ☎ *312/644–0283* ⊕ *www.bridgehousetavern.com.*

12

Bull & Bear. Bull & Bear amps up the testosterone, with a dual focus on sports—the bar's name references two Chicago sports teams—and the stock market. Reserve one of five booths with built-in beer taps (you pay by the ounce), or grab a seat at the bar and catch the game on one of several flat-screen TVs. ⊠ *431 N. Wells St., River North* ☎ *312/527–5973* ⊕ *www.bullbearbar.com.*

Castaways. This breezy, casual bar and grill puts you so close to Lake Michigan that you might consider wearing a swimsuit. Perched atop the North Avenue Beach Boathouse, Castaways creates the perfect setup for lazy, summertime sipping. ⊠ *1603 N. Lake Shore Dr., River North* ☎ *773/281–1200* ⊕ *www.castawayschicago.com.*

Citizen Bar. Everyone's welcome at Citizen Bar, a sleek space with exposed brick walls and traditional bar fare. But the real draw is the huge, multilevel outdoor area—it's one of the city's most coveted spots come summer. ⊠ *364 W. Erie St., River North* ☎ *312/640–1156* ⊕ *www.citizenbar.com.*

Coq d'Or. A dark, wood-paneled room in the Drake Hotel, Coq d'Or has red-leather booths where Chicago legend Buddy Charles held court before retiring. Fine music and cocktails served in blown-glass goblets draw hotel guests as well as neighborhood regulars. ⊠ *Drake Hotel, 140 E. Walton St., Near North* ☎ *312/932–4623* ⊕ *www.thedrakehotel. com/dining/coq-d-or.*

Division Street. For vestiges of the old Rush Street, continue north to Division Street, between Clark and State. The watering holes here are crowded and noisy, and the clientele consists mostly of suburbanites and out-of-towners on the make. Among the better-known singles' bars are Butch McGuire's, the Lodge, and Original Mother's. ⊠ *Chicago.*

Drumbar. Located on the 18th floor of the Raffaello Hotel, Drumbar boasts a delicious, whiskey-focused cocktail menu plus divine city views. ⊠ *Raffaello Hotel, 201 E. Delaware Pl., Gold Coast* ☎ *312/933–4805* ⊕ *www.drumbar.com.*

Fado. Imported wood, stone, and glass are used to create Fado's Irish look. The second floor—with a bar brought in from Dublin—feels more like the real thing than the first. Expect expertly drawn Guinness, a fine selection of whiskeys, a menu of traditional dishes, and live music on weekends. ⊠ *100 W. Grand Ave., River North* ☎ *312/836–0066* ⊕ *www.fadoirishpub.com/chicago/.*

Fodor's Choice ★ **Gilt Bar.** Vintage furnishings and cocktails like the Bee's Knees (gin, lemon, and honey) set the 1920s speakeasy scene at this low-lighted lounge. The food is a major draw here; get in the spirit of indulgence with foie gras and pork liver mousse on toast. Downstairs **The Library**, a handsome book-lined bar, serves cocktails and lighter bites; cash only. ✉ *230 W. Kinzie St., River North* ☎ *312/464–9544* ⊕ *www. giltbarchicago.com.*

Howl at the Moon. The dueling pianists at Howl at the Moon attract a rowdy crowd that delights in belting out popular tunes. Reservations aren't accepted, but party packages are available if you're willing to shell out beaucoup bucks (around $150). ✉ *26 W. Hubbard St., Near North* ☎ *312/863–7427* ⊕ *www.howlatthemoon.com/chicago/.*

Hub 51. Sip cocktails with the after-work crowd in Hub 51's vaulted, loftlike industrial space, and then linger for inventive light bites or more substantial fare. The downstairs lounge, **Sub 51**, has DJ-driven beats, but get there early or reserve a table. ✉ *51 W. Hubbard St., River North* ☎ *312/828–0051* ⊕ *www.hub51chicago.com.*

Hubbard Inn. Billing itself as a "Continental tavern," this two-story River North hot spot pays homage to Ernest Hemingway's travels with classic cocktails and eclectic, globetrotting decor—think Moroccan tiled walls, vintage books, dramatic oil paintings, brass light fixtures, and tables made from reclaimed wood. Small plates are designed with communal dining in mind, though you may want to keep your perfectly balanced Sazerac all to yourself. ✉ *110 W. Hubbard St., River North* ☎ *312/222–1331* ⊕ *www.hubbardinn.com.*

The Motel Bar. The Motel Bar has all the comforts of a real, honest-to-goodness motel bar (TVs tuned to sports, classic cocktails, and a retro color scheme), but the atmosphere is amped-up with sexy, low-rise furniture and a "room service" menu of upscale bites. ✉ *600 W. Chicago Ave., River North* ☎ *312/822–2900* ⊕ *www.themotelbar.com.*

Fodor'sChoice ★ **Old Town Ale House.** Just a stone's throw from Second City, Old Town Ale House has attracted a diverse cast of characters since it opened in 1958, including comedy legends John Belushi and Bill Murray. With eclectic artwork, a mural of bar denizens painted in the '70s, and an on-site lending library, it's a dingy neighborhood bar unlike any other in the city—perhaps the country. Esteemed film critic Roger Ebert called it "the best bar in the world." ✉ *219 W. North Ave., Near North* ☎ *312/944–7020* ⊕ *www.theoldtownalehouse.com.*

Original Mother's. Since the 1960s, Original Mother's has been a local favorite for cutting-edge music and dance-'til-you-drop partying. The subterranean singles' destination was immortalized by Demi Moore, Jim Belushi, and Rob Lowe in the film *About Last Night.* ✉ *26 W. Division St., Near North* ☎ *312/642–7251.*

Pump Room. Ian Schrager revamped the historic Ambassador East Hotel as the affordably chic Public Chicago. In keeping with the democratic pricing, he left the naming of the restaurant to locals, who voted to keep it the Pump Room. In the sleek bar area, complete with gold-leaf ceiling, celebrity spotting still reigns supreme—as it did in the storied spot's heydey, when the likes of Humphrey Bogart and Lauren Bacall occupied Booth One. A separate **Library Bar** off the lobby offers coffee and pastries by day and cocktails at night. ✉ *Public Chicago, 1301 N. State Pkwy., Old Town* ☎ *312/787–3700* ⊕ *www.pumproom.com.*

12

Rockit Bar & Grill. Designer Nate Berkus assembled Rockit's hunter-lodge look: picture wood-plank-framed plasma TVs, antler chandeliers, and brown-leather booths. The crowd, much like the beer list, is diverse and tasteful, and there's a good mix of men and women despite the masculine vibe. Dress to impress. ⊠ *22 W. Hubbard St., River North* ☎ *312/645–6000* ⊕ *www.rockitbarandgrill.com.*

Rush Street. The famous Chicago bar scene known as Rush Street has faded into the mists of time, although the street has found resurgent energy with the opening of a string of upscale restaurants and outdoor cafés. ⊠ *Chicago.*

Fodor's Choice ★ **Signature Lounge.** When it comes to views, the Signature Lounge has no competition. Perched on the 96th floor of the John Hancock Center— above even the tower's observation deck—it offers stunning vistas of the skyline and lake for only the cost of a pricey drink. The ladies' room has an incredible south-facing view through floor-to-ceiling windows. ⊠ *John Hancock Center, 875 N. Michigan Ave., Near North* ☎ *312/787–9596* ⊕ *www.signatureroom.com/TheSignatureLounge.*

Three Dots and a Dash. This Near North Side hot spot specializes in tiki drinks served in a full-on luau environment. The signature cocktail? Bunny's banana daiquiri, which comes in a coconut shell–shaped glass and is garnished with a banana shaped like a dolphin. Don't be thrown off by the back-alley entrance! ⊠ *435 N. Clark St., Near North* ☎ *312/610–4220* ⊕ *www.threedotschicago.com.*

Vertigo Sky Lounge. Trendsetters hit the scene on the 26th floor of the Dana Hotel and Spa for cocktails with penthouse views or gravitate toward the fire pit on the patio. In winter, chill at the outdoor ice bar. ⊠ *Dana Hotel and Spa, 2 W. Erie St., Near North* ☎ *312/202–6060* ⊕ *www.vertigoskylounge.com.*

Zebra Lounge. Small and funky with zebra-stripe lamps and other kitschy accoutrements, this lounge attracts an interesting crowd of dressed-up and dressed-down regulars who come to sing along with the pianist on duty. ⊠ *1220 N. State St., Near North* ☎ *312/642–5140* ⊕ *www. thezebralounge.net.*

COMEDY AND IMPROV CLUBS

Fodor's Choice ★ **Second City.** An institution since 1959, Second City has served as a launching pad for some of the hottest comedians around. Alumni include Dan Aykroyd, Tina Fey, Amy Poehler, and the late John Belushi. It's the anchor of Chicago improv. The revues on the company's main stage and in its smaller e.t.c. space next door are actually sketch comedy shows, but the scripts in these prerehearsed scenes have been developed through improvisation and there's usually a little time set aside in each show for the performers to demonstrate their quick wit. Most nights there is a free improv set after the late show, featuring cast members and invited guests (sometimes famous, sometimes not, never announced in advance). It's in **Donny's Skybox** upstairs that you're more likely to see one of Chicago's many fledgling improv comedy troupes making their first appearance working together on freshly penned material in public. ⊠ *1616 N. Wells St., Near North* ☎ *312/337–3992* ⊕ *www. secondcity.com.*

Zanies Comedy Night Club. Zanies books outstanding national talent and is Chicago's best stand-up comedy spot. Jay Leno, Jerry Seinfeld, and Jackie Mason have all performed at this intimate venue. ✉ *1548 N. Wells St., Near North* ☎ *312/337–4027* ⊕ *chicago.zanies.com.*

DANCE CLUBS

Sound-Bar. Sound-Bar is a labyrinth of nine bars, each with a unique design and color scheme (some even serve matching colored cocktails). Feel like dancing? Join the pulse of Chicago's best-dressed on the huge dance floor. ✉ *226 W. Ontario St., River North* ☎ *312/787–4480* ⊕ *sound-bar.com.*

Spy Bar. Image is everything at this subterranean spot with a brushed stainless-steel bar and exposed-brick walls. The slick, stylish crowd hits the tight dance floor for house, underground, and DJ remixes. ✉ *646 N. Franklin St., River North* ☎ *312/337–2191* ⊕ *www.spybarchicago.com.*

The Underground. Unmarked entrances, servers clad in military outfits, and artillery-case cocktail tables create the illusion of an underground bunker. Sounds strange, but it works—at least according to the celebs and international DJs who make appearances at this subterranean dance club. ✉ *56 W. Illinois St., River North* ☎ *312/943–7600* ⊕ *www.theundergroundchicago.com.*

MUSIC VENUES

BLUES

Blue Chicago. In an upscale part of downtown, Blue Chicago has none of the trademark grit or edginess of the older South Side blues clubs. What is does offer is a good sound system, a packed calendar that regularly features female vocalists, and a cosmopolitan audience that's a tad more diverse than some of the baseball-capped crowds at Lincoln Park blues clubs. ✉ *536 N. Clark St., River North* ☎ *312/661–0100* ⊕ *www.bluechicago.com.*

ECLECTIC

Baton Show Lounge. At Baton Show Lounge, boys will be girls. The lip-synching revues with female impersonators have catered to curious out-of-towners and bachelorette parties since 1969. Some of the regular performers, such as Chilli Pepper and Mimi Marks, have become Chicago cult figures. The more the audience tips, the better the show gets, so bring your bills. ✉ *436 N. Clark St., River North* ☎ *312/644–5269* ⊕ *www.thebatonshowlounge.com.*

Fodor'sChoice **House of Blues.** Though its name implies otherwise, House of Blues actu-
★ ally attracts big-name performers of all genres, including jazz, roots, gospel, alternative rock, hip-hop, world, and R&B. The interior is an elaborate cross between blues bar and ornate opera house. Its restaurant has live blues every night on a "second stage," as well as a satisfying Sunday gospel brunch. Part of the Marina City complex, its entrance is on State Street. ✉ *Marina City, 329 N. Dearborn St., River North* ☎ *312/923–2000* ⊕ *www.houseofblues.com/chicago.*

JAZZ

Andy's Jazz Club. A favorite after-work watering hole with a substantial bar menu, Andy's Jazz Club has live music ranging from swing jazz to bebop. The early-bird 5 pm set is a boon for music lovers who aren't night owls. ⊠ *11 E. Hubbard St., River North* ☎ *312/642–6805* ⊕ *www.andysjazzclub.com.*

Pops for Champagne. This bi-level space is gloriously turned out with a champagne bar, raw bar, sidewalk café, and even a retail space called Pops Shop. The former basement jazz lounge is now home to **Watershed**, a cozy spot with limestone walls focused on Great Lakes regional craft beers and spirits, along with cheese and charcuterie plates. ⊠ *601 N. State St., River North* ☎ *312/266–7677* ⊕ *www.popsforchampagne. com.*

LINCOLN PARK

One of the most beautiful (and bustling) neighborhoods on the North Side of Chicago, Lincoln Park is largely defined by the DePaul students who inhabit the area. Irish pubs and sports bars line the streets, but chic wine bars attract an older, more sophisticated set. Bonus: the constant crowds make this one of the city's safest nightlife destinations.

BARS

Delilah's. A rare dive bar amid Lincoln Park's tonier establishments, Delilah's is dark and a bit grungy. But the bar has a friendly, unpretentious vibe and a standout whiskey selection (more than 300 types are on offer). DJs spin punk and rockabilly. ⊠ *2771 N. Lincoln Ave., Lincoln Park* ☎ *773/472–2771* ⊕ *www.delilahschicago.com.*

Gamekeepers. Full of sports fans and former frat boys, Gamekeepers has more than 40 TVs, three projection screens, and complete satellite sports coverage. There's barely a game it doesn't get. ⊠ *345 W. Armitage Ave., Lincoln Park* ☎ *773/549–0400* ⊕ *www.gamekeeperschicago.com.*

Hi-Tops. Hi-Tops may be the ultimate sports bar. Multiple flat-screen TVs, a lively crowd, and solid bar food keep sports fans coming. ⊠ *2462 N. Lincoln Ave., Lincoln Park* ☎ *773/549–3232* ⊕ *www. hi-topschicago.com.*

Kincade's. Popular Kincade's packs 'em in on two levels with a 10-foot-wide video monitor, several plasma screens, and a bar menu that invites patrons to linger for a game—or three. An outdoor beer garden, pool tables, and French doors that prop open on warm summer days are added bonuses. ⊠ *950 W. Armitage Ave., Lincoln Park* ☎ *773/348–0010* ⊕ *www.kincadesbar.com.*

COMEDY AND IMPROV CLUBS

I.O. Formerly called ImprovOlympic, I.O. is the city's home for long-form improvisation. The signature piece is "The Harold," in which a team of improvisers explores a single audience suggestion throughout a series of stories and characters until they all eventually weave back together to fit with the original audience idea. There's no drink or age minimum. Seating is first-come, first-served, so be sure to arrive early, especially for weekend shows. ⊠ *1501 N. Kingsbury St., Lincoln Park* ☎ *312/929–2401* ⊕ *www.ioimprov.com/chicago/.*

MUSIC VENUES

BLUES

B.L.U.E.S. The best thing about B.L.U.E.S. is that there isn't a bad seat in the joint. The worst thing? The crowds—come early if you want to score a seat. Narrow and intimate, the jam-packed North Side club has attracted the best in local talent since it opened in 1979. Big names such as Son Seals, Otis Rush, Jimmy Johnson, and Magic Slim have all played here. ⊠ *2519 N. Halsted St., Lincoln Park* ☎ *773/528–1012* ⊕ *www.chicagobluesbar.com.*

Kingston Mines. In 1968, Kingston Mines went down in Chicago history as the first blues club to open on the North Side. Though it's since moved to bigger digs, it still offers the same traditional sounds and late-night hours as the original club. Swarms of blues lovers and partying singles take in the good blues and tasty barbecue. ⊠ *2548 N. Halsted St., Lincoln Park* ☎ *773/477–4646* ⊕ *www.kingstonmines.com.*

ECLECTIC

The Wild Hare. This is the place for infectious live reggae, world-beat music, and Caribbean cuisine Tuesday through Sunday. Take a breather at the bar and sip a rum drink or a Jamaican Red Stripe beer. ⊠ *2610 N. Halsted St., Lincoln Park* ☎ *773/770–3511* ⊕ *www.wildharemusic.com.*

ROCK

Lincoln Hall. The owners of Lincoln Hall transformed a former movie theater into an intimate concert space with great sight lines, an excellent sound system, and a wraparound balcony with seating. The booking is always on point, so it's worth taking a chance on a lesser-known band. There's a separate bar and dining area up front for a preshow bite. ⊠ *2424 N. Lincoln Ave., Lincoln Park* ☎ *773/525–2501* ⊕ *www.lh-st.com.*

WICKER PARK, BUCKTOWN, AND LOGAN SQUARE

Hepcats, artists, and yuppies converge on the famed six corners of North, Milwaukee, and Damen avenues, where the cast of Real World Chicago once resided. Previously scruffy and edgy, the area is now dotted with pricey, upscale bars, though the occasional honky-tonk still survives. Logan Square, in particular, has seen an explosion of new nightlife venues in recent years. Those looking for a dance party tend to head to the Debonair Social Club or Slippery Slope, while cocktail connoisseurs brave the wait at the Violet Hour.

BARS

The California Clipper Lounge. After being spruced up by Brandon Sodikoff, one of Chicago's best-known restaurateurs, this 1930s lounge is better than ever. A curving 60-foot-long Brunswick bar still dominates the interior, and tiny booths still line the long room back-to-back like seats on a train. But the look is now cleaner, and the cocktail list is longer (most cost less than $9, so prices are refreshingly old-school). A tobacco shop has been added in the back room, too. Beloved by hipsters who've begun gentrifying the surrounding neighborhood, the lounge is located in Humboldt Park, just west of Wicker Park. ⊠ *1002 N. California Ave., Humboldt Park* ☎ *773/384–2547* ⊕ *www.californiaclipper.com.*

Davenport's Piano Bar & Cabaret. Davenport's, a sophisticated cabaret booking both local and touring acts, brings a grown-up presence to the Wicker Park club scene. The piano lounge is set up for casual listening, while the cabaret room is a no-chat zone that requires your full attention—as well as reservations and a two-drink minimum. ⊠ *1383 N. Milwaukee Ave., Wicker Park* ☎ *773/278–1830* ⊕ *www. davenportspianobar.com.*

Debonair Social Club. In the historic Flat Iron Building, the Debonair Social Club combines visual arts, music, and late-night dining. Upstairs, curated video installations line the walls surrounding the stage-cum-dance floor; the dimly lighted downstairs has a more clandestine feel. ⊠ *1575 N. Milwaukee Ave., Bucktown* ☎ *773/227–7990* ⊕ *www. debonairsocialclub.com.*

East Room. This unmarked "secret" bar carries through with its speakeasy theme—the only sign you're in the right place is the red light above the door. Inside, the lights are dim, the drinks (cash only) are cheap, and the whiskey choices are plentiful. DJs spin funk, house, and other genres; seek out the decked-out elevator room for the best seat in the house. ⊠ *2828 W. Medill Ave., Logan Square* ☎ *773/530-1478* ⊕ *www. eastroomchicago.com.*

Emporium Arcade Bar. Two of America's favorite pastimes—drinking and playing classic arcade games—come together here. You can do both affordably, too. Most games are only 50¢ per play, and no one will bat an eyelash if you select a bottom-shelf beverage. There's also a Logan Square location at 2363 North Milwaukee Avenue. ⊠ *1366 N. Milwaukee Ave., Wicker Park* ☎ *773/697–7922* ⊕ *www.emporium chicago.com.*

Happy Village. Located in Ukrainian Village, this neighborhood institution is known for its cheap beer, Ping Pong tables, and, when the weather cooperates, its massive beer garden. There's no kitchen, but Chicago's own "tamale guy," who sells authentic Mexican tamales out of a cooler, swings by nightly. Be sure to hit an ATM before you arrive because Happy Village is cash-only. ⊠ *1059 N. Wolcott Ave., Ukrainian Village/Wicker Park* ☎ *773/486–1512* ⊕ *www.happyvillagebar.com.*

The Map Room. The Map Room might help you find your way around Chicago, if not the world. Guidebooks decorate the walls of this self-described "travelers' tavern," and the craft beers represent much of the globe. This is a favorite gathering spot for soccer fans, so expect it to be roaring during World Cup season. ⊠ *1949 N. Hoyne Ave., Bucktown* ☎ *773/252–7636* ⊕ *www.maproom.com.*

Fodor'sChoice ★ **The Matchbox.** In West Town near Wicker Park, the Matchbox isn't much bigger than a you-know-what, but the hodgepodge of regulars don't seem to mind. In fact, many claim it's the dark, cramped quarters (we're talking 3 feet wide at its narrowest) that keep them coming back. The crowd spills outside in summer, when wrought-iron tables

12

dot the sidewalk. You're practically required to try the signature drink, a margarita. ⊠ *770 N. Milwaukee Ave., Wicker Park* ☎ *312/666–9292.*

Nick's Beer Garden. Nick's Beer Garden is a neighborhood favorite, especially in the wee hours (it's open until 4 am; 5 am Saturday). Kitschy tropical decor—think palm trees, flamingos, and a surfboard—adds to the appeal. ⊠ *1516 N. Milwaukee Ave., Wicker Park* ☎ *773/252–1155* ⊕ *www.nicksbeergarden.com.*

Northside Bar & Grill. This spot was one of the first anchors of the now-teeming Wicker Park nightlife scene. Locals come to drink, eat, shoot pool, and see and be seen. The enclosed indoor-outdoor patio lets you get the best out of the chancy Chicago weather. ⊠ *1635 N. Damen Ave., Wicker Park* ☎ *773/384–3555* ⊕ *www.northsidechicago.com.*

Rainbo Club. Chicago hipsters and indie rockers have made Rainbo Club their unofficial meeting place. Apart from the working photo booth wedged into a corner, the stripped-down hangout is pretty barren, but drinks are dirt cheap and the upbeat bartenders are willing conversationalists. ⊠ *1150 N. Damen Ave., Wicker Park* ☎ *773/489–5999.*

Rodan. The highly stylized Rodan is a restaurant and lounge that caters mostly to the young neighborhood hipsters who arrive at dinnertime (served until 11 pm) and stay put until closing. The narrow space often feels cramped, but if you can snag a spot at the bar or on a blue-suede banquette, an evening of major-league people-watching is in store. Snacks are served all night, so refuel with a pile of wasabi-tempura fries served with a side of siracha ketchup. ⊠ *1530 N. Milwaukee Ave., Wicker Park* ☎ *773/276–7036* ⊕ *www.rodanchicago.com.*

Slippery Slope. With its giant dance floor, craft cocktails, and dim, red-hued lighting, Slippery Slope has brought a cool, clubby vibe to Logan Square. (It gets bonus points for the Skeeball machines located next to the door.) This place gets especially crowded on the weekends, when the dancing gets serious. ⊠ *2357 N. Milwaukee Ave., Logan Square* ☎ *773/799–8504* ⊕ *www.slipperyslopechicago.com.*

The Violet Hour. The Violet Hour channels a Prohibition-era speakeasy—an unmarked door in the mural-covered facade leads to a mysterious, curtained hallway. Inside, twinkling crystal chandeliers cast a glow on cornflower-blue walls, and extremely high-backed blue leather chairs encourage intimate conversations. Add to that pricey but flawlessly executed cocktails and a sign discouraging cell-phone use, and it's our idea of nightlife heaven. ⊠ *1520 N. Damen Ave., Wicker Park* ☎ *773/252–1500* ⊕ *www.theviolethour.com.*

Webster's Wine Bar. This cozy, candlelit, bookshelf-lined bar is a romantic place for a date. It stocks more than 500 bottles of wine (at least 30 are available by the glass) plus ports, sherries, single-malt Scotches, a few microbrews, and a menu of small tasting entrées at reasonable prices. ⊠ *2601 N. Milwaukee Ave., Logan Square* ☎ *773/292–9463* ⊕ *www. websterwinebar.com.*

The Whistler. If you love unusual cocktails, free live music, and a laid-back vibe, the Whistler is the bar for you. It can get crowded, but downing a Wildcat (a potent drink combining chai-infused bourbon with vermouth, lemon, bitters, and an herbal liqueur) will make you forget any time spent waiting in line. ✉ *2421 N. Milwaukee Ave., Logan Square* ☎ *773/227-3530* ⊕ *www.whistlerchicago.com.*

MUSIC VENUES

BLUES

Fodor's Choice ★ **Rosa's Lounge.** On a given night at Rosa's Lounge, near Bucktown, you'll find Tony, the owner, working the crowd, and his mother, Rosa, behind the bar. What makes the club special is that the duo moved here from Italy out of a pure love for the blues. Stop by and partake in Rosa's winning mixture of big-name and local talent, stiff drinks, and friendly service—the same since it opened in 1984. ✉ *3420 W. Armitage Ave., Logan Square* ☎ *773/342–0452* ⊕ *www.rosaslounge.com.*

COUNTRY

Fodor's Choice ★ **The Hideout.** The Hideout, which is literally hidden away in a North Side industrial zone, has managed to make country music hip in Chicago. Players on the city's alternative country scene have adopted the friendly hole-in-the-wall, and bands ranging from the obscure to the semifamous take the stage. DJs take over Saturday nights after midnight, so come ready to dance. ✉ *1354 W. Wabansia Ave., Bucktown* ☎ *773/227–4433* ⊕ *www.hideoutchicago.com.*

ECLECTIC

The Burlington. Just a few blocks from the heart of Logan Square, this narrow bar has a woodsy vibe and a straightforward menu. In the front room, a rotating roster of DJs plays an eclectic mix of tunes; in the back room, live music from both local and touring acts tends to skew toward punk or noise rock. ✉ *3425 W. Fullerton Ave., Logan Square* ☎ *773/384–3243* ⊕ *www.theburlingtonbar.com.*

Fodor's Choice ★ **The Empty Bottle.** This place, in the Ukrainian Village near Wicker Park, may have toys and knickknacks around the bar (including a case of macabre baby-doll heads), but when it comes to booking rock, punk, and jazz bands from the indie scene, it's a serious place with no pretensions. Grab some grub next door at **Bite Cafe** before the show—odds are you'll be dining next to that night's headliners. ✉ *1035 N. Western Ave., Wicker Park* ☎ *773/276–3600* ⊕ *www.emptybottle.com.*

OFF THE BEATEN PATH **FitzGerald's Nightclub.** Although it's a 30-minute schlep west of Chicago, FitzGerald's draws crowds from all over the city and suburbs with its mix of folk, jazz, blues, zydeco, and rock. This early 1900s roadhouse has both great sound and sight lines. ✉ *6615 W. Roosevelt Rd., Berwyn* ☎ *708/788–2118* ⊕ *www.fitzgeraldsnightclub.com.*

Late Bar. Enjoy late-night music and potent martinis? Late Bar, located along a somewhat lonely stretch of Belmont Avenue, is the place for you. The best time to come is Saturday night, when the club is bumping with New Wave classics until 5 am. Note that this Avondale favorite only accepts cash. ✉ *3534 W. Belmont Ave.* ☎ *773/267–5283* ⊕ *www.latebarchicago.com.*

Logan Square Auditorium. The second-floor ballroom hosts all-ages rock shows put on by the team at the Empty Bottle, plus other live performances and assorted special events. The acoustics aren't the best, but the hip younger crowd it draws doesn't seem to care. For those 21 and over, there's a full bar. ✉ *2539 N. Kedzie Blvd., Logan Square* ☎ *773/252–6179* ⊕ *www.logansquareauditorium.com.*

ROCK

Double Door. Double Door is a hotbed for music in Wicker Park. The large bar books up-and-coming local and national acts from rock to acid jazz. Unannounced Rolling Stones shows have been held here. **Door No. 3,** a lounge with a speakeasy theme, occupies the basement. ✉ *1572 N. Milwaukee Ave., Wicker Park* ⊹ *Main entrance is at 1551 N. Damen Ave.* ☎ *773/489–3160* ⊕ *www.doubledoor.com.*

LAKEVIEW AND FAR NORTH SIDE

Lakeview, Uptown, and Andersonville, all on the Far North Side, have one thing in common: affordability. Unbelievable as it sounds, there are places in the city where $20 stretches beyond the price of admission and a martini. Drink deals are frequently offered at many bars. If you're heading out early, take the El or a bus, but you'll probably want to cab it back to your hotel.

BARS

404 Wine Bar. Enter through rowdy Jack's Bar & Grill to find the serene 404 Wine Bar, a romantic spot filled with cozy nooks. The library-like back room has ornate chandeliers, shelves lined with books, and dramatic oxblood walls. Grab a spot on the patio or near one of two fireplaces and enjoy a glass, flight, or bottle of wine accompanied by a cheese plate. ✉ *2852 N. Southport Ave., Lakeview* ☎ *773/404–8400* ⊕ *www.404winebarchicago.com.*

Blokes & Birds. A departure from the typical Wrigleyville sports bar, this modern public house draws Anglophiles thirsty for a well-poured pint and contemporary takes on classic English pub fare, such as shepherd's pie with stout-braised lamb and fish-and-chips with malt vinegar aioli. (The bar's name is British slang for "guys and girls.") Friday and Saturday nights, sing your heart out in its karaoke lounge. ✉ *3343 N. Clark St., Wrigleyville* ☎ *773/472–5252* ⊕ *www.blokesandbirdschicago.com.*

Cubby Bear Lounge. Diagonally across the street from Wrigley Field stands the Cubby Bear, a Chicago institution since 1953. It is the place where Cub fans come to drown their sorrows in beer or lift one to celebrate. There are plenty of TVs for game watching, plus live music and a menu featuring burgers and other bar food. ✉ *1059 W. Addison St., Wrigleyville* ☎ *773/327–1662* ⊕ *www.cubbybear.com.*

Gingerman Tavern. Up the street from Wrigley Field, Gingerman Tavern deftly manages to avoid being pigeonholed as a sports bar. Folks here take their beer and billiards seriously, with three pool tables and—our favorite part—a list of more than 100 bottles of beer. New and vintage tunes crank out of the jukebox all night long. ✉ *3740 N. Clark St., Lakeview* ☎ *773/549–2050.*

Holiday Club. Rat Pack aficionados will appreciate the 1950s decor at this self-described "Swinger's mecca." Down a pint of beer and scan the typical (but tasty) bar menu as you listen to Frank Sinatra crooning on the well-stocked CD jukebox. ⊠ *4000 N. Sheridan Rd., Far North Side* ☎ *773/348–9600* ⊕ *www.holidayclubchicago.com.*

Fodor's Choice ★ **Hopleaf.** An anchor in the Andersonville corridor, Hopleaf continues the tradition of the classic Chicago bar hospitable to conversation (there's not a TV in sight). The lengthy beer menu emphasizes Belgian varieties and regional microbrews, and the Belgian fare served here far surpasses typical bar food. Don't miss the ale-steamed mussels and delectable skinny fries with aioli on the side. ⊠ *5148 N. Clark St., Far North Side* ☎ *773/334–9851* ⊕ *www.hopleaf.com.*

John Barleycorn. This bar in the heart of Wrigleyville is a popular destination during (and before and after) a Cubs game. When you're ready to dance, there's plenty of space to get down thanks to its massive upstairs dance floor. ⊠ *3524 N. Clark St., Wrigleyville* ☎ *773/348–8899* ⊕ *www.johnbarleycorn.com.*

Marty's Martini Bar. Miniscule Marty's serves up some of the tastiest cocktails in town. Roughly the size of a one-bedroom apartment, the bar can get very crowded, so come early in the night. ⊠ *1511 W. Balmoral Ave., Andersonville* ☎ *773/454–0161* ⊕ *www.martysmartinibar.com.*

Rogers Park Social. It's hard to imagine a bar feeling homier than Rogers Park Social. The community-oriented spot has an impressive menu of craft beers plus fresh cocktails that pack deep layers of flavor into every glass. ⊠ *6920 N. Glenwood Ave.* ☎ *773/791–1419* ⊕ *www.rogersparksocial.com.*

Sheffield's. With a shaded beer garden in summer and a roaring fireplace in winter, Sheffield's spans the seasons. The laid-back neighborhood pub has billiards and more than 100 kinds of bottled beer, including regional microbrews. You can also choose from 18 brands on tap or opt for the bartender's "bad beer of the month" (think a cheap can of PBR). ⊠ *3258 N. Sheffield Ave., Lakeview* ☎ *773/281–4989* ⊕ *www.sheffieldschicago.com.*

Fodor's Choice ★ **Simon's Tavern.** This classic Andersonville bar honors the neighborhood's Swedish roots with its signature drink, *glögg*—mulled Swedish wine, served hot in a mug in winter and in frozen slushie form in summer. The Viking/Midwestern-chic decor is eclectic and dive-y, but in a very good way. This is where the locals hang out. Simon's often hosts live music from area bands as well. ⊠ *5210 N. Clark St., Andersonville* ☎ *773/878–0894.*

Sluggers. Sluggers is packed after Cubs games in the nearby stadium, and the ballplayers make occasional appearances in summer. Check out the fast- and slow-pitch batting cages on the second floor, as well as the pool tables, air-hockey tables, and electronic basketball. ⊠ *3540 N. Clark St., Lakeview* ☎ *773/248–0055* ⊕ *www.sluggersbar.com.*

GAY AND LESBIAN

Fodor's Choice ★ **Big Chicks.** In the Uptown area of the Far North Side, Big Chicks is a striking alternative to the Halsted strip, with a funky crowd that appreciates the owner's art collection hanging on the walls. The fun-loving staff and their self-selected eclectic music are the payoffs for the hike to get here. Special attractions include weekend dancing and free

Bluesman Jimmy Burns singing at Buddy Guy's Legends.

Sunday-afternoon buffets. ✉ *5024 N. Sheridan Rd., Far North Side* ☎ *773/728–5511* ⊕ *www.bigchicks.com.*

Charlie's. A country-and-western dance spot, Charlie's lets you two-step nightly to achy-breaky tunes (club music takes over after midnight). It's mostly a boots-and-denim crowd on weekends. ✉ *3726 N. Broadway St., Lakeview* ☎ *773/871–8887* ⊕ *www.charlieschicago.com.*

Circuit. The biggest dance club in Boystown is a stripped-down hall energized by flashing lights, booming sounds, and a partying crowd. Take a break in the up-front martini bar. ✉ *3641 N. Halsted St., Lakeview* ☎ *773/325–2233* ⊕ *www.circuitnightclubchicago.com.*

The Closet. This compact dive bar—one of the few that caters to lesbians, though it draws gay men, too—can be especially lively after 2 am when most other bars close. Stop by Sunday afternoons when bartenders serve up what are hailed as the best Bloody Marys in town. ✉ *3325 N. Broadway St., Lakeview* ☎ *773/477–8533* ⊕ *www.theclosetchicago.com.*

Hydrate. Hydrate combines a relaxed front lounge with a late-night, high-energy dance floor in the back. Weekly events include drag shows. ✉ *3458 N. Halsted St., Lakeview* ☎ *773/975–9244* ⊕ *www.hydratechicago.com.*

Joie de Vine. Catering to a lesbian clientele, this wine bar has expanded its focus to include craft beer and cocktails. The space itself is cozy, but good design (and sidewalk tables in summer) keeps it from feeling claustrophobic. Sit at the long wooden bar or opposing banquette and enjoy the room's real focal point, a glass-brick wall lighted up in multiple colors. ✉ *1744 W. Balmoral Ave., Far North Side* ☎ *773/989–6846.*

North End. A sports bar with a twist, the North End is a favorite spot to watch the big game or play some pool. Later at night, it has more of a typical gay-bar atmosphere. ✉ *3733 N. Halsted St., Lakeview* ☎ *773/477–7999* ⊕ *www.northendchicago.com.*

Roscoe's Tavern and Cafe. A longtime favorite in the heart of Boystown, Roscoe's Tavern has a lot to offer its preppy patrons, including a jam-packed front bar, a dance floor, a pool table, an outdoor garden, and lively music. The sidewalk café is open May through September. ✉ *3356 N. Halsted St., Lakeview* ☎ *773/281–3355* ⊕ *www.roscoes.com.*

Sidetrack. Focusing on a different theme every night of the week, Sidetrack broadcasts videos on TV screens that never leave your sight. Attractive professionals pack the sprawling strike-a-pose bar and rooftop deck; order a vodka slushie (the house specialty) and join the crowd. ✉ *3349 N. Halsted St., Lakeview* ☎ *773/477–9189* ⊕ *www.sidetrack chicago.com.*

CAFÉS

Intelligentsia. This place was named to invoke the prechain days when cafés were forums for discussion, but the long, broad farmer's tables and handsome couches are usually occupied by students and other serious types who treat the café like their office. Intelligentsia does all of its own coffee roasting and sells its house blends to local restaurants. The North Broadway branch is one of six citywide. ✉ *3123 N. Broadway, Lakeview* ☎ *773/348–8058* ⊕ *www.intelligentsiacoffee.com.*

Kopi, a Traveler's Cafe. In the Andersonville neighborhood, a 20-minute cab ride from downtown, Kopi serves healthy vegetarian fare as well as decadent desserts. It now has a full bar, too. While here, you can browse through a selection of travel books and global gifts. ✉ *5317 N. Clark St., Far North Side* ☎ *773/989–5674.*

Pick Me Up Café. The Pick Me Up combines the charm of a quirky, neighborhood café with the late-night hours of those chain diners. The thrift-store treasures hanging on the walls are as eclectic as the crowd that comes at all hours of the day and night to drink bottomless cups of coffee or dine on sandwiches, appetizers, and desserts. ✉ *3408 N. Clark St., Lakeview* ☎ *773/248–6613.*

Uncommon Ground. The original location of Uncommon Ground is roomy and inviting, with a hand-carved bar and large street-facing windows offering views of passersby. Patrons brave the wait for bowls of coffee and hot chocolate. There's also a full bar and a hearty menu. Perks include two fireplaces, sidewalk tables, and a steady lineup of acoustic musical acts. A second location in the Edgewater neighborhood (*1401 W. Devon Avenue*) gets bonus points for eco-friendliness, with a green roof, solar panels, and tables made from reclaimed wood. ✉ *3800 N. Clark St., Lakeview* ☎ *773/929–3680* ⊕ *www.uncommonground.com.*

COMEDY AND IMPROV CLUBS

Fodor'sChoice **The Annoyance Theatre & Bar.** This is home base for Annoyance Productions, an irreverent group best known for hits like *Skinprov* and *Hitch*Cocktails.* ✉ *851 W. Belmont Ave., Lakeview* ☎ *773/697–9693* ⊕ *www.theannoyance.com.*

Chicago is the undisputed capital of improv comedy.

ComedySportz. ComedySportz specializes in "competitive improv," in which two teams vie for the audience's favor. Book a family-friendly early performance or a late-night show rife with raunchy humor. The space features cabaret-style seating and a full bar. ⊠ *929 W. Belmont Ave., Lakeview* ☎ *773/549–8080* ⊕ *www.comedysportzchicago.com.*

DANCE CLUBS

Fodor'sChoice
★
Berlin Nightclub. A multicultural, pansexual dance club near the Belmont El station, Berlin has progressive electronic dance music and fun themed nights (Madonna is celebrated on the first Sunday of every month, and Björk is honored with a quarterly party).The venue also hosts drag matinees, comedy shows, and vogue-offs. The crowd tends to be predominantly gay on weeknights, mixed on weekends. ⊠ *954 W. Belmont Ave., Lakeview* ☎ *773/348–4975* ⊕ *www.berlinchicago.com.*

MUSIC VENUES

COUNTRY

Carol's Pub. Located in the Uptown area of the Far North Side, Carol's Pub showcased country before it was ever cool. The house band at this urban honky-tonk plays country and country-rock tunes on Friday and Saturday nights; on Thursday and Sunday nights karaoke sessions draw all walks of life, from preppy to punk. ⊠ *4659 N. Clark St., Far North Side* ☎ *773/334–2402.*

ECLECTIC

Beat Kitchen. North Side stalwart Beat Kitchen brings in the crowds because of its good sound system and solid rock, alternative-rock, country, and rockabilly acts. It also serves soups, salads, sandwiches, pizzas, and desserts. ✉ *2100 W. Belmont Ave., Lakeview* ☎ *773/281–4444* ⊕ *www.beatkitchen.com.*

Elbo Room. Elbo Room, a multilevel space in an elbow-shape corner building, has a basement rec-room feel. Talented live bands add a strong dose of nu-jazz, funk, soul, pop, and rock seven days a week. ✉ *2871 N. Lincoln Ave., Lakeview* ☎ *773/549–5549* ⊕ *www.elboroomlive.com.*

FOLK

Fodor's Choice ★ **Old Town School of Folk Music.** Chicago's oldest folk-music school has served as folk central in the city since it opened in 1957. The welcoming spot in Lincoln Square hosts outstanding performances by national and local acts in an intimate-feeling 420-seat concert hall that has excellent acoustics. A major expansion in 2012 added a new, environmentally friendly facility across the street, with a 150-seat performance hall and acoustically engineered classrooms. ✉ *4544 N. Lincoln Ave., Lincoln Square* ☎ *773/728–6000* ⊕ *www.oldtownschool.org.*

JAZZ

Fodor's Choice ★ **Green Mill Cocktail Lounge.** A Chicago institution, the Green Mill in not-so-trendy Uptown has been around since 1907. Deep leather banquettes and ornate wood paneling line the walls, and a photo of former patron Al Capone occupies a place of honor on the piano behind the bar. The jazz entertainment is both excellent and contemporary—the club launched the careers of Kurt Elling and Patricia Barber; the Uptown Poetry Slam, a competitive poetry reading, takes center stage on Sunday. ✉ *4802 N. Broadway Ave., Far North Side* ☎ *773/878–5552* ⊕ *www.greenmilljazz.com.*

ROCK

The Abbey Pub. Located in the Irving Park neighborhood, about 15 minutes northwest of downtown, this place showcases rock, as well as some Irish, Celtic, and country music, in a large concert hall with a separate, busy pub. By day the hall is used to show soccer and rugby games from the United Kingdom and Ireland. ✉ *3420 W. Grace St., Irving Park* ☎ *773/478–4408* ⊕ *www.abbeypub.com.*

Martyrs'. Martyrs' brings local and major-label rock bands to this small, North Side neighborhood sandwiched between Lincoln Square and Roscoe Village. Music fans can see the stage from just about any corner of the bar, while the more rhythmically inclined gyrate in the large standing-room area. A mural opposite the stage memorializes late rock greats. ✉ *3855 N. Lincoln Ave., Far Northwest Side* ☎ *773/404–9494* ⊕ *www.martyrslive.com.*

Metro. Progressive, nationally known artists and the cream of the local crop play at Metro, a former movie palace. It's an excellent place to see live bands, whether you're moshing on the main floor or above the fray in the balcony. In the basement is **Smart Bar**, a late-night dance club that starts hopping after midnight. ✉ *3730 N. Clark St., Lakeview* ☎ *773/549–4140* ⊕ *www.metrochicago.com.*

Schubas Tavern. Built in 1903 by the Schlitz Brewing Company, Schubas Tavern favors local and national power pop, indie rock, and folk musicians. The laid-back, wood-paneled back room is the perfect place to hear artists who are just about to make it big. For preconcert dining,

Harmony Grill serves up regional American comfort food. ✉ *3159 N. Southport Ave., Lakeview* ☎ *773/525–2508* ⊕ *www.lh-st.com.*

PERFORMING ARTS

If you're even mildly interested in the performing arts, Chicago has the means to put you in your seat—be it floor, mezzanine, or balcony. Just pick your preference (theater, dance, or symphony orchestra), and let an impressive body of artists do the rest. From critically acclaimed big names to fringe groups that specialize in experimental work, there truly is a performance art for everyone.

Ticket prices vary wildly, depending on whether you're seeing a high-profile group or venturing into more obscure territory. Chicago Symphony tickets range from $15 to $200, the Lyric Opera from $30 to $180 (if you can get them). Smaller choruses and orchestras charge from $10 to $30; watch the listings for free performances. Commercial theater tickets cost between $15 and $75; smaller experimental ensembles might charge $5, $10, or pay-what-you-can. Movie prices range from $11 for first-run houses to as low as $1.50 at some suburban second-run houses.

PERFORMING ART VENUES

Athenaeum Theatre. The 1,000-seat Athenaeum Theatre, adjacent to St. Alphonsus Church, stages comedy, dance, children's theater performances, and more. ✉ *2936 N Southport Ave., Lakeview* ☎ *773/935–6860* ⊕ *www.athenaeumtheatre.com.*

Auditorium Theatre of Roosevelt University. Designed by notable architects Louis Sullivan and Dankmar Adler, the 4,300-seat, Romanesque Revival–style Auditorium Theatre of Roosevelt University opened in 1899 as an opera house and later became a National Historic Landmark. Known for its perfect acoustics and excellent sight lines, the ornate theater features marble mosaics, dramatic gilded ceiling arches, and intricate murals. (Also of note: This was one of the first public buildings to have electric lighting and air-conditioning.) ✉ *50 E. Congress Parkway, South Loop* ☎ *312/341–2310* ⊕ *www.auditoriumtheatre.org.*

Bank of America Theatre. After debuting as the Majestic in 1906, this 1,800-seat theater became a major stop on the vaudeville circuit. Today, after a series of name changes (from the Shubert Theatre to the LaSalle Bank Theatre to its current incarnation), the plush, red-and-gold venue hosts Broadway in Chicago performances such as *Jersey Boys, The Book of Mormon,* and other traveling shows. ✉ *18 W. Monroe St., Loop* ☎ *312/977–1700, 800/775–2000* ⊕ *www.broadwayinchicago.com.*

Broadway Playhouse at Water Tower Place. Formerly known as Drury Lane, the 550-seat theater in Water Tower Place was taken over in 2010 by the Broadway in Chicago group, which modernized the space and reopened it as the Broadway Playhouse. Its inaugural season included a new production of hometown scribe Studs Terkel's *Working.* ✉ *175 E. Chestnut St., Near North* ☎ *312/977–1700* ⊕ *www.broadwayinchicago.com.*

Back in the day, the Ford Center for the Performing Arts–Oriental Theatre hosted performances by Bing Crosby, Ella Fitzgerald, Danny Kaye, and Billie Holiday.

Cadillac Palace Theatre. Designed by famed theater architects the Rapp Brothers, the Cadillac Palace opened to much fanfare in 1926. The ornate, gilded interior was inspired by the palaces of Versailles and Fontainebleau; restored to its original opulence in 1999, the 2,500-seat space now hosts a wide range of traveling productions. ⊠ *151 W. Randolph St., Loop* ☎ *312/977–1700, 800/745–3000* ⊕ *www. broadwayinchicago.com.*

Chicago Cultural Center. This block-long landmark building houses several performance spaces. The most magnificent is the top-floor Preston Bradley Hall, with its Tiffany glass dome and ornately detailed white marble walls. ⊠ *78 E. Washington St., Loop* ☎ *312/744–6630, 312/744–6630* ⊕ *www.chicagoculturalcenter.org.*

The Chicago Theatre. Since 1921, visitors to the Chicago Theatre, which began as a Balaban and Katz movie palace, have marveled at its stunning Baroque interior. The 3,600-seat auditorium features crystal chandeliers, bronze light fixtures, and murals on the wall and ceiling. Lately it has hosted big-name music acts like Beyoncé and Arcade Fire. ⊠ *175 N. State St., Loop* ☎ *312/462–6300* ⊕ *www.thechicagotheatre.com.*

Ford Center for the Performing Arts–Oriental Theatre. Befitting the name, this former movie palace has a grand, over-the-top Far Eastern decor (think Buddha statues and huge mosaics of an Indian prince and princess). First opened in 1926, it reopened in 1998 after a period of disrepair to accommodate big-name Broadway hits—for several years it served as the Chicago home for *Wicked.* ⊠ *24 W. Randolph St., Loop* ☎ *312/977–1700, 800/775–2000* ⊕ *www.broadwayinchicago.com.*

Goodman Theatre. Founded in 1925, the city's oldest and largest non-profit theater presents an exceptional repertoire of plays each year featuring local and national performers. Works by August Wilson and David Mamet have premiered here, and the Goodman's annual holiday staging of *A Christmas Carol* is a Chicago tradition. ⊠ *170 N. Dearborn St., Loop* ☎ *312/443–3800* ⊕ *www.goodmantheatre.org.*

Joan W. and Irving B. Harris Theater for Music and Dance. Located on the northwest corner of Millennium Park, this 1,500-seat, mostly below-ground theater is a sleek, contemporary space where you can catch music and dance performances by the likes of Laurie Anderson, Magnetic Fields, and Hubbard Street Dance Chicago. ⊠ *205 E. Randolph Dr., Loop* ☎ *312/334–7777* ⊕ *www.harristheaterchicago.org.*

Royal George Theatre. The Royal George is actually a complex of three theaters: a spacious main stage, a smaller studio theater, and a cabaret space. Popular plays and long-running musical comedies are the draw here. ⊠ *1641 N. Halsted. St., Lincoln Park* ☎ *312/988–9000* ⊕ *www.theroyalgeorgetheatre.com.*

Stage 773. Formerly the Theatre Building, Stage 773 showcases new works by up-and-coming playwrights and musical theater talent on three small stages. ⊠ *1225 W. Belmont Ave., Lakeview* ☎ *773/327–5252* ⊕ *www.stage773.com.*

Storefront Theater. This storefront theater, operated by the Chicago Department of Cultural Affairs and Special Events, is an intimate, black-box venue for a diverse array of performances by local theater ensembles. ⊠ *66 E. Randolph St., Loop* ☎ *312/742–8497* ⊕ *www.cityofchicago. org/city/en/depts/dca/supp_info/chicago_culturalcenterpresents.html.*

CHOIR

Apollo Chorus of Chicago. Formed in 1872, the Apollo Chorus of Chicago is one of the country's oldest oratorio societies. Don't miss the annual Handel's *Messiah* if you're here in December. Otherwise, the group performs choral classics throughout the year at area churches. ⊠ *Chicago* ☎ *312/427–5620* ⊕ *www.apollochorus.org.*

Bella Voce. Bella Voce —"beautiful voices," indeed. Formerly known as His Majestie's Clerkes, the 20-person a cappella group performs a variety of sacred and secular music, including everything from early music to works by living composers. Concerts are often held in churches, providing a powerful acoustical and visual accompaniment to the music. ⊠ *Chicago* ☎ *312/479–1096* ⊕ *www.bellavoce.org.*

FAMILY   **Chicago Children's Choir.** A performance by the Chicago Children's Choir is the closest thing we can imagine to hearing angels sing. Its members—ages 8 to 18—are culled from a broad spectrum of racial, ethnic, and economic groups. Most concerts are scheduled during the holiday season and in May. ⊠ *Chicago* ☎ *312/849–8300* ⊕ *www.ccchoir.org.*

Oriana Singers. The small but mighty Oriana Singers are an outstanding a cappella sextet with an eclectic early classical and jazz repertoire. The close-knit traveling group performs from September to June,

periodically in conjunction with the Joffrey Ballet and other Chicago-area groups. ⊠ *Chicago* ☎ *773/262–4558* ⊕ *www.oriana.org.*

CLASSICAL MUSIC

FAMILY   **Chicago Symphony Orchestra.** Under the direction of internationally celebrated conductor Riccardo Muti, the Chicago Symphony Orchestra is a musical tour de force. It has two award-winning, in-house composers and an annual calendar with 150-plus performances. The impressive roster includes regular concerts as well as special themed series dedicated to classical, chamber, and children's concerts. The season runs from September through June. Tickets are sometimes scarce, but they do become available; call or check the website for status updates. If you buy tickets online, use the interactive "Your Seats" tool; it lets you see photos of the stage views from different seats. ⊠ *Symphony Center, 220 S. Michigan Ave., Loop* ☎ *312/294–3000,* ⊕ *www.cso.org.*

Mandel Hall at the University of Chicago. Mandel Hall at the University of Chicago hosts an annual classical concert series featuring a wide range of composers and ensembles. ⊠ *1131 E. 57th St., Hyde Park* ☎ *773/834–0858,* ⊕ *www.leadership.uchicago.edu/mandel-hall.*

Music of the Baroque. Rewind time with one of the Midwest's leading music ensembles. Specializing in Baroque and early classical music, it mounts about eight programs a year, mostly at Millennium Park's Harris Theater. ☎ *312/551–1414* ⊕ *www.baroque.org.*

The Newberry Library. Head to the stately Newberry Library for performances by the Newberry Consort, an early-music chamber group, and other ensembles in Ruggles Hall. ⊠ *60 W. Walton St., Near North* ☎ *312/943–9090* ⊕ *www.newberry.org.*

DANCE

Dance Center of Columbia College Chicago. Thought-provoking fare with leading national and international contemporary-dance artists is presented by the Dance Center of Columbia College Chicago. ⊠ *1306 S. Michigan Ave., South Loop* ☎ *312/369–8300* ⊕ *www.colum.edu/dance-center/performances/.*

Hubbard Street Dance Chicago. Hubbard Street Dance Chicago exudes a jazzy vitality that has made it extremely popular. The style mixes classical-ballet techniques, theatrical jazz, and contemporary dance. Most performances take place at the Harris Theater in Millennium Park. ☎ *312/850–9744* ⊕ *www.hubbardstreetdance.com.*

Joffrey Ballet. Fine-tuned performances, such as the glittering production of *The Nutcracker,* make this Chicago's premier classical-dance company. Treat yourself to one of several annual shows at the Auditorium Theatre of Roosevelt University and help celebrate 60 seasons of superb ballet. ⊠ *Auditorium Theatre of Roosevelt University, 50 E. Congress Parkway, South Loop* ☎ *312/739–0120* ⊕ *www.joffrey.org.*

Muntu Dance Theatre of Chicago. Muntu Dance Theatre of Chicago showcases dynamic interpretations of contemporary and traditional African and African American dance. Artistic director Amaniyea Payne travels to Africa to learn traditional dances and adapts them for the stage. Performances take place at various venues across the city. ⊠ *Chicago* ☎ *773/241–6080* ⊕ *www.muntu.com.*

Trinity Irish Dance Company. Founded long before *Riverdance,*the Trinity Irish Dance Company promotes traditional and progressive Irish dancing. Shows take place at various venues in the city and suburbs. In addition to the world-champion professional group, you can also catch performances by younger dancers enrolled in the Trinity Academy of Irish Dance. ⊠ *Chicago* ☎ *630/415–3382, 877/326–2328* ⊕ *www. trinityirishdance.com.*

12

FILM

Brew and View. The Vic Theatre attracts a rowdy crowd on Brew and View nights, thanks to cheap flicks—both newer releases and cult faves—and beer specials. ⊠ *Vic Theatre, 3145 N. Sheffield Ave., Lakeview* ☎ *773/929–6713* ⊕ *www.brewview.com.*

Facets. Facets Cinematheque presents independent and art films in its cinema and video theater. ⊠ *1517 W. Fullerton Ave., Lincoln Park* ☎ *800/331–6197* ⊕ *www.facets.org.*

Gene Siskel Film Center. New releases from around the globe and revivals of cinematic classics are shown at the Gene Siskel Film Center; the best part is that filmmakers often make appearances at screenings. ⊠ *164 N. State St., Loop* ☎ *312/846–2600, 312/846–2800 hotline* ⊕ *www. siskelfilmcenter.org.*

IMAX and OMNIMAX Theaters. For IMAX and OMNIMAX theaters, go to Navy Pier or the Museum of Science and Industry. ⊠ *Chicago* ⊕ *www. imax.com/oo/navy-pier-imax, www.msichicago.org.*

Logan Theatre. It used to be that folks only came here because of the low ticket prices. But, after an ambitious remodel, the historic 1915 theater is now a neighborhood gem. Expect a well-curated mix of current blockbusters, indie films, and cult classics. ⊠ *2646 N. Milwaukee Ave., Logan Square* ☎ *773/342–5555* ⊕ *www.thelogantheatre.com.*

Movies in the Parks. For a change of scenery, you can watch current and classic films in neighborhood parks courtesy of the Chicago Park District's Movies in the Parks program; flicks run on various evenings June through September. ⊠ *Chicago* ☎ *312/742–7529* ⊕ *www.chicagopark district.com/events/movies/.*

Music Box Theatre. If you love old theaters, old movies, and ghosts (rumor has it the theater is haunted by the spirit of its original manager), don't miss a trip to the Music Box. Certain screenings in the vintage 1929 venue get extra atmosphere thanks to a live pipe organ introduction. ⊠ *3733 N. Southport Ave., Lakeview* ☎ *773/871–6607* ⊕ *www.music boxtheatre.com.*

OPERA

Chicago Opera Theater. This company shrugs off esoteric notions of opera, preferring to make productions that are accessible to aficionados and novices alike. The production of *Nixon in China,* a contemporary American work detailing conversations between the former U.S. president and Henry Kissinger (among others), is a shining example of the Chicago Opera Theater's open-mindedness toward the operatic canon. From innovative versions of traditional favorites to important lesser-known works, the emphasis is on both theatrical and musical aspects. Fear not—performances are sung in English or in Italian with English supertitles projected above the stage. They're held at the Harris Theater in Millennium Park. ⊠ *Harris Theater, 205 E. Randolph Dr., Loop* ☎ *312/704–8414* ⊕ *www.chicagooperatheater.org.*

Light Opera Works. Light Opera Works favors the satirical tones of the distinctly British Gilbert and Sullivan operettas, but takes on frothy Viennese, French, and other light operettas and American musicals from June to early January. Performances take place in Evanston, just north of the city and easily accessible by train or El. ⊠ *Ticket office, 516 4th St., Wilmette* ☎ *847/920–5360* ⊕ *www.light-opera-works.org.*

Lyric Opera of Chicago. At the Lyric Opera of Chicago, the big voices of the opera world star in top-flight productions September through May. This is one of the top two opera companies in America today. Don't worry about understanding German or Italian; English translations are projected above the stage. All of the superb performances have sold out for more than a dozen years, and close to 90% of all Lyric tickets go to subscribers. The key to getting in is to call the Lyric in early August, when individual tickets first go on sale. ⊠ *Civic Opera House, 20 N. Wacker Dr., Loop* ☎ *312/332–2244* ⊕ *www.lyricopera.org.*

THEATER

About Face Theatre. The city's best-known gay, lesbian, bisexual, and transgender performing group has garnered awards for original works, world premieres, and adaptations presented in larger theaters like Steppenwolf and the Goodman. ⊠ *5252 N. Broadway St., Far North* ☎ *773/784–8565* ⊕ *www.aboutfacetheatre.com.*

Bailiwick Chicago. New and classical material is staged at various locations throughout the city by Bailiwick Chicago. ⊠ *Chicago* ☎ *773/969–6201* ⊕ *www.bailiwickchicago.com.*

Black Ensemble Theater. The Black Ensemble Theater has a penchant for long-running musicals based on popular African American icons. Founder and executive producer Jackie Taylor has written and directed such hits as *The Jackie Wilson Story* and *The Other Cinderella.* ⊠ *4450 N. Clark St., Far North Side* ☎ *773/769–4451* ⊕ *www.blackensemble theater.org.*

Briar Street Theatre. Originally built as a horse stable for Marshall Field, Briar Street Theatre is the spot to catch the long-running hit *Blue Man Group.* ⊠ *3133 N. Halsted St., Lakeview* ☎ *773/348–4000* ⊕ *www. blueman.com/chicago/about-show/.*

12

FAMILY **Chicago Shakespeare Theater.** Mounting at least three plays per year, the Chicago Shakespeare Theater devotes its considerable talents to keeping the Bard's flame alive in the Chicago area. The best part? The Courtyard Theater, on Navy Pier, has sparkling views of the city, and seats are never farther than 30 feet from the thrust stage. ✉ *800 E. Grand Ave., Near North* ☎ *312/595–5600* ⊕ *www.chicagoshakes.com.*

City Lit Theater. City Lit Theater Company produces notable staged readings and full productions of famous literary works—by the likes of Henry James, Alice Walker, and Raymond Carver—as well as original material with a literary bent. ✉ *1020 W. Bryn Mawr Ave., Edgewater* ☎ *773/293–3682* ⊕ *www.citylit.org.*

Collaboraction. Actors, artists, and musicians share the stage in Collaboraction's experimental free-for-alls. Of the several performances presented each year, we recommend Sketchbook—a series of 15 to 20 seven-minute-long plays—for its color and energy. ✉ *1579 N. Milwaukee Ave., 3rd fl., Wicker Park* ☎ *312/226–9633* ⊕ *www.collaboraction.org.*

Lookingglass Theatre Company. Staged in the belly of the historic Chicago Water Works building, the Lookingglass Theatre Company's physically and artistically daring works incorporate theater, dance, music, and circus arts. ✉ *821 N. Michigan Ave., Near North* ☎ *312/337–0665* ⊕ *www.lookingglasstheatre.org.*

Fodor'sChoice **Neo-Futurists.** Neo-Futurists perform their long-running, late-night hit
★ *Too Much Light Makes the Baby Go Blind* in a space—oddly enough—above a former funeral home. The piece is a series of 30 ever-changing plays performed in 60 minutes; the order of the plays is chosen by the audience. In keeping with the spirit of randomness, the admission price is set by the roll of a die, plus $9. ✉ *5153 N. Ashland Ave., Far North* ☎ *773/878–4557* ⊕ *www.neofuturists.org.*

Fodor'sChoice **Redmoon Theater.** Telling imaginative, almost magical stories is Redmoon
★ Theater's specialty. The company's "spectacles" take a number of forms but can best be described as madcap theater with a twist—imagine a mix of live music, puppetry, pageantry, and visual art. Some are staged outdoors, others inside a converted Pilsen warehouse called Spectacle Hall. ✉ *Spectacle Hall, 2120 S. Jefferson St., Pilsen* ☎ *312/850–8440* ⊕ *www.redmoon.org.*

Fodor'sChoice **Steppenwolf.** Steppenwolf's alumni roster speaks for itself: John Mal-
★ kovich, Gary Sinise, Joan Allen, and Laurie Metcalf all honed their chops with this troupe. The company's trademark cutting-edge acting style and consistently successful productions have won national acclaim. ✉ *1650 N. Halsted St., Lincoln Park* ☎ *312/335–1650* ⊕ *www. steppenwolf.org.*

Victory Gardens Theater. Known for workshop productions and Chicago premieres, this company stages all of its plays in the impressive 299-seat, proscenium-thrust Biograph Theater (the site of John Dillinger's infamous demise). ✉ *2433 N. Lincoln Ave., Lincoln Park* ☎ *773/871–3000* ⊕ *www.victorygardens.org.*

TRAVEL SMART
CHICAGO

GETTING HERE AND AROUND

Chicago is famously known as a city of neighborhoods. The Loop is Chicago's epicenter of business, finance, and government. Neighborhoods surrounding the Loop are River North (an area populated by art galleries and high-end boutiques), Near North (bordered by Lake Michigan and Navy Pier), and the West Loop and South Loop, both areas with trendy residential areas plus hip dining and shopping options.

Moving north, you'll encounter the Magnificent Mile (North Michigan Avenue), which gives way to the Gold Coast, so named for its luxurious mansions, stately museums, and deluxe entertainment venues. Lincoln Park, Lakeview, Wrigleyville, Lincoln Square, and Andersonville all lie north of these areas, and each has considerable charm.

Neighborhoods west of the Loop are River West, Wicker Park, Bucktown, and Logan Square, the latest place for of-the-moment art, shopping, dining, and nightlife.

Beyond the South Loop lie Chinatown; Pilsen, where long-standing Mexican murals and taquerias intermingle with a burgeoning arts scene; and Hyde Park, home to the University of Chicago and the Museum of Science and Industry.

Traveling between neighborhoods is a relatively sane experience, thanks to the matrix of bus and train routes managed by the Chicago Transit Authority. Driving can be harried, but taxis are normally plentiful in most parts of town.

Chicago streets generally follow a grid pattern, running north–south or east–west and radiating from a center point at State and Madison streets in the Loop. East and west street numbers go up as you move away from State Street; north and south street numbers rise as you move away from Madison Street. Each block is represented by a hundred number (so the

> ### WORD OF MOUTH
>
> After your trip, be sure to rate the places you visited and share your experiences and travel tips with us and other Fodorites in Travel Ratings and Travel Talk on ⊕ *www. fodors.com.*

12th block north of Madison will be the 1200 block).

■**TIP**→ Ask the Chicago Office of Tourism about hotel and local transportation packages that include tickets to major museum exhibits, theater productions, or other special events.

■ AIR TRAVEL

To Chicago: from New York, 2 hours; from Dallas, 2½ hours; from San Francisco, 4 hours; from Los Angeles, 4 hours; from London, 7 hours; from Sydney, 17 hours (not including layovers).

In Chicago the general rule is to arrive at the airport two hours before an international flight; for a domestic flight, plan to arrive 90 minutes early if you're checking luggage and 60 minutes if you're not.

Airline Security Issues Transportation Security Administration. ☎ 866/289–9673 ⊕ *www.tsa.gov.*

AIRPORTS

The major gateway to Chicago is **O'Hare International Airport** (ORD). Because it's one of the world's busiest airports, all major airlines pass through here. The sprawling structure is 19 miles from downtown, in the far northwest corner of the city. It can take anywhere from 30 to 90 minutes to travel between downtown and O'Hare, based on time of day, weather conditions, and construction on the Kennedy Expressway (Interstate 90). The Blue Line El train offers a reliable 45-minute trip between the Loop and O'Hare.

Got some time to spend before your flight? Plenty of dining and shopping options are scattered throughout O'Hare's four terminals. Chicago favorites such as the Berghoff Café, Billy Goat Tavern, Goose Island Brewing Company, Pizzeria Uno, Garrett Popcorn, and Chef Rick Bayless's Tortas Frontera can be found among the usual chain restaurants. Grab that last-minute souvenir or in-flight necessity at an array of shops, including the Field Museum Gift Shop and Vosges Haut-Chocolat. Take young travelers to visit the Chicago Children's Museum's "Kids on the Fly" exhibit. Or spring for a mini-massage from the Back Rub Hub. Wi-Fi is also available throughout the complex.

■TIP➔ If you're stuck at O'Hare longer than you expected, the Hilton Chicago O'Hare (773/686-8000) is within walking distance of all terminals.

Midway Airport (MDW) is about 11 miles southwest of downtown; it's served by Southwest, Delta, AirTran, and Frontier. Driving between Midway and downtown can take 30 to 60 minutes, depending on traffic conditions on the Stevenson Expressway (Interstate 55). The Orange Line El train runs from the Loop to Midway in about 30 minutes.

Some say the more recently renovated Midway has better dining options than O'Hare. With downtown standouts such as Harry Caray's, Manny's Deli, Pegasus On the Fly, and Lalo's Mexican Restaurant all on-site, it's a good point. The Midway Boulevard area in the center of the building features cute shops such as Discover Chicago and Kids Works. Wi-Fi is available throughout the airport.

An extended stay near Midway Airport can be spent at a number of nearby hotels, including the Chicago Marriott Midway (☎ 800/228–9290), Hampton Inn Midway (☎ 708/496–1900), and Hilton Garden Inn Midway (☎ 708/496–2700).

Security screenings at both airports can be fairly quick during off-peak travel times or long and arduous during the holidays.

■TIP➔ Long layovers don't have to be only about sitting around or shopping. These days they can be about burning off vacation calories. Check out www.airportgyms.com for lists of health clubs in or near many U.S. and Canadian airports.

Airport Information Chicago Midway Airport. ☎ 773/838–0600 ⊕ www.flychicago.com/midway/en/home/Pages/default.aspx. **O'Hare International Airport.** ☎ 773/686–2200, 800/832–6352 ⊕ www.flychicago.com/ohare/en/home/Pages/default.aspx.

GROUND TRANSPORTATION

If you're traveling to or from either airport by bus or car during morning or afternoon rush hours, factor in some extra time—ground transport can be slow.

BUS TRAVEL

Shuttle buses run between O'Hare and Midway airports and to and from either airport and various points in the city. When taking an airport shuttle bus to O'Hare or Midway to catch a departing flight, be sure to allow at least 1½ hours. When going to either airport, it's a good idea to make a reservation 24 hours in advance. Though some shuttles make regular stops at the major hotels and don't require reservations, it's best to check. Reservations are not necessary from the airports. Omega Airport Shuttle offers hourly service between the two airports for approximately $45 per person; travel time is approximately one hour. The company also provides an hourly service from the two airports and Hyde Park. The fare is $35 from O'Hare to Hyde Park and $19 from Midway to Hyde Park. GO Airport Express coaches provide service from both airports to major downtown and Near North locations as well as to most suburbs. The ride downtown from O'Hare takes at least 45 minutes, depending on traffic conditions, and the fare is $30, $54 round-trip; the ride downtown from Midway takes at least a half hour and the fare is $25, $44 round-trip. Call to find out times and prices for other destinations.

CAR TRAVEL

Depending on traffic and the time of day, driving to and from O'Hare takes about an hour, and driving to and from Midway takes at least 45 minutes. From O'Hare, follow the signs to Interstate 90 east (Kennedy Expressway), which merges with Interstate 94 (Edens Expressway). Take the eastbound exit at Ohio Street for Near North locations, the Washington or Monroe Street exit for downtown. After you exit, continue east about a mile to get to Michigan Avenue. From Midway, follow the signs to Interstate 55 east, which leads to Interstate 90.

TAXI TRAVEL

Metered cab service is available at both O'Hare and Midway airports. Trips to and from O'Hare may incur a $1 surcharge to compensate for changing fuel costs. Expect to pay about $40 to $45 plus tip from O'Hare to Near North and downtown locations, about $30 to $35 plus tip from Midway. Some cabs, such as Checker Taxi and Yellow Cab, participate in a shared-ride program in which each car carries up to four individual passengers going from the airport to downtown. The cost per person—a flat fee that varies according to destination—is substantially lower than the full rate.

TRAIN TRAVEL

Chicago Transit Authority (CTA) trains, called elevated or El trains, are the cheapest way to and from the airports; they can also be the most convenient transfer. "Trains to city" signs will guide you to the subway or elevated train line. In O'Hare Airport the Blue Line station is in the underground concourse between terminals. Travel time to the city is about 45 minutes. Get off at the station closest to your hotel; or disembark at the first stop in the Loop (Clark and Lake streets), and then take a taxi to your hotel or change to other transit lines. At Midway Airport the Orange Line El runs to the Loop. The stop at Adams Street and Wabash Avenue is the closest to the hotels on South Michigan Avenue; for others, the simplest strategy is to get off anywhere in the Loop and hail a cab to your final destination. Train fare is $2.25, and you'll need to pay by transit card. Transit card vending machines are in every train station. They do not give change, so add only as much as you'd like to put on your card. Pick up train brochures and system maps outside the entrances to the platforms; the CTA's "Transit Stop" app is also helpful.

TRANSFERS BETWEEN AIRPORTS

O'Hare and Midway airports are on opposite ends of the city, so moving between them can be an arduous, time-consuming task. Your best and cheapest move is hopping on the El. You will travel the Blue Line to the Orange Line, transferring at the Clark/Lake stop to get from O'Hare to Midway, reversing the trip to go from Midway to O'Hare. The entire journey should take you less than two hours.

Taxis and Shuttles American United Cab Co. ☎ 773/248–7600 ⊕ americanunitedtaxiaffiliation.com. **Checker Taxi.** ☎ 312/243–2537 ⊕ www.checkertaxichicago.com. **Flash Cab.** ☎ 773/561–4444 ⊕ www.flashcab.com. **GO Airport Express.** ☎ 888/284–3826 ⊕ www.airportexpress.com. **Omega Airport Shuttle.** ☎ 773/734–6688 ⊕ www.omegashuttle.com. **Yellow Cab.** ☎ 312/829–4222 ⊕ www.yellowcabchicago.com.

Public Transit Information CTA. ☎ 888/968–7282 ⊕ www.transitchicago.com.

▌ BIKE TRAVEL

Mayor Richard Daley worked to establish Chicago as one of the most bike-friendly cities in the United States, and it remains that way today. More than 120 miles of designated bike routes run throughout the city, through historic areas, beautiful parks, and along city streets (look for the words "bike lane"). Bicycling on busy city streets can be a challenge and is not for the faint of heart—cars come within inches of riders, and the doors of parked cars can swing open at any time. The best bet for a scenic ride is the lakefront, which has a traffic-free 18-mile asphalt trail with scenic views of the skyline. When your bike is unattended, always lock it; there are bike racks throughout the city.

In 2013, Divvy Bikes, similar to New York's Citibike, launched in Chicago. The network now boasts 3,000 bikes at over 300 stations throughout the city (though there are far fewer, and in some cases none, on large swaths of the South and West sides). You can purchase a 24-hour pass at any of the Divvy stations for $7.50, which allows riders to take unlimited 30- minute rides during that period. Ride for more than 30 minutes at a time, and you'll incur extra charges.

In Millennium Park at Michigan Avenue and Randolph Street there are 300 free indoor bike spaces, plus showers, lockers, and bike-rental facilities offering beach cruisers, mountain and road bikes, hybrid/comfort models, tandem styles, and add-ons for kids (wagon, baby seat, and so on). Bike rentals are also readily available at Bike and Roll Chicago, which has four locations, one at Millennium Park, one at Navy Pier, one at the Riverwalk (at Wacker and Wabash Avenue), and one at the 53rd Street Bike Center in Hyde Park. Bike and Roll Chicago carries a good selection of mountain and cross bikes. Rates start at $10 per hour. The Chicago Department of Transportation publishes free route maps. Active Transportation Alliance maps cost $10. Maps are updated every few years. From April through October, Bobby's Bike Hike takes guests on cycling tours of Chicago. The three-hour tours begin at the Water Tower on the Magnificent Mile and cycle through historic neighborhoods, shopping areas, and the lakefront. A $35 to $60 fee includes bikes, helmets, and guides; book online for a 10% discount.

Information Active Transportation Alliance. ☎ *312/427–3325* ⊕ *www.activetrans.org.* **Bike and Roll Chicago.** ☎ *773/729–1000* ⊕ *www.bikechicago.com.* **Bobby's Bike Hike.** ☎ *312/915–0995* ⊕ *www.bobbysbikehike.com.*

The City of Chicago Department of Transportation (CDOT). ☎ *312/742–2453* ⊕ *www. chicagobikes.org/bikemap.* **Divvy Bikes.** ☎ *855/553–4889* ⊕ *www.divvybikes.com.*

▌ BOAT TRAVEL

Water taxis are an economical, in-the-know way to cruise parts of the Chicago River and Lake Michigan. A combination of working stiffs and tourists boards these boats daily. You won't get the in-depth narrative of an architecture tour, but the views of Chicago's waterways are just as good—and you can't beat the price (about $3 per ticket).

Wendella Boats operates Chicago Water Taxis, which use three downtown docks (Madison Street, Michigan Avenue, and Chinatown) along the Chicago River. The entire ride takes about a half hour, and you'll get to see a good portion of the downtown part of the river. The boats operate seven days a week, April through October. You can purchase tickets at any dock or on the company's website.

Shoreline Sightseeing's water taxis run two routes: the River Taxi cruises between the Willis (formerly Sears) Tower and Navy Pier, while the Harbor Taxi navigates Lake Michigan between Navy Pier and the Museum Campus. Late May to early September, water taxis run from 10 am to 6:30 pm. You can purchase tickets at any dock or in advance on the company's website.

Information Shoreline Sightseeing. ☎ *312/222–9328* ⊕ *www.shorelinesightseeing. com.* **Wendella Boats.** ☎ *312/337–1446* ⊕ *www.wendellaboats.com.*

▌ CAR TRAVEL

Chicago traffic is often heavy, on-street parking is nearly impossible to find, parking lots are expensive, congestion creates frustrating delays (especially during rush-hour snarls), and other drivers may be impatient with those who are unfamiliar with the city and its roads. On the

NAVIGATING CHICAGO

Chicago is a surprisingly well-ordered and manageable city. There are a few city-planning quirks, however, and streets that run on a diagonal, such as Milwaukee, Elston, and Lincoln avenues. These passageways are actually old Indian trails that followed the Chicago River. Chicago also has a proliferation of double- and even triple-decker streets, Wacker Drive being the best-known example. The uppermost level is generally used for street traffic, and the lower levels serve as thoroughfares for cutting through the city rather quickly.

The most helpful landmark to help you navigate Chicago is Lake Michigan. It will always lie on the east, as it serves as the city's only eastern border. Also, look for the Willis Tower and the John Hancock Center, which reach up far enough into the sky to serve as beacons. The former is in the Loop, and the latter is on northern Michigan Avenue.

Chicago's public transit system blankets the city well and is fairly intuitive. Major bus lines include the 151–Sheridan, which runs along the Lakefront; the 36–Broadway, which cuts through the Gold Coast, Lincoln Park, and Lakeview; and the 125–Water Tower Express, which takes a meandering route from Union Station to Water Tower. The train system (referred to as the El, short for "elevated") is a comprehensive network, with eight train lines crisscrossing the city and nearby suburbs. The busiest routes are the Blue Line, which runs from O'Hare Airport into the city through Bucktown and back out again through the Loop; the Red Line, which cuts a north–south swath through the city, crossing through Edgewater, Lakeview, Lincoln Park, the Gold Coast, the Loop, and the South Side; and the Brown Line, which travels from the Far Northwest Side through Lakeview and Lincoln Park, into the Loop, and back up north.

other hand, Chicago's network of buses and rapid-transit rail is extensive, and taxis and limousines are readily available (the latter often priced competitively with metered cabs), so rent a car *only* if you plan to visit outlying suburbs that are not accessible by public transportation.

If you do need to rent one, you'll have plenty of options, from the big chains to luxury options. The common rental agencies regularly stock new models, many with modern amenities (think navigation systems and satellite radio).

Rates in Chicago begin at around $50 a day, $75 a weekend, or $200 a week for an economy car with air-conditioning, automatic transmission, and unlimited mileage. This does not include the car-rental tax and other taxes totaling 20% plus the $2.75 surcharge per rental. If you rent from the airport, expect to pay slightly more because of airport taxes.

The Illinois tollways snake around the outskirts of the city. Interstate 294 runs north and south between Wisconsin and Indiana. Interstate 90 runs northwest to western Wisconsin, including Madison and Wisconsin Dells. Interstate 88 runs east–west and goes from Eisenhower to Interstate 55. Traffic on all is sometimes just as congested as on the regular expressways. Most tollgates are unmanned, so bring lots of change if you don't have an I-Pass, which is sometimes included with rental cars. Even though tolls are double without the I-Pass, it's not cost-effective to purchase one for a couple of days.

The Illinois Department of Transportation gives information on expressway congestion, travel times, and lane closures and directions on state roadways.

GASOLINE

Gas stations are less numerous in downtown Chicago than in the outlying neighborhoods and suburbs. Filling up is about 50¢ higher per gallon downtown, when you can find a station. Expect to pay anywhere between $2 and $3 per gallon of gas (prices at time of writing). Major credit cards are accepted at all gas stations, and the majority of stations are completely self-serve.

PARKING

Most of Chicago's streets have metered parking, but during peak hours it's hard to find a spot. Most parking pay boxes accept quarters and credit cards in increments as small as five minutes in high-traffic areas, up to an hour in less crowded neighborhoods. Prices average $2–$6.50 an hour. Parking lots and garages are plentiful downtown, but they're expensive. You could pay anywhere from $13 for the day in a municipal lot to $25 for three hours in a private lot. Some neighborhoods, such as the area of Lakeview known as Wrigleyville, enforce restricted parking (especially strict on Cubs' game nights) and will tow cars without permits. You won't find many public parking lots in the neighborhoods. Many major thoroughfares restrict parking during peak travel hours, generally from 7 to 9 am heading toward downtown and from 4 to 6 pm heading away. Read street signs carefully to determine whether a parking spot is legal. On snow days in winter cars parked in designated "snow route areas" will be towed. There's a $30 fine plus the cost of towing the car. In sum, Chicago isn't the most car-friendly place for visitors. Unless it's a necessity, it's best to forget renting a car and use public transportation.

ROAD CONDITIONS

Chicago drivers can be reckless, zipping through red lights and breaking posted speed limits. The Loop and some residential neighborhoods such as Lincoln Park, Lakeview, and Bucktown are made up of mostly one-way streets, so be sure to read signs carefully. Check both ways after a light turns green to make sure that the cross traffic has stopped.

Rush hours are 6:30 to 9:30 am and 4 to 7 pm, but don't be surprised if the rush starts earlier or ends later, depending on weather conditions, big events, and holiday weekends. There are always bottlenecks on the expressways, particularly where the Edens and Kennedy merge, and downtown on the Dan Ryan from 22nd Street into the Loop. Sometimes anything around the airport is rough. There are electronic signs on the expressways that post updates on the congestion. Additionally, summertime is high time for construction on highways and inner-city roads. Drive with patience.

ROADSIDE EMERGENCIES

Dial 911 in an emergency to reach police, fire, or ambulance services. AAA Chicago provides roadside assistance to members. Mr. Locks Security Systems will unlock your vehicle 24 hours a day.

Emergency Services AAA Chicago.
☎ 800/222–4357 (AAA–HELP) ⊕ www.aaa.com.
Mr. Locks Security Systems. ☎ 866/675–6257 ⊕ www.mr-locks.com.

RULES OF THE ROAD

Speed limits in Chicago vary, but on most city roads it's 30 mph. Most interstate highways, except in congested areas, have a speed limit of 55 mph. In Chicago you may turn right at a red light after stopping if there's no oncoming traffic and no restrictions are posted. When in doubt, wait for the green. Cameras have been installed at many major intersections in the city to catch drivers who run red lights and commit other infractions. There are many one-way streets in Chicago, particularly in and around the Loop, so be alert to signs and other cars. Illinois drunk-driving laws are quite strict. Anyone caught driving with a blood-alcohol content of.08 or more will automatically have his or her license seized and be issued a ticket; authorities in home states will also be notified. Those with Illinois driver's licenses can have their licenses suspended for three months on the first offense.

Passengers are required to wear seat belts. Always strap children under age eight into approved child-safety seats.

It's illegal to use handheld cellular phones while driving in the city; restrictions vary in the suburbs. Headlights are compulsory if you're using windshield wipers. Radar detectors are legal in Illinois.

▌ PUBLIC TRANSPORTATION

Chicago's extensive public transportation network includes rapid-transit trains, buses, and a commuter-rail network. The Chicago Transit Authority, or CTA, operates the city buses, rapid-transit trains (the El), and suburban buses (Pace). Metra runs the commuter rail.

The Regional Transportation Authority (RTA) for northeastern Illinois oversees and coordinates the activities of the CTA and Metra. The RTA's website can be a useful first stop if you are planning to combine suburban and city public transit while in Chicago.

Information Regional Transportation Authority. ☎ 312/913–3110 ⊕ www. rtachicago.com.

CTA: THE EL AND BUSES

The Chicago Transit Authority (CTA) operates rapid-transit trains and buses. Chicago's rapid-transit train system is known as the El. Each of the eight lines has a color name as well as a route name: Blue (O'Hare–Congress–Douglas), Brown (Ravenswood), Green (Lake–Englewood–Jackson Park), Orange (Midway), Purple (Evanston), Red (Howard–Dan Ryan), Yellow (Skokie Swift), and Pink (Cermak). In general, the route names indicate the first and last stop on the train. Chicagoans refer to trains both by the color and the route name. Most, but not all, rapid-transit lines operate 24 hours; some stations are closed at night. The El, though very crowded during rush hours, is the fastest way to get around (unless you're coming from the suburbs, in which case the Metra is quicker but doesn't run as often). Trains run about every 10 minutes during rush hours, every 30 minutes on weekends, and every 15 minutes at other times. Pick up the brochure "Downtown Transit Sightseeing Guide"

for hours, fares, and other pertinent information. (You can also download it at ⊕ *www.transitchicago.com/assets/1/brochures/13JN_089-DTSSG-WEB.pdf*). In general, late-night CTA travel is not recommended. Note that many of the Red and Blue line stations are subways; the rest are elevated. This means if you're heading to O'Hare and looking for the Blue Line, you may have to look for a stairway down, not up.

The basic fee for rapid-transit trains is $2.25, which must be paid using a Ventra transit card. The basic fare for buses is $2.25 when paying cash (dollar bills or coins, no change given) and $2 when using a Ventra card. Rechargeable Ventra cards can be purchased at CTA station vending machines as well as at Jewel and CVS stores; they can be topped up with any amount or loaded with a pass valid for 1, 3, 7, or 30 days of unlimited travel (costing $10, $20, $28, and $100 respectively). You can also purchase single-ride Ventra cards at any CTA stop.

These easy-to-use cards (which can be shared) are inserted into the turnstiles at CTA train stations and into machines as you board CTA buses; directions are clearly posted. To transfer between the Loop's elevated lines and the subway or between trains and buses, you must either use a Ventra card with at least 25¢ stored on it or, if you're not using a transit card, buy a transfer when you first board. If two CTA train lines meet, you can transfer for free. You can also obtain free train-to-train transfers from specially marked turnstiles at the Washington/State subway station or the State/Lake El station, or ask for a transfer card, good on downtown trains, at the ticket booth. Transfers can be used twice within a two-hour time period.

Buses generally stop on every other corner northbound and southbound (on State Street they stop at every corner). Eastbound and westbound buses generally stop on every corner. Buses from the Loop generally run north–south. Principal transfer points are on Michigan Avenue at the north side of Randolph Street for northbound buses, Adams Street and Wabash Avenue for westbound buses and the El, and State and Lake streets for southbound buses.

Bus schedules vary depending on the time of day and route; they typically run every 8 to 15 minutes, though service is less frequent on weekends, very early in the morning, and late at night. Schedules are available online at ⊕ *www.transit chicago.com.*

Information CTA. ⊠ *Merchandise Mart, 567 W. Lake St.* ☎ *888/968–7282* ⊕ *www. transitchicago.com.*

METRA: COMMUTER TRAINS

Metra serves the city and suburbs. The Metra Electric railroad has a line close to Lake Michigan; its trains stop in Hyde Park. The Metra commuter rail system has 11 lines to suburbs and surrounding cities, including Aurora, Elgin, Joliet, and Waukegan; one line serves the North Shore suburbs, and another has a stop at McCormick Place. Trains leave from several downtown terminals.

Metra trains use a fare structure based on distance. A Metra weekend pass costs $7 and is valid for all-day use on any line except for the South Shore line.

Information Metra information line. ☎ *312/322–6777* ⊕ *www.metrarail.com.*

▌TAXI TRAVEL

You can hail a cab on just about any busy street in Chicago. Hotel doormen will hail one for you as well. Cabs aren't all yellow anymore; look for standard-size sedans or, in some cases, minivans. Available taxis are sometimes indicated by an illuminated rooftop light. Chicago taxis are metered, with fares beginning at $3.25 (including a $1 fuel surcharge) upon entering the cab and 20¢ for each additional 1/9 mile or 36 seconds of wait time. A charge of $1 is made for the first additional passenger and 50¢ for each passenger after that.

There's no extra baggage or credit-card charge. Taxi drivers expect a 15% tip.

▌TRAIN TRAVEL

Amtrak offers nationwide service to Chicago's Union Station, at 225 South Canal Street.

Information Amtrak. ☎ *800/872–7245* ⊕ *www.amtrak.com.*

ESSENTIALS

■ COMMUNICATIONS

INTERNET

Chicago is for the most part a wireless city, with most hotels and coffee shops offering high-speed wireless access. Public libraries are also a good option. Some hotels have a nominal fee (usually less than $10) that gets you online for 24 hours.

■ DAY TOURS AND GUIDES

Chicago Tours. A comprehensive collection of sightseeing excursions by air, water, and land can be found through Chicago Tours, a travel-reservation company offering more than 75 tours, events, and activities. ☎ *888/881–3284* ⊕ *www. chicagotours.us.*

BOAT TOURS

Get a fresh perspective on Chicago by viewing it from the water. The cruise season usually runs from April through mid-November, but monthly boat schedules vary; be sure to call for exact times and fares. One option in particular stands out, though it's a *bit* more expensive than the rest: the Chicago Architecture Foundation river cruise aboard *Chicago's First Lady, Chicago's Little Lady,* or *Chicago's Fair Lady.* The CAF tour highlights more than 50 architecturally significant sights. The cost is $38 ($35 if reserved online, and $30 for select Tuesdays and Wednesdays); reservations are recommended. Shoreline Sightseeing also runs architecture-themed boat tours.

If you're looking for a maritime adventure, you can get a blast from the past on the tall ship *Windy,* a 148-foot ship modeled on old-time commercial vessels. Passengers may help the crew or take a turn at the wheel during several different themed cruises on Lake Michigan. The cost is $25 to $45.

Boat Tours Chicago Architecture Foundation. ☎ *312/922–3432 information* ⊕ *www.*

NEWSPAPERS AND MAGAZINES

Chicago is served by two daily metro newspapers, the *Chicago Tribune* and the *Chicago Sun-Times.* Also be sure to check out the two alternative weeklies, *Chicago Reader,* which comes out on Thursday, and *New City,* which is available on Wednesday. For a glimpse into Chicago's social scene, pick up the free *CS* magazine from kiosks around town. The features-oriented monthly periodical *Chicago* magazine is sold at most newsstands.

architecture.org. **Mercury Chicago Skyline Cruiseline.** ☎ *312/332–1353 recorded information* ⊕ *www.mercuryskylinecruiseline.com.* **Shoreline Sightseeing.** ☎ *312/222–9328* ⊕ *www.shorelinesightseeing.com.* **Wendella.** ☎ *312/337–1446* ⊕ *www.wendellaboats.com.* **Windy of Chicago Ltd.** ☎ *312/451–2700* ⊕ *www.tallshipwindy.com.*

BUS AND TROLLEY TOURS

A narrated bus or trolley tour can be a good way to orient yourself among Chicago's main sights. Tours start at roughly $20 and can last from two hours to a full day. American Sightseeing offers about 30 options, from classic outings to pizza- and blues-themed tours. The double-decker buses of Chicago Trolley & Double Decker Co. stop at all the downtown attractions. You can get on and off the open-air trolleys as you like; these tours vary in price, so call for details. The Chicago Architecture Foundation's bus tours often go farther afield, exploring everything from cemeteries and movie palaces to far-flung neighborhoods.

Bus and Trolley Tours American Sightseeing. ☎ *312/251–3100, 800/621–4153* ⊕ *www.americansightseeingchicago.com.* **Chicago Architecture Foundation.** ✉ *Tour Centers, Santa Fe Bldg., 224 S. Michigan Ave.* ☎ *312/922–3432* ⊕ *www.architecture.*

org. **Chicago Trolley & Double Decker Co.**
☏ *773/648–5000* ⊕ *www.chicagotrolley.com.*

Foreign-Language Tours Chicago Tour Guides Institute, Inc. ☏ *773/276–6683* ⊕ *www.chicagoguide.net.*

SPECIAL-INTEREST TOURS
African-American Black Coutours.
☏ *773/233–8907* ⊕ *www.blackcoutours.com.*

Gangsters Untouchable Tours. ☏ *773/881–1195* ⊕ *www.gangstertour.com.*

Horse-and-Carriage Rides Antique Coach and Carriage Company. ☏ *773/735–9400* ⊕ *www.antiquecoach-carriage.com.* **Chicago Horse & Carriage Ltd.** ☏ *312/988–9090* ⊕ *www.chicagocarriage.com.* **Noble Horse.** ☏ *312/266–7878* ⊕ *www.noblehorsechicago. com.*

WALKING TOURS
The Chicago Architecture Foundation has by far the largest selection of guided excursions, with more than 50 itineraries covering everything from department stores to Frank Lloyd Wright's Oak Park buildings. Especially popular walking tours of the Loop are given daily throughout the year. Chicago Greeter and the affiliated InstaGreeter program (for last-minute weekend visits) are two free services that match knowledgeable Chicagoans with visitors for tours of various sights and neighborhoods.

Information Chicago Architecture Foundation. ✉ *Tour Centers, Santa Fe Bldg., 224 S. Michigan Ave.* ☏ *312/922–3432* ⊕ *www. architecture.org.* **Chicago Greeter.** ✉ *Chicago Office of Tourism, 78 E. Washington St.* ☏ *312/945–4231* ⊕ *www.chicagogreeter.com.*

▮ HOURS OF OPERATION

Neighborhood business hours are generally 9 to 6 Sunday through Wednesday, with later hours Thursday through Saturday. When holidays fall on a weekend, businesses usually close around 4 on the preceding Friday. On a Monday after a weekend holiday, retail businesses are rarely closed but regular businesses often

---

are. Most stores close for Christmas, New Year's, and Easter Sunday.

Chicago museums are generally open daily from 9 to 5, closing only on major holidays; some larger attractions keep later hours (until about 8 pm) one weeknight per week. A number of smaller museums keep limited hours; it's always advisable to phone ahead for details.

Pharmacies might open as early as 8 am and close as early as 5 pm, but many shut later (anywhere from 6 to 10 pm). Major chains have outposts that are open 24 hours.

▮ MONEY

Compared with large cities like San Francisco or New York, costs in Chicago are fairly reasonable—though the sales tax here (9.25%) is one of the highest of any U.S. city. Restaurant, event, and parking prices are markedly higher in the Loop than in other parts of Chicago.

ATMs are plentiful. You can find them in banks, grocery stores, and hotels, as well as at drugstores, gas stations, and convenience stores.

Prices throughout this guide are given for adults. Substantially reduced fees are almost always available for children, students, and senior citizens.

▌ SAFETY

The most common crimes in public places are pickpocketing, purse snatching, jewelry theft, and gambling scams. Keep your wallet in a front coat or pants pocket. Close your bag or purse securely and keep it close to you. Also beware of someone jostling you and of loud arguments; these could be ploys to distract your attention while another person grabs your wallet. Leave unnecessary credit cards at home, and hide valuables and jewelry from view.

Although crime on CTA buses and trains in general has declined, recently robbers have been targeting El travelers with smartphones; keep your phone and other portable electronic devices out of sight on train platforms. Several additional precautions can reduce the chance of your becoming a victim: look alert and purposeful; know your route ahead of time; have your fare ready before boarding; and keep an eye on your purse or packages during the ride. Avoid taking public transit late at night.

The city has gained a reputation in recent years for being particularly violent. While certain parts of Chicago are plagued by gun violence, they are largely segregated on the West and South Sides in areas that have long struggled with deep, intergenerational poverty. The city's tourist areas remain generally quite safe.

▌**TIP→ Distribute your cash, credit cards, IDs, and other valuables between a deep front pocket, an inside jacket or vest pocket, and a hidden money pouch. Don't reach for the money pouch once you're in public.**

▌ TAXES

At restaurants you'll pay approximately 10% for meal tax (thanks to special taxing initiatives, some parts of town are lower than others).

The hotel tax is 16.4% in the city, and slightly less in suburban areas.

In Chicago a steep 9.25% state and county sales tax is added to all purchases except groceries, which have a 2.25% tax. Sales tax is already added into the initial price of prescription drugs.

▌ TIME

Chicago is in the central time zone. It's 1 hour behind New York, 2 hours ahead of Los Angeles, 6 hours behind London, and 16 hours behind Sydney.

Time Zones Timeanddate.com. ⊕ *www. timeanddate.com/worldclock.*

▌ TIPPING

You should tip 15% for adequate service in restaurants and up to 20% if you feel you've been treated well. At higher-end restaurants, where more service personnel per table must divide the tip, increase these measures by a few percentage points. An especially helpful wine steward should be acknowledged with $2 or $3. It's not necessary to tip the maître d' unless you've been done a very special favor and you intend to visit again. Tip $1 per checked coat.

Taxi drivers, bartenders, and hairdressers expect about 15%. Bellhops and porters should get about $1 per bag; hotel maids about $1 to $2 per day of your stay; and valet-parking attendants $1 or $2 (but only after they bring your car to you, not when they park it). On package tours, conductors and drivers usually get about $2 to $3 per day from each group member. Concierges should get tips of $5 to $10 for special service.

▌ VISITOR INFORMATION

The Chicago Convention and Tourism Bureau is a great place to start planning your visit to the Windy City. The organization's website is a veritable gold mine of information, from hotel packages to sample itineraries, event calendars, and maps. You can also call the toll-free number to speak with a travel consultant. The Illinois Bureau of Tourism offers detailed information about what to do and see in Chicago and is especially helpful if your travel plans will take you outside the downtown area. Once you're here, you can count on Choose Chicago's civic visitor centers in the Chicago Cultural Center and Macy's on State Street. They are stocked with free maps, local publications, and knowledgeable staff to help you out.

Contacts Chicago Convention and Tourism Bureau. ☎ *312/567–8500, 877/244–2246* ⊕ *www.choosechicago.com.* **Choose Chicago, Chicago Cultural Center.** ⊠ *77 E. Randolph St., Loop* ⊕ *www.choosechicago.com.* **Choose Chicago, Macy's.** ⊠ *111 N. State St. , Macy's, Lower Level, Loop* ⊕ *www.choosechicago.com.* **Illinois Bureau of Tourism.** ☎ *800/226–6632* ⊕ *www.enjoyillinois.com.*

ONLINE TRAVEL TOOLS
ART
For a preview of the Art Institute of Chicago, check out ⊕ *www.artic.edu.*

NEWSPAPERS AND MAGAZINES
The websites of the city's daily newspapers, the *Chicago Tribune* and the *Chicago Sun-Times*, are great sources for reviews and events listings. The *Chicago Reader*'s site is rich in arts reviews, while *Metromix Chicago* and *Time Out Chicago* thoroughly cover Chicago's dining and entertainment scenes.

Contacts Chicago Reader. ⊕ *www. chicagoreader.com.* **Chicago Sun-Times.** ⊕ *www.suntimes.com.* **Chicago Tribune.** ⊕ *www.chicagotribune.com.* **Metromix Chicago.** ⊕ *chicago.metromix.com.* **Time Out Chicago.** ⊕ *www.timeoutchicago.com.*

INDEX

PHOTO CREDITS

NOTES

NOTES

NOTES

NOTES

NOTES

NOTES

NOTES

ABOUT OUR WRITERS

Jenny Berg, a Chicago-based lifestyle editor and writer, updated the Where to Stay chapter this edition. She covers events for *BizBash*, weddings for *CS Brides*, and contributes beauty and fashion features to publications such as *Refinery29* and *Racked*. Her favorite parts of hotel life include room-service breakfast; if "visiting spas" can be counted as a life passion, it's hers.

Joseph Erbentraut is an editor at the *Huffington Post* and lives in Chicago's Uptown neighborhood. His work has also been featured in publications including *Village Voice*, *Chicagoist*, *Gapers Block*, and the *Windy City Times*. He loves to splurge on a night out, but will always have a place in his heart for the city's many holes-in-the-wall and dive bars. He updated the Lakeview and Far North, Pilsen, Hyde Park, Shopping, and Nightlife and Performing Arts chapters this edition.

Carly Fisher, our Where to Eat updater, is a food writer with a lifelong love of Chicago—especially the hot dogs and Mexican food. She can be found praising eats in places like *Food & Wine*, *Bon Appetit*, *Saveur*, and *McSweeney's*. She always has room for dessert and worships her grandmother's cooking.

Neil Munshi, a reporter for the *Financial Times*, is based in Chicago and updated the Experience and Travel Smart chapters this edition.

Roberta Sotonoff, an award-winning travel junkie, writes to support her habit. Her family often complains that she spends more time with gate agents than with them. Her work has been published in dozens of domestic and international newspapers, magazines, websites, and guidebooks. She never tires of exploring her hometown of Chicago. For this edition, she updated the Loop, Near North and River North, Lincoln Park and Wicker Park, and Day Trips from Chicago chapters.